AMERICA'S GREATEST BLUNDER

ALSO BY BURTON YALE PINES

Back to Basics
The Traditionalist Movement That Is Sweeping Grass-Roots America

Mandate for Leadership III

Out of Focus
Network Television and the American Economy

AMERICA'S GREATEST BLUNDER

The Fateful Decision to Enter World War One

BURTON YALE PINES

RSD PRESS | NY, NY

RSD Press
New York, New York
U.S.A.
www.americasgreatestblunder.com

GreatestBlunder@gmail.com

ISBN-13: 978-0-9891487-3-3
LCCN: 2013916387

Book Design by Kristeen Ott

Cover image courtesy of Library of Congress,
Prints & Photographs Division, WWI Posters, LC-USZC4-9736

Back cover photo by Bill Keefrey, Ft. Lauderdale, FL

Printed in the United States of America

For Helene, of course,

and

To the Memory of

George L. Mosse
Professor of History, University of Wisconsin
Who taught me to research and respect the lessons of history

and

Richard M. Clurman
Chief of Correspondents, Time-Life News Service
Who taught me the discipline and skills of rigorous reporting

ACKNOWLEDGMENTS

With great pleasure I extend my deep gratitude to Samuel Vaughan and Theron Raines, both legendary editors, whose incisive suggestions immensely improved my narrative; to Richard Heffner, long-time producer and host of Public Television's "The Open Mind," whose buoyant encouragement kept me at the too often frustrating tasks of finishing and publishing this book; to the research rooms' staff at the New York Public Library; to Professors George L. Mosse, Michael Petrovich, Harvey Goldberg and their associates at the University of Wisconsin (Madison) Department of History who, in the grand Frederick Jackson Turner spirit, trained me in the craft of historical research and analysis; to Richard M. Clurman, Time-Life News Service Chief of Correspondents, and my colleagues at *Time Magazine* who taught me how to report events in ways accessible to the broad public; to five generations of World War One historians whose impressive research and provocative analyses allowed me to draw the conclusion central to the book's thesis; to Jason Eiker-Wiles whose sharp proofreading eye and wry wit helped push me across the finish line towards publication; to the creative and encouraging staff of Hillcrest Media which designed the book's exterior and interior layouts; and to the members of the World War One Historical Association and the vast universe of World War One enthusiasts on Twitter, LinkedIn and elsewhere on the Web whose effervescent fascination with all aspects of that great conflict convinced me that someone, somewhere would be interested in what I was writing.

CONTENTS

INTRODUCTION

A FATEFUL AMERICAN DECISION AND THE CENTURY PIVOTS

I T WAS APRIL 5, 1917 and characteristically cloudy along almost the full 475-mile line running from the North Sea to the Swiss border. It was a line of brutal devastation, of rows upon rows of fortified trenches, dividing two massive military machines, millions of men in each, which had battled and bloodied each other for almost three years. For almost as long they had been stalemated and deadlocked along that line, known as the Western Front, despite hurtling unprecedented numbers of troops at each other in one massive offensive and counteroffensive after another, suffering unprecedented casualties, counted not in the tens or even hundreds of thousands but in the millions, in futile attempts to break their deadlock.

The following day, that deadlock would start coming undone. On that day, April 6, 1917, the United States entered what was being called The Great War, bringing its extraordinary industrial and manpower resources to the side of Britain and France and against Germany. With that decision, America transformed the conflict into a true world war. More significant, much more consequential, with that decision America transformed the war from a conflict that not only, as historians long have recognized, dropped the curtain on the 19th Century and its optimistic belief in perpetual progress, but simultaneously raised the curtain on a new century, one that was to be cursed by almost nonstop war and tension.

With today's enviable and indulgent perspective of a century's hindsight, it can be said that America's decision to enter the Great War was one of history's rare pivot points. As the few others before it—an English monarch accepting the Magna Carta, Luther nailing his theses to a church door, thirteen British colonies declaring independence and Napoleon carrying the French Revolution across Europe—it too changed history profoundly. The dispatch to Europe of more than two million American doughboys, as they affectionately became known, sharply tilted the balance on the stalemated Western Front and, in effect, won the war against Germany. This allowed Britain and France to impose a punishing peace on the vanquished, thus setting in train events and actions that helped make the 20th Century the West's most destructive as it subsequently suffered the horrors of Nazism, the devastation of yet a second great and even broader war and the often terrifying tensions and at times bloodshed of a Cold War. Without America's 1917 entry into Europe's war, the 20th Century would have been extraordinarily different: No punishing Versailles peace treaty, no humiliation of Germany, no toxic German drive for revenge, no Hitler, no World War Two and likely no Cold War. Entering Europe's war truly was a gigantic and fateful American decision. As it turned out, it was America's greatest blunder of the century.

The April 6 declaration of war against Germany was no surprise. America had been inching toward it for many months. Yet, three years earlier, when the war had erupted in Europe on August 2, 1914, it would have been a wild, long-shot bet that America would enter it at all. Far from it. And were America to do so, it was no sure thing that it would enter against Germany. At war's onset, Washington immediately proclaimed its neutrality and vowed to treat all belligerents equally, showing no favor to any, as President Woodrow Wilson promised the nation and the world. Had that promise been kept, 20th Century history would have been enormously different. But Washington, almost from the war's first days, began backpedalling, skewing and undermining its neutrality, treating Britain and its allies with understanding and leniency (and giving them extensive economic support) while treating Germany with unrelenting rigidity. How and why genuine neutrality withered, despite its almost unanimous backing by the American public, and how and why America turned against Germany are the first half of the tale of how America's entering the war transformed the century.

This half of the tale is a fabric of many interwoven strands: of skilled British propaganda in America trouncing German propaganda, distorting and even fabricating facts to convince the American public that Germany was America's enemy and that Germans were committing unspeakable atrocities and behaving as barbaric Huns; of growing American banking, manufacturing and farming dependence on sales to Britain and France, with the simultaneously growing fear that a British or French defeat or even setback would destroy profits and plunge America into deep recession; of a Wilson policy that putatively prohibited all American loans to every belligerent but in fact opened a spigot of dollars to the Allies (as Britain, France and their allies were known) while completely shutting out Germany; of actions that selectively defended America's freedom of the seas, protesting strongly and issuing ultimatums against German submarine attacks on shipments of goods to Britain and France while looking the other way when Britain's massive naval blockade prevented American ships from, as custom and law entitled them, reaching German ports.

The second half of the tale relates how America changed the dynamics on Europe's battlefield. By entering the Great War, America dramatically shifted the balance of forces against Germany, ultimately ending the stalemate on the war's Western Front. This half of the tale begins even before the troops arrived in Europe. The mere prospect of America, with its seemingly bottomless reservoir of manpower, mobilizing an army of millions—named the American Expeditionary Force or AEF—instantly cast its shadow on the European battlefield. Indeed, many historians argue convincingly that the certainty that vast numbers of Yanks were coming immediately influenced the combatants' military plans and strategies. And then, when the doughboys started arriving by the shipload, then began training in camps in France and then began going onto the line, they made not only a difference. They made the key difference. It wasn't just a matter of their bravery, though by every account they (as had the British, French, German and Russian troops for three years) fought bravely, their ranks full of individual heroes; and it wasn't just a matter of superior American tactics or leadership, though both tipped the scales in particular battles (but, in other battles, proved no better than the stale British/French tactics which had been unable to break the deadlock).

Rather, the decisive factors—at the battles of Cantigny, Belleau Wood, St. Mihiel, Meuse-Argonne and other places whose names became instantly familiar to those back at home and landmarks in America's military history—were the sheer numbers and enthusiasm brought to the field by the arriving doughboys and their officers. In striking and crucial contrast to the British, French and Germans who then were fielding their third or maybe even fourth generation of recruits, those who repeatedly had been rejected as defective in the war's early years, those who otherwise would have been judged far too young or too old or too infirm to fight and those who now were exhausted and weary, the Yanks and their officers were fresh, eager and represented the best of American youth.

Most were, in one way or another, heroic Sergeant Yorks. When they went to battle, even in those early, troubling encounters with the German Imperial Army when American training, tactics and leadership were found wanting and green, they impressed all with their energy. "Lusty arrogance" was one admiring description of them. Within months, as they gained experience and understanding of the Western Front's unique pock-marked, barbed-wired and trench-encrusted battlefield, that energy and their numbers would make the difference that counted. It broke the stalemate and won the war—a judgment that may spark finger-wagging from offended British and French, but which a century's perspective can make with great confidence.

By ending the stalemate, the U.S. guaranteed not only a British/French victory, but a victory that was overwhelming in its devastating finality. It guaranteed that there would be no mediated end to the conflict, no negotiated tradeoffs, no compromises, but rather what turned out to be an imposed harsh armistice and an even harsher peace, which even then was seen almost guaranteed to sow seeds of future conflict. It guaranteed that what would result certainly would not be Wilson's long proclaimed American goal—a "peace without victory," a peace with neither victor nor vanquished, "a peace between equals"—but just the opposite. What emerged from the later Versailles peace conference were triumphant victors on one side and a defeated Germany on the other, brought to its knees and saddled with a huge financial burden and political and psychological humiliation. It meant, not only in hindsight but recognized at that time too, that the infant, fragile democracy just taking root in Germany, by being forced to accept this painful peace, would be wounded severely; in hindsight we know that it was wounded fatally.

Though declaring war on April 6, 1917 was agonizing and obviously painful for Wilson and Congressional leaders, as the following pages describe, they ultimately felt that it was justified and, more importantly, served America's interests well. Yet even here, their case was weak. In his speech to Congress asking for war, judged by many historians as among the most eloquent orations of any president, Wilson was unable to depict Germany as any threat to American security or interests—because it wasn't. He didn't even try.

Instead he urged his nation to go to war to defend and advance lofty ideals, including, in one of history's most memorable presidential phrases, to "make the world safe for democracy." We know, of course, that it did not.

Much more important, we also now know that the decision by Woodrow Wilson and the 65th Congress to take America into Europe's Great War on the British and French side shaped the fate of most of the rest of the century in the West and, indeed, for much of the world. From that decision of April 6 flowed the actions that made Nazism a possibility, along with all the horrors and agony inflicted on mankind by the Nazis, including a World War Two and a collapse of Germany in 1945 which opened half of Europe to nearly a half-century of Soviet domination and subjected America and much of Western Europe to a trying, costly and at times very bloody Cold War.

And if America had not declared war? What then? History offers guidance towards an answer. Without America's intervention, the Great War's exhausted belligerents almost certainly would have been forced—by the mounting food and other shortages on their home fronts, by their looming economic bankruptcies, by the plunging morale and rising restlessness of their populations and frustrated despair of their political leaders and by the fast-dwindling supply of fresh manpower for their armies—to drag themselves, however distastefully, to a negotiating table. There they would have ended the conflict as all of Europe's continent-wide wars had been ended since the Thirty Years War of 1618-1648, by compromises and tradeoffs.

With such a compromise peace, it in hindsight is possible to speculate, though, of course, not state with certainty, about several crucial subsequent developments: that the movement towards constitutional monarchy in Germany, which had been gaining momentum before the war, would have accelerated and a democratic Germany would have emerged in Central Europe; that the Austro-Hungarian Empire, seething with subjected nationalities verging on revolt, well may have begun its peaceful devolution, marked certainly by sporadic violence but no longer smoldering as Europe's tinderbox; that there would have been a more manageable burden of international postwar debts and financial reparations (very possibly, no reparations at all), hence sparing the West those financial uncertainties and severe distortions that derailed economic growth and, in great part, contributed to the cascade of events triggering the stock market, currency and bank crashes and even, perhaps, the Great Depression.

All of this, understandably, falls into focus only through a century's hindsight and is highly speculative. The following pages, in fact, will not linger on the details or permutations of such "what if" speculation. What is not speculative, however, is that American intervention in the war changed history's course. And it is nearly impossible to imagine a worse, uglier, more self-destructive course than that which the 20th Century took. To render such judgment is not necessarily to point a finger of blame at the American policymakers who took the nation into the war. There were no villains. No American president, individuals or groups or forces are "guilty" or share "responsibility" for the horrifying history that flowed from America breaking the military deadlock in Europe. Rather, there were flawed policies, inept policy executions, massive ignorance, persistent inconsistencies and even hypocrisies, but no evil intents.

The result, however, was a huge mistake: a fateful decision with extraordinary consequences. A full century later, when other mistakes, still fresh in the memory, have taken America into wars, it remains intriguing and illustrative (possibly even useful) to ask anew those quintessential historical questions of "How did this happen?" of "How did America end up fighting a war it never thought it would fight and in which no national interests were at stake?" and of "What difference was made by America's fighting?" The following pages are a 21st Century stab at exploring answers.

CHAPTER 1

—————⟫⊙⟪—————

STALEMATE ON THE WESTERN FRONT

W HEN THE WAR BEGAN IN summer 1914, nearly all the generals and government leaders on both sides believed that it would be a swift conflict. As German Kaiser Wilhelm II was reassuring his armies that they would be back home before autumn's leaves fell, the mobilized French troops confidently were shouting "á Berlin" as they headed towards the front. British Prime Minister Herbert Asquith told colleagues that the war would be over "in a few months," while one of his senior officers was predicting a war of "three months if everything goes well, and perhaps eight months if things do not go satisfactorily."

Such short war expectations were not unreasonable. After all, each European conflict since Napoleon's defeat almost exactly a century earlier had been brief. The Franco-Prussian War of 1870-71, the Continent's last major hostility, triggered when France attacked Prussia, lasted about nine months, while the land battles of the Russo-Japanese War of 1904-05, considered by military planners to have been a very long war, was over in just fifteen months. Meanwhile, the industrialization that had swept the Continent since Napoleon also argued for a short war, since it was widely assumed that modern economies could not afford an extended conflict.

Sure there were skeptics. British Foreign Minister Edward Grey (commonly known to history as Lord Grey) seems to have been expecting a very long conflict since, just a few days after the war's start, in what is often called the war's most-remembered quotation, he said to a colleague: "The lamps are going out all over Europe. We shall not see them lit again in our time." In Germany, generals as early as 1895 warned of prolonged warfare, which would be, in Chief of the German General Staff Helmuth von Moltke's words ten years later, "a long wearisome struggle…which will utterly exhaust our own people, even if we are victorious."[1] Yet, so powerful was the notion of the short war that Germany's carefully crafted and re-crafted strategy, known as the Schlieffen Plan, rested completely on the premise that German forces would defeat the French in six weeks, allowing German divisions then to pivot and speed east by rail to fight the Russians. In its precision, the Schlieffen Plan called for the defeat of France by a certain time—Day 42 after mobilization of German forces.

Convinced of the certainty of a short war, none of the combatants were prepared for a long one. Though all except Britain had raised and trained large citizen armies, none had geared their industries and farms for sustained conflict. The German General Staff, for example, had enough grain, meat and industrial raw materials on hand for just nine months and confidently felt that to be sufficient. They stockpiled no copper, nickel, zinc nor other key metals needed for weapons and ammunition.

As they faced off against each other in August 1914, the two sides were not at all equal. Germany and its Central Powers allies of Austria-Hungary, Bulgaria and Turkey were inferior in population and economies to the Triple Entente or the Allies—France, Great Britain, Italy and Russia. British historian Niall Ferguson, in his acclaimed 1998 study *The Pity of War: Explaining World War I*, has calculated the combatants' relative strengths. According to him, the Central Powers' combined population at war's start was about 144 million, not even one-fourth of the Entente's 656 million (including Belgium, Serbia and Britain's colonies and dominions). And while the Central Powers were to be able to send the historically staggering number of 25 million troops into battle during the four-year war, this was to be far short of the 32 million fielded by the other side. Similarly lopsided was economic muscle: Germany and its allies in 1913 produced nineteen percent of the world's manufacturing compared to twenty-eight percent for the Entente.[2]

Not only was the German side inferior in population and economic strength, it also was, by key measures, less militarized than its opponents—something that may surprise those accepting the "militaristic German" stereotype. Writes Ferguson: "The most militarized society—in the sense of the proportion of the population under arms—in pre-war Europe was undoubtedly France: 2.29 percent of the population were in the army and navy." Next came Germany, at just a bit more than half France's rate, with 1.33 percent under arms, trailed by Britain's 1.17 percent. Moreover, German military outlays measured both in per capita terms and as a share of public spending were less than Britain's and France's.[3] Such French and British economic and population advantages, of course, would count for little in a short war. But as the war dragged on they became an increasingly important (though not conclusive) factor.

The New Reality – A Long War

A short war, however, is clearly what this conflict seemed certain to be in the weeks after July 28, 1914, when Austria-Hungary's declaration of war on Serbia triggered the spiral of alliance-induced war proclamations and military mobilizations which propelled what had been a regional Balkans squabble into the first continent-wide conflagration since Napoleon. Those August weeks saw what the experts call a war of maneuver: sweeping and rapid movements, penetrations into open country, brazen dramatic thrusts. German troops pushed rapidly through Belgium and then into France, penetrating, by September 4 (Day 35 of the Schlieffen Plan), to within thirty-five miles of Paris. Two days earlier, the panicked French had transferred their seat of government, as they had forty-four years earlier in the Franco-Prussian War, to the safety of more distant Bordeaux. Inside Paris was chaos. Preparations were being made to blow up the Eiffel Tower and Seine bridges, to clear fields of fire for artillery and to conscript laborers to do that work. What haunted the French and thrilled the Germans was the seemingly impending replay of 1871, when Prussian troops marched into Paris and imposed on France a peace that returned to Germany the Alsace and Lorraine areas which France had taken by stages throughout the 17th Century.

But August 1914, for all of Germany's swift and systematic gains, definitely did not repeat 1871. To be sure, the French Army and the British Expeditionary Force (the BEF, as it ultimately legendarily became known) had been on almost constant retreat, suffering staggering casualties. But the retreat had been orderly; discipline had held, weapons had been saved and the armies were falling back on their own lines of communication. Top French commander Joseph Joffre, amidst others' panicking, had very much kept his cool. At each step, as his forces pulled back, they made the Germans pay a huge price. Joffre was calculating that ultimately the invaders would over-extend themselves and that a gap would open in their advancing line; when that happened, he reasoned, he would counterattack ferociously.

He was right. And counterattack the French and British did—at the very eleventh hour, just moments before the Germans would have arrived at the gates of Paris. (Yes, Paris still had gates. World War One expert John Keegan writes that, "Paris, in 1914, was still a fortified city, surrounded by walls and a girdle of forts.") Almost as rapidly as the Germans initially had thrust deep into France, now astoundingly the French and British rolled them back, retracing, as Keegan writes, their "steps over the ground won in bitter combat during the last two weeks."[4] This culminated in what history records as the first turning point of the war, the early September epic bloodletting of Wagnerian drama and intensity called the Battle of the Marne, named after the river defining the region. There, over two million men clashed for eight days. By the time the fighting stopped, 500,000 of them were dead or wounded. Never before had history witnessed such carnage so swiftly. But, in what Scottish military historian and Oxford University Professor Hew Strachan calls "one of the truly decisive battles of history," the counterattack in the Marne River region succeeded; it halted that seemingly inexorable German advance.

Germany's grand, carefully studied, meticulously tweaked and extensively rehearsed Schlieffen Plan for a swift victory over France had crumbled. There was no way to deny it. So, on September 14, German Chief of Staff Moltke in effect admitted that the advance was over, ordering his troops to fortify and defend their positions on the heights above the river system just beyond the Marne, the deep and wide Aisne. Though none of the generals on either side could know it at the time, the war of movement and momentum had ended. Along the Aisne Valley maneuver gave way to stasis and attrition as two now relatively balanced forces faced off against each other. The Germans were strong enough to halt the French-British counteroffensive but not strong enough to mount a successful new offensive. The British and French were strong enough to block further German advances, but not strong enough to push through the German lines and send what would be splintered German armies into retreat.

Occupying some 4,000 square miles of Belgium and France, the Germans began digging in. Literally digging in. Over the months, they dug deeper and deeper—as did the British and French armies facing them. In mirror lines of trenches stretching 475 miles from the Bec de Canard on the Swiss border to Nieuport-Bains on the North Sea, this became what history knows as The

Western Front, a term that still chills the spines of British, French, Germans and others who know even just a bit about the human agony that was World War One.

Some thirty months later, in April 1917, when America declared war on Germany, the two sides' positions barely had changed.

What did change was the landscape they occupied. It became what later generations would call a moonscape. Its barren devastation testified to the monstrous battles that raged across its face and the monstrous losses these battles claimed, surpassing even the horrendous tolls of the war's opening months. The Western Front would become history's worst and most sustained killing fields. Thus, though stalemated the battlefield was, stagnant it was not. Gargantuan clashes for four years were waged there; millions of soldiers rushed forward and fell back. In what several generations of historians later concluded was stubborn (and often ignorant) folly, British and French commanders (at times with their political superiors looking on in paralyzed horror) season after season launched one gigantic offensive after another against the increasingly better-entrenched Germans.

It is impossible to read the accounts of contemporaries and by every subsequent generation of amateur historians and professionals without being stunned by their uniform incredulity at the senselessness of the generals' strategies and tactics and at the enormity of the human physical and mental sacrifice. Even in our day, historians who already have read endlessly of the war and thus may be expected to be inured to the pointless suffering are still palpably moved by it. Prominent in these accounts are the names of the Western Front's great battles. They remain, to this day, familiar to Europeans, inscribed in the war memorials and monuments in every town square and on city hall walls: The First Ypres. The Somme. Verdun. The Second Ypres. The Nivelle Offensive. Passchendaele.

The aim of these battles always was the same, to puncture the enemy's lines and then break into open country, thus allowing a cavalry-led campaign of maneuver in which superior skills of generalship plus bravery of the troops at last would turn war's tide. The pattern too always was the same: First came the enormous assembling of arms and troops (and horses, of which some eight million were killed in the war); then multi-day or even multi-week artillery bombardment to "soften" enemy positions; then a "creeping artillery barrage" rolling just a hundred yards or so ahead of the assaulting forces, ostensibly (but always failing) to clear the field; and then, finally, the tidal wave of infantrymen, rifles aslant, bayonets up, lugging some sixty pounds or more of equipment, surging (or, as Keegan writes, "plodding") over the ground between the opposing trenches, the space that had become known as no man's land, typically 200 to 300 yards wide, but sometimes only twenty-five yards wide.

Then the advance always sputtered, as the infantry waves clambered into the barbed wire, entangling themselves and becoming easy targets for the opposing trenches' machine guns. And then, inevitably, the enemy counterattacked, regaining the few hundred yards that the advancing troops may have captured in the offensive's initial hours. When it was all over, almost no land would have changed hands. The only change was further devastation to the landscape and further human toll.

What made advances nearly impossible and so costly were three complementary developments: trenches, barbed wire and machine guns. They shifted the battlefield advantage from the Napoleonic offensive to the defensive. The signature of the Western Front was the trench. To be sure, World War One did not invent it; Union and Confederate soldiers had dug in deeply in Virginia and Maryland during America's Civil War, just as had soldiers a few decades earlier in Portugal during Napoleon's campaign. But only on World War One's Western Front did trenches define the battlefield.

First came the front line trenches to protect soldiers from shells and to create a concrete nest from which to fire at attacking troops; behind these were back-up trenches, support trenches, communications trenches, supply trenches, side trenches with kitchens and first aid stations, latrine trenches, trenches with officers' quarters often outfitted (mainly on the German side) with wallpaper and rugs. In some areas, Germans dug as many as ten rows of trenches, one behind the other, so that even if the British or French overran the first line, they encountered another and then another. Ultimately, reckons American military historian Robert Cowley, 60,000 miles of trenches in aggregate were dug on the Western Front. Life in these trenches became the nightmare that defined the war for a full generation of British, French and Germans. Simple words capture the unrelenting agony of trench life: rats, trench fever, oozing mud, trench foot, lice, giant roaches, gangrene, rotting cadavers, stinking dead horses, dysentery.

By themselves, the trenches would have been no more than a classic shield, protecting soldiers and allowing them to peek up and fire. But the Western Front's trenches were vastly more than shields. With the machine gun, an American Civil War invention, combined with barbed wire, invented by American cattlemen to contain their herds, the trenches became emplacements for deadly weapons that transformed the battlefield. First, the barbed wire, which invariably survived prolonged artillery shellings, entangled and slowed the attackers; then the torrent of machine guns firing 1,000 bullets per minute scythed down everything before them. Together, barbed wire and the machine gun, explains British military historian Gary Sheffield in his 2001 study of the war, gave the defender the battlefield advantage. Defending soldiers in trenches offered a smaller target to the attacker, were harder to locate and more difficult to hit with a bullet. By contrast, the attacker was forced to expose his entire body to enemy fire.[5]

All this decreed vulnerable and thus anachronistic the waves of oncoming bayonet-wielding infantry and sword-thrusting cavalry that had been fielded so successfully by Napoleon, U.S. Grant and other celebrated 19th Century generals. Now, the machine gun shattered their classic battlefield tactics and stopped the assaulters in their tracks. The tragedy was, writes John Ellis in his *The Social History of the Machine Gun,* "the generals never came to terms with [the machine gun]. Time and time again they threw their men forward, confident that this time a little bit more preparation, a few more men, and an extra dash of sheer courage would suffice to break the enemy's will to resist. They never realized that they were not fighting his 'will', but his machine guns." Those generals, British historian and journalist A.J.P. Taylor says, simply "stared" at the trenches, "impotently and without understanding. They went on staring for nearly four years."[6] The result, over and over again, was slaughter. This the green American doughboys tragically were to discover in spring 1918 as they, in America's earliest appearances on the European battlefield, marched in almost parade-ground formation across the landscape at Cantigny and Belleau Wood while unbelieving German machine-gunners opened fire, easily and efficiently slicing down the approaching Yanks.

In these clashes, field guns in staggering numbers fired what earlier would have been an unimaginable number of shells. In preparation for what was called the Second Ypres Offensive, for instance, the British in May 1916 fired more than one million rounds; the German counter-fire closely equaled that. Looking back, military historians conclude that it was the artillery battle more than anything else that made the war so violent and costly in lives, as increasingly refined shells killed and maimed vast numbers trying to find refuge in the trenches and traverse no man's land.

The senseless carnage was obvious to those on the battlefield. One French regimental commander, for instance, in the mid-1915 Battle of Artois, reports military strategy expert Douglas Porch, "watched helplessly as two of his companies were entangled in the undestroyed enemy wire and annihilated."[7] There were times, such as at the September 1915 Battle of Loos, when the oncoming soldiers (in this case, fresh, young British recruits) were such easy targets and so easily killed that the Germans, writes German military history expert Dennis Showalter, became "disgusted with the killing [and] ceased firing on their own initiative."[8] A full year later, when the British launched their gigantic offensive at the Somme, apparently little had been learned and thus little changed. As the Germans in their concrete-encased machine-gun nests astonishingly watched, British infantrymen climbed out of their trenches, formed long rows and began marching slowly almost shoulder to shoulder upright as if on parade across the battlefield, prompting a German gunner later to write: "When we started to fire we just had to load and reload. They went down in their hundreds. We didn't have to aim, we just fired into them."

Calling such carnage "senseless" is no loose use of the word. It was senseless because strategy and tactics that had failed were used again and again even though the sacrifice yielded almost nothing. The four-and-a half-month Battle of the Somme, launched by the British and French on July 1, 1916, which Keegan calls Britain's "greatest military tragedy" ever, which Cowley rates as "the bloodiest battle in history" and which a German captain concluded was "the muddy grave of the German field army," brought three million men onto the field. One-third of them became casualties. Wounded or killed (many by drowning in the mud) were 450,000 British, 200,000 French, 400,000 Germans. Cowley coldly estimates the fatalities at "about 7,000 corpses per square mile."[9] And yet, when British Commander in Chief Douglas Haig finally gave in to outraged pressure from his subordinates in the field and from his government in London and halted the offensive on November 18, 1916, the furthest line of his advance was only seven miles forward of where he had begun on July 1; in most sectors no gains had been made at all.

What lessons were drawn from this? Seemingly none. When British, French and Russian commanders met at a summit in late 1916 to plan the next year's operations, the broad strategy was unchanged. To be sure, Allied offensives inflicted massive—and, as it turned out, devastating—losses on the Germans; the problem was that losses were equally devastating to the French and British (and Australians, Canadians, New Zealanders and others who loyally answered the call to fight, they said, for their British Empire). Lessons were drawn only later, in the following Great War. Then, according to General Dwight Eisenhower, the Supreme Commander of U.S. and other allied armies, "Our guiding principle was to avoid at all cost the freezing of battle lines that might bog down our troops in a pattern similar to the trench warfare of World War I."[10]

Verdun's Mutual Suicide

No battle in the public's mind then, and now, symbolizes the war's massive and devastating losses more than 1916's ten-month struggle by the Germans to capture, and by the French to hold, Verdun. No battle looms greater in history, no loss more tragic, no devastation more complete. If, after nearly a full century, one word can still evoke World War One's seemingly insatiable appetite for lives and destruction, the closed-minded rigidity of its generals and the extraordinary bravery and tenacity of its soldiers, it's Verdun. Nothing casts a longer, darker shadow. Memoirs, novels, poems, histories, movies all attempt to get their arms around the epic bloodletting, to portray and make sense of it.

This great battle began on February 21, 1916, as a massive German offensive against the Verdun Fortified Region, the rings of twenty fortresses encircling the town of Verdun. Initially, Germany's aim, like the British and French offensives, was to break through the lines and then wipe up the splintered and fragmented opposing forces. Like those other offensives too, it sputtered after early gains. Within days attackers ran head-long into ferocious French resistance and a wall of machine gun fire. Citing a historian of Verdun, Ellis writes in his study of machine guns: At Verdun "it was as simple as this: three men and a machine gun can stop a battalion of heroes."[11] Their advance having faltered, the Germans changed goals. General Erich von Falkenhayn, the attack's architect, declared a new purpose: "to compel the French to throw in every man they have. If they do so the forces of France will bleed to death." And, he later added, when "it is clear to the eyes of the French people that, militarily, they have nothing to hope for, then will their limit [of endurance] be surpassed." The French readily took the bait and vowed to hold Verdun. For France's military commanders and political leaders, its loss was unacceptable; it would have inflicted psychological and morale blows they feared their nation could not survive. To be sure, ironically, Verdun and its fortresses actually had scant military value. At stake, rather, was France's ability to demonstrate that it still was strong enough to prevent yet more of its soil from falling to the Germans.

The battle thus was joined. The Germans sought to bleed the French and the French were ready to bleed and bleed if that's what it took to hold Verdun. Even after continual bashing against each other for months with no gains, neither side was ready to stand down. The Germans deployed every single one of their reserve divisions, while two-thirds of the French Army fought, at some moment, to hold Verdun. To pound the French, the Germans lugged in, on specially built rails, a dozen of their fearsome Gamma Guns, the world's most powerful howitzers, known to history as "Big Berthas," blasting away at the fortresses with shells weighing nearly one ton each. The forts didn't crumble. The French too fielded powerful artillery, including hundreds of their envied 75mm cannon, its revolutionary design enabling it to move around the battlefield and fire twenty rounds of shrapnel shells a minute. Both sides together fired some 50 million artillery shells in the battle; their legacy of devastation today is still visible to anyone walking the area, as have done generations of French and Germans, as if on a pilgrimage.

By December 15, with both sides exhausted and Verdun still in French hands, the fighting stopped. Writes B.H. Liddell Hart, who fought with the British at the Somme and later became one of the war's most influential chroniclers: Verdun "was France's supreme sacrifice and her supreme triumph."[12] Just about all historians of all generations agree. But at what price? Casualty figures from such a marathon conflict can't be precise and, understandably, omit the hundreds of thousands of French and Germans psychologically deeply scarred, whose despair and anger helped shape their societies and their politics in succeeding decades. It is reckoned that 162,000 French died at Verdun, with another 215,000 wounded. German losses were a bit lighter (unusual, because attackers typically lose more men than defenders): 143,000 Germans dead and 194,000 wounded.[13] By comparison, U.S. fatalities in all of World War One were 114,000, in World War Two 405,399, in Korea 36,516 and in Viet Nam 58,151.

At Verdun, the Germans lost their best trained and most experienced troops. Concludes Laurence Moyer in his account of Germany during the war: "After Verdun, the German Army was never the same... Its impact on the home front was...extensive."[14] The same could be said for the French; indeed, its dismal World War Two showing, collapsing in 1940 before Nazi troops in just five weeks (actually, faster than the Schlieffen Plan's World War One timetable) in part was Verdun's legacy. This eerily was foreshadowed by the words of French General Henri-Phillipe Petain, whose own World War Two role as what many still see as the Nazi puppet leader of Vichy France made him one of the most controversial and vilified leaders in French history. Wrote Petain: "My heart leapt as I saw our youths of twenty going into the furnace of Verdun. But...when they returned...their expressions seemed frozen by a vision of terror, their gait...betrayed a total dejection; they sagged beneath the weight of horrifying memories."[15]

Verdun's carnage was so monumental in great part because Verdun went on for months. So did the war's other signature battles. And while Europe surely was no stranger to massive armies charging at and killing each other and suffering huge losses, in no previous war had the battles raged so long. Previously, climactic battles had occurred on one day, maybe two. But World War One was different. What distinguishes it (and, later, World War Two) from its predecessors is not so much the extraordinary casualties per day, but that there were so many of those days. Writes Hew Strachan in a 2003 *Foreign Affairs* article: "Losses occurred every day—and night—of the year...Fighting was continuous; it was never really all quiet on the Western Front."[16] This fighting, moreover, no longer had the goal of defeating the enemy in a final, defining battle; rather it now sought victory simply by a wearing down, by attrition, what the French called "nibbling" (*"grignotage"*). France's General Joffre declared: "We shall kill more of the enemy than he can kill of us." The trouble was, so many were killed on both sides that attrition had become akin to a mutual suicide pact.

By the opening months of 1917, when America was nearing its decision on whether to join the conflict, the Great War was still deadlocked on the Western Front. And on that front is where the war was to be won or to be lost. Of course, in the war's first thirty months epic battles had raged elsewhere—at Tannenberg and Gallipoli, in the Balkans, throughout the Middle East and in the North Sea where Britain's Grand Fleet and Germany's High Seas Fleet at Jutland fought to pretty much a draw in what was history's grandest naval confrontation until the World War Two mammoth Pacific Ocean battles between the American and Japanese navies. And, of course too, battles of legend were fought in the east by Russia's huge armies against Germany and Austria-Hungary, at moments (as in the June 1916 Brusilov Offensive) scoring astounding victories and forcing Germany to rush eastward scores of divisions from the Western Front.

It is not to diminish the suffering and sacrifice of these battles to say that they mainly were important, in the end, by how they affected the Western Front. And on the Western Front stalemate continued—and continued—breeding (as should be expected) discontent and anger, as soldiers increasingly saw themselves as being fed perpetually into a meat grinder for no ostensible purpose. This anger most dramatically erupted in the French Army in May 1917, just weeks after America had declared war on Germany and was beginning its own mobilization. French soldiers began balking. They refused to attack, refused to become still more purposeless mincemeat. They would hold the line, they said, to defend their homeland, but they wouldn't attack. No more.

Triggering this mutiny (called "acts of collective indiscipline" by the French command) was the collapse of France's April 1917 Nivelle Offensive, yet one more grand effort to escape from attrition and to pound through German lines. It had been sold to the French government and hyped to the French public by France's new Western Front commander, Robert Nivelle, as a different kind of offensive, "a mass of maneuver" sure to achieve victory within forty-eight hours and force the Germans to turn heel and retreat from France. It didn't. Instead, it replayed the film everyone already had seen—and seen repeatedly. Once again French (and Germans too, of course) were killed and wounded in staggering numbers, with little to show for it.

This was the straw breaking the back of French troop discipline. The French infantryman, the "poilu"—or "hairy one" (a term of endearment conveying not only the recruits' rustic, rural, unsophisticated background but also that, in the trenches, they seldom shaved)—had decided he had enough. The "terrible ordeal," writes Keegan, "was simply no longer bearable by those at the bottom of the heap." On May 6, some of them refused the order to advance, sparking a fast-spreading mutiny which ultimately involved some 35,000 soldiers in about half of France's divisions, inspiring the poignant 1935 novel and 1957 film *Paths of Glory*. In the weeks following, others refused similar orders to advance, declaring that while they were ready bravely to man the trenches and prevent Germans from pushing further into France, they would not go on the attack. Some shouted, "Down with the war"; some got drunk; some didn't bring their weapons with them; some marched on Paris, looting along the way. The French command struck back hard at the protestors: 3,427 were court martialed, 554 sentenced to death, forty-nine actually executed by firing squad. The mutiny collapsed. Yet it shook to the core the French government and military command. Petain, now the new French Western Front commander, by and large called off all further French offensive action, telling his British counterpart, Douglas Haig, that he no longer should count on French forces to help in British offensives, saying, in effect, "I don't have an army." The British, who had rushed to the Continent in August 1914 to save France, were now on their own. For nearly all of the following year, the French barely budged from their trenches.

There they would stay, waiting for America's young men, its boys, to arrive. Only then, when millions of Yanks would take to the field in France, could the stalemate be broken and only then could an offensive be launched capable of smashing through German lines.

CHAPTER 2

AMERICA WATCHES A WAR

HERE WAS NO SENSE IN America (or elsewhere, for that matter), when the war in Europe erupted in August 1914, that this ever would become America's war. Throughout its history, after all, the U.S. resolutely had refused to get involved in Europe's battles. Many Americans could recite by heart George Washington's 1796 Farewell Address admonition imploring the nation "to steer clear of permanent alliances with any parts of the foreign world," a sentiment undergirding generations of Americans' near-universal support for isolationism and echoed nearly a century later in Grover Cleveland's 1885 presidential inaugural address rejecting "any share in foreign broils." When Europe exploded, therefore, President Woodrow Wilson's first response was to proclaim the nation's neutrality and declare that Europe's war "cannot touch us."[1]

Even had Wilson toyed with the notion of taking sides (which he certainly did not), it would not be clear which side America would favor. Looking back a century from our day, it may be hard for us to understand how thoroughly divided were American sympathies in 1914. There were, naturally, deep feelings for and bonds with the British—through the obvious elements of common language, shared democratic values and systems and a great deal of intermingled history. But American feelings for and bonds with Germany were nearly as strong and nearly as historically grounded. Wilson recognized this when, in his neutrality message to the Senate just after the start of the war, he said that in origin most Americans came "chiefly from the nations now at war." As such, he continued, it "is natural and inevitable that there should be the utmost variety of sympathy... Some will wish one nation, others another, to succeed in the momentous struggle."

Pro-British sentiment, predictably, was strongest on the East Coast and amongst America's social, cultural and economic elite, an extremely influential group which a half-century later was nicknamed, usually derisively, WASPs—for White Anglo-Saxon Protestants. They not only saw themselves as the New World torchbearers of everything grandly British, but also had myriad economic, family, social and even religious ties to the United Kingdom. Wall Street, in particular, was strongly bound to London, and even Paris, by countless economic interests, arrangements and deals. Most prominent was J.P. Morgan and Company. It not only had the lucrative contract to serve as the sole agent purchasing munitions and other supplies in the U.S. for Britain and France, but also was linked by family to British aristocracy. Morgan Partner Thomas Lamont, a true titan of Wall Street, after the war candidly admitted: "Our firm had never for one moment been neutral... From the very start we did everything we could to contribute to the cause of the Allies."[2] Studies have found similar pro-Allied sentiments among America's college professors, public school teachers and clergymen.

Favoring the British side also were America's top politicians. Wilson himself, who had shown almost no interest at all in foreign affairs before becoming president in 1913, is said to have known or cared little about any foreign country other than Britain. Teddy Roosevelt, the dashing and charismatic former president who still influenced much of the nation's political opinions, after briefly calling for U.S. neutrality, early on threw his formidable and muscular support behind the Allies—the British and French. As president, after all, he had championed what later generations would call America's "special relationship" with Britain, espousing, writes American historian William C. Widenor, "an Anglo-American combination dominating the world in the interest of civilization."[3]

As for the media, which in those days mainly meant newspapers and magazines, those taking a side overwhelmingly fell into the pro-Allied camp. A *Literary Digest* poll of 367 editors published on November 14, 1914, found that 242 respondents were neutral, 105 favored the Allies and only twenty favored Germany.[4] Meantime, America's two most influential newspapers, the *New York Times* and the *New York World*, the source of much of the foreign news carried by other papers around the country, were strongly anti-German. From the start, therefore, the pro-British, thus pro-Allied, forces in America were formidable.

But so were the pro-Germans.

America's largest immigrant group, it perhaps now is forgotten, was the German, with the 1910 Census recording 8,262,618 who checked Germany as country of origin—nearly nine percent of the nation's 92 million population. To this add another 15 million Americans estimated to come originally from German stock. This means that over a quarter of the American population in 1914 had some affinity for Germany. Indeed, the German stamp was readily in evidence, with huge communities in Chicago, Cincinnati, Cleveland, Columbus, Dayton, Des Moines, Milwaukee, New York City and St. Louis, all with their influential local social and political clubs and churches (at least 6,000 Lutheran congregations nationwide). Meantime, some 500 German-language dailies and weeklies were being published in America, with New York City alone boasting eight dailies and five weeklies. Giving added clout and political muscle to all of this was the two million-strong National German-American Alliance, whose members all were American citizens; it was perhaps the largest ethnic organization in U.S. history. The Alliance published leaflets and launched an ambitious national publicity campaign to keep America from supporting the Allies, including dispatching speakers to oppose U.S. arms sales to Britain. Its backers on Capitol Hill even managed to introduce resolutions to ban arms sales to all combatants in the war. And in Manhattan, Germans marched down Broadway singing "Deutschland Ueber Alles."

Second only to the Germans in size as an immigrant group were the Irish, with 4,504,000 checking Ireland as country of origin in the 1910 Census. By 1914, they were playing leading roles in America's labor movement, wielding enormous influence in the U.S. Roman Catholic Church and were beginning to take control of big city politics. What counted for Germany was that almost all America's Irish were deeply hostile to Britain. The *Gaelic-American,* the *Irish World* and other Irish newspapers, a number of which began receiving ads from German firms, incessantly attacked Britain and strongly and repeatedly urged Irish-Americans to take actions to prevent Washington from leaning towards London. Organizations such as the United Irish-American Societies, among other things, mobilized their members to demonstrate at cinemas, forcing them to cancel British propaganda movies, while the American Truth Society, an Irish-led group (with many German members), acted to counter British propaganda directly.

Then there was the Russia factor. This was no small matter. Poles, Jews and Finns, also huge immigrant communities, all had fled to America to escape Tsarist Russia's dark and brutal repression. Surely they would oppose any U.S. help for hated Imperial Russia, the key ally of Britain and France in the war. And indeed they did. Meirion and Susie Harries, in *The Last Days of Innocence,* describe these communities' strong opposition to Russia and cite efforts by Russian Jews in Cincinnati "to raise a volunteer regiment to fight the Tsar." More broadly, according to a study of American Jewish attitudes during the war, "immigrant Jews prayed that the 'more civilized' Germans would free their oppressed brethren in Eastern Europe from Russian persecution." So widespread was hatred of the Tsar and his pogroms that Jacob Schiff, a very prominent Jew and head of one of New York's leading banks, on October 19, 1914 wrote to a German Foreign Office official that: "The sympathies of a majority of American Jews, who are in the main of Russian origin, are on the side of Germany."[5] The Russia factor also played a role beyond immigrant communities, influencing many liberals and Progressives, a key (and perhaps dominant) component of the electoral coalition giving Wilson his 1912 presidential victory. They were extremely troubled by any U.S. actions helping the Tsar and his autocracy, which they regarded (correctly) as vastly less democratic and more oppressive than the Kaiser's Germany. In fact, only after revolution in March 1917 toppled the Tsar did many Progressives rally to Wilson's increasing hostility to Germany.

American ties to and sympathies with the belligerents thus clearly were divided at the war's outbreak. Whether the pro-Allied or pro-Central Powers forces in America were equally matched may be unanswerable. But it is certain that a pro-British and Allied tilt was far from inevitable or desirable. It even could be argued (statistically and theoretically) that if the U.S. were to favor any side it would favor the German, though this was never even remotely possible nor ever considered. The reality of August 1914 was that no tilt at all would be America's best policy. Each camp in the U.S. was large enough to make it politically unappetizing for any official to take sides in the European conflict. And no officials were tempted to do so. Within hours of the war's start, the U.S. made this explicitly clear with the official "Proclamation of August 4, 1914" stating: "I, Woodrow Wilson, President of the United States of America...do hereby declare and proclaim...a strict and impartial neutrality." He forbad Americans to "take part, directly or indirectly" in the war, requiring them to "remain at peace with all of the said belligerents." Two weeks later, in an August 19 message to the Senate, he elaborated, declaring

that the "United States must be neutral in fact as well as in name…
We must be impartial in thought as well as in action."

Wilson had powerful motives for insisting on neutrality, beyond mirroring the divided sympathies of the American populace. As the many historians who over the decades have analyzed Wilson seem to agree, he apparently truly was dedicated to peace and long sympathized with and had a wide following among American pacifists. His Secretary of State was the very popular William Jennings Bryan, three-time Democrat presidential candidate and, more important, a leading pacifist, as were powerful Democrats on Capitol Hill, such as Representative Claude Kitchin of North Carolina, who soon would become House Majority Leader. Wilson, moreover, had bold plans for extending his already far-reaching domestic policy agenda, such as abolishing child labor, setting the eight-hour working day for railroad workers, slashing tariffs, introducing an inheritance tax and creating an ambitious farm loan program. He rightly feared these all could be delayed or even derailed by U.S. involvement in war. "Every reform we have won," he said, "will be lost if we go into this war."[6]

Wilson's neutrality policy was cheered across a wide political spectrum. He was supported by 878 of the nation's 897 major newspapers. Backing him unreservedly were political powerhouses from all parties. The reflexively pugnacious Teddy Roosevelt, who relished opportunities for flexing the nation's military muscles (and who had no love for Wilson, having been defeated by him in the 1912 elections), made it clear that he strongly felt that the U.S. should stay out of Europe's war, calling the notion of American intervention "folly" and a "frightful calamity." He feared that a solid victory by either side would upset the European equilibrium, though he soon changed his mind and began pushing for increasingly broad American backing for the Allies.

Wilson—and Roosevelt—were echoed by their many supporters in the still powerful, though fading, Progressive movement. Progressives were loath to divert any policy focus from such favorite domestic aims as limiting immigration, banning child labor, advancing women suffrage, imposing a graduated income tax on the wealthy, establishing a central bank via the Federal Reserve System and regulating the railroads. Equally crucial, Progressives and Populists were very vocal about their deep suspicions of the role played in triggering the war by what they called, variously, international financiers, banking interests or capitalists. And since Progressives and Populists typically saw London as the headquarters of international finance, there was absolutely no reason, they argued, for the U.S. to take any actions favoring Britain. Writes Thomas Knock in his well-regarded 1992 study of Wilson: For the feminists, liberals, pacifists, socialists and social reformers, "peace was essential to change—to the survival of the labor movement and of their campaigns on behalf of ...social justice legislation in general." An America at war would jeopardize these causes.[7]

Agreeing with this would be the Socialists, whose candidate in the 1912 presidential elections was Eugene V. Debs. He had received 901,000 votes, a very impressive six percent of the electorate. By 1914, more than 1,000 Socialists were holding office in 340 municipalities in half of the states. For Debs and his Socialists, the European war was nothing more than a violent family squabble among capitalist and imperialist nations which should not be supported by working men and women. For America to join the war was unthinkable for Debs.

Overlapping the Progressives and Socialists was the peace movement, including what became the Women's Peace Party founded by social work pioneer Jane Addams in January 1915, specifically to rally opposition to the war and any American participation in it. In a year it had signed-on 40,000 members. As the war progressed, the peace and women's movements invoked themes of motherhood to prevent the U.S. from entering the conflict. This theme resonated astoundingly. Example: The December 1914 recording "I Didn't

Raise My Boy To Be A Soldier" became an instant hit, with subsequent sheet music sales skyrocketing to 1915's Top Ten list. The sheet music's cover is headlined "A Mother's Plea For Peace"; below this headline is a seated white-haired mother hugging a son as war clouds gather in the background. The lyrics begin: "Ten million soldiers to the war have gone, who may never return again. Ten million mothers' hearts must break." Then comes the refrain, repeated several times: "I didn't raise my boy to be a soldier. I brought him up to be my pride and joy. Who dares to place a musket on his shoulder, to shoot some other mother's darling boy? ...There'd be no war today, if mothers all would say: I didn't raise my boy to be a soldier."[8]

Though the song triggered a sizeable backlash, was denounced as being unpatriotic and prompted, in the style of that day, sharp-edged parodies (such as "I Did Not Raise My Boy To Be A Coward"), its immediate and year-long popularity reflected America's broad support for neutrality. So nearly unanimous and strong was political, media, social and popular backing of neutrality that British Ambassador to the U.S. Cecil Spring-Rice in early 1915 cabled home that were the U.S. to declare war on Germany there would be "a strong probability of civil war" in America.

Thus, as the war began in Europe, it seemed certain that it would not become America's war. That it eventually did so and that America thirty-one months later declared war on Germany, joined the Allied side and mobilized four million troops was a decision that profoundly influenced subsequent history, setting the course for the 20th Century in the West.

Strangely, in terms of the bloody battle itself, as is clear in the previous chapter, there was much less reason for America to enter the war on April 6, 1917 than there had been in the conflict's opening weeks, when Germany's swift advances made it seem that a Teutonic victory was assured. By early 1917, the battlefield was frozen, rigidly stalemated, with its 60,000 miles of elaborate concrete trenches along its 475-mile front. Both sides—the Allies and the Central

Powers—were exhausted, their reserves of manpower and stockpiles of weapons running low, their war-driven debts running high, their home fronts tired of sacrificing their sons and increasingly dubious of the competence of their military and political leaders. There was no danger of the kind of German triumph that could have upended the European balance of power, giving Berlin the sort of hegemony that (rightly) worried American military and geopolitical strategists. At most, the success of one side or the other's offensive somewhat would have shifted lines on Europe's map. Paris was no longer in danger of falling; London never was; and there was no fear of the war spreading. There was, after all, no Pearl Harbor, no 9/11; no direct attack on America by Germany and no attack on any American ally (because, after all, America had no "allies").

So why, in a fateful April 6, 1917 decision and action, did once determinedly neutral America declare war on Germany? The answer is found in the fabric of interwoven threads, which, over the thirty-one months, persuaded America that Germany was a dangerous predator aggressor, that Britain and France needed saving and that only America could save them. These threads included:

- Britain's skilled propaganda campaign in the U.S. aimed at bringing America into the war by portraying Germany as the aggressor and (unfairly, as history has concluded) as a perpetrator of disgusting atrocities;
- Germany's flawed and ham-fisted propaganda efforts in the U.S. aimed at keeping America neutral;
- Growing American economic reliance on sales of war materiel, food and other goods to Britain, France and Russia;
- German submarine attacks on shipping, designed to break Britain's strangling blockade of Germany but which, by killing some Americans, outraged the American public, convincing it that Germany was an international thug which could not be allowed to win the war;

- The Russian Revolution of March 1917, which overthrew the Tsar and introduced some democracy into Russia, thus eliminating the repressive autocracy that had been making it difficult for U.S. liberals and Progressives to back the Allies;
- Washington's lenient response to London's harsh wartime actions, contrasted with its very tough response to Berlin's, which gradually made a mockery of neutrality, inexorably nudging the American public toward viewing Germany as *the* enemy.

Dueling Propaganda

Nothing was more effective in eroding and ultimately ending American neutrality than the British propaganda campaign. It was subtle, sharply focused and waged on several fronts. Part was active propaganda. And part was simply controlling the information flow into America about the war. As the conflict raged on Europe's battlefields, there was very little that Americans read about the war or heard about it at public lectures and meetings not controlled or heavily influenced by London. Surely, at no time in history— neither before nor since—has a foreign country so shaped American perceptions. What Americans thought they knew about the war, about Germany, about the Allies, about the battlefield, about troop actions and behavior, about atrocities and war crimes, about war aims, about home front conditions all were colored deeply by London's propaganda. In what became an intense, though ultimately one-sided, propaganda duel, judge some historians, "Germany was beaten more decisively than on the field of battle." British success at misinformation and disinformation would have impressed greatly the later Soviet Cold War masters of the craft.

Certainly none of what Britain did was illegal; nor, in the context of London's absolute necessity to mobilize all resources to fight a war, was it unacceptable or even unfair or even inappropriate.

It violated no international conventions of good conduct. If it served British war ends, Britain was entitled to lie, distort the truth, mislead. That Britain (and France), in the end, lied more effectively than did Germany (and the Central Powers) is a credit to Britain. But that doesn't obscure the crucial fact that the target of the lies was America and those being lied to were Americans who, as it was, were relying greatly on these British lies as they were making up their minds about what America should do about the war. And it consequently doesn't obscure the crucial fact that when America decided to join the British side against Germany that decision rested, to a great extent, on British-manufactured false information and phony data.

To start, London physically controlled just about all war news reaching U.S. shores. Within days of the war's outbreak, the British cable ship *Telconia* sliced the two trans-Atlantic telegraph cables linking Germany to America. Several months later, the only remaining link, a Liberia-to-Brazil cable jointly owned by Germany and the U.S., also was cut by the British. Reported the *New York Times* on August 6, "Until direct cable service is restored, all word of happenings in Germany must pass through hostile countries." The cable remained severed throughout the war. This actually prompted Berlin unashamedly to beg the American public to understand Germany's predicament. Declared German Imperial Chancellor Theobold von Bethmann-Hollweg in a statement to the Associated Press carried on page one of the *New York Times* on August 23, 1914: "Germany is completely cut off from the rest of the world, and can neither send out news nor receive it... The German people will be profoundly grateful for every effort to disseminate the real truth."

That London could move so quickly to snap the German cables indicates just how long and thoroughly the British had been planning to control information flow to America. For the rest of the war, explains Stewart Ross in his 1996 study, *Propaganda for War: How the United States Was Conditioned to Fight the Great War of 1914-1918,* Germany had to rely on radio or mail to get its message to

America. Neither was secure. British warships intercepted and read all mail crossing the Atlantic, even on neutral ships. Even on American ships.[9] As a result, just about all journalists' war dispatches had to be transmitted via British-controlled cables. Imposing massive censorship, which intensified during the war, London systematically blocked any news favorable to the Central Powers and unfavorable to the Allies.

Adding to Britain's control of cable traffic was its strong influence on news content itself. In 1914, American newspapers posted few American reporters abroad, instead staffing their European bureaus with locals and relying on overseas papers and magazines for information. Typical was even the *New York Times*; its London bureau chief, Ernest Marshall, was British, as was most of his staff, all of whom strongly backed Britain in the war. And since just about all U.S. papers covered Europe from their London offices, the reporting from wartime Europe being read by Americans in American newspapers actually was being written mainly by Britons—who, understandably, favored their country.

Even those correspondents committed to balanced reporting found the task made nearly impossible by the British Defense of the Realm Act. DORA, as it was known, was passed by Parliament just one week after the war's start and imposed a stifling censorship regime by making it illegal for Britain-based correspondents, such as those working for American papers, to send home any news unfavorable to the Allies. And though American journalists in London were extremely unhappy about the limitations imposed on them and continually tried to circumvent them, they had little success. Writes Horace Peterson in his 1939 study of wartime propaganda: "The American correspondents in Europe did attempt to send unbiased news to their papers. They struggled against the restrictions imposed on them by the British but to no avail." Peterson cites an Associated Press reporter who, in 1915, estimated that seventy-five percent of dispatches written by American correspondents were blocked by British (and French) censors.[10]

The result of Britain's propaganda and censorship operations: American newspapers, by and large, certainly unintentionally, became megaphones for the British war effort. Within a month of the war's outbreak, nearly every English-language paper in the U.S. was following the British line. Concludes Ross: "Tainted news stories and feature articles of imaginary battlefield successes, biased concepts of the war's origins, and atrocity sensations were on the front pages."[11] (To be sure, London's censors also greatly controlled what their fellow Britons knew of the war. In fact, in a moment of extreme candor, British Prime Minister David Lloyd George in December 1917 told a reporter that: "If the people really knew, the war would be stopped tomorrow. But of course they don't—and can't—know.")

British propaganda strategy extended far beyond controlling the news flow. Britain also sought to influence American opinion directly, and did so through an elaborate and sophisticated campaign with a headquarters in London and an operations center in Washington. British operatives used, and perhaps pioneered, techniques which decades later would become common public opinion-bending methods routinely employed by American lobbyists, trade unions, business associations, think tanks, political parties and partisan organizations and all others advocating or opposing a cause. The British used "direct mail" campaigns, sent celebrity surrogates on the road to make speeches around the U.S., supplied a steady stream of articles, interviews and even cartoons to hundreds of small-town newspapers unable to afford their own correspondents, commissioned and published heavily slanted books, pamphlets and articles dressed up as unbiased and academic studies, deployed influential and high-ranking Britons to lobby personally American opinion makers, conjured up tainted (or totally phony) statistics to support every British position on the war—and more.

All of this was done secretly, with London denying repeatedly that it was doing anything to influence American opinion. By contrast, as described below, the German propaganda effort was conducted openly by German officials in the U.S., mainly via the German Embassy and consulates and through the ubiquitous German-American associations, and thus was easily dismissed by the American public as being biased. The headquarters of the British propaganda campaign, officially called the War Propaganda Board but known to history mainly as Wellington House, was the ostensible London base of an insurance firm. (Its existence and location became known only long after the war.) Head of what internally was termed the American Ministry of Information was Sir Gilbert Parker, a name that became very familiar to academics in the years after the war as they researched and analyzed British wartime information practices. Parker's mission was unambiguous: to bring America into the war on Britain's side.

Parker eventually had a staff of fifty-four, who, among other things, with the help of the British Embassy, consulates and agents in the U.S., compiled a list of 260,000 Americans targeted to receive British-produced disinformation. Topping the list were American academics, bankers, businessmen, editors, lawyers, politicians and public officials who received "personal" letters signed by Parker. Also targeted by British propaganda, as outlined in a November 1914 memo, were American public libraries, lawyers' offices, school teachers, universities, hotels, railway reading and smoking cars, men's and women's clubs and doctors' and dentists' waiting rooms. British diplomats in America actually were mobilized to visit those venues to drop off pamphlets and other propaganda. According to Jonathan Epstein in his study of German and British propaganda during the war, they were later honored for making "one of the most significant contributions of the Foreign Office" to the propaganda campaign.[12] British celebrities and prominent Americans, meanwhile, continued to be recruited to write and lecture across the U.S.

Their main technique was soft propaganda. Their central theme was that Britain and America were peas of the same pod, similar in endless respects. By sharp and ugly contrast, they repeated over and over that Germany was alien to America and savage, determined to assemble a global empire threatening to the U.S. The message was that Germans were "Huns" and "barbarians"; that the German Emperor, the Kaiser, was a degenerate villain and criminal; that Germany alone was responsible for starting the brutal war; that German spies were infiltrating America. Popular British science fiction writer H.G. Wells, for instance, wrote propaganda pamphlets stressing that his country actually was serving U.S. interests by "fighting a war against Kruppism," a shorthand term, well understood then by many Americans, for German industrial might and domination. Wellington House, meantime, commissioned books and pamphlets depicting Germans as dangerous militarists. One Wellington House technique, described by Epstein, was to translate into English and distribute in the U.S. books by "extreme German nationalists, militarists and exponents of *Machtpolitik* [policy based on power] such as von Treitschke, Nietzche and Bernhardi." This later was seen by analysts, writes Epstein, as a "brilliant move" because it reinforced Britain's argument that Germany was alien to the peaceful values shared by Britain and America.[2-30] Wells echoed this in another of his pamphlets, hammering that Britain's wartime goal was "disarmament and peace throughout the earth." Foreshadowing Woodrow Wilson's later slogan that the war was a "war to end all wars," a Wells pamphlet of August 14, 1914 was entitled *The War That Will End War*. In all, Wells wrote five propaganda books during the war.

No British propaganda success was more spectacular nor had more impact than its tale of horrifying German atrocities. To this day, those who may know a little about the war or at times think a bit about it likely reflexively assume that German troops committed unspeakable acts against individuals and towns. In fact, that was almost entirely untrue. Though German troops at times acted brutally in the war's early months (as did British, French and

Russian soldiers), extensive historical research has found that almost all the stories about German atrocities were lies and distortions, many fabricated by Wellington House. Dressed up as news reports and academic investigations, London spread accounts of German barbarism that included, writes Ross in his study of wartime propaganda: "The crucified Canadian soldier, the women whose breasts were cut off after being ravished, the German corpse factory where glycerine was distilled from the bodies of dead German soldiers."

To illustrate stories purportedly about Germans terrorizing Belgians, British papers carried photographs from pre-war Russia of Jews and others being terrorized in pogroms. The photos were doctored, substituting Germans for the Tsarist troops.[14] The most widely circulated stories, according to Laurence Moyer in his 1995 history of Germany during the war, depicted Germans raping nuns and chopping off both hands of Belgian youth so that they'd never be able to fight against Germany in future wars. These and other British fabrications triggered such *New York Times* headlines as: "DANISH CHILDREN SHOT. Said To Have Been Executed Because They Cried 'Vive la France'"; "GERMANS, HE SAYS HE SHOT REFUGEES"; and "BOYS WITH HANDS CUT OFF."

These reports, pure lies, outraged the handful of American journalists actually in Europe covering the opening months of the war. Five of them, reporting for the Associated Press, the *Saturday Evening Post*, the *Philadelphia Public Ledger*, the *Chicago Tribune* and the *Chicago Daily News*, jointly sent home a dispatch strongly repudiating the atrocity stories. Carried on the *New York Times* front page on September 7, 1914, their dispatch declared: "In spirit of fairness we unite in rendering German atrocities groundless…we are unable to report a single instance unprovoked reprisal… Numerous investigated rumors proved groundless." Throughout their subsequent careers these reporters stood by their statement.[15] The truth, however, made no impact. As London kept drumming its theme of atrocities by barbaric Germans, that theme kept running in American newspapers.

The most successful operation of this very successful campaign was what history remembers as the Bryce Report, named after its chairman, James Bryce, a former British ambassador in Washington and the author of a history of the U.S., thus enhancing the report's credibility in America, particularly among America's East Coast elite and opinion makers. Officially known as the *Report of the Committee on Alleged German Atrocities* and released on May 13, 1915 in thirty languages, it professed to be an academic and impartial finding that Germany, without doubt, committed repeated atrocities. It was, according to many historians, "the most powerful and enduring example of World War I propaganda." Thomas Knock's study of Wilson deems it "the crescendo of a systematic propaganda campaign to overcome American neutrality."[16] The trouble was, the Bryce Report was a big lie.

The Report claimed that the Committee's investigators had uncovered some 1,200 acts of German barbarism and cruelty, including the crucifixion and decapitation of prisoners of war, gang rape and the sexual mutilation of Belgian and French women, the hacking off of children's fingers and—what still lives in popular mythology of the war—the horrifying German bayoneting of Belgian infants. That nearly every bit of this was concocted and that nearly every witness interviewed was pro-British was not known to the public at the time. Only later, writes Knock, was "much of it...proved to be fictional." Adds Dennis Showalter, onetime president of the American Society for Military History and often called the dean of military historians: "The Kaiser's army fought by recognized rules and conventions about as well as did its enemies. Germans, like all combatants, committed a significant number of battlefield atrocities. These, however, were part of the 'filth of war' as opposed to systematic policy, and were subject to heavy penalties if officially discovered."[17]

But these balanced verdicts on alleged German atrocities,

of course, came much too late to affect American attitudes. In May 1915, the Bryce Report's release triggered a public relations tsunami. It was acclaimed in America and much elsewhere as the credible, painstaking work of a board of distinguished objective scholars who carefully sifted evidence and interrogated impartial witnesses—and by doing so unearthed behavior inconceivable by ostensibly civilized Europeans. It implanted in many American minds the indelible notion of barbaric and evil Germans at the gate, held back only by British and French soldiers, the forces of good. Concludes Knock: "The report created a sensation. Germany would never fully recover from the revulsion that swept the U.S."[18]

Feeding this, though inadvertently, were the highly publicized appeals for funds and clothing by Herbert Hoover's Committee for Relief in Belgium, the Cardinal Gibbons Fund for Catholic Children, The Belgian Kiddies Fund and various other American efforts to help those suffering economically in German-occupied Belgium. To raise money, the groups denounced Germany and highlighted its treatment of Belgians. Ultimately, it seems, most Americans decided that there was a huge moral difference between the two sides in the war. (This was reinforced, of course, once America declared war on Germany and launched its own anti-German propaganda campaign; according to British historian Niall Ferguson, several Liberty Loan posters urging Americans to buy bonds to finance the war "used images of scantily clad Belgian nymphs at the mercy of Simian Huns.")

British propaganda, in the end, overwhelmed Germany's. Yet, none of this could have been predicted at the war's outbreak, when German propagandists seemed to have an upper hand. Germany had a slew of advantages. To start, as noted earlier, those of German origin comprised America's largest ethnic group and were influential in their communities, thus capable of spreading and echoing the Berlin point of view. Then there was the network of the earlier-mentioned

Lutheran churches and German-American organizations plus the 500 or so German language daily and weekly newspapers, all of which were potential valuable megaphones for Berlin.

Of advantage too was the legacy of America's generally cordial relations with Germany (and the varied German states before German unification in 1871), at least until the decade or so before the war. Never had American soldiers fought a German state, a point stressed repeatedly by Germany's propaganda articles, pamphlets and posters. By contrast, emphasized German propagandists, America had battled Britain in the American Revolution and in 1812 and contended, at times very acrimoniously, with British challenges to the Monroe Doctrine in Latin America. And in that traumatic conflict to keep America unified, the Civil War, still vivid in many memories, what side had London favored, asked German publications. The Confederacy, they correctly answered.

Germany also could make points by appealing to several of America's large non-German immigrant groups and arguing, rightly, that their historical enemies were now Germany's enemies. German propaganda aiming at the Irish, for instance, constantly hammered away at Irish grievances against London. The Germans, in a huge propaganda barrage, exploited what history knows as the Easter Rising when, for a full week in April 1916, militant Irish republicans occupied sites in Dublin, including city hall and the main post office, and proclaimed Ireland's independence from Britain. The subsequent fighting left dead 116 British soldiers and about three times as many Irish republicans. These bloody events, understandably, were followed closely by America's Irish, fueling their long-simmering hatred of London. Raising their tempers even further was the uprising's aftermath, when the British military in Ireland arrested some 3,500 republicans and sentenced ninety of them to death by firing squad, fifteen of whom ultimately were executed. The Easter Rising was Britain's most serious propaganda setback and Germany played it up relentlessly. German propagandists, writes Epstein, stressed that "in this war, Ireland has only one enemy. Let every Irish heart, let every Irish hand, let every Irish purse be with Germany."[19]

German propaganda similarly targeted America's Jews, arguing that it was German soldiers who now were fighting those same Tsarist troops who routinely had attacked and massacred Jews in countless pogroms. Germany branded the Russians as "half-cultured Tartars" and "Asiatics." Meantime, Germany's U.S. Ambassador, Johann von Bernstorff, wrote the editor of New York City's Jewish paper *Der Tag* that "Germany is offering the Jews in Russian Poland openly and without reservation everything that they have been deprived of under the Russian regime." In both the Irish and Jewish communities, as well as among German-Americans, Germany's arguments found traction. This so irritated Wilson that, in early 1916, he began slamming what he called the "hyphenates"—German-Americans, Irish-Americans, Jewish-Americans and their likes, accusing them, in a series of speeches, of "pouring poison into the veins of our national life."

Germany's top propaganda advantage was that it had, surely, the easier case to make. It needed simply to urge Americans to continue doing what they already were doing: to take no sides, to remain neutral, to stay true, as the German argument put it, to the great American tradition of fair play. Treat Germany and its allies the same way you treat Britain and its allies, entreated the Germans. America had no real quarrel with Germany, they argued, and thus no reason to go to war. By contrast, the British propaganda campaign's task was much harder; it had to change American attitudes and actions drastically, convincing Americans to send their sons into battle.

In the war's early months, Berlin moved rapidly to exploit its propaganda advantages, opening the German Information Bureau in Manhattan and distributing throughout the U.S. hundreds of pamphlets, books, speeches, official documents and anthologies of war poetry and fiction and, of course, photographs, which needed no translation. Every day, the Bureau sent a "fact sheet" to hundreds of American newspapers and opinion makers. Like the British, the Germans compiled mailing lists of influential Americans, though the German list of 60,000 was about one-quarter the size of the British. Movies depicting heroic and victorious German soldiers at the front were given at no charge to cinemas and were widely screened. Staffers in Berlin and in Manhattan, writes Epstein, "mined American history to find examples of British offenses against" the U.S. They emphasized the British class system and love of aristocracy and how much that offended the democratic virtues at America's heart.[20] Berlin also boosted and funded what later generations would call "front organizations," ostensibly unbiased, neutral groups which, however, in various ways advanced the German line. Such organizations included the American Neutrality League, Friends of Peace and the American Humanity League (all opposing U.S. arms exports), the American Embargo Conference, the American Independence Union (urging the U.S. to remain neutral to avoid being dominated by Britain), the American Organization of Women for Strict Neutrality, the Labor National Peace Council (seeking to disrupt munitions production) and the German University League (organizing pro-German college faculty).

Yet, overall, the German propaganda campaign failed. America, after all, entered the war on the Allied side. To be sure, German propagandists bumped up against America's East Coast elite's pronounced preference for London. Study after study, beginning almost as soon as the war had ended, catalogues in detail the long-standing pro-British inclinations and sympathies of the great majority of America's authors, essayists, journalists and other opinion-makers. Almost nothing Berlin's public relations operatives, no matter how skilled, could do could change that. Language obviously also was a problem for German propaganda. While the network of German-language newspapers and Lutheran

Churches was a valuable conduit for Berlin's message on the war, almost everything via them was delivered in the German language, thus seldom reaching America's vast majority of English-speakers whose minds Germany would want most to affect.

Berlin's biggest problem turned out to be its ineffective propaganda; to use a modern phrase, the Germans were tone deaf to the American public. Example: While it was a solid idea to launch a weekly newspaper whose masthead proclaimed "Fair Play for Germany and Austria," it did not help that it carried the official red and black seals of Germany and of Austria-Hungary and was called "*The Fatherland*," a name clearly signaling that the publication was German in content and ownership and thus could be treated (and dismissed) as a biased propaganda vehicle. The same was true about the myriad, at times well-written and well-produced, German propaganda pamphlets and other publications; many actually carried the stamp of the Imperial German government. Press releases making the German case, meantime, were issued by the German Embassy and consulates and often were written by the German military's War Press Office, while speakers on the lecture circuit (surpassed only by newspapers and magazines as a means of influencing American public opinion) often were German government officials. Perhaps Germany could be respected for being so honest and upfront about its propaganda operations, making little effort to disguise their source. But the price paid was the enormous loss of the essential aura of impartiality that lends credibility and hence persuasiveness.

British propaganda, by contrast, operated in such extraordinary stealth that those receiving its message had no idea that it was being produced and managed by Wellington House. So secret was the British effort that not until after the war was its existence revealed to Parliament. Writes Stewart Ross: "Nearly all Americans…would fervently come to believe that only the Germans were trying to subvert U.S. public opinion."[21] Similarly they would believe that only the Germans were capable of atrocities, ignoring or dismissing German reports, some true and many fabricated, of savage behavior by British, French and Russian soldiers. And though, according to Niall Ferguson, "British troops shot many of the German soldiers they captured...against both military regulations and codes of honour," the world heard nothing about it.[22] Nor did it hear that the French bombing of the German city of Karlsruhe hit a circus and killed eighty-two German children and many adults. Writes Moyer: "No word of French 'baby-killers' found its way into the world's newspapers... By war's end, the Allies had conducted more raids on German towns than Germans had on British towns... Most of the world never heard of the British bombings of Dusseldorf and Cologne."[23] The world also knew little about the widespread hunger, malnutrition and even some starvation inflicted on the Germans by the extensive British naval blockade, which illegally stopped even the ships of neutral nations (including the U.S.) from bringing foodstuffs and basic materials to Germany.

With a century's perspective, there is no quibbling that in telling their respective stories, the British succeeded astoundingly and the Germans, equally astoundingly, failed.

America's Shifting Views of Germany
Britain's adroit propaganda efforts fell upon fertile ground. The American audience, even before the war started, gradually but increasingly had been growing displeased with and suspicious of Germany's international behavior and thus susceptible to believing the worst about Germany. This marked a dramatic and remarkable shift in American attitudes. For a full century and more after the American Revolution, U.S.-German relations had been extremely warm, even cordial. Americans not only seemed to admire Germany and appreciate its accomplishments, they seemed to like Germany and its people.

This cordiality had begun, in fact, before the American Revolution. Historian Manfred Jonas writes in his 1984 study analyzing centuries of U.S.-German relations that the American colonies cheered Prussia's Frederick the Great when he sided with them in the critical French and Indian War and they further admired him as "the champion of Protestantism—and therefore liberty and enlightenment." Widely admired too and celebrated as a hero of the American Revolution was Frederick Wilhelm von Steuben, the former Prussian General Staff officer who became George Washington's chief of staff, author of the Continental Army's basic drill manual and innovator of the army's extremely deadly bayonet tactics. Von Steuben is a name even today memorialized across America in statues, parks, roads, schools, public buildings, a postage stamp, U.S. Navy warships, county names, annual parades and even a TV miniseries.

Right after the colonies' victory over England, Prussia was quick to demonstrate its warm feelings, signing important treaties of trade and friendship with the newly independent United States. Later, in America's Civil War, Prussia, unlike Britain and France, refused to remain neutral and immediately backed the Union. (By contrast, French Emperor Napoleon III backed the Confederacy.) Germans, writes Jonas, flocked to the U.S. Legation in Berlin to volunteer for the Union Army and became, via the Frankfurt stock exchange, the heaviest foreign buyers of Union bonds. In the U.S., nearly 200,000 native-born Germans signed up with the Union Army while two Union divisions were comprised entirely of Germans.

America eagerly returned the favor, enthusiastically applauding Prussia's battlefield victories over Denmark in 1864 and Austria in 1866, which extended Berlin's rule over more Germanic states. U.S. Secretary of State William H. Seward lauded Prussia's 1867 creation of the North German Confederation as "the North German United States," predicting that its flag "will be hailed with peculiar pleasure" in American waters. American support continued three years later when Prussia was fighting France, after Napoleon III first declared war on Prussia. Following its crushing victory over France in 1871, Prussia unified the German states, created a German nation and proclaimed the German Empire. As they watched Prussia fight France, a majority of U.S. newspapers backed Berlin, with the very influential *Harper's Weekly Magazine* "being especially pro-German."[24] This Franco-Prussian war, writes Clara Eve Schieber in her 1923 landmark study of American attitudes towards Germany before 1914, was seen as a battle for German unity, not unlike the U.S. Civil War's battle for national unity. Reflecting such sentiments was famed American author Louisa May Alcott, writing to her mother: "I side with the Prussians, for they sympathized with us in our war. Hooray for old Pruss!"[25]

And when Prussia took Alsace-Lorraine away from France, Washington remained silent despite fervent pleas from Paris for the U.S. to object. In the following decades, very little irritated U.S.-Germany relations—not in Latin America, where U.S. and British interests had been clashing, nor in Asia, where neither Germany nor the U.S. (in contrast to Britain, France, the Netherlands and other European states) had any desire to establish major colonies and possessions; all Washington and Berlin wanted was access to trade and commerce.

Adding to the glowing feelings were the policies of Otto von Bismarck, Chancellor of the newly minted German Empire. He carefully cultivated good relations with the U.S. and was widely, and deservedly, admired in America as a progressive and a liberalizer. (Americans' later revulsion at the name "Bismarck" is a flawed backwards reading of history, tarnishing earlier German leaders for the outrages and crimes of the Hitler and Nazi regime.) America watched approvingly as Bismarck reformed Germany, introducing civil marriage and secularizing education. He won further points when Germany, mediating a U.S.-Britain clash over the boundary between British Columbia and the Washington Territory, awarded the disputed land to the U.S.

Americans' warm view of Germany was reinforced by admiration for Germans who had settled in the U.S. Well-remembered, for instance, was Carl Schurz, who had fought as a brigadier general for the Union in the Civil War and later became the first German-born U.S. Senator (representing Missouri as a Republican). German liberals who had fled to America after the collapse of the 1848 Europe-wide revolutions had become advocates of reform in their new communities, strongly opposing slavery, for example. Meanwhile, Germany's schools and universities were winning high marks and deeply influencing development of American universities. By 1914, America's leading professors of history, psychology and the sciences either were German or had trained in German universities. The same could be said of prominent composers, musicians, philosophers and writers.

Such good feelings, however, did not last. American-German cordiality began shifting, hardening, by the end of the century. The specific cause, say historians who have studied the matter, was a bunch of pinpricks: diplomatic differences, military blustering, the pomposity of new German Emperor Wilhelm II and so forth. More important, they note, was an unavoidable underlying cause: the simultaneous emergence in the 19th Century's last decade of both the United States and the German Empire as major world economic, geopolitical and military players, ambitious newcomers to the big power scene. It was probably inevitable that they would, and did, find themselves bumping into each other.

The pinpricks easily are identified. One was Samoa, a cluster of islands south of the equator halfway between Hawaii and New Zealand, where in the late 1880s Washington and Berlin clashed over minor differences. At one point three U.S. and three German warships tensely faced off each other for several months, a confrontation resolved only when a cyclone destroyed all the ships. Meantime, German soldiers had landed on some of the islands, raising their black-white-red Imperial flag. American papers reported extensively, at times inflamingly, on the lingering episode, blasting German behavior as "high-handed." All this, concludes Schieber, was the "first definite friction with Germany and the earliest appearance of any general American sentiment of suspicion and distrust against Germany." Ultimately the islands were divided, creating American Samoa and German Samoa.

A second pinprick involved the 1898 Spanish-American War, from which a victorious U.S. claimed the Philippines as a colony. In the conflict, Berlin was seen as a supporter and supplier of Spain. (Britain, by contrast, was the only European power to back Washington.) Particularly provocative, it appeared, was Berlin's dispatch of five Imperial Navy warships to Manila Harbor to protect German nationals and interests in the Philippines; this squadron actually was larger than that commanded by America's Admiral George Dewey, whose ships had sunk or captured the entire Spanish Pacific fleet. When German ships refused to honor Dewey's blockade of the harbor, he fired a warning shot across a German bow. This all was covered almost nonstop by U.S. journalists. Writes Jonas: "The alleged perfidy of the Germans in the Philippines was told and retold in numerous articles and books and embellished in each new version." The result: A sharp uptick in Americans' anti-German sentiment.[26]

A third pinprick was in Latin America, obviously regarded by the U.S. as its backyard and protected, in the American mind, by the Monroe Doctrine. Americans grew suspicious in 1901 when German warships began surveying Venezuela's coastal waters. Suspicion became anger when Berlin dispatched warships to force Venezuela to repay debts owed to German businesses; ultimately, the warships sank Venezuelan vessels and bombarded a port. Seeing this as a direct challenge to the Monroe Doctrine, American public sentiment rallied to Venezuela's cause, denouncing Germany for "browbeating" an innocent South American country. Tellingly, the once strongly pro-German *Harpers Weekly* was one of the sharpest German critics. Similarly alarming to Americans was the appearance of German warships off Haiti, again to force payments owed to

Germany. Meanwhile, the flow of German emigrants to Argentina, Brazil and Chile alarmed many Americans as a deliberate Berlin plot to colonize South America.

By themselves, these pinpricks and other minor irritants scarcely would have moved the needle of American sentiment against Germany. It was behaving no different than other countries, including the U.S. What they importantly did, however, was offer tangible examples for the gnawing American notion that no longer were U.S. and German interests as comfortably aligned as they had been. That was correct. As the two most formidable emerging world powers, America and Germany, deliberately or not, at times would be stepping on each other's toes, getting in each other's way. The trouble was, this was so exaggerated by media reporting that Imperial Germany was perceived as a serious threat.

Take the matter of colonies—which America near the end of the century had been acquiring rapidly, despite the more benign, less imperialistic name it gave to its control of the Philippines, Puerto Rico and Samoa. As other European powers had been doing for decades (even centuries), Germany now also sought to plant its flag overseas and gain protected trading arrangements. But coming late to the colonial game, Berlin found little on the world's map that hadn't already been tagged by Europe's big powers and even by such puny powers as Belgium, Denmark and the Netherlands. To Germany, getting footholds in Africa or China, meager as they were, was simply doing what others to a much greater extent had done. So was building a German Navy to protect its lines of communications to those colonies and its trade routes. So was exerting some global influence. But to Americans, all this was a sure sign that Germany had expansionistic if not aggressive and, in the buzzword of the day, "hegemonic" intents. Theodore Roosevelt (first as president and then again later) and powerful Senator Henry Cabot Lodge, both vociferous champions of U.S. expansion abroad, were among the first to warn that Germany threatened American interests. And by 1910 the War Department (a precursor to today's Department of Defense) had plans for defending North America from a German attack.

Historian Ross Gregory in his 1971 study of America's intervention in World War One explains: "There was a popular notion that countries anxious to seize more territory were acting in a greedy and dangerous way for orderly civilization. Britain and the United States often looked with disapproving eye on less satisfied nations seeking a larger share of the management of the world. Germany was one of those."[27] Adds Jonas: "It was not that either [the U.S. or Germany] sought advantages at the expense of the other. But both sought similar advantages at the same time, and their rival ambitions led to conflict over differences, both real and imaginary."[28]

Conflicts there also were over trade, triggering the kind of American testy accusations and dire predictions that a century later some Americans would be making against first Japan and then China. To be sure, the economic growth of newly united Germany was phenomenal, as was America's growth and as had been Britain's at the dawn of the industrial age. By 1913, Germany was a manufacturing powerhouse, producing nearly three times as much steel, then the key measure of economic might, as was Britain (though a quarter less than was America). Germany accounted for thirteen percent of global trade, just behind Britain's fifteen percent, but ahead of America's eleven percent. German inventors, chemists and other scientists were developing hosts of new products and techniques which rapidly were transforming manufacturing. Among these were chemicals, dyes for clothing, electrical engineering techniques, fertilizers that revolutionized food production, Siemens electrical generators, Solingen knives, Adler typewriters, Zeiss Tessar lenses, AGFA photo chemicals, Bayer aspirin, Bechstein pianos, Rosenthal porcelain, Faber lead pencils. All those new icons of quality and market dominance testified to the expanding muscle of German industry. So did the Nobel prizes increasingly won by Germans.

And so too did the seemingly inexorable emergence of German as the international scientific language.

With German goods flooding onto the world market, America (as well as Britain, France and others) felt the sting of competition. Not surprisingly, Germany was accused, writes Schieber, of being an "unfair competitor—making vast quantities of cheap, even shoddy goods, in order to crowd out the better yet more expensive manufactures of her rivals." The U.S. Tariff Commission received many complaints alleging Germany's unfairness. Former Commission member Frank J. Sheridan later described some of these. There was "jealousy and resentful feeling...due to inroads made by German competition in a number of American industries," he recalled in 1918. "Strong statements charged that Germany had been practicing various methods of unfair competition...including threats to cut prices and drive American manufacturers out of business; dumping; deceptive imitations and use of trademarks...imitation of articles and especially by undervaluation" of the German currency.[29]

Such accumulated prewar worries and grievances against Germany, authentic or exaggerated or even contrived, combined with Germany's wartime disadvantages in propaganda and public relations all had serious consequences as the war was playing out to the American audience. In the battle for the American mind, in its quest to keep America neutral, Berlin could neither blunt the British anti-German propaganda assault nor effectively portray Britain and its Entente allies as being guilty of the same behavior and motives for which Germany was being denounced.

German U-boats and American Attitudes

No factor was more devastating to Germany's standing in America and none contributed more to America ultimately declaring Germany an enemy than Berlin's broad waging of submarine warfare.

It was the perception and then conviction that German deployment of submarines to attack shipping, commercial and even passenger ships as well as military, had crossed the line of behavior acceptable for a modern, civilized nation. More than anything else it convinced the American public that Germany was a brutal, aggressive nation, a predator roaming the neighborhood that had to be stopped. To be sure, the story about German submarines, its U-boats, definitely had two sides. But Americans heard only one. Unfolding over two years, it inflamed their passions and turned them angry and ready ultimately to heed those calling for war against the German Empire.

That empire's Imperial Navy at first deployed its submarine fleet, the world's best, to attack Allied warships, then expanded the campaign to cargo and other commercial vessels and then to passenger ships believed to be carrying weapons, munitions and other war materiel. Whatever its strategic and military value, this was, from the start, a public relations catastrophe. Accounts of ships being sunk without warning by an unseen foe and accounts of crews hurtling overboard and frantically scrambling to cling to life and then, eventually, drowning, horrified Americans—and others, including Germans. There seemed something unfair about it, a violation of long-understood rules of combat conduct, an offense to the honor of combatants. It seemed like a sneak attack by cowards, a mugging of an innocent stroller in a dark alley, a stabbing in the back. British propaganda, understandably, pounced on it, repeatedly blasting submarine attacks as uncivilized and yet further proof of Teutonic barbarism.

Yet Berlin viewed submarine warfare as an acceptable and appropriate naval response to the tight, and ever tighter, naval blockade Britain had thrown around Germany, interfering with neutral shipping and inflicting great deprivation and suffering on Germans. German U-boats simply were trying to prevent, argued Berlin correctly, supplies, weapons and munitions from reaching Britain and its allies, just as Britain was blocking supplies from

Germany. "England wants to starve us. We can play the same game," bluntly declared Alfred von Tirpitz, the commander (and founder) of the Imperial Navy in a December 1914 interview with a reporter from the *New York Sun*. Why, asked German leaders repeatedly, using more diplomatic language than did von Tirpitz, did Washington not vigorously protest Britain's blockade, a kind of starvation warfare against the German people, as much as it protested German submarine warfare? Their question lingered, hanging in the air, unanswered.

Nothing more powerfully typifies the impact on American opinion of German submarines than did the torpedoing and sinking of the British trans-Atlantic luxury liner RMS *Lusitania* by U-boat U-20 on May 7, 1915, killing 128 Americans. This, writes historian H.W. Brands, "caused a dramatic shift in American perceptions of the war. Previously, the conflict had been about other people; now it was about Americans."[30] That America remained out of the war for two years after the sinking testifies to how sensibly reluctant Americans and Woodrow Wilson were to join the European bloodletting. At the same time, however, the Wilson Administration's reaction to the tragedy for the first time revealed a bias toward Britain which would grow only more extreme. While America after the *Lusitania* tragedy remained technically neutral, it was a neutrality increasingly asymmetrical and unbalanced. Germany consistently was held to higher standards and stricter restrictions than was Britain.

To this day, nearly a full century later, fascination with the *Lusitania* keeps bubbling. Simply mentioning the ship's name still sparks images, warranted or not, of German military outrages and inhumanity. That the tragedy still intrigues the public is confirmed by the nearly 600 *Lusitania*-themed books for sale by Amazon.com, the U.S. online retailer. Through the decades, the sinking has been investigated and studied and speculated about over and over, and yet the fascination and (minor) controversies endure. As recently as

December 2008, deep divers exploring the wreckage just a few miles off the Irish coast claimed to have discovered a new piece in the *Lusitania* puzzle which, if true, could help explain why the ship sank so quickly with so many passengers perishing and could corroborate (though not necessarily excuse) Germany's justification for the attack.

Much about the sinking is straightforward and undisputed.

- The *Lusitania* was on its return voyage to Liverpool from Pier 54 in Manhattan, carrying 1,257 passengers and 702 crew.
- It was traversing waters declared by Germany a "war zone," known to be patrolled by German submarines. In fact, German authorities in the U.S. had been warning Americans of the dangers of traveling on British and other Allied ships because they could come under German attack, just as German ships were being attacked by the British Royal Navy, which had proclaimed all of the North Sea a "war zone" and had mined its waters.
- Just nine days before the *Lusitania* steamed out of New York harbor, the German Embassy placed an ad in fifty U.S. newspapers, appearing beside a *Lusitania* ad, stating: "NOTICE! TRAVELLERS intending to embark on the Atlantic voyage are reminded that a state of war exists between Germany and her allies and Great Britain and her allies; that the zone of war includes the waters adjacent to the British Isles; that…vessels flying the flag of Great Britain, or any of her allies, are liable to destruction in those waters and that travellers sailing in the war zone on the ships of Great Britain or her allies do so at their own risk."
- After being warned by the Royal Navy command of heightened dangers in the area, based on radio intercepts of German submarine movements, the *Lusitania's* captain took such protective actions as closing watertight doors, posting extra lookouts and ordering a blackout. He did not, however,

engage in such standard submarine-defense maneuvers as steaming at maximum speed or zigzagging. (Some accounts report that the captain did not want to rattle the glasses in the parlor or interfere with passenger deck games.)

• Just a bit after noon on May 7, submarine U-20, steaming on the surface at full speed, low on fuel and heading back to Germany with just a single remaining torpedo, spotted the *Lusitania* about 800 yards ahead. Lieutenant Walther Schweiger, the U-20 commander, ordered his ship to dive and his crew to battle stations. The lone torpedo was fired, striking the *Lusitania* just below the bridge and exploding. A few minutes later, a second, much more powerful explosion racked the ship, the cause of which remains one of World War One's lingering mysteries and controversies.

• Within eighteen minutes, the *Lusitania* had sunk. Dead and missing were 1,198 passengers and crew, including the 128 Americans.

• The sinking shocked world opinion, not only in Allied and neutral nations, but also inside Germany and its Austro-Hungarian and Turkish allies.

In the uproar following the tragedy, Germany insisted that the *Lusitania* was a valid and appropriate military target because its holds were transporting huge quantities of ammunition to Britain. It was the igniting of this volatile cargo, argued Germany, that explains the ship's second, more violent, explosion. That may in fact have been true. Postwar investigations and the 2008 diving expedition at the wreckage found evidence of millions of rounds of American-made Remington .303 bullets. Even so, it does not explain why Berlin would attack the Atlantic's premier passenger ship just to destroy some small munitions and risk triggering world outrage, particularly in the U.S.

Whatever the merits of Berlin's rationalization and whether

or not the attack was planned by the Imperial Navy high command (it almost certainly was not) or was the opportunistic decision by U-20's Lieutenant Schweiger, the attack on the *Lusitania* was a public relations disaster for Germany. It is one thing to argue, correctly, that Americans had no legal right to expect safe passage while traveling on a belligerent's ship in a war zone and that by doing so they knowingly and willingly thrust themselves into harm's way; it is a very different thing to argue that this entitled Germany deliberately to attack an easily recognizable passenger ship and kill civilians and crew. Germany may have been within its wartime rights to have done so, but it was enormously stupid. Writes Ross Gregory: "The sinking was one of the most important events of the period of [American] neutrality. It resurrected charges of German brutality. For the first time, many Americans began to consider the possibility that their nation might have to take part in the war."[31]

Americans studying the list of drowned fellow-citizens began to feel that the war was edging closer to home. Among the famous dead were wealthy socialite Alfred Vanderbilt, industrial titans Arthur Henry Adams (president of U.S. Rubber Company) and Albert Hopkins (president of Newport News Shipbuilding and Drydock Company) and writer and philosopher Elbert Hubbard and his wife, women's rights activist Alice Moore Hubbard.

Nudging America closer to war the *Lusitania* sinking may have done, but it still did not push the nation over the edge. Wilson initially stressed the urgent need to remain neutral and his countrymen agreed, remaining far from ready or eager to fight in Europe. Though East Coast newspapers brutalized Germany and demanded some kind of tough U.S. retaliatory action, the rest of the nation was decidedly calmer. A survey of about 1,000 editorials written within three days of the sinking found fewer than a half-dozen suggesting war with Germany. And when Teddy Roosevelt, then six years out of the White House, urged Congressional

Republicans to push for a strong policy to protect Americans on the high seas, he was rebuffed.

The sinking's greatest blow to American neutrality probably was its triggering the exit from the Wilson Administration of William Jennings Bryan, the Secretary of State who consistently had been imploring (even pestering) Wilson to be more evenhanded in dealing with the Allies and the Central Powers. If there were one prominent genuine champion of neutrality in America, it was Bryan. Though his influence on Wilson was limited (his high cabinet post mainly was a reward for his crucial backing of Wilson in the 1912 presidential election), he remained immensely popular in the Democrat Party and among Populists.

In the term used decades later, Bryan had a strong and solid constituency. His voice counted for something. In response to the sinking, Bryan sought restraint and balance; willing to reprimand Germany, he also wanted Wilson to reprimand Britain for its wide naval blockade which interfered with America's freedom of the seas and with its legal right to ship food to German and Central Powers civilians. He was very angry, moreover, that London had been using the U.S. flag to disguise its vessels. Britain should stop interdicting the shipments of foodstuffs, he said, and limit the mining of international sea lanes, while Germany, in turn, should curtail its submarine attacks. In addition, he urged Wilson to warn Americans not to travel on belligerents' ships. To Bryan, "Germany has a right to prevent contraband going to the Allies, and a ship carrying contraband should not rely on passengers to protect her from attack—it would be like putting women and children in front of an army."

Wilson strongly disagreed, insisting that Germany apologize for sinking the *Lusitania*, compensate American victims and promise no future similar attacks. In a May 13 note to Berlin, drafted with the help of Robert Lansing, the State Department's second-ranking official and strongly sympathetic to Britain, Wilson declared that Americans had the right to travel safely on any ship, heading anywhere and that

Germany should stop attacking commercial vessels, even those of belligerents. In a second note, on June 9, Wilson rejected German assertions that Britain's blockade was illegal and inhuman and that the *Lusitania* was carrying munitions. A final Wilson note was sent July 21; it, in effect, was an ultimatum, threatening that the U.S. would regard any further attacks as a "deliberately unfriendly" action. This was more than a hint that such actions could prompt an American declaration of war on Germany.

Such tough Wilson language was too much for Bryan; failing to temper the second note, he resigned in open protest on June 8. The following day, Wilson named Lansing Secretary of State, a post he then held for nearly five years. Gone was the champion of neutrality; in his place was a skilled diplomat and Washington operator who was emotionally committed to the Allies and believed America should be fighting alongside Britain. Indeed, in his memoirs Lansing later admitted that after the *Lusitania* sinking he always had the "conviction that we would ultimately become the ally of Britain." And on July 11, 1915 he wrote in his diary: "Germany must not be permitted to win this war and to break even."[32] Lansing's emergence at the State Department's helm and America's harsh response to Germany's torpedoing of the *Lusitania* symbolized the start of America's pronounced tilt towards Britain and its allies, a tilt that increasingly, with a few hiccups, would intensify. Gradually, incrementally, "neutrality" would lose most of its legitimate meaning. Step by step, even the pretense of evenhandedness would fade. This was signaled clearly by Washington's extraordinarily different responses to Germany's submarine warfare and to Britain's naval blockade of Germany.

Though the *Lusitania* tragedy brought German U-boat warfare to Americans' attention, submarine warfare already had been raging for eight months, starting September 5, 1914, when Germany's U-21 sank the British light cruiser *Pathfinder* off the British Isles. Eight days later, Britain retaliated; one of its subs, the

E9, sank a German light cruiser in the North Sea. These, however, were minor clashes. September 22 was different. It brought the startling demonstration of just how powerful a weapon a submarine could be. On that day, a single German U-boat, the U-9, a mere 493-ton ship, torpedoed and sank three British cruisers near the Netherlands. The attack's dramatic math could not be ignored: A tiny German ship with a crew of just twenty-nine destroyed three armored British warships weighing 12,000 tons in aggregate, killing 1,400. To Berlin, this math demonstrated how extremely lethal and cost-effective its U-boat fleet could be, even though the ships were slow, flimsy and thin-hulled. Until this time, few had viewed submarines as weapons operating on their own. Suddenly the underwater attack boat was seen as a major weapons system.

Almost from the start, the U-boats' public relations problems were obvious. They went beyond the submarine being seen as a back-alley mugger or engaging unfairly and unsportingly in sneak attacks. Much worse, the submarine, by its own nature and limitations, could succeed only by violating established naval warfare conventions. Explains Hew Strachan in his highly-regarded 2003 study of the war: "The laws of war at sea expected the submarine to behave the same way as a conventional warship... She had to surface, give notice of her intention to sink a vessel and allow time for the crew to abandon ship."[33] This created a problem for submarines, a huge problem: Were the submarine to conform to these established practices, it would be placing itself in extraordinary danger. With its slow speed and fragile hulls, it easily was pierced and severely damaged by even light arms fire and quickly sank if rammed by a larger ship. To obey conventions would mean that the submarine could not attack unless it surfaced; to surface exposed the submarine to near certain destruction.

London quickly exploited these U-boat limitations. It covertly armed merchant ships, enabling them to fire on surfaced subs, and trained their crews to ram them. It flew the flags of neutral countries on British-owned commercial vessels, whose hulls had been reinforced with armor and whose decks carried concealed guns. And it launched its notorious Q ships—in effect warships, manned by Royal Navy gun crews, disguised to look like freighters flying neutral flags, with armaments hidden behind specially disguised trap doors. Their explicit purpose: to deceive U-boats seeking to comply with naval law and entice them to surface. When the U-boat did come up and its crew, in accord with the law, started boarding a putative merchant ship to check its cargo for contraband, the Q ship tore off its mask, unveiled its guns and destroyed the U-boat and killed its crew. Q ships, writes B.H. Liddell Hart, the legendary analyst of the war (in which he fought as a British Army captain), "were equipped with torpedo tubes, depth charges, and guns concealed behind collapsible bulwarks... [Their crew] simulated panic...and thereby lured the molesting submarine to the surface within close range." To Liddell Hart, the U-boat's dilemma was clear: "The more merciful the U-boat, the greater danger it ran; the less heed it paid to the nature of its target and the rescue of those on board, the more its safety and success were assured."[34]

Q ships even dared masquerade as American merchant vessels—and did so frequently. Such was the *Baralong*. Flying the U.S. flag, its hull painted red-white-and-blue, on August 19, 1915 it approached Germany's U-27 which was about to destroy a British merchantman but first had surfaced, following the law, to help the merchantman's crew safely disembark. Apparently trusting the U.S. flag, U-27's crew paid the approaching *Baralong* little heed. Then the *Baralong*, according to Ross Gregory, "suddenly hoisted the British flag, fired, and quickly sank the U-boat. The *Baralong's* crew then turned on the German seamen floundering in the water and brutally shot as many as were in sight."[35] At this there was no outrage in America, though Berlin reasonably might have expected Washington to protest loudly and forcefully Britain's exploiting the American flag to entice within range a German submarine and then destroy it and its crew. Instead, Washington's rebuke to London was very mild. America seemed deaf to Berlin's explanation that British ships flying the American flag were putting genuine U.S. vessels in danger from U-boat attacks.

The submarine's importance grew as the war moved through its first two years. With the ground war's Western Front now frozen in standoff, oceans became the sole arena for combatant maneuver, bold moves and swift initiative. It was where Britain's Grand Fleet and Germany's High Seas Fleet were expected to wage Wagnerian-scale battles, which could determine the war's outcome. In the years before the war, both fleets, each eagle-eyeing the other, had expanded ferociously, each building great numbers of the massive "Dreadnaught"-class battleship, named after a British behemoth launched in 1906 whose all big-gun armaments ignited the British-German naval arms race which fueled mounting pre-war tensions.

When they confronted each other, however, the huge British and German surface fleets, like the massive ground armies, also ultimately found themselves in a standoff. After shadow-boxing for more than a year, the two fleets finally faced off in epic battle on May 31, 1916 in the North Sea near Jutland, Denmark. The resulting Battle of Jutland (called Skagerrak by the Germans), history's largest and costliest (in lives lost) naval battle until the massive World War Two American-Japanese battleship and aircraft carrier clashes in the Pacific, ended in what essentially was a draw (though most historians give a slight edge to the British). German ships proved stronger than the British, their firepower and accuracy superior. But they were so badly damaged that their High Seas Fleet commanders never again let them venture far from German waters. Thus, though Britain's Grand Fleet failed in its explicit strategic goal of destroying the German Navy, it did cork it up, preventing the Germans from operating in the high seas. Yet the Grand Fleet was nearly as corked up, forced to stand guard making certain that the German ships did not venture out. The result: The only German ships capable of offensive warfare were submarines. After Jutland, concludes John Keegan, "Germany's attempt to win a decision at sea would be conducted exclusively through the submarine arm."[36]

Berlin well understood and wrestled with the dilemma posed by its submarines, repeatedly and agonizingly debating how to use them. On the one hand, U-boats were the sole weapon system with even a remote chance of blunting Britain's naval blockade of Germany and carrying the sting of war to Britons beyond the Western Front. As such, many in Germany's top decision-making circles, including leading economists, pushed for expanded and even unrestricted submarine attacks against all shipping of potential value to Britain and its allies. On the other hand, some top officials urged (even begged for) caution, arguing that Germany should do nothing to antagonize America and bring it into the war. Typical was Imperial Chancellor Theobold von Bethmann-Hollweg who in June 1915, following the *Lusitania* sinking, ordered U-boat commanders to stop firing on passenger ships and neutral ships, declaring: "In doubtful cases it is better to let an enemy merchantman pass than to sink a neutral."

Kaiser Wilhelm at times sided with one group, at times with the other. The result was a zigzag submarine policy, with periods of aggressively deploying U-boats against a broad range of targets alternating with periods of extreme circumspection. Even during aggressive periods, though, according to American and British naval records cited after the war by Admiral William Sims, who commanded all U.S. Navy forces in Europe during the war, U-boat officers often behaved extraordinarily humanely, rescuing the crews and passengers of torpedoed ships and even towing them close to the coast.

Americans knew nothing of the U-boat debate raging in Berlin. Had they known, they may have formed a more nuanced view of Germany. But little of what was happening in Berlin made it into American newspapers since so few American journalists were reporting from there. In the dark too, it seems, was official Washington, unaware that Germany's leaders, including the Kaiser, were far from closed-minded and monolithic on the matter of

U-boat warfare and were, in fact, susceptible to U.S. pressures and very much concerned about U.S. sensibilities. The man who should have been keeping Washington informed, U.S. Ambassador to Germany James Gerard, a wealthy New York City Tammany Hall machine politician, dismally failed to do so and is widely judged by history as having been massively incompetent at his post. Though Wilson apparently made no secret of his disdain and contempt for Gerard, even referring to him in correspondence as "this idiot," he made no move to replace him. Had the U.S. a more skilled diplomat in Berlin, Washington's (and America's) attitudes and responses to Germany could have been much different. Testimony to Gerard's shortcomings and shallow analysis was his memoirs, *My Four Years in Germany*, published in 1917 and made into a popular and influential movie the following year. In his book he wrote that Germans' heavy eating and drinking "had made the people more aggressive and irritable and consequently ready for war."

What is clear from the record is that Berlin so feared U.S. intervention in the war that it bowed to just about all of Washington's U-boat protests and accepted just about all of Washington's demands. When a U-boat sinking of the British passenger liner *Arabic* on August 19, 1915 killed two Americans, a furious Wilson threatened to break relations with Germany unless it stopped all attacks without warning on unarmed passenger liners. Berlin acquiesced, promising not to sink passenger ships without giving warning and rescuing passengers. Berlin unofficially also halted almost all U-boat attacks on non-military vessels. It acquiesced again (and apologized) seven months later when, after a March 24, 1916 U-boat torpedoing of the French ferry *Sussex* in the English Channel killed four Americans, Wilson demanded that U-boats abide by conventional war rules and thus surface and warn ships before attacking them. Berlin bowed, accepting all conditions. Writes Gregory: "The United States hardly could have asked for more." And to Wilson-expert Knock, this so-called *Sussex* pledge "was the greatest diplomatic triumph of

Wilson's first administration."[37]

Indeed, so cautious had German U-boat commanders become by mid-August 1916 that, according to German Foreign Minister Gottlieb von Jagow, one submerged U-boat in the English Channel had allowed forty-one ships to pass unmolested even though the U-boat commander was certain that they were carrying ammunition and soldiers. American historian (and later, 9/11 Commission member) Ernest May explains that it became German policy "to carry on the U-boat war at whatever pitch the United States would allow."[38]

In bowing to Wilson's demands, Berlin hoped and diplomatically and publicly pushed for balance in U.S. policy, insisting that Wilson similarly insist that Britain abide by international law and stop blockading neutral shipping from reaching Germany. Berlin was dismayed to discover that while Wilson was outraged at Germany's disregard for international rules of naval conduct, he was not nearly so at Britain's similar actions, which, like Germany's, put civilians at risk, infringed on neutrals' rights and made a mockery of freedom of the seas, a principle long at the heart of American foreign policy.

Responding to Britain's Blockade of Germany

The British blockade began almost as soon as did the war. In October 1914, British ships started mining the North Sea, that water mass touching Britain, Germany and Scandinavia, through which all ships to or from Germany must pass. The mining meant that American, Scandinavian and all other neutral ships had to use the English Channel, requiring them to take aboard British Admiralty pilots and submit all cargo to British inspection. As they were launching their mining operation, British officials feared and expected a searing American protest. None came. While Scandinavian governments objected vigorously, Washington simply sent a note to London, described by American historian Ross Gregory as "the friendliest sort of reminder that Britain should be conscious of American neutral rights." That was it. "There appeared no demand," adds Gregory, "that Britain cease any trade restriction, no hint of retaliation."[39] The following month, London declared the entire North Sea a war zone. Four months later, on February 4, 1915, Berlin retaliated by proclaiming all waters around the British Isles a war zone.

Britain rigorously enforced the blockade. Its ships stopped copper heading for Italy, tungsten and graphite heading for America and meat heading for the Netherlands. This was particularly punishing to perishables because London, ignoring traditional rules that warships must halt and search neutral merchantmen at sea, required inspections in ports. Sometimes ships awaiting inspection languished for weeks or even months in British docks. Thus the meat never reached the Dutch, rotting instead in Liverpool. So important was the blockade to Britain that it actually created a Ministry of Blockade. This new cabinet-level post, according to Ernest May, "applied every screw to neutral trade... Practically no measure of economic warfare...was left unused."[40] British warships, for instance, began seizing and inspecting almost all mail from America to Europe, even mail addressed to neutral countries and even diplomatic pouches. American companies suspected that proprietary information in the inspected letters was being given to British competitors. Later, London "blacklisted" eighty-seven U.S. firms, accusing them of trading with Germany and other Central Powers; as a result, neutral ships carrying these firms' cargoes were denied coal at British-controlled ports around the world. British warships, again in violation of international norms, also halted and its sailors forcibly removed from American ships passengers suspected of helping Germany.

London's control of Atlantic shipping was almost total. Note Edwin Borchard and William Lage in their 1937 study of American neutrality: "Scarcely a ton of cargo left an American port from 1915 to 1917 without control of a British agent."[41] It even seemed that London was specially targeting American vessels, determined to prevent them from carrying any goods, non-military as well as military, to Germany, though American shippers had every legal right to do so. Blocked entirely, for instance, were the huge amounts of copper and cotton that America before the war had been shipping to Germany and upon which Germany relied for its industry. Traditionally, well-established maritime law would require Britain to prove that a neutral's cargo was contraband. But London flipped the law, instead demanding that neutral captains prove that their ships carried no goods of value to the Central Powers armies. Openly, therefore, Britain was violating America's rights as a neutral. In May's assessment, it was "an unending series of small injuries" to American interests.[42]

Not so small were the injuries inflicted on Germany's civilians. By the end of 1915 they were cut off from almost all the outside world as German freighters and other German commercial ships were driven from most of the high seas, having been captured or having fled into neutral ports where they languidly rolled in the waters. This led, writes Liddell Hart in a 1930 study, to "the semi-starvation of the German people."[43] Other historians agree, describing wartime Germany as "a great European nation living as a starving pauper." And Niall Ferguson, in his pioneering 1998 comparison of the belligerents' economic ability to wage the war, judges that the damage from Britain's naval blockade "was undoubtedly severe." Not only did it cut off food imports, but, more importantly, blocked supplies of nitrates and other components of fertilizer, sharply reducing the output of German farms.

By spring 1915, bread rationing had spread all through Germany; a few months later, Berliners were limited to one-half pound of bread per person per day, one-third below the prewar consumption level. Butter, cooking oils, lard and milk were running short in the larger cities. In late 1916, full-fledged rationing kicked in, vastly reducing even further individual consumption of bread, butter, eggs, fats, milk, potatoes and sugar; the meat ration, at a half-pound per week per person, was just one-fifth the prewar intake level. Short too were supplies of coal and cotton. "By the end of 1916," says Laurence Moyer in his account of wartime Germany, "for most [German] citizens it had become a time of eating meals never entirely filling, living in under-heated homes...walking with leaky shoes. It meant starting and ending the day with substitutes for nearly everything." And when it rained, clothing made from paper (since American cotton was blockaded) disintegrated. This situation is confirmed by the U.S. Consul General in Dresden, who reported to the State Department on November 4, 1916 that: "There is virtually no meat, butter, eggs, or sugar to be had and very few vegetables and very little milk... Each inhabitant is allowed an egg a week... We are supposed to receive 9 ounces of meat a week, but in fact we get about half of that."

Health eroded. German youngsters stopped growing, with rickets afflicting nearly forty percent of them. Overall medical care deteriorated from shortages of disinfectants, catgut for sewing wounds, camphor, menthol, operating gloves, cotton gauze and even soap. Widespread were intestinal disorders, chronic anemia and tuberculosis. "For all this," concludes Moyer, "the British blockade was responsible."[44] Ultimately, great numbers of Germans seem to have died from the blockade, if not directly from starvation then from undernourishment and malnutrition.

Though exactly how many is uncertain (Ferguson doubts that few direct starvation deaths can be confirmed), a postwar December 1918 German report puts overall blockade-caused fatalities at 762,796 and an official British report sees an even higher number, 772,736. At the Krupp factories, for example, worker mortality rose from 4.1 per thousand in 1914 to 8.7 per thousand in 1917. To be sure, all belligerents' civilian populations suffered; Russians, in fact, probably suffered most. In the west, however, no civilians were hit harder than Germans. And while the British after 1916 were prohibited from feeding food to pigeons or throwing rice at weddings, "they were spared," according to Roger Chickering's 1998 history of Imperial Germany, "the shortages of food and fuel in the degree that Germans endured."[45]

The tenacity with which Britain waged blockade warfare irritated and even angered Washington—but not enough for Wilson to deploy the kind of language nor threaten the kind of action he reserved for Germany and its U-boat campaign. Still, on occasion, the blockade sparked tension, straining Washington-London relations. There were several reasons for this. In part, the blockade genuinely seemed to offend Wilson's sense of humanity because it hurt innocent civilians. In part too, it clearly violated international norms and law, an edifice which Wilson, a distinguished political scientist, deeply revered. And in part, the blockade severely damaged large sectors of the U.S. economy dependent on exports to Europe. Such major exporters as southern cotton-growers, mountain states copper miners and Middle West meatpackers in the early stages of the war yelled loudly. They bombarded their representatives and the State Department with demands that Congress and the Administration defend America's freedom of the seas and force Britain to allow American ships to carry goods, as entitled by international law, to Germany and neutral countries.

Though Wilson occasionally did seem on the verge of doing something against Britain, in the end nothing solid came of it. One example: In early 1915, after Britain declared all of the North Sea a war zone and Germany declared the waters around the British Isles a war zone, Wilson proposed that Germany not attack merchant vessels in the war zone if Britain allowed food to be shipped to Germany. Berlin accepted; London refused; and Washington dropped the matter. Another example: In October 1915, Wilson sent London a note complaining about the U.S. ships being detained in Britain for cargo inspection. Yet, explains Gregory, the note was "relaxed and leisurely compared with the urgent treatment given the submarine question." Missing was any threat of reprisal, any hint at ultimatum. And, just in case London mistakenly thought that the note actually signaled Wilson's anger, Secretary of State Lansing, in effect winking, told a Boston newspaper that the note was not to be taken seriously, that it merely was "a political safety valve…it would certainly not be pressed." In addition, it seems that often before sending protest notes to the British Embassy in Washington, the State Department would alert British Ambassador Cecil Spring-Rice, assuring him that the protests were simply pro forma and not to be viewed as serious.

No British action so riled Washington as the July 1916 blacklisting of the eighty-seven American firms, thereby denying to them their rights under international laws of commerce. Gregory judges it "the greatest mistake of British diplomacy during the period of American neutrality." It set Wilson fuming. Yet he did nothing. In fact, though a very angry Congress passed laws giving the President authority to retaliate against the blacklist, such as turning back from U.S. ports ships of any nation discriminating against American commerce, he never acted. He even ordered the State Department to make no threats to London. And once again, it was Secretary of State Lansing who signaled privately that Britain really had no reason to worry about Washington, assuring the British ambassador that Congress' new law was mainly a domestic political matter and that Wilson would never use it. To make certain, it seems, that history understood where he stood, Lansing wrote in his diary: "On no account must we range ourselves even indirectly on the side of Germany, no matter how great the provocation [from the Allies] may be."

By the end of 1916 it was apparent that Wilson was rejecting any notion of equivalence in dealing with the belligerents' sea war, completely dismissing the argument that better German behavior could be conditioned on better British behavior. In the end, concludes May, Wilson "did in fact acquiesce in the blockade…

[and] accepted the limitation of American trade with neutral Europe." Wilson insisted "that the Germans obey international law regardless of what their enemies did. And he chose to threaten war if Germany failed to comply."[46]

This Wilson double standard has perplexed historians. There is no doubt that Wilson clearly realized that both Britain and Germany were violating American rights, even acting with hostility against America. There is just as little doubt that this angered him. As late as March 20, 1917, he complained to his cabinet about "German militarism on land and England's militarism on sea." Yet, he simply could not get himself to take action against Britain. As such, in all the months leading up to its intervention in the war, explains diplomatic historian Daniel Malloy Smith, America "made no formal objection to the [British] mining zone, [but] when the German government retaliated with the submarine zone, the United States was to demand the strictest compliance with its interpretation of international law." Germans were warned, continues Smith, that they were to be held to a "strict accounting" for American ships and lives lost to German submarines, though "Great Britain was not threatened with drastic countermeasures."[47] Moyer agrees, writing: "German submarines had attempted to disrupt British lifelines, resulting in worldwide revulsion at the tactics used. The British Grand Fleet passively and unobtrusively cut off German lifelines to the world in ways which scarcely raised an eyebrow."[48] This double standard's stigmatizing Berlin as the war's main villain, a judgment now dismissed and deplored by almost all historians, became yet another nudge turning Americans against Germany.

Had German propaganda been more effective, Americans may have learned about the British blockade and may have recognized that both the Royal Navy and Imperial Navy similarly were engaging in unconventional and even extreme naval warfare. But Americans were hearing only the anti-German side. After the war, assessing his nation's propaganda failures in America, Count Johann von Bernstorff, Germany's ambassador to the U.S. until war was declared on Germany, lamented that his country had failed to portray "the suffering of our children, women and old people as a result of the British hunger blockade."

Neutrality Bleeds from a Thousand Cuts

As 1916 ended, America was still technically, formally, a neutral nation, but its practice of neutrality had shifted away from any common meaning of the word and very far away from Wilson's August 19, 1914 vow to the Senate that America "must be neutral in fact as well as in name." Against Germany, Washington invoked the strictest letter of accepted international norms of neutrality. Against the British, French and Russians, Washington bent neutrality and, increasingly, cast a blind eye on outright violations. At the end of 1916, therefore, it probably seemed ages since the Wilson Administration's autumn 1914 actions when neutrality indeed had meant neutrality, when the President had tried so hard to be evenhanded that he kept silent and did not protest Germany's invasion of Belgium, that he blocked Britain's buying ship and submarine parts from American suppliers and obtaining loans from American banks and that he changed ship registry laws to make it actually easier for German ships to register as American.

So very different was it now. Neutrality was bleeding from a thousand cuts—the skilled, persistent British propaganda campaign, the inept efforts of Germany to tell its valid story, the shock of a *Lusitania* sinking, the seeming unfairness and brutality of German submarine warfare, the ignorance of the suffering inflicted on German civilians by the British blockade, the near-silence from Washington at London's violation of America's freedom of the seas and rights to trade with anyone, the drumbeat press coverage of putative German atrocities, the mainly one-sided reporting of the war and its battlefields—and the gradually emerging fact that the American economy inexorably was becoming tied to the Allies.

America was shifting ever closer to siding, in some way, with the Allies. This certainly cheered and was cheered on by Secretary of State Lansing, who wrote in his diary in September 1916: "Nothing... can move me from my fixed purpose to remain on friendly terms with Great Britain... I only hope that the President will adopt the true policy which is 'Join the Allies as soon as possible and crush the German Autocrats.'" That at a time when Germany had not threatened America, not attacked America, restrained its submarine warfare in deference to America, asked no favors of America other than it remain neutral and, in fact, was as deadlocked and frozen on Europe's battlefield as were Britain and France. Just such a deadlock was exactly what Wilson once had favored, seeing it as the war's best outcome. With remarkable prescience he told the *New York Times* shortly after the war started that the chances of peace "will be happiest if no nation gets the decision by arms." He warned that an "unjust peace...will be sure to invite future calamities."[49]

History now knows just how right was Woodrow Wilson in this judgment. The tragic—and agonizingly consequential—story of 1917 will be that he abandoned his historic insight and took America into a war in which millions of American doughboys broke the deadlock, thereby, to use Wilson's words, inviting "future calamities," vastly greater and more horrible than Wilson ever could have imagined.

CHAPTER 3

CHOOSING WAR

"He kept us out of war!"

WITH THAT SLOGAN PLASTERED IN hundreds of thousands of banners, headlined on more leaflets and proclaimed from even more campaign buttons and signs across America, President Woodrow Wilson in summer and fall 1916 asked Americans for a second White House term. And with that slogan in mind, voters on November 7 gave it to him, rewarding him for keeping America at peace. It had been a close election and tough fight, with Wilson defeating Republican challenger, two-term New York Governor and Supreme Court Justice Charles Evans Hughes, by a mere 594,188 popular votes (of over 17 million cast) and a tight 277 to 254 Electoral College margin. So close was the outcome that not until November 22 did Hughes send his concession telegram. And even then, California was still counting ballots.

Throughout the election campaign, Europe's war and America's policies towards it had dominated, overwhelmed, every other issue, despite a peeved Wilson's attempt to focus on his considerable domestic policy accomplishments. These included child labor laws, taxing the wealthy, easy rural credits and naming liberals to the Supreme Court, which had shifted America markedly leftward and began constructing what later would be called the welfare state. But these played second fiddle in the election campaign. It was the war that was on everyone's mind. From the campaign rhetoric, from the editorials, from the party flyers, one thing was absolutely clear: No one (or, just about no one) wanted America to go to war. "Neutrality became the reigning passion during the summer and autumn of 1916," writes Wilson expert Arthur Link. "It...invaded the national conventions and controlled the writing of the party platforms, and made captives of both Wilson and his Republican opponent." Thomas Knock, also a respected Wilson scholar, agrees, calling the election "a referendum on neutrality."[1] And it was a referendum which Wilson apparently continued to back. After the election, in a January 17, 1917 note to one of his closest advisers, he declared emphatically: "There will be no war. This country does not intend to become involved in this war... It would be a crime against civilization for us to go in."[2]

So what happened? How, just a dozen weeks later, on April 2, 1917, could Woodrow Wilson stand at the House of Representatives rostrum and ask, demand, a joint session of Congress for the authority to take America into war? What changed in those weeks? How did America, so seemingly determinedly neutral in so short a time find itself heading into war? Not only into war, which easily could have meant merely helping Britain and France financially and with war supplies, but furiously mobilizing to send more than two million of its sons into the Western Front's human meat grinder. How did this happen? It's a question that has spawned generations of historical research, analyses and debate.

In shaping answers, historians point to a number of new factors tipping the scale towards intervention. One was the March 1917 collapse of Russia's brutally repressive Tsarist monarchy, removing a main obstacle that had been souring Progressives, liberals, Jews, Poles and other immigrant groups on any notion of backing the Allies, of which Russia was one. The end of Tsarist rule, commented Secretary of State Robert Lansing, "removed the one objection to affirming that the European War was a war between democracy and absolutism."[3]

A second factor was a string of revelations about German spying in the U.S., including agents' efforts to spur factory work stoppages on goods and munitions being produced for the Allies and efforts in warehouses and even ports to delay or destroy goods (including infecting horses and mules) heading for the Allies. Other German agents attempted to deny the Allies goods by buying and then warehousing huge quantities of strategic materials, such as acids and other chemicals needed for explosives.

By autumn 1915, after reviewing wire taps on the German and the Austro-Hungarian embassies' phones, Wilson was complaining that America was "honeycombed with German intrigue and infested with German spies." Historian Gary Mead calculates that from the start of 1915 to the start of 1917, there were at least eighty-eight "suspicious accidents and acts of proven sabotage" by German agents in America. One German was convicted of blowing up a bridge, while others were known to have attempted, unsuccessfully, to destroy Canada's Welland Canal and a Canadian Pacific Railway tunnel, key links in the British supply route to America's Midwest. Though British espionage in America surely was as active as German (though not so destructive, since America was neither producing anything for nor shipping anything to Germany because shipments would have been intercepted by the British naval blockade), the public heard nothing about British spying; Germany thus was seen as the sole perpetrator of shady nefarious activities on American soil.

Another, more personal factor tilting America towards war was Wilson's great disappointment at his failure to broker a peace. From the start, he pictured himself and America as the powerful trustworthy outsider bringing the misbehaving, warring sides to a negotiating table, just as had his great rival Teddy Roosevelt in 1905, when his efforts to end the Russo-Japanese War landed him a Nobel Peace Prize the following year. At times, Wilson's secret peace efforts seemed to be making modest progress, with Berlin somewhat more ready than London or Paris to consider a deal. (Germany, of course, had more to gain from a mediated solution since its forces were occupying enemy territory, some of which Germany expected to keep.) Mainly, however, Wilson's mediation dug dry wells. Despite the battlefield stalemate whose costs mounted daily, each side still flirted with notions that it could win the war—or at least a significant battle that would improve its position at a negotiating table. There also was the tragically ironic factor that the worse the carnage grew, the worse grew mediation's appeal. Explains military historian and onetime Director of the U.S. Army Military Institute Rod Paschall, "By 1917, so many youths had been sacrificed that any kind of compromise would appear unworthy and even dishonorable."[4]

Wilson nonetheless kept trying, concluding in late December 1916 that the war was so stalemated that the belligerents at last would respond to him. Going public, in what actually was the first-ever open intervention in European affairs by a president, he offered what history rightly judges a bold and balanced initiative. He asked both sides to state their war aims (neither had yet explained precisely what it sought from the war) and he indicated that he favored a peace without annexations or indemnities. When this effort failed, Wilson realized that mediation was at a dead-end. In its place he decided that were America to exert any substantial influence at whatever talks ultimately ended the war, then America would have to become a belligerent. Washington could not sit on the war's sidelines, he and others reasoned, and then expect to wield clout at a peace conference. His envisioned conference, importantly, would conduct genuine negotiations and produce real compromises. This point he made forcefully in a January 22, 1917 speech to the Senate, proclaiming that the war should end with a "peace without victory."

Yet mediation's failure, the exposure of German spies and the fall of Russian Tsardom, even all together, would not have propelled America into war in spring 1917. Of much greater, determining weight were three other factors:

- The first was the mounting economic dependence of a now prospering America on sales to Britain, France and Russia. The war was spiking American exports, which soared from $691 million in 1913 to $4.333 billion for the twelve months ending June 1916, the vast bulk of this heading for Allied ports. Simply put, many influential Americans were concluding that the nation's economy could not survive an Allied defeat or even setback.

- A second was the so-called "Preparedness Movement," launched right after the war began. Mainly an ad hoc, volunteer affair, it sought to bolster the nation's anemic military by training citizens to fight and by increasing defense spending—just in case America found itself at war. As preparedness advocates stumped the country and paraded in cities pleading for readiness and a bigger army and navy, indirectly they were making the case for and winning converts to the necessity of America joining the war.

- Last, and the most significant factor in the immediate sense, was Germany's expansion of submarine warfare. As pain and agony mounted inside Germany from the British naval blockade, German military leaders insisted that Berlin at last must retaliate and unleash its submarines to impose on the British Isles the same kind of deprivation that Britain's Royal Navy was inflicting on Germany. To the rejoinder by the German Chancellor and other civilian leaders that this almost certainly would trigger a U.S. declaration of war against Germany, the German admirals and generals were dismissive, countering that American neutrality was such a sham that America in effect already was in the war on the Allied side.

Ultimately Kaiser Wilhelm agreed, approving what would be known as unrestricted submarine warfare, a green light for U-boats to attack all ships in the war zone, including American, carrying goods to any German adversary.

Looking back from a century's perspective, these strands, woven together, help sketch America's route into Europe's war, thereby transforming it into a world war. But that was far from apparent as 1917 began. Then the country had just come off that bruising, hotly contested election season and was preparing for a second Wilson term. That Wilson won because of his strong affirmation of neutrality is beyond doubt. He polled particularly well among those most opposed to the war: labor, farmers, pacifists, women and socialists. The *International Socialist Review*, for example, lauded Wilson for keeping America's working class off the battlefield. The powerful Republican senator from Massachusetts, Henry Cabot Lodge, attributed Wilson's triumph to his attracting rural and Scandinavian Republicans. "They went over to Wilson," bemoaned Lodge, "on the one cry that he kept us out of war."

That cry had been repeated in the presidential campaign endlessly by the Democrats. Their themes, phrasing and hot-button lines began taking shape in the oratory at their June 1916 National Convention in St. Louis. There Kentucky Senator Ollie James was cheered hysterically for twenty minutes when he declared that Wilson had defended the nation's honor "without orphaning a single American child, without widowing a single American mother, without firing a single gun, without the shedding of a single drop of blood." To the *New York Times* reporter covering the convention, "the effect was simply electric" when the keynoter, former Ohio governor Martin Glynn, exclaimed that it was "true Americanism to bear with provocation and settle disputes without war... It is the duty of this nation to avoid war by every honorable means. The policy of neutrality is as truly American as the American flag."

Later, campaign buttons would proclaim, "War in Europe, Peace in America – God Bless Wilson." In Washington State, Democrats targeted mothers of young sons in publicizing the battle of Verdun's long fatality lists, promising that Wilson would spare American mothers similar grief. And in his own campaign statement, Wilson darkly warned that a Hughes victory would draw America "in one form or another into the embroilments of the European war." The GOP is the war party, Democrats endlessly charged.

That charge was unfair. Though Teddy Roosevelt was barnstorming the nation urging vigorous American support for the Allies, he was a GOP outlier. In the 1916 primaries, particularly in the West, according to George Mayer's history of the Republican Party, GOP voters chose delegates running on a peace platform, while Roosevelt's bellicosity "frightened many people."[5] Later, at the party's June convention in Chicago, at Henry Cabot Lodge's insistence and to placate the Midwest's and West's anti-war feelings, the GOP Platform sounded a decidedly dovish tone. Without equivocation it advocated "maintaining a strict and honest neutrality between the belligerents in the great war in Europe." Lodge even had struck from the platform planks that would have called for increasing the army to 250,000 men and for building the world's largest navy. In his campaigning, Hughes himself was no saber-rattler, avoiding as much as possible Europe's war, focusing instead on America's recent battles with Mexico's Francisco Pancho Villa, accusing Wilson of not doing enough to bring order to Mexico.

Those voting for Hughes, therefore, clearly were not voting against neutrality. In many instances it was quite the opposite. Particularly in agricultural and minerals exporting states, they voted Republican because they were angry at how unbalanced Wilson's brand of neutrality had become, with its tolerating British warships interfering with American shipping and violating America's freedom of the seas. Hughes, in fact, hammered at this issue throughout the campaign.

Strong neutrality sentiment extended beyond the election rhetoric season. This is evident from Wilson's approval of an astounding March 1917 memo sent by his most senior adviser, Edward House (a Texas politician known to history as "Colonel House," though he never served in the military), to British Prime Minister David Lloyd George and chief of British intelligence in the U.S. William Wiseman, the key liaison between Wilson and the British government. In what today is called the "back channel," Colonel House had established through Wiseman a White House line of communication to Britain's leaders. This memo explained that Americans were not enthusiastic about entering the war and that the "mass of the people" did not back the Allies strongly. In fact, continued the memo, very many Americans actually were hostile to Britain because of its blockade of Germany and its blacklisting and subsequent penalizing of U.S. firms doing business with Germany and its allies. The House memo could hardly have been more explicit when it told Lloyd George: "The people of the United States wish to be entirely neutral as far as the European war is concerned," though it added that the Wilson Administration has always "been entirely sympathetic to the Allies."[6]

"Great Prosperity is Coming."
Though the vast majority of Americans continued to desire and support neutrality into 1917, Washington's version of that neutrality, as the previous chapter recounts, had become profoundly unbalanced. This is the verdict of Wilson-scholar Arthur Link who concludes in his essay "Wilson and the Struggle for Neutrality" that "American neutrality did work greatly to the benefit of the Allies."[7] Nowhere was this more pronounced than in economic matters, where the tilt toward Britain and France became so overwhelming— and obvious—that a senior Wilson adviser even complained to the French that the Allies were not appreciating America's favoring them.

At first, the war had wounded the U.S. economy severely. Already in a recession in summer 1914, America immediately took an enormous hit as European markets for its goods shut almost completely. For instance, the price of cotton, a major U.S. export, within months of war's outbreak plummeted fifty percent, from 12 cents a pound to 6 cents, with cotton bales piling sky-high at America's docks. Falling too were exports of copper, meat, oil and steel, while textile manufacturers no longer could obtain highly prized German dyes. One indication of how much the U.S. economy was faltering: New railway construction fell to its lowest mileage in a half-century. Urban unemployment surged, reaching eleven percent in April 1915 (in New York City it was 16.3 percent). Ships feared venturing into the seas, not knowing which lanes were safe and which were mined and dangerous. Currency markets, predictably, convulsed. So did the world's stock markets. The New York Stock Exchange closed on July 31, 1914, not to reopen for full trading until April 1, 1915, an eight-month closure absolutely implausible today.

In relatively short time, however, the war's initial economic pains became healthy gains as the belligerents turned to America for funds and goods to fight and to feed and clothe their people. As the world's, by far, largest neutral economy, it was natural for America to profit from the war as its farm and factory output grew increasingly essential to those fighting. Since maritime law gave the U.S. the right to ship any goods to any customer anywhere, America should have become the mega-bazaar for all belligerents. It did not. With British warships keeping American and all other vessels from German ports, Germany was able to buy almost nothing. As a result, Britain, France and Russia were the sole belligerent customers for American goods, understandably spawning American interests vested in Allied success. From summer 1915 onwards, writes Link, America became "the storehouse and armory of the Allies...for the simple reason that Great Britain and not Germany controlled the seas."[8]

The U.S. fast became the main financier of Britain's

military operations, the key supplier of food to the British and an essential source of munitions for the British forces. Signs of this were everywhere in America. New plants were opening across the nation. Shipyards were running at capacity, as were machine tool manufacturers. Exports were soaring as shiploads heading for Allied ports delivered American chemicals and metals for munitions, explosives, firearms, cartridges, barbed wire, howitzers, Lee Enfield rifles, railroad cars, trucks, tires, motorcycles, horses, mules, saddles, boots, cotton, wool, canvas, leather, rubber, steel rails, generators, canned meat, beer and even submarines. American shipbuilding, mainly to replace Allied merchantmen sunk by U-boats, quadrupled between 1914 and 1917, while wheat exports surged an astounding 683 percent and sugar an even more astounding 3,833 percent.[9] Britain, France and Russia soon were buying forty percent of their war materiel from the U.S. During Britain's 1916 massive Somme offensive, for example, three-quarters of its light field artillery shells came from America.

To handle all of this, London, as early as May 1915, began stationing purchasing missions in America; one specialized in grains, another in munitions and a third in general goods. Their staffs, numbering at least 1,600 (by April 1917), went to American factories, selected and inspected products and accompanied shipments on freight trains and loading docks to prevent theft and sabotage. That these missions violated international law prohibiting belligerents from establishing a supply base inside a neutral country was ignored by Wilson.

So explosive were exports to the Allies that they not only propelled America out of its deep 1914 recession, they ignited a boom. Just one year after the European war's start, an effusive William McAdoo, the U.S. Treasury Secretary, wrote Wilson that "high prices for food products have brought great prosperity to the farmers, while the purchasers of war munitions have stimulated industry and have set factories going to full capacity... Great prosperity is coming."[10] Seconding this were similarly ebullient statements by War Secretary Newton Baker and hosts of other officials, economists and financiers.

And it was not only sales to the Allies that were firing up this welcome prosperity. Surging too were U.S. exports to Latin America, Asia and other markets that the British (and, to an extent, the French) had to abandon because they needed all of their available ships to transport munitions, food, troops and other war necessities. In Brazil, for instance, imports from the U.S. jumped to first place from third, displacing Britain which, before the war, had enjoyed a dominating two-to-one advantage. Overall, calculates historian Edward B. Parsons, America nearly doubled its share of world exports between 1913 and 1920, from 13.5 percent to 25.1 percent.[11]

Predictably, as America's booming manufacturing and banking sectors were growing increasingly dependent on sales and loans to the Allies, they also were growing increasingly fearful that an Allied defeat, or even military reversal, would crush the boom and jeopardize loan repayments. This created a huge and expanding powerful interest group pushing Washington to help the Allies. This need not mean, as some analysts conclude, that America's declaration of war was a plot by Wall Street to save its loans to the Allies. Or that America fought the war "to protect our investment in Allied bonds." Nor need it mean, as socialists have charged, that America's wartime policy was driven purely by capitalists seeking profits. Invoking plots and conspiracies gratuitously inflames and confuses the matter.

Yet, there is no denying that by 1917 the American economy and some American banks (notably J.P. Morgan) were so hooked on Allied trade that they would suffer grievously were the Allies to lose. The importance of the "economic link between the Allies and the United States…is almost impossible to exaggerate," writes historian Ross Gregory, honored by his profession with one of its most prestigious awards. "For the Allies it came to be the difference between life and death, for the United States, at least, between prosperity and depression." Hew Strachan concurs. Author of an acclaimed recent multi-volume history of the war, he writes that by 1917 "the United States could not now afford to countenance an Entente defeat." Britain's financial collapse, Strachan concludes, "would have triggered economic crisis in the United States."[12]

Numbers make Gregory's, Strachan's and other analysts' case. When the war began, merchandise exports were six percent of America's gross national product; two years later that had doubled to twelve percent, giving exports the largest share of the economy for any year for which data were then or still are available. The details tell an even more dramatic story. U.S. trade with the Allies in 1914 was $825 million; as early as 1916, it had jumped 400 percent. By contrast, in that same period America's $170 million in trade with Germany and its allies had plummeted ninety-nine percent. Also in that time, while Britain's share of U.S. exports rose from 24.22 percent to 35.24 percent, and France's share rose from 5.93 percent to 14.50 percent, Germany's share collapsed from 13.45 percent to 0.01 percent.

From such a flood of exports to Britain and its allies, Americans were paying off their foreign debts, transforming the U.S. by 1916 from a debtor into a creditor nation and accumulating most of the world's gold. The new debtors were the once-rich Allies and Central Powers. To pay for their American purchases, the Allies first liquidated their foreign currency reserves, then their gold and then their foreign investments, lands and other holdings. With few assets left, they started borrowing. Initially, when most everyone still believed that the war would be short, London was a ready banker, its loan windows profitably open to France and Russia. Soon, however, London's cash too was running low.[13]

Now only America had pockets deep enough to fund the Allied war machines. And America did. By mid-1915, New York had become banker to the Allies, with J.P. Morgan prominently in the lead. In a sense, certainly not unique to the World War One era, American banks began giving Allied nations the money to buy goods from American factories (a situation not much different at its core from 21st Century China buying U.S. Treasurys, thus enabling the U.S. to fund America's trade deficit with China so that Chinese factories could run full throttle and keep Chinese workers employed). In theory and under law, of course, Wall Street's banks could be tapped by any belligerent. But that was only theory. In reality, Berlin was shut out. With British warships interdicting all cargoes heading for Germany, no prudent banker would finance a German purchase of American goods that almost certainly could not be delivered to Germany.

Were America to be evenhanded, Washington strongly would have been protesting the British blockade, backed by threats of punitive economic action. After all, Washington now enjoyed increasing leverage over the Allies, as they were becoming almost totally economically dependent on America. An October 1916 report prepared for the British government declared flat out that without the U.S., Britain could not continue the war. And the following July, the head of Britain's mission in America wrote: "We are down on our knees to the Americans."[14] But Washington's leverage for ending or tempering the British blockade was never deployed, nor even seriously considered. By the start of 1917, Washington had become reconciled, however uncomfortably, to London's persistent violation of America's freedom of the seas.

Reconciled too was Washington to America's mounting economic dependency on the Allies. This is apparent from the wink-wink nature of the Wilson Administration's policy on war loans. When confronted by the choice of either enforcing neutrality or funding Allied purchases of American products, Wilson again sacrificed neutrality. Technically, all those mounting loans to the Allies were prohibited. They had been so since Secretary of State William Jennings Bryan, just days after the war began in 1914, ordered U.S. bankers not to fund combatants. "Loans by American bankers to any foreign nation which is at war are inconsistent with the true spirit of neutrality," read the official State Department statement. But just two months later, after American bankers and Allied governments protested vigorously that without loans the Allies could not buy American goods, the White House caved. In effect, Wilson winked, instructing the State Department to inform America's bankers orally that while they certainly could not lend money to any belligerent, there would be no objection if credits were extended. It was a difference without a difference. And it opened America's cash spigots to the Allies.

Less than a year later, in September 1915, Washington dropped the pretense that "credits" were different from "loans," permitting outright loans to the war's belligerents. A chief advocate for this was Robert Lansing, now Secretary of State. In an alarmist September 16 letter to Wilson, Lansing warned that America would suffer greatly unless Wilson immediately lifted the ban on Allied loans. Without loans, predicted Lansing, Allies would halt their American purchases, resulting in a "restriction of [American] outputs, industrial depression, idle capital, idle labor, numerous failures, financial demoralization and general unrest and suffering among the laboring classes." All this, Lansing need not even imply, would be in the year leading to the November 1916 elections and Wilson's bid for a second term.[15] Though Wilson went through the motions of balking, insisting that the loan ban stay on the books, he again winked, again instructing the State Department to assure bankers, again orally, that the U.S. government would not block loans to belligerents. As a result, according to Niall Ferguson's calculations, though American financial institutions by April 1917 had loaned $2.16 billion to the belligerents (about $41 billion in today's dollars), only $35 million of that had gone to Germany.[16]

This was applauded by American businessmen. "We profit by helping the Allies," candidly exclaimed a *Journal of Commerce* November 1915 article, "and we can afford to sacrifice something even of our rights in not hindering them." The resulting export profits strongly influenced how Washington came to view the war. This is meticulously documented by political scientist Benjamin Fordham in his study of exports and American intervention, presented at the American Political Science Association's 2005 annual meeting. After examining export flows and correlating them with House of Representatives and Senate voting patterns, Fordham told his fellow political scientists that "an analysis of data on the wartime export boom and congressional voting offers substantial evidence that economic factors shaped the political environment in which the war was debated."[17]

By the start of 1917, therefore, the economics of the war was dramatically Janus-faced. On one side, the Allies were receiving massive shipments of arms, ammunition, food and manufactured goods from America and the loans with which to pay for them; on the other, Germany, though legally entitled to the same commerce and financing, was completely cut off by the British blockade, its civilian population suffering brutally. This had been the result of a pair of Washington policies: The first was its refusal to take the tough action to enforce real neutrality by penalizing London for blocking U.S. ships from reaching Germany; the second was to permit the credits and loans to the Allies which then gradually aligned American economic interests with Allied fortunes on the battlefield. (This growing economic dependence on the Allies so concerned the Federal Reserve Board that, on November 28, 1916, it instructed member banks to stop buying foreign treasury bills and warned Americans "to consider carefully" their foreign investments.) Janus-facing had enormous consequences. It certainly meant, concludes Fordham, that when Wilson would be deciding, as he soon would be, how to respond to increased German submarine attacks on shipping, he would be influenced "by the fact that [those attacks] menaced such a substantial part of the American economy."

Hence these attacks had to be stopped. But there was a graver consequence, identified by Ross Gregory and other World War One historians: America's substantial economic backing of the Allies forced Germany to intensify its efforts to stop goods from reaching the Allies and to break the British blockade. Germany attempted this mainly by unleashing its submarines. Writes Gregory: It was U.S. shipments to Britain and France "that brought on the submarine warfare. Without American assistance to the Allies, Germany would have had no reason to adopt a policy injurious to the interests of the United States."[18]

That is an extraordinary conclusion, supported—from a century's perspective—by a reading of the historical record. It was Berlin's decision in early 1917 to wage what was called unrestricted submarine warfare, described later in this chapter, which triggered first America breaking relations with Germany and then declaring war on Germany. Yet that Berlin decision may well have been just a frustrated last-gasp response to those Washington policies driven, in large part, by America's growing economic ties to the Allies.

Sounding a Preparedness Tocsin

While deepening reliance on sales to the Allies gradually (and, in retrospect, inexorably) was convincing American manufacturers, exporters, banks, economists and policymakers that their nation should join the Allies in the war, another phenomenon similarly was influencing a broader public. It was the "Preparedness Movement"—a call for expanding the army and navy and for requiring all young men to receive military training. Its most prominent advocate was that untiring cheerleader, Teddy Roosevelt, who repeatedly and with fiery rhetoric decried and bemoaned what he saw as America's feeble ability to defend itself.

Roosevelt was right. While America certainly was one of the world's great nations by 1914, it certainly wasn't a great power.

Its economic growth and output for decades had been dazzling; its population soaring; its scientific, industrial, farm and even cultural creativity winning mounting global admiration and respect. But its military was puny: an army of about 100,000 men (smaller than some Balkan countries); a navy of thirty-one mainly obsolete, pre-Dreadnaught-class battleships; a ragtag state militia of 120,000. More puny still was its weaponry, so much so that in the months after America declared war on Germany recruits were drilling with broomsticks rather than rifles and machine guns. America, as Roosevelt and his fellow preparedness boosters kept saying, was unprepared for war.

What they meant was that the nation was unprepared for a land war. But then, of course, there was little reason America should have been. Though it was a cliché that the Pacific and Atlantic Oceans were impregnable moats protecting America, like most clichés it was rooted deeply in some fact. Indeed, not until the late 1950s, with Soviet deployment of intercontinental ballistic missiles, was continental America in danger of serious attack. Its border with Canada had been peaceful for a century; and while threatening actions by Mexican troops and independent armed bands at times required a U.S. Army response (particularly after the unrest unleashed by the 1910 Mexican Revolution), they did not require a huge American military establishment. After all, the 1898 Spanish-American War, for all the bravado of Rough Riders charging up San Juan Hill, was won with just 18,000 troops; the major force in that conflict was the then (though not in 1914) formidable U.S. Navy.

Still, as the Great War introduced new tactics and new weapons, it was prudent for Americans to take stock of their army and navy. It also was prudent to ask by early 1916 how large an army, navy and air service (as it was then called) America needed were it suddenly required to defend its interests and even itself. In theory, preparedness and neutrality need not be in conflict. Preparedness could be viewed and supported (and was by most) as a purely defensive action, implying no desire to intervene in Europe's war. As it played out, however, the tom-toms beating for military preparedness also prepared Americans for entering the war. The more the public heard from speeches and read in popular magazines and books and saw in gripping, action-filled (silent) movies arguments that America must become militarily stronger, the more accustomed and receptive did it become to arguments that America must fight.

Introducing preparedness to the American mind, particularly to policy and public opinion makers and the educated, was what history knows as the Plattsburgh Movement, named for Plattsburgh, the upstate New York town where it began. There, beginning in 1913 but accelerating enormously after the war's start and the May 1915 sinking of the *Lusitania*, Leonard Wood, former Army Chief of Staff and still the service's senior major general, launched a summer camp for upper and middle class men, mainly in their thirties and forties. Its aim: to expose them to the discipline, rigors and doctrines of rugged army training so that if the army suddenly needed to expand, they could fill crucial junior officer ranks. By the time America entered the war, some 16,000 men had been trained in Plattsburgh and similar camps around the nation. Whether their training actually prepared them much for their eventual wartime billets is uncertain; it probably did not. What is certain is that these well-placed and influential cadres left the summer camps convinced that preparing soldiers to fight was a long process which America had not yet begun. One Plattsburgh alumnus, cited by John Finnegan in his exhaustive 1974 history of the Preparedness Movement, concluded: "The most valuable lesson that we learned is that of our own incompetence."

August 1915 dramatically brought Plattsburgh to America's attention. Some 1,300 businessmen, professionals and notables, most arriving from New York City's Grand Central Station on a train dubbed the Business Men's Camp Special and all paying their own ways, poured into the austere Plattsburgh camp, with its sixteen rows of tents. Among them were New York City's mayor, its police commissioner, a J.P. Morgan partner, the Episcopal Bishop of Rhode Island and three sons and a cousin of Roosevelt, who along with Wood was Plattsburgh's biggest booster. For five weeks they drilled and marched in their olive fatigues, supervised by forty West Point graduates and 200 army enlisted men. They ended with a nine-day hike, forty-two-lbs. packs on their backs. Evenings, assembling in a hall or gathering around campfires, they listened to an eloquent (even charismatic) General Wood describing America's military shortcomings, potential enemies' strengths and the vulnerability of the nation to attack. Explains Finnegan: "Some of the most influential men in the country were learning firsthand the complexities of soldiering, the efficiency of West Pointers and the failure of American military policy."[19]

Carrying the message of the nation's military vulnerabilities to even more Americans were a number of civilian defense organizations whose development paralleled and in a few cases preceded the Plattsburgh Movement. Though funding was always tight, their voices were loud and strong. Their message, echoing Wood and Roosevelt, was unwavering: Germany's invasion of Belgium dramatically demonstrated what befalls a nation unprepared to defend itself. While generally carefully avoiding pointing to any power as a potential enemy, these groups left little doubt that such an attack easily would succeed. Among the most visible and active groups were the American Defense Society, League to Enforce Peace, Aero Club and Navy League.

The most influential group, agree Finnegan and other historians, was the Manhattan-headquartered National Security League, headed by 1904 Democrat Presidential candidate Alton Parker and boasting Roosevelt and Boston Mayor James Curley as among its some 100,000 members in its seventy chapters (mostly on the East Coast). The League enjoyed one advantage over the other groups: It could count on financial support from such Wall Street titans as

Cornelius Vanderbilt and Simon Guggenheim. At its December 1, 1914 founding meeting in New York City's Hotel Belmont, League members heard a U.S. Army major warn that Germany was planning to invade America as soon as it defeated Britain.

Such sense of approaching catastrophe typified the League's outlook, rhetoric and policy prescriptions. It demanded that Wilson and Congress act immediately to build the world's largest navy, to increase vastly the size of the army to 500,000 and, in a call taken up by all of the Preparedness Movement, to follow the example of most European countries (except Britain) by instituting Universal Military Training and Service (generally known as UMT&S), requiring every young American male to serve in the military. In contrast to other groups, the National Security League wasn't shy about explicitly targeting Germany as the source of America's greatest peril. Its speakers fanned across the nation and its lobbyists worked Capitol Hill warning endlessly that the Allies were about to collapse and that America was next on Berlin's hit list, with invasion just about imminent.

In major cities, the League organized parades; the grandest was its May 13, 1916 Citizens' Preparedness Parade in Manhattan. By the *New York Times*' precise reckoning, high-stepping along Fifth Avenue were 135,683 marchers, including 3,287 women, 728 Spanish-American War veterans and 8,000 bandsmen in more than 200 bands. "Every band in New York City has been engaged, as well as more than fifty fife and drum corps," wrote the *Times*. "Fifth Avenue is aflutter with flags from end to end…while nearly every building has been decorated, in nearly every instance, with American flags exclusively. Over the roof of the Ritz-Carlton, hundreds of red, white and blue electric lights have been strung." Within a month, 350,000 preparedness backers were marching in ten other cities' parades, more than 100,000 alone in Chicago, where telephone operators were costumed as parts of a huge American flag, which seemed to float down the street. Finnegan writes: "America had become preparedness conscious."[20]

Influential organizations in diverse fields helped raise this consciousness, such as the National Association of Manufacturers, the newly-founded U.S. Chamber of Commerce and the National Academy of Sciences, which set up the National Research Council to coordinate militarily-useful studies. The National Education Association, initially deaf to the preparedness clarion, by mid-1916 reversed itself, declaring that public school students should be getting military training. Women too clambered aboard, establishing the Women's Section of the Movement for National Preparedness and the Women's Section of the Navy League. Most ambitious and committed was the National Woman's Special Aid Society, preparing for what it was certain was the coming war by compiling lists of sewing clubs and nurses and outfitting cottages to be used as military hospitals. In New York City, members of the American Women's League for Self-Defense donned uniforms and drilled weekly at the medieval fortress-style Ninth Regiment Armory on 14th Street.

Meantime, ten chairmen of the American Medical Association's divisions, along with seventy-nine presidents of state medical associations and representatives of ninety-five medical schools, strongly voiced support for universal military training. As did, it appears, many of those who would be conscripted and trained by it. In polls, 1,112 Yale students backed UMT&S, with 228 opposing; at Harvard it was 860 for to 339 against; at Princeton 503 for to ninety-two against; and at the University of Pennsylvania, 936 for to fifty against. Unwilling to wait for universal military training, some Harvard students formed their own drill battalion, while Yale actually organized four field artillery batteries to practice with the Connecticut militia. Other young men went further, going to war immediately. Some went to Europe to fight, like the 15,000 or so Americans who responded to British and Canadian recruiters in the U.S. and joined Allied armies. And some went to fly, like the scores, mainly college-educated and middle class, who formed the American

Escadrille, later renamed the Lafayette Escadrille, and spawned tales of dashing war plane heroics in France which live to our day.

Amplifying the preparedness tocsin warning of America's inability to defend itself were the day's mass media. In Finnegan's view, preparedness had become "part of American popular culture. It filled the newspapers and flooded the streets. The advertisements for innocuous products featured soldiers or battleships, and men's clothing stores put out uniforms displays."[21] Most of the country's widely circulated magazines and large urban newspapers began calling for expanding the armed forces, so that, as Finnegan calculates, "by the end of [1915] less than a dozen newspapers of any size in the whole country opposed defense increases." Magazines featured alarmist articles with such titles as "Our Undefended Treasure Land" and "The Invasion of America." The lurid cover story "Get Ready" depicted a German occupation of America's eastern states, with the region renamed "New Prussia" and major cities now called "Kulturplatz," "Hyphenburg" and "Schlauterhaus." In this fantasy, America's West was occupied by Japanese.

Book publishers, for their part, released from 1915 to early 1917 some sixty titles trumpeting preparedness arguments. A few were quite scholarly, but most were extremely sensationalist, such as the very popular John Bernard Walker's *America Fallen! The Sequel to the European War* and Hudson Maxim's *Defenseless America*, both released in 1915. Walker, a respected editor of *Scientific American,* grippingly portrays an America invaded by 200,000 battle-tested German soldiers who effortlessly capture Boston, New York City and Washington, while German warships sink the U.S. fleet in the "Battle of the Caribbean." Finally, when the president of a defeated America is forced to pay the Germans a $12 billion indemnity (about a quarter-trillion of today's dollars), his chief of staff consoles that it is "the cost of being taught the great national duty of preparedness." Echoing this, but more lurid, was Maxim's extremely influential and popular book. It flatly predicts that war is inevitable and that when the invaders overrun America, "our wives and our daughters and our sweethearts would be commandeered to supply the women and song" to sate the invaders.[22]

Movies, though still novel, but with swelling and mesmerized audiences, made the most dramatic and terrifying case for preparedness, portraying an America not only militarily weak and thus inviting attack, but an America actually under attack. Most renowned was 1915's *The Battle Cry of Peace*, based on Maxim's *Defenseless America*. Its message was dramatic and convincing, building to crescendo scene by gripping scene. An enemy naval fleet bombards and pulverizes New York City while the attacking ships remain smugly and safely beyond range of the city's defensive coastal guns; shells slam into crowded Times Square, scattering panicked citizens; waves of enemy bombers set Long Island homes aflame; hordes of spike-helmeted enemy troops land, line up Americans to be machine-gunned and threaten to ravage American women.

Moving Picture World in its August 21, 1915 issue says of *The Battle Cry of Peace*: "Tragedy is piled upon tragedy, culminating in the most poignant scene of all—a mother's shooting of her daughters to save them from drunken soldiers." *Variety's* August 13 review declares that the film "from a pictorial standpoint is a revelation. There are a score of panorama scenes, some of which have been taken from hydroplanes flying over New York, which are little short of wonderful." After its Manhattan Vitagraph Theater premier, where the screen's actions and agonies were intensified by a full orchestra and a massive organ, by sounds of roaring mobs and screaming women coming from behind the screen and with General Wood and other luminaries in attendance, the film played to huge audiences nationwide plus at special meetings in Washington and many state capitals.

The film's significance immediately was recognized. The *New York Times* review of August 7, 1915 described it as "an animated, arresting, and sometimes lurid argument for the immediate and radical improvement of our national defenses... It is designed to make many a person in each audience resolve to join the National Guard, the American Legion, the National Security League, and the Navy League, forthwith. Thus is the rising propaganda for greater preparedness carried into the movies." And to *Variety*, "*The Battle Cry of Peace* comes into the field at a moment when every American is faced with the realization this country is in a general state of what is termed 'unpreparedness.'"[23]

Beyond the articles, books and movies, the Preparedness Movement was picking up even more support by morphing far from a simple call for revitalizing America's army and navy. It also was becoming a call, embraced by a great many who otherwise would have paid scant attention to military matters, to make over American society and revitalize America's soul, thus tapping into the Progressive movement's powerful guilt/redemption undercurrent. For two decades, Progressives, including Woodrow Wilson and to a considerable extent Teddy Roosevelt, had been preaching to a vast and receptive audience, admonishing that despite (or because of) America's mounting wealth, embarrassing and sordid conditions still festered unacceptably and unfairly in the nation – child labor, frightful sweatshops, greatly unequal distribution of incomes, exploitative and atavistic industrial and banking trusts and monopolies and more. This audience, America's growing urban middle and upper classes, not only began agreeing that America needed Progressive-style reform, but also began feeling uneasy, perhaps apologetic, even perhaps guilty, about personally reaping so many benefits of the nation's economic advances while so many fellow citizens were not. Such middle and upper class unease (and guilt) explains in great part the Progressive movement's astounding success in mobilizing voters and enacting sweeping reforms.

It also may explain the Preparedness Movement's broadening

popularity. Preparedness promised both sacrifice and redemption, a return, said many, to the Puritan era's pre-materialist moral code, which tragically had faded in the subsequent generations' easy living. "Universal military training," explains Finnegan, "now seemed a panacea for America's social and economic ills, making the nation fit for competition in peace as well as war." It was a means of toughening what many bemoaned as the increasingly flabby, undisciplined Americans and misbehaving teenagers.

Military training would take up, as an economist put it, "the slack of idleness" and the "hoodlum period" of late adolescence. It would sweep, promised others, "boys off street corners and out of saloons," promote respect for authority and the work ethic and reduce frightening divorce rates and the scandal of husbands deserting wives. Others claimed that it would slash government waste and rid cities of political bosses. For Cardinal James Gibbons, Baltimore's longtime archbishop and America's most influential Roman Catholic cleric, military training would restore order and respect among youth. This argument unsurprisingly resonated among teachers and principals who welcomed the discipline that military training would bring to their classrooms. Others saw it combating "slovenly labor and serious crime" and even unleashing the "virile strength of manliness." Overall, writes Michael Pearlman in his 1984 history of preparedness and Progressives, a dose of military training would "develop a new and better American manhood."

Efficiency too would improve. Historian John Chambers tells of a Philadelphia department store executive observing that attendance at a Plattsburgh-like training camp made his employees "more alert and taught them to think quickly and obey instinctively." General Wood boasted that six months at a training camp boosted worker efficiency fifteen percent to thirty percent. Then there were those convinced that such training would meld the masses of new immigrants into American society, or, as it sometimes was put, would "yank the hyphen out of America." Most notably championing this was Columbia University President Nicholas Murray Butler, a onetime outspoken pacifist who now embraced universal military training and America's entry into the war because they were to be a "unifying force of national necessity and conscious national purpose" that would solve the problem of diverse ethnicity. General Wood agreed, promising that military training would "bind together all classes of society into one common purpose." Leading liberals, meanwhile, like essayist Walter Lippmann and *New Republic* editor Herbert Croly celebrated preparedness as a way to deepen government's role in the economy and society and "advance the cause of social welfare policy."

Whatever the varied and growing rationales for preparedness, whatever its expected benefits, however (in Finnegan's view) "exaggerated and silly as it sometimes was," the movement was a great success, ultimately drawing Wilson into its ranks and forcing Congress to fund a larger army and navy. To be sure, preparedness support was far from universal. A phenomenon primarily of the cities, and even of the middle and upper classes, it was opposed by much of rural America (particularly the National Grange and National Farmers Union) and its powerful representatives on Capitol Hill. Farmers were suspicious of militarism, distrusted the corporations backing preparedness and hated the thought of paying the added taxes needed for a bigger army and navy. Also opposing were pacifists (the American Union Against Militarism, with branches in twenty-one cities), liberal Democrats in the states and in Congress (Wilson's initial base of support), socialists, organized labor (except for Samuel Gompers, the country's top union leader), many women's and suffragist groups such as Jane Addams' Women's Peace Party and some southerners who cringed at training Blacks to use arms. Meantime, many immigrants opposed because, after all, they had fled their native countries specifically to escape conscription.

But such opposition barely slowed the preparedness juggernaut. By December 1915, stung by attacks that he was timid and with an election less than a year away, Wilson knew that he had to get in front of the parade. Teddy Roosevelt, a potential Wilson opponent in the 1916 election, had been deriding the president as one of the "professional pacifists…flubdubs and mollycoddles… every soft creature, every coward and weakling," while Roosevelt's former Secretary of State Elihu Root was mocking that Wilson "first shakes his fist and then he shakes his finger."[24]

Wilson had to respond, and did. Declaring that America required "reasonable preparedness" to protect national honor and Western hemisphere security, he sent Congress what, after extraordinary wrangling and bargaining, would become the National Defense Act of June 3, 1916 and the Naval Appropriations Act of August 29, both giving preparedness advocates most, though not all, of what they wanted. The army's strength was doubled to 216,000 men and 11,450 officers; the ranks of its generals climbed from thirty-six to fifty-four; navy capital ships were doubled to sixty; a Reserve Officers Training Corps (ROTC) was created for colleges; and the militia, to be called the National Guard, was boosted to a potential 457,000 and, importantly, would be supervised closely by the Regular Army, would take an oath to the United States as well as to the state in which each unit was raised and could be ordered into national service by the president in an emergency. Additionally, the president in wartime could take over the nation's factories.

Glaringly missing from the legislation, however, was that core preparedness demand: universal military training. This omission made one big thing very clear. Neither Wilson nor Congress was ready to declare that America needed a mass army. Nor were they ready to declare that America soon would be fighting; the doubling of the army was spread over five years, the naval expansion at least six. In that respect, the Preparedness Movement did little actually to prepare America militarily for the war it soon was to enter. What it did do, and this was historically vastly more significant, was to prepare the public—once so fervently neutralist—for entering Europe's war and doing so with massive force. So inoculated had Americans become by preparedness rhetoric, images, parades, warnings and theatrics, that when provoked by a last straw of German military action, they abandoned their neutrality in a flash and reacted ferociously. Such a last straw provocation was to come within months, when, in early 1917, Berlin again unleashed its U-boats.

Germany Unleashes Its Submarines

From the war's start, submarines had posed a conundrum for Berlin. U-boats were the one German weapon advantage, the sole effective means of retaliating against the British Navy's blockade strangling Germany and inflicting hardship on German civilians in ways unimaginable in Britain and France. Yet, as Chapter 2 explains, the U-boats immediately created a huge public relations problem, particularly in America, where they were viewed, because of their stealth, as a sneaky, unfair means of combat and darkly were called "Assassins of the Sea." Wilson, in particular, denounced them as "inhumane," as "a cruel and unmanly business" and as assaults on "humanity," in contrast to the British blockade which he explained repeatedly was merely inflicting material damage.

But U-boats needed their stealth. Without it they exposed themselves to enormous danger. Were they to act like a traditional warship, observing maritime law and custom by first surfacing before attacking, they made themselves, with their thin hulls, flimsy construction and slow speed, extraordinarily vulnerable. When rammed by a merchant ship or when fired at with even small-caliber guns by a merchant ship's crew, the U-boat would sink. In deciding whether to deploy its U-boats, therefore, Berlin throughout the war had to balance their significant military stealth advantage against the cost of enraging America and, perhaps, bringing it into the war against Germany.

Neither London nor Paris faced a conundrum anything like this.

As a result, German submarine policy had zigzagged, punctuated by periods of U-boats inside the war zone firing without warning at merchant vessels and even passenger liners (like the *Lusitania* in May 1915) to periods of extreme circumspection, with Berlin bowing completely to Washington's demands and allowing even enemy ships to pass safely and quietly. Such circumspection marked the months after the March 24, 1916 U-boat torpedoing of the French ferry *Sussex* in the English Channel. Four Americans onboard died. Although Germany was within its legal rights to declare a war zone around Britain in retaliation for the British blockade of Germany and for Britain's declaring the North Sea as a war zone, and although the *Sussex* was, after all, a ship flying the flag of a belligerent enemy, and although the four American victims knowingly were traveling on a belligerent's ship in a war zone, the sinking infuriated Wilson. So much so that Berlin, greatly fearing that he would take America into war against Germany, did whatever it could to placate the American president. Germany promised that its U-boats, before attacking merchantmen, would surface, would warn the target ship and then would allow the ship's crew to escape, even though this greatly endangered the U-boat. And that's exactly what Germany mainly did, in effect throttling back its U-boat action and removing submarine warfare as an irritant and provocation in U.S.-German relations.

By the start of 1917, this was changing; the U-boat conundrum cost-benefit balance had begun shifting towards the benefit. Several realities were driving this. One was that the pain inflicted by the British blockade steadily was intensifying and only could be softened, reasoned Berlin, by a German retaliation inflicting sufficient counter-pain to force Britain to loosen its grip.

A second reality, related closely to the first, was a growing acceptance of the military command's argument (ultimately proved wrong) that its expanded and vastly improved submarine fleet, now numbering more than 100 boats, unrelentingly could attack all shipping in the war zone around the British Isles and thus cripple Britain. Citing data generated by German academic research institutes, the admirals and generals insisted that by sinking 600,000 tons of Britain-bound shipping each month, that country would be brought to its knees within a half-year, long before America, should it enter the war, would be able to raise and train an army and ship it to Europe. By then—and the military command was very sure of this—with Britain out of the war, Germany would be able to concentrate its forces against France and defeat it. As it happened, none of this played out as predicted. Far, very far, from it. But that would come later. At the start of 1917, the need to puncture the British blockade, with the added possibility of driving Britain from the war, seemed to German leaders a plausible and even necessary course of action.

Making it more plausible and acceptable was a third reality. It was huge; in retrospect, it was decisive. It was the spreading German official and public feeling that though greater U-boat aggressiveness could turn America formally against their country, America in fact already had turned against it and was behaving so hostile that Germany had little to lose by antagonizing the U.S. For months influential German admirals and generals had been hammering this point, declaring unequivocally to Chancellor Theobald von Bethmann-Hollweg, an opponent of expanded U-boat attacks, that there would be "no real change for Germany" were America to become openly hostile since it all along had been waging its "secret war" against Germany. In August 1916, the U-boats' most prominent and persistent champion, Admiral Henning von Holtzendorff, dismissed concerns about bringing America into the war, declaring to the Chancellor that America "scarcely can engage in more hostile activities than she already has done." And by January 8, 1917, the enormously powerful and respected Chief of the German General Staff Paul von Hindenburg flatly stated that things with America "cannot be worse than they are now."[25]

Increasingly, the German public was agreeing. Anger at America's unbalanced neutrality and dismay that Wilson had done nothing against Britain to defend American ships' rights to deliver food and other non-military goods to German ports was fueling popular support for lifting restrictions on U-boat actions in the war zone. It isn't fair, Germans began saying, that America denounces U-boat attacks as wrong, even immoral, but then allows Britain to wound Germany exactly as German U-boats would be wounding Britain. This mounting popular backing for full-scale submarine warfare, wrote French politician and expert on the blockade Louis Guichard in 1929, was "the feverish, mad reaction of a besieged people in danger of starvation." Even the hapless U.S. Ambassador in Berlin, James Gerard, picked up on and reported to Washington about the growing German public anger. He later wrote in his memoirs that "no German ever forgets" that the U.S. sells arms to the Allies and that "American supplies and munitions killed his brother, son or father."

Ringing ever truer to the German ear was Admiral von Holtzendorff's argument that Germany had the right to demand that America and other neutrals "put up with our measures just as they tolerate those of the English." Nearly a century later, historians find this case plausible. Writes Hew Strachan, arguable today's most eminent World War One authority: "From Germany's perspective the United States, although nominally neutral, had become a covert belligerent in economic terms. Thus [Germany] could calculate that the decision…to adopt its own form of economic warfare, the unrestricted use of submarines, had no penalty."[26]

Approval of unrestricted U-boat attacks spread across Germany's political spectrum, backed not only, predictably, by rightist German political parties and its press and by the pro-military groups, but also now by socialists and by such influential centrist media as the daily *Berliner Tageblatt*, Jewish-owned and edited and long a leading champion of liberalism and democracy.

"The most popular military campaign of the entire war" is how historian Laurence Moyer, in his history of Germany during the conflict, describes the public mood after restrictions on the U-boats had been lifted. And a Lower Saxony daily detected that "a sigh of relief is going through the German people."[27]

Berlin, however, did not easily come to its U-boat decision. Though not well known at the time, and certainly not in the U.S., which had scant information about anything happening inside German policymaking circles, the historical record reveals that an enormous U-boat debate raged in Berlin, with Kaiser Wilhelm in the middle. Arrayed against the admirals and generals and their demands for immediate unrestricted U-boat action was much of the civilian leadership, including the still influential Chancellor Bethmann-Hollweg, Foreign Minister Arthur Zimmermann (fortified by impassioned dispatches from his ambassador in Washington, Count Johann von Bernstorff) and leaders of the Reichstag's left and center parties.

But since the earlier overriding concern for keeping America out of the war was fast receding, the U-boat decision now would turn on a single calculation: whether Germany and its military forces would be better or worse off were Berlin to lift the restrictions on U-boat actions. With the Western Front frozen and still devouring hundreds of thousands of lives in senseless offensives and counteroffensives; with the huge German and British surface fleets at a standoff, the former bottled up in German waters and the latter largely tied down guarding and preventing them from breaking out; and with the German home front enduring vastly greater pain than the British or French, the Kaiser made his calculation and decreed that unrestricted U-boat warfare offered benefits exceeding its costs.

Of course, the actual decision process was not nearly so methodical, clear, neat and rational. It was influenced enormously by emotions, harangues, exaggerations, intrigues, intimidations and, perhaps most important, ignorance and naiveté—all since chronicled and dissected by generations of historians. Yet stripping away those contending influences and atmospherics, what remained was that simple German calculation. And from that was the decision made, the orders given. To the U-boat commanders went instructions that on February 1, 1917 they should attack all merchant ships in the war zone (but not, of course, on the high seas). And to Count Bernstorff in Washington went the instructions to call upon Secretary of State Lansing on January 31 to inform him that unrestricted submarine attacks in the war zone would begin the next day. In this cable to Bernstorff (relayed via the U.S. Embassy in Berlin since Britain had cut all undersea telegraph links between the U.S. and Germany), Chancellor Bethmann-Hollweg acknowledged: "I am well aware that with our action we run the risk of bringing about the break and perhaps war with the United States. We are determined to accept this risk."

As instructed, on the afternoon of January 31, a very nervous and dismayed Bernstorff arrived at the State, War and Navy Building (today's Old Executive Office Building) next to the White House. This Imperial German ambassador was noticeably trembling when he said to Lansing: "I am sorry to have to bring about this situation, but my government could do nothing else." He then handed Lansing the official German note. It formally notified the United States that on the following day U-boats would begin operating in the war zone without restriction, attacking all ships, including American, suspected of carrying goods to any of Germany's adversaries. After reading the note in silence, Lansing said to Bernstorff, who was seated beside the Secretary of State's desk, that it was an "unfriendly and indefensible act." Bernstorff then rose, as did Lansing; as the two diplomats shook hands, tears came to Bernstorff's eyes, prompting Lansing to feel, as he later wrote in his diary, compassion for the German.

But Lansing also had to feel pleased, perhaps even delighted. If his letters and diary accurately reflect his views, as they must, then for nearly two years he had wanted and tirelessly sought for America to join the Allied ranks in the war. He was widely known to regard German leaders as undemocratic, evil and immoral. Just a month before, in fact, according to Arthur Link and a host of other historians, Lansing had sabotaged a major Wilson effort to mediate a peace, secretly advising London and Paris how to respond to Wilson in ways certain to force Berlin to reject the mediation. And that's exactly what London and Paris did. Link, an undisguised admirer of Wilson, regards Lansing's behavior as "one of the most egregious acts of treachery in American history" and believes that Wilson was "unaware of the full degree of Lansing's disloyalty."[28]

Lansing, of course, soon was to see his desires for war fulfilled. Had William Jennings Bryan remained Secretary of State, history may well have been quite different.

Wilson's first response to the notification of unfettered U-boat attacks was to break diplomatic relations with Germany. On February 3, at 2 p.m., a State Department lawyer arrived at the German Embassy on Massachusetts Avenue. There he formally declared to Bernstorff that because there is "no alternative consistent with the dignity and honor of the United States... The President has, therefore, directed me to announce to your Excellency that all diplomatic relations between the United States and the German Empire are severed." Though Wilson invited the other neutral nations to break with Germany, none followed his lead—except for a very young Republic of China. Eleven days later a saddened Bernstorff, having served eight years as ambassador, boarded the Danish liner *Frederik VIII* at Hoboken pier and sailed homeward, where, by and large, he was snubbed by officials because he was seen as pro-American. That he was well regarded in America was true. His send-off was extremely warm, with a large crowd of journalists and well-wishers surrounding him at the pier, with papers around the country printing friendly farewell articles and with ships in New

York harbor sounding whistles of safe journey. For now, German interests in America would be looked after by the Swiss, who also would be keeping their eye on American interests in Germany.

Then Wilson waited, almost in seclusion, much of the time, in fact, in his bedroom—a presidential withdrawal unthinkable today. First he told aides that he could not be disturbed because he had a severe cold; then he just stopped accepting callers, maintaining what Wilson scholar August Heckscher calls an "impenetrable facade."[29] He interacted with the outside world almost exclusively via his wife Edith. From historical accounts, it seems that he was waiting and closely watching, hoping that Germany would do something to give him cause not to take the next step: a declaration of war.

After all, he reasoned, twice before had Berlin reined in U-boat actions after strong Washington protests; perhaps it would happen again. But Berlin no longer was wrestling with the U-boat conundrum, no longer calculating the tradeoffs between the gains from U-boat attacks versus the likelihood of war with America. In essence, the Kaiser and the Chancellor both had decided that there no longer were tradeoffs. Manfred Jonas, in his history of U.S.-German relations, explains that Bethmann-Hollweg was now persuaded that in the past he "had given in more than enough to the American viewpoint and had obtained little or nothing in return." This time Germany was not going to give in.[30]

And Germany did not. With their new battle orders, the U-boats aggressively began patrolling the high seas for Allied ships and in the war zone around Britain for all ships. Two days after the launch of unrestricted submarine warfare, U-boats torpedoed and sank twelve merchantmen, one of them American. On March 18, three more American ships in the war zone—*City of Memphis, Illinois* and *Vigilancia*—went down. In all, fourteen Americans died. Meantime, understandably wary of U-boats, American captains balked at braving the war zone; they kept their ships safely in America's home harbors, where goods destined for Britain and

France began piling up, prompting frantic calls for supplies from London and Paris. For Wilson, all this was too much to bear.

Compounding Wilson's mounting anger at Germany was the bizarre incident known as the Zimmermann telegram, the January 16, 1917 dispatch sent by German Foreign Minister Arthur Zimmermann to Mexico's leaders offering them an alliance should America go to war with Germany. This was Zimmermann's proposal: In exchange for Mexican armed forces creating disturbances on America's border to tie down American military resources, Germany would support the return to Mexico of Texas and other territory taken by the U.S. This was a bold, audacious and foolish move. ("An incredibly inept German maneuver," is the judgment of Jonas.) Though it differed little in concept from the many deals that London and Paris were offering a score of countries in what are called the "secret treaties," the Zimmermann proposal, after all, specifically would harm America and thus specifically guaranteed American fury were the deal to become known, as it almost certainly would. To be sure, it would take effect only if America declared war on Germany; Zimmermann was not proposing an alliance that would allow Germany first to declare war on America. But those subtle details were technical and minor at the time, and remain so today.

London was first to learn of Zimmermann's proposed deal when it intercepted and decoded, as it had been doing since the war's start, the wireless transmissions from the German Foreign Ministry. British leaders immediately recognized that the telegram almost surely would push the U.S. ever further to viewing Germany hostilely. After nearly a month of sitting on the information, surely waiting for the moment when it would have the greatest impact on American policymakers and the American public, London finally passed the telegram's transcript on to the State Department, which then sat on it for a full week before releasing it on March 1. The enormous subsequent indignant press and public uproar, with screaming headlines and petitions supporting war, is not unimaginable; it, in fact, was predictable and understandable, particularly since America was extremely sensitive about the security of its border with Mexico. Fresh in the public's mind was the messy campaign of the just withdrawn expeditionary force which Major General John J. Pershing had led into Mexico to punish Pancho Villa for attacking some U.S. border communities. The Zimmermann telegram was thus incendiary, emblazing in the public mind that the German indeed was the treacherous, scheming Hun.

W...A...R

For all of the pyrotechnics sparked by the Zimmermann offer to Mexico, its actual impact on American policy was nearly nil. It did not have to push or nudge America into war. For that the die already had been cast. As a proximate cause for it, unrestricted submarine warfare was the key. And it was in response to the resumed U-boat attacks that Wilson, on March 20, met with his cabinet. He asked for, and unanimously received, support for his next step, a call to Congress to convene in special session on April 2, to receive from the president "a communication concerning grave matters of national policy." There was little doubt that this grave matter would be a request for a declaration of war, proclaiming Germany the enemy of the United States.

In many respects, particularly from a century's perspective, that would seem a puzzling development. Germany had not declared war on America. For the thirty-one months since the start of the war, Germany had made numerous concessions and taken numerous steps to persuade America to remain neutral. And when, earlier in the war, U-boats did kill some Americans, they were traveling on belligerent ships at time of war in a war zone. And even when, after the unrestricted submarine campaign had begun and American ships themselves were targeted and torpedoed, those ships were in the war zone, not on the high seas, and were steaming toward Allied ports with cargoes almost certainly beneficial to the Allies.

To be sure, as some historians do, it can be argued that the killing of Americans had forced Wilson's hand. That is certainly an understandable explanation of his action. But it assumes that Wilson, in calculating America's own tradeoffs, concluded that retaliating for the pain inflicted on America by U-boat casualties justified the cost and consequences of a likely war. It assumes too that Wilson believed that the government always must protect its citizens traveling anywhere, even if they voluntarily journeyed into harm's way. But that is an argument finding little historical support. Indeed, legendary U.S. diplomat George Kennan states in his history of American diplomacy that a president may have the "privilege to defend the rights of our citizens to travel on belligerent vessels, but it is hardly a duty."[31]

It could be said, of course (and often is), that the loss of even a single American life demands an honor-saving response. In the heat of the moment, resisting this argument may be very difficult. But from the vantage of our day, we may more dispassionately be able to reason, as political scientist Benjamin Fordham's paper does, that Wilson's response was neither warranted by nor appropriate to the costs inflicted by unrestricted U-boat warfare. Fordham calculates that from the war's August 1914 start to April 1917, when the U.S. entered the war, 236 Americans had been killed by U-boats. Of these, however, explains Fordham, "all but 14 embarked on ships flying the flags of belligerent states when they were attacked. From the perspective of December 7, 1941 or September 11, 2001— not to mention the 53,402 American combat deaths sustained in [World War One] itself—these losses are not especially large."[32]

But they loomed large in spring 1917 and in Wilson's April 2 speech to Congress. In requesting that the House and Senate send him a declaration of war to sign, Wilson invoked a catalogue of reasons and motives. Several times did he bring his audience—Members of the House and Senate, the entire Supreme Court and Cabinet, the Diplomatic Corps (with the British, French and Russian ambassadors in formal attire) and scores of distinguished Americans and foreigners—to its feet, filling the House chamber with hurrahs. Some of them were led, unimaginable in our day, by an arm-waving Chief Justice of the Supreme Court who wore a tiny American flag in his lapel.

Hurrahs too have been offered up over the decades by those many historians who judge Wilson's words one of the nation's great presidential orations. Yet a review of the 2,700-word address now finds it puzzling and troubling. Missing from it is any litany of alleged wrongs committed by Germany against America to warrant America's going to war. Missing is the indictment charging Germany with counts meriting retribution. The standard for such an indictment, of course, is America's Declaration of Independence, listing one after another the many injustices and pains inflicted by England's George III on the colonies. Even today, nearly a quarter-millennium later, that Declaration's indictment rings true, convincing any reader that the colonies had a right and were right to raise an army and revolt. Closer to our time, some twenty-four years after Wilson's speech, Franklin Roosevelt, at the same rostrum, needed point only to the skeletons of American warships still smoldering in Pearl Harbor to make the convincing case that America had to go to war against Japan. There was no question that Japan had attacked America and posed an unacceptable danger to the nation.

But such was missing from Wilson's eloquent and moving plea. All he could point to, and did so repeatedly, was a single German action: deploying U-boats to sink ships in the war zones around Allied ports. America was going to war, said Wilson, because those U-boats had trampled on America's neutrality. Nothing was said about British warships similarly trampling on neutrality by preventing American merchantmen from reaching German ports, even though Wilson had complained as recently as February 2 at a cabinet meeting that "both [sides] had been equally indifferent to the rights of neutrals." Secretary of State Lansing, in fact, later admitted "that in 1917 we had as good, if not better, legal grounds for fighting Britain as for fighting Germany."[33] Wilson, in truth, could not offer a litany of German transgressions against America because no transgressions existed. Indeed, in appearing before the Senate Foreign Relations Committee shortly after the war, he acknowledged that he would have taken America into war whether or not Germany had committed, in the words of a senator, any "act of war or any act of injustice" against America or its citizens.[34]

Instead of justifying war as a way to stop Germany from allegedly grievously harming America (and to punish Germany for it), Wilson in his call for war justified it as an opportunity for America and other nations to improve the world or, as he put it in one of American history's most memorable phrases, "to make the world safe for democracy." Using words and concepts deeply familiar and powerfully resonant to his generation of Progressive reformers and to a public nurtured on soaring sermon-like Progressive rhetoric and cadence (the very concepts and rhetoric that would launch Prohibition within a year), Wilson told Congress that war was justified because it would be a "vindication of right, of human right"; it would "vindicate the principles of peace and justice in the life of the world as against selfish and autocratic power"; it would be a "fight thus for the ultimate peace of the world and for the liberation of its peoples"; and it would be a fight against "an irresponsible government which has thrown aside all considerations of humanity and of right and is running amuck."

This indeed is, as Wilson's many admirers state, a grand and eloquent vision, so much so that it has given a name, "Wilsonian," to a whole school of policymakers and scholars who still, in our day, on the left and even on the right, argue that American foreign policy must be driven by high ideals. Wilson, writes an admirer, took America into war to establish "a regime of liberty in the world." From all we know, Wilson strongly believed and was motivated by such ideals.

But it was more than just Wilsonian or Progressive ideals, of course, that was about to send young Americans to kill Germans. There also was a fabric of realities that had made war against Germany an acceptable American policy: The reality that many Americans, influenced by British propaganda, had concluded that Germans were evil and barbaric Huns who deserved to be fought; the reality that American industry, farms and banks had much to lose from an Allied defeat; the reality that East Coast policymakers, media and academics had, from the start, favored Britain and France; the reality that such senior Wilson advisers as Edward House and Secretary of State Robert Lansing repeatedly were assuring London and Paris that America was not at all neutral but really on their side; and the reality that the broad American public, thinking that their nation was neutral and thus angered that this neutrality allegedly was being violated by Germany, never realized how far that neutrality had tilted.

It was a stark reality also that by spring 1917 Woodrow Wilson, little versed in the power plays of foreign affairs, never considered using his growing leverage to press London for concessions, particularly a loosening of its blockade of Germany, an act that could have stopped U-boat attacks on American ships. Deploying such leverage was never contemplated, even though Britain and France, confronting bankruptcy, desperately needing American loans, raw materials and munitions to fight the war and American food to feed their people, had become very susceptible to American pressure. Nor did Wilson impose (or even request) conditions on London and Paris in exchange for bringing his nation to battle on their side.

What was not a reality was that Germany in 1917 posed a strategic threat to the United States. It did not. And Wilson, according to all the documents, diaries, papers and speeches, never once indicated that he regarded Germany as a military or security threat. He did not. Whatever German aggrandizing, expansionist, aggressive visions may have been entertained at one time by some, or even many, of Germany's leaders (German historians have been debating this ferociously for a half-century), however nasty and oppressive a victorious Germany might have been to those it might conquer, whatever problems a German-dominated Europe might have posed for America, none of that was the reality of April 1917; they were not even a possibility or a distant dream for Berlin. Germany, like Britain, France and Russia, was exhausted and impoverished. The only reality at that date was the extraordinarily bloody and costly stalemate that the war had become, with the sole certainty that no nation would emerge victorious or even healthy and that all would emerge weak and wounded and disillusioned. It is this reality of stalemate that would be changed by America's declaration of war.

...

Late on April 4, the Senate voted 82-6 to declare war on the German Empire; two days later, on April 6, so did the House of Representatives, 373-50. This joint declaration then was sped to the White House by messenger, who interrupted Wilson's lunch. The president, leaning on the chief usher's desk, signed it at 1:18 p.m. Immediately a Navy lieutenant ran out onto the White House lawn and by hand waves sent a prearranged message to another officer waiting across the street at a Navy Department window. At once, the signal was relayed to every U.S. Navy ship and shore installation: "W...A...R."

America was at war and Germany formally was declared an enemy of the United States.

The declaration of war was the dramatic admission that neutrality had failed. The trouble was, for which the 20th Century paid the price, neutrality had not really been tried. True neutrality would have seen the U.S. exporting and lending to the Central Powers as well as to the Allies. True neutrality would have seen Wilson as tough on the Allies as he had been on Germany. It would have had Wilson issuing ultimatums to Britain to end its blockade of neutral shipping and to end its violation of America's freedom of the seas, just as he had issued ultimatums to Germany about submarine attacks. And true neutrality, most consequential, would have allowed the European combatants to fight to exhaustion and then end their war as all Europe's continent-wide wars had ended since the 1648 Peace of Westphalia concluded the Thirty Years War—with a negotiated settlement.

The declaration of war against Germany (similar declarations would follow against the Austro-Hungarian Empire and the other German allies within two weeks) was to become the pivot of 20th Century history, determining, as it did, the European war's outcome. Yet, even at this late moment, the consequences of that declaration of war need not have been so cosmic. At that moment there were still possible limits to how much and in what ways the U.S. would help Britain and France fight Germany. In fact, Wilson himself remained so wary of British and French war goals that he emphasized that America would fight Germany not as Britain's and France's "ally" but simply as an "Associate Power."

More important, it was not at all foregone that America actually would send troops to the battlefields. Wilson's April 2 address to Congress said not a word about American soldiers going to and fighting in Europe. And four days later, when Thomas Martin, the Virginia Democrat who chaired the Senate Finance Committee, was told in hearings that the War Department might need funds to dispatch an army to France, he exclaimed: "Good Lord! You're not going to send soldiers over there, are you?" Then he warned: "Congress will not permit American soldiers to be sent to Europe." Some members of Wilson's cabinet were certain that America's main contribution would be limited to loans and supplies to the Allies, while a February 1917 War College Division study predicted that were war to come, America's initial contribution would be economic and naval forces. Meantime, Treasury Secretary McAdoo viewed dollars as "substitutes for American soldiers."[35] Had they been right, the war's end still may have been an Allied victory, but surely not the devastating victory, with the devastating peace, that it was to be.

But they were wrong. Almost immediately Washington began mobilizing the nation. And it was this mobilization, eventually putting some 3.7 million men into uniform and shipping more than half of them to the Western Front, which set the West's course for the rest of the century.

CHAPTER 4

∋⊅●⊂∈

MOBILIZING THE NATION

"The most unfit army the United States has had since the Revolution."

"From a military point of view, America is nothing."

"I do not think that it will make much difference
whether America comes in or not."

THE FIRST STATEMENT IS BY an American popular magazine in 1914; the second by a German Navy officer in early 1917; the third by the Chief of the British Imperial General Staff just days before America declared war.[1] In their unanimity, they were not far off the mark. While the question for the world no longer was would America get into the war, it now was the equally pressing: Could America fight the war? The safe answer would be "No." After all, this was the endlessly repeated message of Preparedness Movement advocates.

And they were right. The United States was not at all prepared to fight in spring 1917. Its highest-ranking officers were five major-generals and they barely had an army to lead. Compared to the more than six million British, French, Belgian and German troops battling on the Western Front, the U.S. Regular Army was tiny, numbering a minuscule 127,000, not even enough to replace Britain's losses in its brutally costly mid-1917 offensive to capture Passchendaele in Flanders (where the unrelenting slaughter became, and remains, with Verdun, the eternal symbol of the Great War's insatiable appetite for life).

By size, the U.S. Army ranked seventeenth in the world, along with Chile, Denmark and the Netherlands and smaller than some Balkan countries. It had, calculates military historian Rod Paschall, 3,000 trucks but needed 85,000 to fight in Europe; 600,000 modern rifles but needed 2.5 million; fewer than 1,500 machine guns but needed tens of thousands; 544 modern artillery pieces but needed thousands; no military aircraft at all suitable for the Western Front; no flamethrowers, gas masks or trench mortars and few of the 15,000 pigeons required by the Signal Corps. Incalculable were its shortages of horses and mules, still the battlefield's main means of transport.[2] Sorely lacking too were the fleets of ships required to carry a huge army and its equipment across the Atlantic and the logistical troops and logistical systems needed to support those troops once they arrived.

Washington, moreover, had no blueprints or contingencies for fighting an offensive war and certainly not for sending troops overseas. All military planning (except "War Plan Green," for possible action in Mexico) had been for defense, mainly for the navy to repel at sea, hundreds of miles from America's coasts, possible attacks by enemy armadas, such as the British and Japanese, or for the army's formidable 12 in. coastal guns and huge mortars to fire on approaching enemy vessels. And while the navy since the start of the century had been preparing for possible action against Germany ("War Plan Black"), it assumed that Berlin's first step would be to seize a West Indies base from which the German fleet then would attack the U.S. East Coast—and be repelled by U.S. warships. In his memoirs, Secretary of War Newton Baker recalls that America was so unprepared for a major war that he had to buy obsolete rifles from Canada, use "leftovers of the [Spanish-American] war...and ransack the museums of city police departments for confiscated 'concealed weapons.'"[3] It truly was, as eminent military historian B.H. Liddell Hart has declared, "a giant armed with a penknife." Or, as other experts have put it, more a constabulary than a fighting force.

Adding to the Regular Army's deficiencies, as Gary Mead quips in his history of American forces in the war, surely tongue partially in cheek, it "was led by elderly men who had made their mark as fighters against Indians."[4] Even less kind, though characteristically probably aiming more at shock than precision, is iconic chronicler of the U.S. military S.L.A. Marshall. He was an infantryman in the war, later a chief U.S. Army historian and then author of thirty books about U.S. forces in action, stretching from World War One through Viet Nam. In his view, when the U.S. declared war "the average man in the ranks never attended high school. The average officer was a West Pointer, more knowledgeable about cards than about Field Service Regulations and the tactical problems of the Western Front."[5]

To be fair, it wasn't quite so bad. Enlisted men were subjected to hard drills, harder discipline and were regarded as tough and high-spirited. Their officers had seen combat against (admittedly ragtag) forces in Cuba, Mexico and the Philippines and had a look at some modern fighting, observing, for instance, the 1904-1905 Russo-Japanese War. Members of that American mission included a Captain John J. Pershing and a Second Lieutenant Douglas MacArthur. Yet no U.S. officers since the Civil War had organized or led anything as large or complicated as a division; the regiment, about 3,900-men strong, not the 25,000-men-plus division, was the army's basic organizational unit. And though the Western Front, where Americans soon would be fighting, had come to be defined by its layers of solidly-protected trenches embedded with tens of thousands of machine guns, the U.S. Army had given scant thought to trench warfare tactics. It still viewed the horse cavalry as its most important unit and rifle marksmanship as its most important skill. (It was a matter of great pride that the army's M1903 Springfield bolt-action was regarded, correctly, as the world's finest rifle. In fact, through the Korean War it remained the sniper's weapon of choice.) The top

American forces, as always, were the Marines, but they numbered only 15,500 and were scattered about the world in the nation's overseas possessions and in areas of recent U.S. intervention, such as Central America, where most probably would have to remain.

The blinding truth on April 6, 1917 was that if the U.S. declaration of war was to do more than supply and finance British and French armies and if it actually was a declaration that Americans were heading overseas for combat, Washington would have to mobilize the nation. An army—a huge army—would need to be recruited and then trained and then supplied and then shipped to Europe. Dozens of reception and training centers would have to be built in the U.S. and base camps built in Britain and France. Factories would have to shift from their civilian consumer output to rifles, machine guns, artillery, ammunition, tents, blankets, field kitchens and the thousands of other items devoured in enormous quantities and at unprecedented speed by the mass armies fighting the world's first industrial-age war. And, of course, needed still were huge numbers of harnesses and shoes for the tens of thousands of horses and mules required for transport. (The typical U.S. Army regiment counted 325 mules and sixty-five horses plus 161 horseshoers, saddlers, waggoners and mechanics.)

So gargantuan were the tasks that the smart money bet would be against the U.S. doing all of that fast enough to make a difference on the European battlefield. It would have been the prudent bet. As it turned out, it would have been a losing bet.

There were, to be sure, a rash of speed bumps, potholes, crack-ups and scandals on the road of America's rush to mobilize. At the time, these problems loomed as catastrophes, igniting public outrage and congressional investigations. In the end, however, what is extraordinary is that the Wilson Administration ultimately managed to field and supply eighty divisions, create an air corps and even deploy a fledgling tank company, commanded by a young

Lt. Colonel George C. Patton, Jr. (His tanks, though, were French-designed and -made.) Within just a bit more than a year of America's declaration of war, not only had its army swollen to 3,700,000 men, but nearly 300,000 of them each month were arriving at British and French ports. The cost may have been great—in dollars, in economic dislocation and inefficiencies, in infringements (at times savage) of the nation's constitutionally protected individual liberties—but the undeniable fact is that America mobilized in what, in retrospect, was an astonishingly short time.

It was a mobilization running on three parallel fronts: creating the mass army; converting the economy to war output; and ensuring, at times strong-arming, public support for the war. These successes merit history's admiration. But they also had enormous and troubling consequences. The fresh and robust American army divisions changed Western Front dynamics, allowing Germany to be crushed in a lopsided defeat; the creation at home of a "war economy" with its food rationing, fuel shortages, black markets, high taxes and painful inflation then angered Americans who, understandably, blamed Germany for these hardships; and the revved-up popular war support was nurtured on an unrelenting and explicit anti-Germanism which conditioned Americans to view Germany as such an extraordinarily evil and barbaric enemy that it would deserve to be humiliated and treated harshly by the victors. In mobilizing America for war, therefore, Woodrow Wilson unavoidably mobilized those American strong feelings and attitudes which later were to overwhelm his efforts for a compromise peace.

Raising a Mass Army
When Wilson signed the declaration of war and proclaimed that America would become an "Associate Power" of the Allies, all U.S. Army planning was in the hands of a General Staff numbering just fifty-one, of whom only nineteen actually were allowed to be in

Washington at the same time. This long had been mandated by Congress which, with wary eyes on 19th Century European coups, feared that allowing too great a concentration of military officers in the capital risked a martial takeover of government. With America now at war, this tiny staff faced massive tasks. Not only had it to expand the army's ranks by millions, but it also had to decide where and when to deploy these forces.

The answers then were not nearly as obvious as they now may seem. Prudent assumptions argued, as did all of the General Staff, that America should not ship its troops abroad until they were trained and equipped well enough to confront a first-class enemy (quite different from the Mexicans and Indians whom they had been fighting) and had competent officers to lead them. Meaning: It would be at least a year before large numbers of Americans could reach the battlefield and longer, possibly not until late 1919 or maybe even 1920, before a major offensive could be launched. After all, Britain had taken nearly two years to recruit and deploy a mass army. Of course, the Regular U.S. Army's 127,000 or so soldiers could be dispatched quickly. But to do so would be a grave mistake, the General Staff's war-planners maintained, with reason on their side. These experienced troops and officers, they insisted, were most needed at home to train the hordes of incoming recruits. The overwhelming military consensus, then, was to train soldiers fully before deploying them.

Where they were to be deployed was another question. Wilson, the generals and Congress all were appalled by the horrendous French and British battlefield losses, most recently during the disastrous French Nivelle Offensive and equally disastrous 1916 British Third Somme Offensive, inflicting 420,000 British casualties, 200,000 French and 500,000 German. Of great concern too were the continuing mutinies in half of France's divisions. Why would America send its youth into the Western Front meat grinder where, for all the sacrifice, nothing had been gained? In the eyes of Army Assistant Chief of Staff Tasker Bliss, writes historian Michael McCarthy, it would be a "mass butchering of green American troops." Moreover, Wilson was telling his aides that "the American people would not be willing to continue an indefinite trench warfare."[6] Rather than on the Western Front, mused some military planners and Wilson (though not General Staff heavyweights), Americans perhaps should fight elsewhere, such as against Turkey, a key German ally, or against Bulgaria, another German ally or even on the Eastern Front, alongside the Russian troops now campaigning under the new flag of a Russian Republic. All these options, at least in theory, were on the table and remained under some consideration through the end of 1917.

And all horrified the British and French, whose very high-level delegations had arrived in Washington just weeks after Wilson declared war on Germany. They were greeted with great hoopla—a cavalry escort, banners, flags, honking wagons and autos and even invitations to address Congress. Their message was as clear as was their urgency. They were asking, actually begging, for an immediate injection of fresh bodies into their Western Front lines. Heading the British mission were Foreign Secretary Arthur Balfour (a former Prime Minister) and Lt. General Tom Bridges; and heading the French mission were former Premier René Viviani and Marshal Joseph Joffre, extremely famous in America as the "Hero of the Marne" commander who halted the 1914 German invasion.

It was a very impressive, muscular lineup. Bridges wasted no time in asking for permission to recruit Americans directly into the British Expeditionary Force and in pleading for a full American division (which, of course, didn't yet exist) to be dispatched immediately to France. This should be followed shortly, he implored, by a half-million additional men shipped "to our depots in England to be trained there, and drafted into our armies in France" and then sent onto the line in just a bit more than ten weeks. Arrival of the Yanks would boost British and French morale enormously, he argued, while "the sight of the Stars and Stripes on the continent will make an impression on both" the Allies and the Germans.

Even more important, the British generals were telling each other but not, of course, the Americans, was the feeling, as expressed by Chief of the British General Staff William Robertson to a fellow general, that "it would be a good thing to get some Americans killed and so get the country to take a real interest in the war." For his part, France's Joffre appealed for "men, men, men." He had very specific plans for them: They were to be called "Auxiliary Troops" and to be incorporated into French units where they would be commanded above the rank of captain by French officers. In addition, he wanted 50,000 Americans to work on French railways and in hospitals and shops.

The undisguised desperation obvious in the Allied appeals first puzzled then shocked the Americans. Having had little source of war information except that coming from Allied upbeat propaganda or passing through British and French censors, America believed that despite the huge losses the war was going reasonably well for the Allies. Now, for the first time it was learning the truth. The Allied armies were not crushing the Germans; the Western Front was hopelessly deadlocked; the home fronts were staggering under collapsing morale and rising anti-war activity; French Army mutinies were symptomatic, not an aberration. This all was news, not only to America's public, but also to its officials.

While the Wilson Administration pondered the Allied requests, the British and French missions were making a huge splash in America. They crisscrossed the country by train, giving interviews, making speeches, building support. Balfour addressed Congress, with Wilson listening in the galleries; Joffre addressed the Army War College, with Secretary of War Newton Baker in the audience, visited West Point and paid his respects to the Abraham Lincoln gravesite in Illinois. And both delegations journeyed to

Mount Vernon to place wreaths at George Washington's tomb.

All of this vigorous lobbying, however, yielded only a bit of what the Allies wanted. Wilson and the U.S. Army General Staff were very cool to the notion of allowing the Allies to recruit American troops directly in the U.S. and even more cool to sending any soldiers to Europe before they were trained properly. And outright opposed were they to integrating Americans into Allied units under Allied officers. Absolutely "no" to that. Still, Wilson knew he must acquiesce to some British and French requests, calculating that if he expected to influence the ultimate peace arrangements he would need troops on the ground as soon as possible. Were America to be a player in ending the war, it would have to endure, as McCarthy calls it, "a large share of the fighting and dying."[7] Without consulting his generals, who would have opposed him, Wilson bowed to Allied pressure, ordering the immediate dispatch of troops to France. He had made the decision: Americans were to fight on the Western Front and they would start arriving immediately.

It was, however, to be but one division of about 25,000 men, hastily stitched together from existing units. It was a token, a symbol, at best a down payment on the masses ultimately to follow. It was little more than the ante needed to stay in the game. Named the American Expeditionary Force, or AEF, the U.S. military operation in Europe was to be led by John J. Pershing, fifty-six, the most junior of the army's major generals, who had just finished commanding the controversial "punitive" campaign in Mexico. (By year's end, Congress would award Pershing two more stars, making him a four-star, thus a full, general, allowing him to deal as an equal with his Allied counterparts.) Passed over for AEF commander and greatly pained by the snub was Major General Leonard Wood, much Pershing's senior, father of the Preparedness Movement and probably America's best-known, most-capable and highest-regarded military leader.

Pershing was selected, according to Arthur Millett's study of U.S. strategy in the war, because he "was the most physically vigorous and tested field commander among the major generals," had a demonstrated ability "to handle complex diplomatic and operational problems" and was respected for his energy, intelligence and field and staff experience. It also did not hurt that his late wife's father was Senator Francis Warren of Wyoming, a powerful Republican. Agreeing with his fellow officers, Pershing was adamant that his troops should not fight until they were ready, and then should fight only as American units in an American Army commanded by American officers under the American flag. On this, he had received very specific instructions from Secretary of War Baker: The AEF was to be "a separate and distinct" part of any campaign with the Allies. That insistence would become and remain through the entire war a huge matter of U.S. acrimonious contention with London and Paris.

For the moment, however, the British and French were delighted that American soldiers eventually would fight on the Western Front and that some would be arriving soon, signaling that America's declaration of war had teeth. As an advance party, Pershing and a 187-man entourage of officers (including George Patton, Jr., then still a captain), orderlies, clerks, translators and three reporters on May 28, 1917 boarded the White Star Line's passenger liner SS *Baltic* in a densely fogged New York harbor. Five days before leaving, Pershing had met briefly at the White House with Wilson for what historians agree was a discussion of no great consequence, limited to formalities and pleasantries and with actually almost no talk of the war. It was to be the last time Pershing spoke to the president during the war. Wilson gave his commander an almost blank check to organize his forces and fight the war as he best thought, though Wilson throughout the war did remain deeply involved in broad military decisions, with nearly daily briefings from War Secretary Baker. Pershing later wrote that the "entire freedom" he was given was "unique in our history." Onboard ship, Pershing and his staff reviewed and made endless lists of the tasks confronting them (billeting, training, organization of a headquarters staff and so forth) and attended lectures on European battlefield conditions by British officers. The Americans also took French lessons.

After ten days at sea, on June 8, the *Baltic* arrived at Liverpool, where banners, local notables and the Royal Welsh Fusiliers with their mascot (a goat) gave Pershing a rousing welcome. He immediately recognized and appreciated the poignant symbolism of the Fusiliers' presence; it was the unit which, 142 years earlier, had fought the American rebels at Bunker Hill. When his staff disembarked, they became the first American troops ever to land in Europe. Later, in London, the pace quickened: meetings with King George V, Prime Minister David Lloyd George, top British generals and admirals and a forty-two-year-old Winston Churchill. From the King, Pershing received an extremely cordial welcome and was told that "the Anglo-Saxon race must save civilization."[8]

Then, after four days in the British capital, it was on to France. The group's arrival in Paris on June 13 triggered a tumultuous, almost hysterical welcome along the full two-mile route from the railway station to Pershing's temporary headquarters at the Hotel Crillon. Writes Edward Coffman in his military history of the war: "Parisians thronged the streets shouting 'Vive l' Amerique,' pelted the completely surprised Americans with flowers, and surged toward them to shake or just touch hands." Pershing recalled that women "threw flowers until we were literally buried" and that he had to respond to the cheering crowds at his hotel by repeatedly being "forced to appear on the portico of my apartment." In the following days, the Americans returned the affection, with Pershing making what Coffman calls "the right gesture" by visiting Napoleon's tomb, bowing and kissing Napoleon's sword and then visiting Lafayette's tomb.[9]

Two weeks later, on June 26, a second and much more muscular down payment began arriving. A fourteen-ship convoy carrying about 14,500 men delivered to France's Atlantic port of St. Nazaire the first contingents of a hastily assembled U.S. Army

1st Division. Some were Regular Army (wearing their Mexican campaign uniforms), one battalion was Marines and the rest were raw recruits, whom Pershing kindly called "sturdy rookies." The division's assistant chief of staff was George Marshall.

After disembarking, the soldiers headed by train, in forty-eight boxcars, for their makeshift camps and billets, many of them stables and barns, to begin learning from French trainers about trench warfare and other Great War disciplines. Their routine's most notable interruption came on the Fourth of July, when Pershing took a battalion of his best marchers to Paris to lead them on a festive, exuberant three-mile parade from Les Invalides to the tomb of Marquis de Lafayette. That is where a Pershing aide, paying tribute to Lafayette's valuable service in the American Revolution, loudly declared "Lafayette. We are here!"—words that became the universally recognized affirmation of America's readiness to fight for the Allies. All along the parade route French cheered, screamed, waved American flags and tossed more flowers. Not knowing exactly what to call the Americans, many French dug into their memories for the one name they could associate with the U.S. and came up with the vigorous image of a cheerfully assertive former president; thus inspired, they yelled excitedly: "Vive les Teddies."

As an AEF nickname, "Teddies" did not stick. Nor did "Amex," preferred by the U.S. command as a shortening of American Expeditionary Force. Nor did the attempt by the British and French troops to call the Americans "Sammies," the obvious friendly diminutive for Uncle Sam. "Yanks," of course, a natural and universal tag (accepted even by southern boys) was used often in the war. But in short time and after a bit of debate, chronicled in the pages of the U.S. Army newspaper *Stars and Stripes*, one affectionate AEF nickname topped all others: "doughboy." Initially it just meant a U.S. Army infantryman, but soon applied to all AEF troops, including Marines, Air Service and even Pershing himself. It admiringly connoted heroism, grit and toughness. (British infantrymen popularly were called "Tommies," and had been since the mid-18th Century. French soldiers were called "poilu," meaning "hairy" or "scruffy" ones, because those in the trenches rarely shaved.)

Though the etymology of "doughboys" is somewhat disputed, both Gary Mead and Laurence Stallings in their separate doughboys histories give most weight to the explanation that its pedigree stretched back to the army's battles along the Rio Grande. Because infantrymen there often became powdered white from the adobe soil dust, they derisively were called "adobes" by the much more elegant and elitist U.S. Cavalry. The term, according to this interpretation, quickly shortened to "dobies" and ultimately to "doughboys."[10]

The July 4th Paris parade was great public relations, but that's about all it was. The cheering French, clearly expecting the "Teddies" to rush immediately to the trenches, were to be disappointed. It would be nearly a year before an AEF unit of any significant size would go to battle. Before the French (and British) publics truly would be able to cheer great numbers of arriving Yanks destined for the Western Front, the AEF would have to be recruited and trained. Pershing's arrival, the ship convoy bringing the 1st Division's first units and the parade were just teases. The real war effort was still in Washington, and just getting underway. There the most pressing task was raising the army.

It almost immediately became clear to Wilson and the War Department that America's traditional means of building its army through volunteers was not going to give Pershing the million men he initially requested (a number which soon grew to three million). Though the declaration of war generally had been met by public approval, the recruiting offices had not seen floods of volunteers after the first weeks' enthusiasm. To be sure, there was some high-profile volunteering. Teddy Roosevelt, probably not surprisingly, was quick to act, proclaiming a readiness to reprise his role as Rough Rider commander and lead a division to Europe, which, he declared, he would recruit and outfit himself. For a number of good reasons, including the likelihood that he would be uncontrollable, the War Department politely declined the offer.

Roosevelt's enthusiasm, however, was not contagious. Nationwide, just 73,000 men initially volunteered. To fill AEF ranks something else had to be done. Conscription was the only option. Explains John Chambers in his study of the draft in America: "Only the draft could produce an enormous mass army and do so at a planned and predictable rate…with a steady flow of replacements."[11]

Yet conscription was a very troubling notion. The nation's only previous general draft was during the Civil War, just a bit more than a half-century earlier. It had not gone at all well and had left many scars. Widespread opposition had ignited bloody draft riots in two dozen cities, starting in Pittsburgh and spreading to Boston, Albany, Rochester and other East Coast communities. New York City in July 1863 was rocked for four days as armed anti-draft demonstrators marauded through lower Manhattan, burning down draft headquarters and attacking the homes of the mayor and draft officials. After six army regiments finally restored order, at least 120 protestors were dead (estimates range as high as 1,200). It was, by far, the worst public disorder in Gotham's history and was still fresh in memory.

Beyond the rioting, and as important to Wilson and the War Department as they contemplated conscription, were the Civil War draft law's inequities, which had sparked near-universal public bitterness. The wealthy, for example, could avoid service by hiring substitutes to go in their stead or by paying a $300 fee for exemption (that was more than a half-year's average blue-collar earnings). For many, writes Chambers, the Civil War had become "a rich man's war, but a poor man's fight."[12]

If the AEF were to rely on a draft, it would have to differ dramatically from the Civil War's. And it did, proving so successful that it became the template for World War Two and beyond. Authorizing a draft was the Selective Service Act which, despite early and almost unanimous Democrat Party opposition and after weeks of contentious hearings and debate, was passed overwhelmingly by Congress on May 18, 1917. It explicitly established a "liability for military service of all male citizens" and banned anyone from purchasing an exemption or hiring a substitute. All conscripts, moreover, would serve not a fixed, limited term but for the "duration" of the conflict. The process was called "selective" because it established a mechanism for selecting who would go into uniform and who would be exempted if their skills were needed in industry, government or farming or if their families depended on them. Selecting the recruits and the exempted would not be distant and faceless Washington bureaucrats but some 4,647 local draft boards staffed with friends and neighbors. To further soften the sting, the government avoided the terms "draft," "conscript" and "conscription," using, instead, "servicemen" and "selectee."

Specifically, an immediate selective draft was authorized from a pool of all males aged twenty-one to thirty (later expanded to eighteen to forty-five). These men were told to appear at their local boards on Tuesday, June 5, 1917, between 7 a.m. and 7 p.m., to register, or, as it was put, to enter their names on "lists of honor." And just about all of them did. That day, some 9,660,000 young men turned up and received their green cards as proof of registration. Not only were there no riots, there was no opposition at all, save for some skirmishes in backwoods Arkansas, Montana and Texas. Seven weeks later, on July 20, a blindfolded Secretary of War Baker drew from a glass bowl the first of 10,500 numbers in a national draft lottery (it was #258) which called 687,000 men to arms. Each state and territory had been assigned a quota based on its population; New York, for instance, had to supply 122,424 recruits; Texas 48,116 and Alaska 710. They were paid $30 per month ($434 in today's dollars), comparable to the earnings of an unskilled laborer. Festivities and hoopla sent the first draftees off to their training camps. In New York City, with bands blaring, some 2,000 marched down Fifth Avenue past the mayor and governor while in the South, writes Chambers, "parades often were led by Confederate war veterans in their faded uniforms."[13]

By war's end, 24,234,021 men had registered (of the 54 million total male population), with 2,810,296 of them drafted. Conscripts ultimately accounted for seventy-two percent of the AEF, the rest were volunteers and career army. Together, all those mobilized comprised twenty percent of males ages eighteen to forty-five; Britain, by contrast, mobilized sixty percent of that age cohort. The average American recruit, calculated from the mountain of draft-generated statistics (which proved a boon to America's budding sociology profession), was white, in his early twenties, unmarried, had little education beyond some primary school, was 5 ft., 7.5 in. tall and weighed 141.5 lbs. About one-fifth of them were foreign-born. Since the Civil War, average height had not changed, while weight was up 6.5 lbs. It is estimated that 2.4 million to 3.6 million men dodged the draft, some by heading to Mexico and Canada, but most by simply hunkering down, mainly in Appalachia and in backcountry Illinois, Louisiana and Missouri. Tens of thousands of them subsequently were caught in the waves of "slacker raids" when Justice Department officials, according to Meirion and Susie Harries in their history of America at war, swept into "hotels, cafes, saloons, dance halls, poolrooms" and asked to see the green registration card of every male appearing to be of draft age. Those convicted of draft evasion faced up to one year in prison.

The recruits ultimately were formed into divisions of about 25,000 men (twice the size of British and French divisions). These mirrored America's staggering and unprecedented heterogeneity, something that worried the British and French and confounded the Germans when they took doughboy prisoners. Example: The troops of the 77th Division, almost all from New York, spoke forty-two different languages or dialects, including Cantonese, German,

Italian, Mandarin, Turkish and Yiddish. Its own theme song ran: "The Jews and the Wops/The Dutch and the Irish Cops/They're all in the Army now." Particularly perplexing to the Germans were the fourteen Choctaw Indians deployed on the front as field telephone operators, talking in their native tongue in what was, in effect, undecipherable code. Confounding too was the 32nd Division, mainly from Michigan and Wisconsin, whose troops often spoke German better than English. Missing from the diversity, of course, were Blacks; the military's strict racial segregation meant that drafted African-Americans would have to serve in what were organized as all-Black units, mainly the 92nd and 93rd Divisions.

Training the AEF recruits, for which there had been absolutely no blueprint, was agonizingly chaotic. Some thirty-two sprawling training cantonments very quickly were built, sprinkled about the nation, each containing about a thousand structures. Long rows of front line, support and reserve trenches had to be dug. In them, tutored by British, Canadian and French veterans, the recruits would practice, typically at night, for their upcoming Western Front combat. Everything was in short supply—or no supply. For the 89th Division training at Camp Funston, Kansas, for instance, there was neither a single modern rifle nor field artillery piece. Instead of uniforms, the recruits wore overalls and in place of guns and cannon they used sticks and sawed off telephone poles. In drastically short supply too were the officers to train or lead the swelling masses of enlisted men, so much so that Britain and France hurriedly dispatched 700 officers to the U.S. to help. In abundant supply, by contrast, were the Progressives who voluntarily worked in the camps organizing group singing, theatrical performances and baseball leagues and, most enthusiastically and repeatedly, warned about the evils of alcohol and prostitution.[14]

Erecting the cantonments and outfitting a huge army should not have been expected to be, nor was, much different or less ugly than any other government works project before then or since. Inefficiencies, duplication, incompetence, corruption, extravagance, patronage and cronyism were rife. So was waste, massive waste— such as the $840 million ($12.1 billion in today's dollars) spent by the War Department in an attempt to build thousands of airplanes with almost nothing to show for it by spring 1918 or the costly shipbuilding program which launched no ships. Meanwhile, Capitol Hill began hearing from constituents angrily complaining that their sons at the training camps in the cold of winter had only summer clothing, unheated barracks and no heavy blankets, that their living conditions and plumbing facilities were primitive and unsanitary, that buildings were shoddy and that diphtheria, measles, meningitis, pneumonia and scarlet fever were spreading rapidly in the overcrowded conditions.

Angry constituents spawn angry lawmakers. Expressing outrage, Congress launched five major investigations in mid-December 1917, summoning War Department officials and cantonment commanders to testify. After listening to three weeks of explanations, Senate Military Affairs Committee Chairman George Chamberlain, a Democrat from Oregon, blew up, exclaiming: "We are still unprepared. The military establishment of the United States has broken down. It has almost stopped functioning." The senatorial outrage was warranted, but, it soon became clear, the verdict was not. America's mobilization had not stopped functioning and, with some reorganization and tinkering, began functioning better—so much better that within a half-year it was sending Pershing up to 300,000 very fresh doughboys a month. So smoothly had the draft begun manufacturing soldiers that America, as John Chambers observes, found itself, most assuredly unintentionally, making and fulfilling "an open-ended commitment to send American troops to the Western Front."[15]

Revving the Economy for War

Mobilizing the economy was as crucial as mobilizing manpower, and in many respects more problematic. Federal fiat, after all, almost immediately forced men into uniform. But for months after war was declared, Washington lacked power to force Detroit to manufacture military trucks instead of Model-T Fords or Hudsons. The whole notion of fiat, moreover, was very troubling, not only to conservatives, but also to the left. Neither Wilson nor the Progressives who strongly influenced him wanted a huge federal apparatus to command what later would be called a "war economy." They understandably feared that such a concentration of authority in Washington, empowering bureaucrats, would trample individual liberties. Scaring them too was the likelihood that the resulting apparatus would be dominated by the very industrialists and financiers whom they had reviled and demonized over the years as obstacles to their ambitious domestic reforms. Still, a Leviathan of some sort also was not without its charms for Progressives. Because they long had dreamed of turning over economic decision-making to cadres of bright reformist experts, there was a strong appeal in the notion of committees, commissions, councils and administrations, all motivated by high ideals and embracing Progressive principles, running America.

Initially, Wilson relied mainly on persuasion and volunteer committees of corporate executives to get the nation's factories and farms to produce what the AEF needed and to coordinate the railroad system and shipping lines to ensure that this output efficiently reached the U.S. military and the British and French. By and large, the War and Navy Departments and other agencies supplying the AEF had to compete for goods in a free market. That worked poorly. Bottlenecks, backlogs, inefficiencies and a dozen other predictable potholes created huge shortages of key materials needed to train the AEF and send it to Europe. In addition, promised output of machine guns, artillery and other weapons for Britain and France fell behind schedule and, worse, competed in priority with the AEF.

Building the ships desperately needed for transporting the AEF to Europe, in particular, was nearly paralyzed by chaotic management and supply networks.

For other items, military demand had to bid against the American consumer. Railroad lines became so clogged by January 1918 that a federal official threatened to halt all factory production east of the Mississippi River for four days to give the transportation network time to untangle. Coal distribution also was a problem, in part because of a railway car shortage; as a result, coal was becoming scarce (with its price soaring) just as the nation was heading into what turned out to be the unusually cold winter of 1917-1918. Watching all of this with horror was Congress, which then did what Congress reflexively does; it held hearings. At them, Wilson Administration officials repeatedly were berated and angrily charged with massive incompetence. The charges were on target.

Wilson didn't need Congressional pressure to conclude that the volunteer light touch was failing. Obvious was it that America could not fight an industrial-age war with its insatiable appetite for supplies and munitions unless its economy was fully revved for and focused on war. And that required the coercive power of government. Such power is ultimately what Wilson demanded and a reluctant Congress granted. Gone was any pretense of restraining the Leviathan. To the contrary, Progressives and liberals, many of them fervent pacifists, quickly warmed to and cheered the new order in Washington. As a later generation snidely might put it, they learned to love the war. These groups, writes historian and authority on progressivism Allen Davis, began seeing the war-spawned agencies as "a climax and culmination of the movement for social justice in America."[16] The influential liberal essayist Walter Lippmann was typical; he marveled that war-induced reforms would put the U.S. "at the threshold of a collectivism which is greater than any as yet planned by the Socialist Party." Herbert Croly, editor and co-founder of *The New Republic*, agreed. He told his readers that "under the stimulus of the war & its consequences there will be a chance to focus the thought & will of the country on the high and fruitful purposes such as occurs only once in many hundred years."[17]

Croly got it right. In the name of mobilizing the nation, Wilson was able to raise taxes on the wealthy, win an eight-hour day and collective bargaining for many workers, expand women's rights and launch a host of what were called social experiments. The war became such an incredible boon for reformist policy proposals that historians call the period the "flowering of Progressivism" and a "social engineer's utopia." Prominent Progressives were delighted. For example, Edward Devine, head of the New York Charity Organization Society, cheered what he termed the "luxuriant crop of new agencies springing up" and declared that "it is all very exhilarating, stimulating, intoxicating." Another Progressive leader, cited by Allen Davis in his essay "The Flowering of Progressivism," exuberantly proclaimed: "Laissez faire is dead… Long live social control."[18]

Control, indeed, kept growing. In short time, the federal government began running more of America and American lives than ever before. Suddenly Americans encountered, as a necessity of fighting a war, an ever-lengthening list of things they could not do or, conversely, must do. Life became an obstacle course of annoying pinpricks, inflicting on every American the pain of war. And for this pain, understandably, Americans would blame Germany and it thus would ultimately spark an American insistence on revenge.

Wherever Americans turned, new federal agencies, boards, committees, administrations and authorities, with battalions of experts, seemed to be issuing reams of edicts and regulations. A Food Administration was controlling food output and consumption; a Capital Issues Committee was regulating investment; a War Trade Board was controlling imports and exports and keeping supplies from Germany; a Railroad Administration was regulating railways; a War Finance Committee was ensuring that industry had the money to convert from civilian to military output; a Fuel Administration was fixing the price of coal (which enjoyed a near-monopoly on powering America); an Alien Property Custodian was seizing real estate, factories, securities, patented process and other property owned by Germans and by those suspected of sympathizing with Germany; a War Labor Board was trying to prevent labor disputes by setting a minimum wage and recognizing labor's right to organize; a Shipping Board was decreeing shipping rates and expanding the U.S. freighter fleet; a Grain Corporation was stabilizing the price of wheat; a Sugar Equalization Board was doing the same for sugar—and that was just the start. There were many others. They all acquired very sharp teeth in August, 1917 when the Lever Food and Control Act (named for its sponsor, Representative Frank Lever, a South Carolina Democrat) gave Wilson power to take over and run factories and fix prices.

This power he wielded broadly, particularly through what became the most muscular new agency, the War Industries Board. As a result, Detroit began making tanks and aircraft engines instead of passenger cars, the Akron Tire Company began producing army cots and Black and Decker began turning out gun sights. Civilian activity too was targeted. The Food Administration, for instance, asked every woman to sign a card pledging "to carry out the directions and advice of the Food Administrator." There were voluntary meatless Tuesdays (though eating poultry and game was okay) and wheatless Mondays and Wednesdays, bolstered by such exhortations as, "Don't let your horse be more patriotic than you are—eat a dish of oatmeal!" But exhortations were not enough. Food rationing ultimately was imposed, followed almost immediately, as happens always under rationing and price controls, by infuriating and demoralizing gray and black markets. As consumer goods ran short, prices soared, with the cost of living jumping seventy-four percent from 1917 through 1920.

Inflation was not the only economic hardship imposed by the war. So was the need to pay for it. Americans were asked to dig deep and then deeper in their pockets to fund the conflict's unprecedented bill, ultimately about $31.3 billion (including the $9.5 billion loaned to the Allies), equal to $452 billion in today's dollars. That was more than France or Russia or any other nation, except Britain and Germany, spent on the conflict. From 1916 to 1918, the annual federal budget soared from $742 million to almost $14 billion. Clearly, the tariffs and excise fees on which the federal government for more than a century had relied for three-quarters of its revenues could not underwrite the war. New revenue sources urgently were needed. At first they were voluntary and then became mandatory, through a new device, authorized in 1913 by the Sixteenth Amendment, called the income tax.

To spur voluntary war contributions, Washington launched what was to be the most successful federal government advertising campaign to that time. Americans were urged to buy what Treasury Secretary William McAdoo called "Liberty Loans," federal government bonds paying 3.5 percent to 4.25 percent interest. In five bond drives Washington raised $21.5 billion directly from the public. The bonds were pitched by volunteers in every nook of the nation, including by pastors from their pulpits on "Liberty Loan Sundays." The pointed message typically combined appeals to patriotism with threats of shame. McAdoo put it directly. At a California Liberty Bonds rally, he declared that anyone who didn't buy one was "a friend of Germany... A man who cannot lend his government $1.25 per week at the rate of 4% interest is not entitled to be an American citizen." The pitch worked. All five bond issues were over-subscribed.

Not so voluntary was the War Revenue Act passed by Congress on October 3, 1917, after a half-year of heated debate. Though Washington had been taxing some individual and corporate incomes very modestly since the adoption of the Sixteenth Amendment, this new Act was the first attempt to raise significant federal sums by direct taxation. It boosted rates that had ranged from one percent to seven percent on a progressive income scale to one percent to twelve percent. So successful did this prove, so willingly did Americans seem to pay this tax that Washington never looked back; income taxes became the main federal source of money. After the war, three-quarters of federal revenue would come from the income tax rather than from tariffs and excise taxes.

Fighting the war also nearly quintupled the national debt and for the first time propelled it into eleven figures, jumping from $5.7 billion in fiscal 1917 to $14.6 billion the next year and $27.4 billion in fiscal 1919. A more telling view of such macro figures is to calculate the debt as a share of gross domestic product. It more than tripled from 9.6 percent of GDP in fiscal 1917 to 34.9 percent in 1919—a huge leap, but, actually, much below the 116 percent in 1945, in the depth of World War Two, and the sixty-nine percent in pre-recession 2008.[19]

Big government, high taxes and legions of bureaucrats enforcing myriad regulations, therefore, ultimately were created to support an America at war. And it worked well enough. The U.S. economy began humming, becoming what in a future world war would be called "the arsenal of democracy," outfitting and supplying the mass army whose deployment on the Western Front would change the course of a war. But this economic mobilization came at a price. As inconveniences, hardships, deprivations, frustrations and worse kept mounting on individual Americans and businesses, the nation was told that it all was Germany's fault. For Americans, therefore, German-inflicted suffering began even before many doughboys had landed in Europe, to say nothing of being shot at.

Igniting "White-Hot" Public Support
Home front mobilization went beyond bond rallies, taxation and funding the war. Urgently important too were igniting public backing for the war and keeping it high-pitched. That was the goal

of three intense parallel campaigns: a fervent, heated propaganda appeal to patriotism, an equally fervent ad hoc assault on all things German and a drive via law and intimidation to crush (including by imprisonment and vigilante hangings) any dissent. In every war, such government actions are understandable and many are even legitimate. In every war too, such actions to varying degrees careen out of control and cross lines long established by tradition and law, inflicting pain and leaving a contentious legacy.

America's prosecution of World War One was no exception. It did have, however, exceptional consequences. The constant home front drum beat—in posters, movies, billboards, pamphlets and books, ads, lectures, church pulpit sermons, songs—which demonized Germany and all things German, which warned of imminent German attack on America and of German spies penetrating deeply into the nation, which blamed Germany solely for starting the war and committing barbaric atrocities and which insisted that America and democracy would be safe only when Germany and its Prussian militarists were smashed, molded an American public mindset determined to impose the most oppressive terms on an eventually defeated Germany.

Though those harsh terms at war's end were to be dictated by the British and French, there was little resistance from an American public and Congress which for two years had been stirred into anti-German frenzy. What began for Wilson, and for him personally seemed to remain, as a vision of a negotiated "peace without victory" and without "vanquished" was transformed by his policies and his Administration's actions into the reality that Americans would accept nothing short of a victory that severely punished, even stomped on, its declared enemy. To be sure, Wilson eventually began worrying about this, condemning on July 26, 1918, the "mob spirit which has recently…shown its head amongst us." But he did nothing to stop it.

Such an anti-German mob spirit would not have been easily predicted when Wilson took America into war. Though Americans had been prepared for a declaration of war by the escalating tensions with Germany, there still was little sentiment that Germans were an enemy whom Americans had to kill. Reflecting this was the tepid volunteering for the army. This mood was sensed by Britain's Washington Embassy which, in a May 23, 1917 memo, advised London that "there is evidence that in many localities the people have only entered the war with reluctance." This definitely did not mean that there was serious or even modest opposition to America at war. Very much to the contrary. The powerful German-American organizations and the German-American press, whose reporting and editorials had favored Germany while America was formally neutral, immediately proclaimed their fervent patriotism and backing of U.S. policy as soon as war had been declared. As for the prewar pacifists, only a few groups persevered, mainly the Socialist Party, anarchists, the New York State Woman's Peace Party and the United Mine Workers. Historian Susan Zeiger writes: "With U.S. entry into the war, many peace organizations virtually collapsed overnight."[20]

But lack of opposition did not translate into war enthusiasm. To inspire that, Wilson unleashed his powerful rhetoric, repeatedly portraying America's going to war not merely as a response to what he called aggressive and dangerous "Prussianism," but more so as a righteous, even moral, endeavor of which Americans could be proud. The nation was not, exhorted Wilson, fighting a typical war. It was not a war of European-style militarism or imperialism or balance of power politics. Rather, he declared over and over again, it was a "people's war," a war "to make the world safe for democracy" and—with a phrase that then (and still) most captured public attention and specifically was designed to comfort Progressives and pacifists fearful that they were betraying their principles by supporting the war—it was a war to bring a very long-lasting peace, a "war to end all wars." To that Progressives responded "Amen," with the *New Republic* proclaiming that the Great War had become "the thinking man's war."[21]

But even Wilsonian rhetoric, in that golden age of oratory,

could not alone spark and then sustain mass war support. For this Wilson, on April 14, just eight days after declaring war, established the Committee on Public Information, explicitly giving it the role of "censorship and publicity." He did this by Executive Order, thus bypassing Congress. For its entire two-year existence the CPI was headed by crusading Progressive journalist George Creel, an ardent Wilson supporter who had worked in both of his presidential campaigns; he was appointed personally by and reported to Wilson.

Creel declared that his aim was to work up the public to "one white-hot mass" consumed by "fraternity, devotion, courage and deathless determination" to back the war, to buy Liberty Bonds and to report any suspicious pro-German activities. At a hearing he told Congress, which always was cool to him and his work, that the CPI would make Americans realize that they are in "a holy war, and a war in of self-defense." Earlier he had warned that "reckless journalism…is a positive menace when the nation is at war."

So prominent and ubiquitous was Creel that to his contemporaries and to history the Committee on Public Information was and is known simply as the Creel Committee. Under his control it conducted, agree historians seemingly unanimously, the most extensive and intrusive government effort to manipulate public opinion in American history. And it greatly succeeded, whipping up Creel's desired "white-hot mass" support for the war. Yet there was a very dark side to the work of Creel, who today would be called a Propaganda Czar. Many historians document how his zeal at times morphed into a fanaticism which recklessly trampled individual liberties.

By today's lights it may be difficult to conceive the sweep of Creel's writ. He was granted massive federal power and arm-twisting to run a propaganda machine which touched just about every American household. Its muscle, intrusiveness and arbitrary actions probably differed little from the extensive British and French efforts to keep their own publics supporting a war that was taking hundreds of thousands of lives. Still, any federal agency or operation as unfettered as was the CPI would be unacceptable in 21ˢᵗ Century America.

Raw statistics only hint at the extent of its campaign. Some 150,000 academics, actors, artists, lecturers and writers were hired to produce and deliver the Committee on Public Information line by writing pamphlets, designing and printing posters, delivering patriotic pep talks wherever Americans gathered, placing ads in newspapers and magazines, producing and distributing short features and full-length movies, publishing a daily official U.S. Government newspaper, drawing cartoons, creating postcards and ghost-writing newspaper and magazine stories and even books ostensibly authored by prominent Americans. In addition, Creel oversaw a Division of News, Film Division, Bureau of State Fair Exhibits, Labor Publications Division, Advertising Division, Pictorial Publicity Division, Speaking Division, Women's War Work Division, Division of Work with the Foreign Born and similar units.

In its short two-year existence, calculates Stewart Ross in his 1996 study of American propaganda during the war, the Creel Committee wrote, mimeographed and distributed 6,000 news releases and produced 60 million copies (some sources say 75 million) of its more than 100 books and leaflets. Included were *The Kaiserite in America: One Hundred and One German Lies, A War Message to the Farmer, The Government of Germany, How the War Came to America, Conquest and Kultur: Aims of the Germans in Their Own Words* and *The German-Bolshevik Conspiracy.* Happy to help the CPI distribute its output was a vast number of such public agencies and private groups as the Agriculture Department, American Federation of Labor, U.S. Chamber of Commerce, and YMCA. Some pamphlets were reprinted whole in newspapers.

The publications' themes were simple and direct, differing little from some of those of the Preparedness Movement: Germans by nature are warlike; Germany is undemocratic; Germany is the greatest menace on earth; and America is threatened by "the pied pipers of Prussianism." In Creel Committee ads sadistic German soldiers thrust bayonets into civilians, toss bare-breasted women to the ground and crucify men on doors. One ad reads: "The poison cannot be dammed up, it must be cut out else this monstrous thing called Kultur will fasten its hideous self on all the world." The storyline of the Committee on Public Information book *Why America Fights Germany* tells of 50,000 German troops landing in New Jersey, grabbing beer and wine, pillaging and burning the post office and stores, demanding a million dollars, throwing a Catholic priest and Methodist minister into a pig sty, lining up in front of the local bank and shooting fifty leading citizens and hanging an old woman for trying to conceal $20. Through all of this the invaders laugh. In Committee on Public Information *School Bulletin #3*, Treasury Secretary McAdoo tells schoolchildren that they must do their part to ensure that "the military despotism for which the Kaiser stands will be swept away," while an official federal "war study course" for elementary schools instructs teachers to tell their pupils that America was fighting "to keep German soldiers from coming to our country."

Anti-Germanism intensified as America's mobilization accelerated. Some forms of this prejudice were harmless and silly, such as refusing to serve pretzels in taverns or changing the names of "frankfurters" to "liberty sausages," "dachshunds" to "liberty dogs," "sauerkraut" to "liberty cabbage," "hamburgers" to "liberty steaks"—and even "German measles" to "liberty measles." Some forms were stupid, such as banning German language instruction in public schools and even universities, removing German books from libraries, canceling concerts in Washington and elsewhere by Austrian-born violinist Fritz Kreisler and dropping German works from performances by the Chicago Grand Opera, New York Metropolitan Opera, Philadelphia Orchestra, Pittsburgh Symphony and other ensembles because such music had been branded dangerous German propaganda. Some anti-German forms were simply mean, as when Creel Committee-inspired vigilantes forced German-Americans to kiss the American flag and painted yellow the houses of German-Americans suspected of not buying enough Liberty Bonds. And some forms were just transparently opportunistic, such as the Anti-Saloon League's attacks on German brewers and its warnings that opposing liquor prohibition was the same as supporting the Kaiser.

But much anti-Germanism was more serious, with very serious consequences, conditioning Americans to believe that Germany deserved to be punished severely. Recycling British propaganda's fabricated stories of German atrocities, for instance, one Army recruitment poster screamed "THEY CRUCIFY" and depicted a father and baby murdered by Germans; another headlined "THEY MUTILATE" and depicted a Belgian child with severed arms. Posters directly produced by the Committee of Public Information's Division of Pictorial Publicity portrayed Germans as sub-humans, rapists and pillagers and depicted German soldiers dragging a young girl.[22]

Meantime, vitriol flowed freely from pulpits. Leading liberal Congregationalist theologian Lyman Abbott, for example, exclaimed that he hated Germany "because it is a robber, a murderer, a destroyer of homes, a pillager of women." He boasted, "I do well to hate it." Another clergyman, Newell Dwight Hillis, pastor of a large Brooklyn Congregational church, attracted huge crowds on his nationwide lecture tours by graphically detailing and showing gruesome photos of falsified German atrocities. "Mad dogs" is how he described German soldiers as he demanded that "all civilization must unite to kill" them. Hillis won considerable attention by endorsing a proposal by some American surgeons to sterilize 10 million German soldiers so that, he declared, "civilized cities, states and races may be rid of this awful cancer." Publishing Hillis' attacks on Germans were *The Christian Century*, *Christian Work* and other religious magazines.

And then there was the unrelentingly fiery shirtsleeves preaching of William "Billy" Sunday, the most influential American evangelist of his time. Overflow audiences thrilled to his passionate sermons describing Germans as a "weazen-eyed, low-lived, bull-neck, low-down gang of cutthroats of the Kaiser" and as a "great pack of wolfish Huns whose fangs drip with blood and gore." His signature line: "If you turn hell upside down, you'll find 'Made in Germany' stamped on the bottom." Covering these sermons, the *New York Times* headlined: "Billy Sunday Fires Hot Shot at Kaiser."[23]

Such themes were magnified and their impact intensified in wildly popular movies encouraged by the Creel Committee. These movies also were probably partly prompted by Hollywood's determination to demonstrate its patriotism and value to the war effort, to escape being declared "nonessential" and shut down for the war's duration. Most of the films, writes historian Michael Isenberg in his 1981 study of the war's portrayal in movies, "endorsed the axiom that the wearer of the German uniform was invariably a drunk, a looter, or a rapist... If looting, killing, and mindless destruction was their business, rape was their sport."[24] Stewart Ross adds that the "films were typically absurd fiction: sneaky German spies in closets and behind hedges, sadistic German soldiers coming ashore in America and attacking defenseless young women (who were then rescued by brave young American males)."

A sampling of Hollywood's wartime output offered by Ross includes: *For Liberty* (a German officer murders an American boy), *Till I Come Back To You* (Belgian children are abducted to Germany as slave laborers), *To Hell with the Kaiser* (doughboys capture the Kaiser and force him to salute Gen. Pershing), *The Kaiser's Finish* (the Kaiser's illegitimate son returns to kill his father), *Me und Gott* (a Hoboken deli owner tries to persuade his son to blow up a U.S. munitions plant) and *The Hun Within* (a German immigrant's son becomes a German spy).

Most famous—or notorious—is *The Kaiser, the Beast of Berlin*. Ads for it urged: "Come and hiss the Kaiser! Everybody's doing it!"[25] The film's title accurately describes plot and message. Premiering in Manhattan on March 9, 1918, it became a smash box-office hit, making, boasted its distributor Universal Studios, a "landslide of money." In the seventy-minute silent black-and-white film an evil, nasty Kaiser warns the American ambassador that after Germany wins the war it will "stand no nonsense from America." But later, when hearing that America has entered the conflict, the Kaiser grows horribly shocked and demoralized. All this leads to a happy ending: Germany's defeat and the Kaiser's imprisonment by the Belgian king. (So highly is this film regarded that it is on the American Film Institute's list of the "Ten Most Wanted" lost films.)[26]

Even audiences at more mainstream films got a potent Creel Committee jolt. They heard from Creel's shock troops, the 74,500 Four Minute Men (plus an auxiliary women's division) trained to deliver a powerful and uplifting message in the four minutes it took to change film reels in cinemas. Those who spoke longer were dropped from the rolls. It was impossible to avoid their message since, writes Ross, they "were a nightly feature in virtually every movie house across the nation." So popular were some Four Minute Men that cinemas even advertised particular speakers' appearances at screenings. Beyond cinemas, Americans encountered Four Minute Men at churches, synagogues, schools, granges and concert halls, on trains and street corners and in factories, mills, mines and logging camps. Ross counts thirty-eight separate speech topics, some obviously designed to build passion for the war, others simply to win cooperation in the broad war effort, such as by conserving food, donating binoculars to the navy, buying Liberty Bonds and understanding why the new income tax was needed. By war's end, it has been precisely calculated, Four Minute Men gave 7,555,190 speeches to a 314,454,514 aggregate audience (in a population totaling 103 million).[27]

Four Minute Men pep talks were stirringly upbeat. But mobilizing war support also had its dark, on occasion very dark, side: a raft of federal laws and ad hoc vigilante actions designed to smother all criticism and dissent. Such measures, of course, were neither unprecedented nor necessarily wrong. America, in its centuries-long history making it even in 1917 the world's oldest, most enduring liberal democracy, at times had (and since has) faced genuine, serious subversion and espionage threats. At these moments, tough responses are prudent and even reasonable. The trouble is that they almost always, to lesser or greater extent, ultimately veer off course, inflicting individual pain and societal injury. During World War One, federal actions to counter perceived internal threats sped so far off course that they became what history near-unanimously judges as the most serious assault on Americans' individual liberties since the Alien and Sedition Act of 1798 made it a crime to publish "false, scandalous, and malicious writing" against the federal government or its officials.

Wilson closely followed the 1798 model, warning that sedition and dissent gravely undermined America's ability to fight the war. Dissent thus had to be stifled. Though he and Creel did not get all the repressive tools and extensive censorship they had sought, Congress did give them broad authority to restrict speech and press freedoms. This included:

- The Espionage Act of June 1917, imposing up to twenty years in prison for saying anything or sending materials through the mails that, in the opinion of officials, would aid the enemy, incite rebellion in the armed forces or obstruct the draft.
- A law of October 1917 requiring all foreign-language newspapers to submit translations of their war-related copy for review by Creel Committee-appointed boards, which then judged whether the copy violated the Espionage Act.
- The Trading with the Enemy Act of October 1917 censoring all civilian mail, cable, radio, news reports and other communications with foreign countries, with Creel

chairing its Board of Censors.

- The Sedition Act of May 1918 imposing fines and up to twenty years in prison for what officials perceived as "disloyal, profane, scurrilous, or abusive language about the form of government of the United States, or the Constitution of the United States, or the flag of the United States, or the uniform of the Army or Navy." This included writing, publishing or even saying anything criticizing the government or opposing Wilson Administration actions and policies.

These laws were a sweeping assault on established American liberties. To help enforce them and to ferret out what were said to be German agents, saboteurs and sympathizers, the Justice Department deputized a quarter-million vigilantes in at least 600 cities and towns, arming them with quasi-official badges identifying them as the "American Protective League-Secret Service," prompting Americans to believe that they actually were federal law enforcement officials. Helping the American Protective League were even less-official groups such as the American Defense League (veterans of the Preparedness Movement), the Sedition Slammers, the Boy Spies of America and the Terrible Threateners.

With Creel cheerleading their actions, they literally patrolled streets to interrogate those voicing anti-war or other ostensibly seditious views, stopped suspicious-looking people, tapped telephones, opened mail, shadowed those with German-sounding names, broke into German-American homes, launched "slacker raids" on suspected draft-dodgers or deserters, investigated those appearing to live in greater luxury than their incomes seemed to warrant, vetted jury panels to exclude pro-Germans and turned-in government employees thought to be disloyal. Whatever materials they found were delivered to the Justice Department's Bureau of Investigation, the FBI's forerunner. For Creel, the American Protective League vigilantes were not enough; to them he added Committee on Public Information ads in mass-market publications asking readers to report to the Justice Department those who spread "pessimistic stories... cries for peace, or belittles our effort to win the war."

Newspapers were huge American Protective League boosters, with the *New York Times* imploring its readers to report any suspicious behavior and the *Washington Post*, according to an Ohio University History Department study, suggesting that occasional lynchings were justified as a means of silencing "enemy propaganda." Other newspapers became Creel Committee targets, particularly the socialist press which, by and large, was silenced. At colleges, meanwhile, questionable faculty utterances and actions led to quick dismissal. Setting the repressive campus tone was Columbia University President Nicholas Murray Butler, declaring in June 1917 that "what had been tolerated became intolerable now. What had been wrong-headedness was now sedition. What had been folly was now treason." To all this a very satisfied U.S. Assistant Attorney General John Lord O'Brian, head of the Justice Department's War Emergency Division, remarked that the nation never before had been so effectively policed.[28]

As intrusive as they were, these laws and activities did not unleash a reign of terror or a witch hunt. To assert they did exaggerates what happened. Nonetheless, it is easily imagined how loose interpretations of the sedition and espionage laws' language by over-zealous vigilantes, the bigoted or those simply wanting to settle personal scores could—and did—strip individuals of their freedoms and the protection of law. Well reported, of course, was the high-profile jailing of such war-opponents as Socialist Party leader (and five-time presidential candidate) Eugene V. Debs and anarchist conscription-foe Emma Goldman and the arrests for suspected disloyalty of Boston Symphony Orchestra Conductor Karl Muck (a German) and Cincinnati Symphony Orchestra Conductor Ernest

Kunwald (an Austrian).

Beyond them, however, and just as deplorable, were thousands of ordinary citizens who were apprehended, of whom 1,050 were convicted and imprisoned, some for doing no more than criticizing Wilson or spreading what was deemed depressing accounts of the war. More telling were the hundreds of reported cases of vigilante harassment and bullying, such as tarring and feathering or painting German-speakers yellow, flogging and even shooting those deemed insufficiently enthusiastic about Liberty Bond drives, stoning delivery wagons of German-American firms and driving to suicide those fearing vigilante attacks. Most sensational was the April 1918 mob-lynching of Robert Prager in southern Illinois because he was suspected (wrongly) of being disloyal and planning to dynamite a coal mine.

At any moment in history these actions and their individual consequences would be shameful. In the context of World War One, the consequences were much more serious. The inflamed public passions that prompted and, perhaps more important, permitted such violation of liberties testify to the Creel Committee's astounding success at igniting anti-German frenzy—and at a time when Germany had yet to harm America very much. After all, American troops had barely begun to fight Germans on the Western Front and so far had suffered almost no deaths at German hands; there were no long casualty lists yet being published in U.S. newspapers or posted in town squares, and there were yet very few American war widows or grieving Gold Star mothers. And, of course, Germany had not even attacked America. Still, Creel Committee campaigns managed, long before American involvement in the war deepened, to transform Americans, few of whom had been anti-German, into Creel's desired "white-hot mass," hating and determined to punish an enemy. What this did, with serious consequences, was prevent any public discussion of reasonable U.S. peace aims, thus undermining Wilson's ability, at war's end, to push alternatives to the humiliating terms Britain and France imposed on the defeated Germany.

By the start of 1918, America's sprint to mobilize had covered great ground. Huge numbers of young men were being conscripted and trained. An industrial goliath was beginning to spew out massive quantities of weapons and war supplies. And a huge public—then, as now, the world's third largest—was becoming convinced that Germany was its deadly enemy. From all this, the shadow of an emerging American military colossus was lengthening over Europe. Yet, two crucial questions remained. Would the Yanks arrive in Europe in time and in sufficient numbers to make a difference? And, how well would these raw, unseasoned troops, including the tens of thousands of newly-minted officers, fight? These questions, as 1918 began, could not be answered by Washington or London or Paris with any confidence. Answers would have to wait for far greater numbers of doughboys actually to land in Europe and actually to march into combat.

For this, however, the Germans were not going to wait; they felt that they already had their answers. Field Marshal Paul von Hindenburg and General Erich Ludendorff, Imperial Germany's top generals and the powers behind the civilian government, had concluded that it made no difference how well the Americans would fight. For them, the mere prospect of an American Expeditionary Force landing by the shiploads in France was extraordinarily alarming. At the least, it would weigh the Western Front's balance of forces sharply against Germany. This conclusion prompted them (some could say, stampeded them) to toss what John Keegan, a leading World War One historian, calls, "Germany's last roll of the dice"—a gamble that a series of bold offensives in early 1918 could transform the Western Front before too many Americans arrived. It was a roll of the dice forced only and explicitly by the imminent arrival of the doughboys. This German gamble and the Allied and American response to it were to determine, suddenly and quickly, after years of stalemate, how and when the Great War was to end. And thus also determine the course of the still young century.

CHAPTER 5

DOUGHBOYS HEAD FOR THE WESTERN FRONT

WHILE THE MONTHS FOLLOWING AMERICA'S declaration of war against Germany were changing America profoundly, little was changing on the Western Front. The carnage continued and the casualties soared. But the lines shifted barely at all. Layers of hardened trenches, barbed wire and machine-gun emplacements, reinforced and improved over three years, still faced each other for more than 400 miles, separated by the 50-yard to 500-yard-wide killing field known as no man's land. This "trenchlock" (to use British military historian Gary Sheffield's term), which had paralyzed the front since Germany's August 1914 invasion of Belgium and France had been halted and somewhat pushed back, continued through 1917 and into 1918.

But that was not for want of Britain and France trying to break it. One after another, the two countries' generals launched ambitious and grand offensives, as if perversely to demonstrate that they had learned little in three years of war. These offensives sent staggering numbers (almost inconceivable today) of men into battle, often more than a million on each side each time. "Never had Western society exposed so much of its youth to battle," writes Rod Paschall in his 1989 study of Germany's defeat.[1] By comparison,

World War Two's D-Day invasion of Normandy marshaled a small fraction of that, about 380,000 troops and civilians: the 160,000 ground forces who actually landed on the beaches, the 196,000 sailors and merchantmen who delivered and supported them and the 24,000 who parachuted or were air-lifted behind German lines. As further comparison, 550,000 American troops were in Viet Nam at the 1969 peak of U.S. combat there, while about 140,000 were in Iraq in 2006. These numbers, seen as huge in their day, never even closely approached the towering levels fielded and put at risk in a single battle by the Great War's generals.

There was an eerie and, for the Allied home fronts, horrifying repetitiveness to these battles. Each time a new offensive was announced there was the promise that "this time" would be different; "this time" improved and innovative tactics would puncture the German trench lines and force the battle into open field where the attacking Allies would triumph. But each time "this time" merely replayed "last time." The offensive failed, with nothing to show for the massive effort except, on both sides, still more casualties, with numbers of the dead, wounded and captured climbing into the hundreds of thousands. At best, a few miles would be gained. "Mounting casualties for minimal advantage." That's how Hew Strachan coolly puts it in his monumental history of the war.[2] It was onto this front that America's doughboys began arriving, first to be trained and then to fight.

Nivelle and Passchendaele

"Mounting casualties for minimal advantage" was indeed the storyline of the April 1917 offensive devised by France's new commander in chief, General Robert Nivelle, and launched just ten days after America entered the war. His ultimate failure to deliver a promised quick victory is what triggered the widespread French troop mutiny described in Chapter 1. Reckoning that

1916's marathon bloodletting at Verdun had severely weakened German forces, Nivelle convinced the French government that he now, in a single brutal strike, could destroy the German Army and end the war. He would unleash, he declared in what all agreed was his eloquent and enormously persuasive manner, a new kind of lightning-fast offensive: a massive artillery bombardment followed by unprecedented phalanxes of infantry swiftly pushing over the battlefield; a "mass of maneuver," as he described it, which would snowball into an attack of extraordinary violence. "I can assure you," he proclaimed repeatedly, "that victory is certain. The enemy will learn this to his cost." To demonstrate his confidence and win his government's approval, he vowed that if victory did not come within forty-eight hours he would call off the offensive. For his attack, known to history both as the Nivelle Offensive and the Chemin des Dames Offensive, he deployed the gargantuan force of 1,200,000 men in fifty-three divisions and support units, including 132 of the battlefield's newest and, it was assumed, most promising weapon—tanks.

It began with French artillery pounding German positions, thundering nearly nonstop for two weeks. Then, early on April 16, Nivelle ordered his infantry out of its trenches and over the top, sending wave after wave across no man's land in frontal attack, what military historian S.L.A. Marshall describes as "bearing a surprising resemblance to past patterns that had dismally failed." What they encountered was disaster, a "new carnival of slaughter," as Marshall puts it.[3] The French artillery bombardment, for all of what a much later generation of generals would call its "shock and awe," failed to destroy the German position, leaving intact much of the German entrenchment and guns. Intact too was the concertina barbed wire, eight feet high in some places; and it now was entangling and slowing the advancing poilus, channeling them towards open areas where they became easy targets for the many surviving concealed German machine-gunners.

Slowing them also was the legacy of their own artillery barrage, which had so ripped up the landscape that it was now nearly impassable. Almost immediately, writes Paschall, "French infantrymen were being scythed down by the forward German machine-gun outposts." Adds John Keegan: "It was a massacre."[4] Nivelle's tanks, meanwhile, overweight and underpowered, sputtered; within a day, 121 of them were out of action. Casualties on both sides climbed rapidly and enormously, and the offensive faltered. There was no breakthrough, no sign of Nivelle's promised "rupture." The German Army had not been broken. Yet, despite his promise to halt within forty-eight hours if he did not succeed, he kept on, pressing his men forward. For many of them, this was the last straw. They had been assured that this would be their final sacrifice, the battle that would end the war and send them home. When it was clear that it would not, tens of thousands balked, sparking the mutiny that ultimately spread to half of all French divisions. On April 29, a horrified French government, in effect, fired Nivelle, forcing him to report to Henri-Philippe Petain, the new chief of the general staff. Petain formally ended the offensive on May 9. Nivelle's forty-eight-hour offensive had turned into more than three weeks of death and ruin.

It also ended France's fighting for nearly a full year. French troops would man their trenches, hold their lines, repulse German probes and launch limited attacks, but little more. As an independent offensive force, France was out of the war. "The French," recorded British Commander in Chief Douglas Haig in his diary, "are a broken reed." And when British Prime Minister David Lloyd George, after the collapse of the Nivelle Offensive, confronted Petain, asking him to deny "for some reason or other you won't fight," the French general remained silent. The best his armies were to do was to preserve the stalemate on the two-thirds of the Western Front that they held—until the arriving Americans would change the battlefield arithmetic. Relying on America to win the war, in fact, was France's open, explicit policy. In the wake of the Nivelle Offensive catastrophe and the resulting troop mutinies, Petain, now promoted to commander in chief, rejected any notion of launching a major attack, saying unashamedly that he was waiting for "tanks and the Americans." Had he a better sense of English-language rhythms, he might have said "tanks and Yanks."

The British saw no need to wait. Just two months after the Nivelle Offensive's collapse, Britain's generals launched their own massive thrust. Looking back from a century's vantage, it can only be wondered, "What were they possibly thinking?" The planning, the promises, the tactics, the casualties all were, in essence, a replay of earlier grand offensives and even of the very recent Nivelle Offensive. So was the outcome, which left the battlefield barely changed. Huge efforts and casualties were expended to gain mere yards. This 1917 British Expeditionary Force (BEF) assault formally was known as the Third Battle of Ypres; but history remembers it much better as the Passchendaele Offensive, named after the Flanders village and ridge whose capture was the goal of the excruciating four-month campaign.

For Britain's postwar generations—and, indeed, for many Britons still today—the single word "Passchendaele" triggers an intake of breath, a catch in the throat, a reflective silence, moistened eyes and a slow shake of the head. It became for the British what "Verdun" is for the French. Few are the words so freighted with horror and anger as "Passchendaele," shorthand for what was and is still regarded as the British military command's World War One senseless and profligate sacrifice of an entire generation. This too has been the judgment of historians across the decades: "The gloomiest drama in British military history," (B.H. Liddell Hart, 1930); "Not one thing of importance had been achieved," (S.L.A. Marshall, 1964); "The bloodbath of mud and despair...synonymous with British callousness," (Rod Paschall, 1989); Britain's "most notorious land campaign of the war," (John Keegan, 1998).[5]

The offensive's architect was Haig. Unlike Nivelle, new to his top command post, Haig had been British commander in chief for almost two years and would remain so through war's end. It had been Haig who, in summer 1916, almost exactly a year before his Passchendaele campaign, conceived and launched the Battle of the Somme, which, after four months of brutal fighting merely had pushed back the Germans six miles. Yet, it had cost Britain a half-million dead, wounded and captured.

Now, a year later, Haig was going at it again. His aims seemed reasonable: capturing a key German railway junction, shattering German trench defenses and forcing the battle into the open, inflicting so much loss and pain on the German Army that it would retreat and perhaps even quit the war. Simultaneously, a British Navy amphibious operation was to capture what was thought to be German submarine bases on the Belgian coast from which attacks ostensibly were being launched against Allied shipping. (Actually, as the British discovered, the submarines were not in Belgium at all, but at ports in Germany.) Yet the aims of all Western Front grand offensives also initially seemed sensible. What made no sense was the expectation that, in the front's entrenched environment, such aims could be achieved. And the Flanders field on which Haig in 1917 chose to fight probably made least sense of all.

For three years, the Germans there had been reinforcing their positions and refining their defensive tactics. Confronting any potential attackers now were nine layers of German trenches, obstacles and firing positions, including concrete bunkers for machine-gunners, what British troops began calling "pillboxes." This created one of the strongest German positions on the entire Western Front. Making any assault even more difficult, the naturally swampy landscape's elaborate drainage system, meticulously built and tended carefully over the centuries by Belgian farmers, had been severely damaged by the war's shelling. Any rain thus threatened to turn this battlefield into a bog. And Haig's troops were, to their great misfortune, to suffer rain. Weeks and weeks of it.

Haig's key tactical challenge, as Keegan explains, was the same as in prior major offensives: for his artillery to so crush German guns and other defenses that his attacking infantry quickly could seize battlefield positions from which they could repel the inevitable ferocious German counterattack. For this Haig had deployed 2,300 artillery pieces, easily out-gunning the Germans' 1,500. In a ten-day mid-July barrage, British guns fired nearly four million shells at German lines, four times greater than the number fired in preparation for 1916's Somme campaign. It was, judge experts, a "bombardment without precedent in history." With his thirty-six divisions, his thousands of cannon and his war planes and tanks, writes Paschall, a West Pointer, "Haig had the greatest assembly of combat power that the British Empire had ever fielded." And this was strengthened even more by six French First Army divisions, the units least weakened by the mutinies.

Then, on July 31, at what history precisely records as 3:50 a.m., the preparatory artillery barrage was deemed to have done its job and the British ground assault began. Within hours, so did trouble. Crucial communications between British gunners and infantry, essential for aiming artillery shells so that they would land just ahead of the advancing lines, broke down as cables everywhere were cut. Low clouds, meanwhile, prevented British observer planes from relaying British infantry positions to the gunners. Haig's forces were reduced to relying on runners and carrier pigeons, but they helped little. As a result, there was almost no coordination between the guns and the infantrymen, who thus had to slow their advance on the eleven-mile front to avoid being hit by their own artillery. By 2 p.m., before the British had reached defensible positions, the Germans were counterattacking.

Then the rain began—and seldom stopped.

It rained for most of August and again through October and November. At times it was torrential; always it was steady. Since the extraordinary shelling had destroyed the dikes and just about everything else that had remained of the land's drainage system, the rainwater rapidly pooled, turning the battlefield into a muddy swamp; in many places its consistency resembled quicksand. Official reports, diaries and observers chronicle how the muck gummed up rifles and machine guns and swallowed tanks, how infantrymen literally crawled into battle and then couldn't find solid ground on which to stand or kneel when firing their rifles, how the wounded thought they were reaching safety by dragging themselves into holes and then drowned as the water rose, how horses and mules suffocated after sinking into the mud, how soldiers became afraid to sleep. A German soldier wrote in his diary: "We fear the mud at night more than we do Tommy. You just slide a little and disappear forever." To Britain's B.H. Liddell Hart, himself a veteran of the war (though not of Passchendaele), it was a "bath of mud and blood."[6] He tells of a senior British officer, near the offensive's end, visiting this Flanders battlefield for the first time, looking at the morass and bursting into tears, crying out: "Good God, did we really send men to fight in that?"[7]

Haig indeed had. Week after week his artillery thundered and his Tommies climbed out of trenches to try to push further over the sodden, glutinous landscape. Progress, if any, was barely measurable. And week after week too losses mounted; so too did pressure on Haig from a shocked government in London, urging him to halt the offensive. He repeatedly resisted, refusing to stop fighting, insisting—very wrongly—that the Germans were so exhausted that they were about to retreat. To shore up his own increasingly fatigued forces, in early September he sent Australian, Canadian and New Zealand divisions into the line. Their men too died and were wounded in staggering numbers. August, September and October had passed, yet Haig persisted.

Finally, on November 6, his troops captured Passchendaele Ridge and Passchendaele village, now just a pile of stones. His original plans had called for these to be taken on the offensive's day one. Four days later he halted the campaign, ordering his men into defensive positions. Nothing of strategic value had been gained, nor almost anything of tactical value. But much had been lost: Tommy morale, confidence in Haig's leadership and, of course and most tragically, a shocking number of lives. Precise casualty counts remain, even now, murky. Best estimates are that some 70,000 Australians, Britons, Canadians and New Zealanders were killed in the offensive; over 170,000 were wounded. German losses were just as great or even greater. By comparison, America's losses in the entire Viet Nam War were 58,209 killed in combat and by related causes; in the entire Korean War, 53,686 Americans died; and on that bloody July 1-3, 1863 battlefield at Gettysburg, the combined Union and Confederacy dead totaled about 7,500.

The failures of the Nivelle and Passchendaele Offensives hung over the Western Front as America's soldiers began arriving. There they would find that while the lines barely had changed in three years, the troops certainly had. Gone were the enthusiasm and optimistic high spirits of the war's opening months. Gone was the aggressive determination to launch campaigns to drive the Germans out of Belgium and France. In their place (on both sides) were persistent exhaustion and gnawing demoralization—among the infantrymen who, by the millions, were the expendable fodder in the front's huge clashes and also among the junior and even senior officers. And there was anger, so much so that when doughboys, some months later, began taking front line positions, French and British troops at times snarled at them, berating them for needlessly prolonging a hopeless war.

To this hopelessness and the extraordinary carnage of 1917, the French poilus, "the hairy ones" as infantrymen fondly were known, had responded with their mutiny. The British too were to mutiny, not in the ranks, but at the very top. British leaders began balking at sending Haig still more soldiers for the Western Front's killing fields. Writes Britain's John Terraine, author of more than a dozen books on wars: "Some members of the British Government had become well-nigh hysterical about the casualties of a manpower war;" the 2,000,000 dead and wounded by 1917's end was "a figure beyond all previous experience or imagining."[8] So much sacrifice for so little gain so horrified Prime Minister Lloyd George that he denied Haig's requests for full replacements to make up the Passchendaele losses. By early 1918, Lloyd George was holding back at least 200,000 new conscripts in Britain, ostensibly for shipbuilding, munitions manufacturing, food production and "home defense," rather than entrust them to his commander in chief. After the war Lloyd George did not change his mind about what he viewed as Haig's profligacy with men, nor was he ever able to shake his own sense of guilt for not having halted the Passchendaele slaughter. He wrote: "Our men advanced against the most terrible machine gun fire…and they fell by the thousands in every attack. But divisions were sent on time after time to face the same slaughter in their ranks."[9]

Lloyd George's dismay reflected his home front's. In Britain and the other combatants civilian suffering was deepening. As the battlefield's Moloch-like appetite devoured workers from industries that had been making consumer goods, a growing list of essential and otherwise common items was in increasingly short supply. Manpower allocations for consumer-goods industries ranked a distant third, according to historian Gail Braybon, behind the armed forces and behind the factories turning out munitions, trucks, planes, ships and other military products. The message to civilians was that they simply would have to keep tightening their belts.[10] No belts were tighter than in Germany, suffering from the double blow of its own declining domestic consumer output and the British naval blockade stopping almost all imports. Meat, eggs and milk were very scarce, while fruits and vegetables had just about disappeared from German markets. So much cotton and other fabrics were needed by the military that clothing was strictly rationed; German women, for instance, were allowed a wardrobe of only one Sunday dress and two workday dresses and two pairs of shoes. Men, in effect, were drafted into war production. Under the so-called Hindenburg Program, introduced in late 1916 to mobilize the economy totally, all men aged seventeen to sixty not fit for military service had to go work in war-related industries.

Adding to home front pains everywhere were rising taxes and inflation, plus the serious contraction of individual liberties, as special police units on both sides were clamping down on any hint of dissent. The greatest pain, of course, was inflicted by the staggering battlefield toll. The official black-bordered notices with their long lists of the dead, along with the return home of the wounded and maimed, unsettled and touched every community and family. The reaction in all home fronts was anger and a surging feeling that the killing had to be stopped; there were strikes in Britain, France and Germany, various peace resolutions adopted by powerful political organizations and, of course, revolution in Russia and the toppling of a Tsar.

But the war did not stop. It simply was, on the Western Front, at 1917's end, frozen. It would remain so until the following spring when the specter of a gathering tsunami of arriving American troops set in train battlefield actions that would end the Great War faster and more completely than anyone could have guessed.

Doughboys Start Arriving

Though some 14,000 doughboys, about half of the 1st Division, may have arrived in France in time for that July 4th, 1917 parade in Paris, it would not be until the following year before American troops in any significant numbers would land in Europe and be ready for combat. By October 1917, the American Expeditionary Force in France numbered just 65,000; at Christmas, it was still a modest 129,000, comprising four combat divisions and support units: the 1st and 2nd Divisions (filled by Regular Army and Marines), the 26th Division (New England National Guardsmen) and the 42nd Division (known as the "Rainbow Division" because of its varied composition, drawing together National Guardsmen from twenty-six states and the District of Columbia).

At 1917's end, these troops had yet to see any real Western Front action. To be sure, the 1st Division had tiptoed into the hot war—a bit. On October 23, at 6:05 a.m., a battery from its 6th Field Artillery fired the first official American shot of the war, sending shells from a French cannon towards the general direction of German lines, with unknown results. Eleven days later, in the early hours of November 3, the division got America's first taste of real combat. Some of its units, on their ten-day rotation to train with the French Army in a muddy Lorraine sector that had been quiet for three years, were attacked under the cover of heavy fog and smoke by a 213-man Bavarian trench-assault party. S.L.A. Marshall believes that the Germans discovered that AEF units had moved in and thus "intended to humiliate them." In the fifteen-minute clash, five doughboys were wounded, eleven captured and three killed: a corporal and two privates. One was shot, one had his throat slashed, one's skull was bashed. They became World War One's first American fatalities. That afternoon they were buried nearby, with a French general saluting and French gunners firing volleys. They became national heroes. The Bavarians, for their part, suffered two dead and seven wounded and lost one deserter to the AEF. The doughboys, in this their debut skirmish of the Great War, apparently did well enough; the attack's leader, a Lieutenant Wolf, later reported that "the enemy was very good in hand-to-hand fighting."[11]

But this lone 1st Division scuffle with the enemy impressed no one. What appeared like America's agonizingly slow AEF buildup distressed the British and French who desperately wanted massive American reinforcements on the Western Front, particularly after the huge Allied losses in the year's Nivelle and Passchendaele Offensives. The Allies did not hide their ire. British troops began referring to dud shells as "Wilsons," because they failed to explode. The *London Times'* Charles Remington, perhaps Britain's most prominent war correspondent, caustically asked a U.S. intelligence officer: "After more than eight months of being in the war, you haven't really fired a damned shot! ...When is something actually to be done in the fighting line?" A few months later, when the U.S. formally had been in the war a full year and 163 doughboys already had been killed, that number still looked pitifully low to some. "Too ineffective for words," was the verdict on America's battlefield contribution by French General Ferdinand Foch, soon to be named generalissimo of all Allied and American forces. French Premier Georges Clemenceau, writing after the war though surely echoing earlier sentiments, bemoaned that "while large bodies of American troops remained idle...my country's fate was every moment at stake on the battlefields." And, recounts Pershing biographer Donald Smythe, when an American serviceman accidentally ran over and killed a Parisian with an auto, "the French jeered that the Americans were killing Frenchmen sooner than they were Germans."[12]

To such criticism Pershing didn't really demur, admitting at the start of 1918 that he suffered "much embarrassment" at the slow arrival of his forces. In truth, he was much more frustrated than embarrassed. After all, the real damage of a slow buildup was that it set back his timetable for reaching his key aims: creating completely-equipped American divisions, then grouping the divisions into several corps and then, as the ultimate goal towards which he single-mindedly and relentlessly pushed, forming these corps into a genuine powerful American Army, operating independently in its own battlefield sector, under the American flag, commanded by American officers.

In retrospect, the criticism was unwarranted; the AEF buildup wasn't all that slow. Unlike the other combatant nations, which had large standing armies, established military training and supply structures and (except for Britain) well-oiled conscription and mobilization systems, America was starting from absolute zero. First the prospective American soldier had to be drafted by Selective Service, then sent to the hastily-built and often still incomplete cantonments scattered about the U.S., then organized into units, then trained, then loaded onto ships (mainly at Hoboken's piers in New York harbor) and then, once in France, handed over to British and French officers in quiet areas for more training.

Meanwhile, the War Department in Washington and Pershing and his staff at the AEF's headquarters in Chaumont, a city of 15,000 about 150 miles east of Paris, had to craft the infrastructure and systems to supply, feed, care for and medically treat the several million troops expected ultimately to be based in France. They had to calculate how much they needed of horses, cars, trucks, coal, lumber, food, medicine and hundreds of similarly essential items—and then figure from where these were to be obtained. In France, among many other things, Pershing had to build wharves to receive his doughboys and lay railway tracks for the twenty-five carloads of supplies required daily by each AEF combat division. All of that took time and lots of it (as it did in Britain, for example, when it introduced a draft) and was subjected to the delays of infuriating but unavoidable bureaucratic squabbling and inefficiencies. By some comparisons, in fact, the AEF readied itself for battle as speedily as had other armies. It fielded a five-division-strong army corps within a year, just about as long as it had taken Canada to deploy a corps and Britain to send into major battles the first of its new, so-called Kitchener Army recruits. In fact, London originally had not planned to send its Class of 1915 recruits into combat until 1917; the AEF did much better than that.[13]

Of all the pieces in the AEF deployment machine, none turned out to be more critical, none constricted the bottleneck more, than transport availability for carrying the doughboys across the Atlantic. Was the U.S., it could be asked, expending huge efforts and spending vast sums on raising an army destined never to reach the battlefield? Concludes Smythe: "The whole future history of the AEF rested on the question of ships."[14] And ships were in painfully short supply. For one thing, America actually had a very small troop-carrying ship capability. Despite Yankee Clipper legends and other vaunted seafaring traditions, the U.S. merchant marine was tiny. Pershing in mid-1917 calculated that if only U.S. vessels were to be used it could take as much as four years to bring 900,000 soldiers to Europe. For another thing, and much more important, German submarine attacks were taking a huge toll of the British bottoms carrying food and war-related supplies to the Allies; as such, London was loath to fill its remaining ships with American soldiers rather than with essential goods. So desperate were the British and French for American supplies that London for months refused to allocate sufficient shipping (the term used was "tonnage") to transport doughboys. Rather, London was begging, urging, demanding that U.S. shipyards enormously accelerate their output of new vessels.

Pershing, on his part, was begging, urging, demanding London to assign more British tonnage to transporting doughboys. He peppers his memoirs with excruciatingly detailed accounts of his pained (at times angry) exchanges with the Allies, to the very end of the war, over their shipping tonnage allocations. On June 11, 1917, for instance, just as he first was arriving in Europe, he told Chief of Britain's Imperial General Staff William Robertson that he needed more ships to bring over AEF troops. "Entirely out of the question," snapped Robertson.

This exchange was to become typical. Typical too, in later months, would become London's use of its tonnage leverage to insist that its ships deliver only the kind of doughboys the Allies wanted, mainly infantrymen and machine-gunners to replace fallen Allied soldiers. In contrast, Pershing wanted much more, all those needed to create and support a full AEF Army: not only infantrymen but also artillerymen, truck drivers, horse handlers, cooks, engineers, nurses, telephone exchange operators and workers to run railways, construct wharves and warehouses, fell trees and saw lumber. There even were times, according to Pershing, when London argued that arriving doughboys should be assigned to British rather than French battlefield sectors because they had been brought to battle in British hulls. Passage in these ships, of course, was not free; London charged the U.S. $81.75 per man. And that, America was told, was a bargain. Originally London was demanding the $150.00-per-man commercial shipping rate, but Washington refused to pay it.

So linked was tonnage to the AEF buildup that the War Department actually ordered the Selective Service to pace the draft to the number of conscripted young men who could be carried to Europe. For this reason, through April 1918 the War Department was calling up only about 116,000 per month instead of the 250,000 sought by Pershing. By late spring 1918 this changed dramatically. Deliveries of doughboys began soaring. Responsible for this in part was the Department's determination to squeeze sardine-style ever more doughboys into each ship by, among other things, assigning three to a bunk, with three eight-hour sleeping shifts.

Much more important was the sharp tonnage improvement, first because of effective Allied naval defenses against German submarines and then because of vastly increased U.S. shipyard output. America's troop-carrying capability jumped spectacularly from a mere thirteen ships with 94,000 aggregate tons in July 1917 to, at war's end, 616 ships with over 3.5 million tons. Of these ships the grandest actually once was Germany's 54,000-ton SS *Vaterland*, the world's largest ocean liner, whose owners had boasted it was "the greatest of the world's greatest liners." At war's start in August 1914, the ship happened to find itself in New York harbor. There it remained (not daring to risk steaming back to Germany and be attacked by British warships) until it was seized by the U.S.

Navy when America declared war on Germany. Renamed the USS *Leviathan*, its nineteen Atlantic roundtrips under the American flag carried nearly 120,000 doughboys to Europe.

In all, U.S. ships delivered forty-six percent of the more than two million doughboys who landed in Europe; forty-nine percent sailed in British ships; the rest were carried by Dutch, French and Italian ships. Military historian James Hallas calculates that four of every five doughboys sailed from Hoboken piers, with most of the rest sailing from Newport News, Virginia. By summer 1918, nearly 10,000 doughboys were landing in France each day and the U.S. draft rate had jumped to 373,000 a month. Pershing now was talking about a three-million-man army and a 400,000-per-month draft. Those numbers would make the AEF bigger than the British Expeditionary Force and would begin to rival in size the French Army, which, after all, was defending its homeland.

Pershing Battles for Control of His AEF

With the AEF pouring into France, two huge questions had to be confronted: How were the doughboys to be trained and where were they to fight? To both, Pershing had very definite answers and stuck to them with unwavering stubbornness. His forces, he declared, were not going to bog down and be chewed up by those static tactics of trench fighting which already had eradicated a generation of British, French and Germans. This trench battlefield Pershing hated before he arrived in France and would grow to hate it more with every passing day. Instead of merely learning to survive in trenches, he wanted his doughboys to be trained in what he called "open warfare," which would unleash swift battlefield charges of infantrymen especially skilled in firing their lethal rifles. Nonsense, retorted the British and French generals. Though they agreed that open warfare was an admirable ideal, they argued it was totally unsuited to a battlefield now defined by rows of elaborate trenches whose machine guns easily were annihilating attackers charging across barbed-wire strewn fields. This Pershing-Allied disagreement over how to train the doughboys smoldered throughout the war.

So did the question of where the doughboys were to fight. To Pershing there was only one answer: They would fight on the Western Front, in a sector of their own, as an American Army commanded by Americans. And so doing, he declared, they would defeat the Germans and win the war. To this the British and French could hardly object. But it was, they forcefully countered (at times, pleaded), a matter of timing. They feared that if the AEF were to delay extensive combat until it could organize and train as its own full-size army, then it would not be ready to contribute much until late 1919 or even early 1920.[15] What they desperately needed, insisted the Allies, was help now. With their huge losses, they argued that Americans had to replace depleted British and French units immediately and thus had to enter Allied ranks in British and French sectors and serve under Allied officers and British and French flags. Absolutely unacceptable, rejoined Pershing and his superiors at the White House and War Department. Americans were not being drafted, they said (though not publicly) just to become more fodder for failed Allied offensives.

The matter of where and under whose command the Americans would serve was, of course, moot until they were trained for the Great War's battlefield. All agreed that the doughboys were strong, enthusiastic ("lusty arrogance" was one description), energetic, well-disciplined and possessed admirable physiques. One French officer even told Pershing that "Americans had the advantage over Frenchmen because of their long legs and large feet." And like the Australian, Canadian and New Zealand forces, the arriving Americans were applauded for their aggressiveness and eagerness for combat. But eager doughboys needed training. AEF recruits were extraordinarily green and their newly minted officers, many of them alumni of the Preparedness Movement's Plattsburgh training camps, just as extraordinarily inexperienced. This included the very senior officers. None of them, not even Pershing, had ever commanded anything as large and complex as a division, to say nothing of an even larger corps or much larger army. As late as May 1918, more than a year after the U.S. entered the war, a French command memo was complaining that AEF officers "have either everything to learn, or only possess elements of theoretical instruction."

This applied to even the 1st Division. Though composed of Regular Army troops who ostensibly had seen combat in Mexico or elsewhere, most of the division's men and officers in fact were recent volunteers. The army's experienced officers were being held back in the U.S. to instruct the conscripts flooding into the War Department's cantonments. Overall, fewer than half of the Regular Army's original officer cadre was ever to make it to the Western Front; they were needed at home for training. And there were not even enough of them for that. Washington thus had to ask Britain and France to help train the AEF. As a result, hundreds of British and French officers began arriving at the cantonments as "advisers." For much of the first year of America's participation in the war they set the tone for and most of the substance of doughboy education. They declared, and just about all agreed, that as much as Pershing may favor open warfare, his troops had to be prepared for Western Front reality. That meant training for the trenches.

This kind of training intensified once the doughboys, after six months or so of basic instruction in the U.S., arrived in France. Their destination, via railway boxcars (for which the AEF was billed by French railways), was the Western Front's so-called quiet sectors where they were to learn trench combat first-hand from French and British forces. Though the doughboys were led by U.S. officers up to company level, actually they were serving under the British and French, whose officers commanded the larger battalion and regiment units. As the first to arrive in France, the 1st Division became something of a template for doughboys who followed. Lacking proper barracks, the division's men were scattered among small villages and billeted, as were many French soldiers, in farmhouses and unheated barns within earshot of the front's booming guns. Officers slept in beds in houses, the rest on hay or fodder in haylofts. Pershing, who once led General Petain up ladders to inspect these billets, proclaimed the accommodations "fairly comfortable." Most doughboys would disagree.[16]

The 1st Division's tutors, at least at the start, were among the best France could offer—officers from the elitist 47th Division, a French infantry mountain unit known as the Chasseurs Alpins, or Alpine Hunters. Most of the day they drilled 1st Division men in dummy trenches, leaving them little time for the shooting-range rifle practice which Pershing wanted stressed. Instead, explains Gary Mead in his doughboy history, the French trainers emphasized that "the most important skill was how to duck into a shell-hole, peep over the top, lob a grenade and then scamper back a few yards to one's own trenches."[17] Ditto, recalls Laurence Stallings, an AEF officer on the Western Front (and later a successful Hollywood screenwriter and Broadway playwright whose credits include, among others, *What Price Glory* and *Northwest Passage*), who writes that because neither the British nor the French "saw much usefulness in the rifle in trench warfare," they taught the doughboys how to use flamethrowers, bayonets, grenades, mortars and shovels and how to deal with gas attacks and barbed wire.[18]

Pershing, predictably, was not happy with these training arrangements, unavoidable though they were. It was bad enough, he complained, that the Allies were instructing his men in the U.S.; it was worse that this was continuing in France. For one thing, he worried greatly that the Allied troops' deflated spirits and trampled morale would be contagious. He branded the French divisions "worn and weary" and groused that they failed "to set an example of the aggressiveness which we were striving to inculcate in our men." In his memoirs he writes that, except for what he dismissively calls "the details of trench warfare," training by the Allies "was of little value" and that it "retarded our progress."[19] He put it bluntly in a July 28, 1918 cable to the War Department, informing Secretary Newton Baker that "training with these worn-out French and British troops, if continued, is detrimental... The morale of the Allies is low and association with them has a bad effect on our men... The fact is that our officers and men are far superior to the tired Europeans."[20]

For another thing, and much more unsettling to Pershing, he felt his troops were learning failed trench tactics instead of the essential skills for his kind of warfare. On few topics did Pershing feel more strongly (and passionately) and speak out more readily than on open warfare's virtues. And on few topics would history judge him to be so wrong. But open warfare's test and its cost in doughboy lives would come later. For now, for Pershing, it was the cure for what he saw as the debilitating frozen tactics of the Western Front: of frustrated troops and commanders, in essence, incessantly banging their heads against an impenetrable wall of trenches, each time suffering huge casualties, each time further depleting their nations' manpower, each time resulting in continued stalemate and deadlock. Explains Rod Paschall, Pershing and his generals had concluded that the Allies were "obsessed with the safety of the trenches and cowed by machine guns...and fatigued by Western Front conditions."[21] All that would be changed, Pershing promised, by open warfare doing just what its name conveyed, forcing enemy soldiers out of their trenches into the open where they would be engaged and defeated by an attacker's superior tactics and skills.

The key open warfare skill, for Pershing, was not mastery of Western Front-style artillery barrages, grenade throwing, trench digging or barbed wire emplacing. It was good old-fashioned marksmanship. It was the infantryman's highly accomplished use of what Pershing extolled as the most effective battlefield weapon: the rifle, with its extraordinary firepower potential and the deadliness of a rapid charge with fixed bayonet. It exploited, he insisted, the AEF's competitive advantages: the American soldier's aggressiveness, self-reliance, independent character, readiness to maneuver and exceptional skills as a sharp-eyed sharp-shooter and skirmisher, honed over decades on America's frontier and farms, in Indian wars and in combat in Mexico and the Philippines. It was, Pershing writes with confidence, precisely what he had learned at West Point and had not forgotten. Surely cheering him as a reflection of this American aggressive spirit was the doughboy-penned poem published in the February 15, 1918 *Stars and Stripes,* the U.S. Army eight-page weekly which he launched to boost morale. It reads, in part: "With bayonet and shot and shell, We will give the Kaiser hell; Jab 'em, jab 'em, Shoot and stab 'em."[22]

This sort of aggressiveness he contrasted with what he describes as the British and French doctrine of "the cautious advance of infantry" where the infantryman "did not rely on his rifle and made little use of its great power." He was right. Trench fighting relied on artillery, grenades and satchel charges, not the rifle. His disdain, even contempt, is barely veiled when he notes that because of their long time in the trenches "both the French and British were poor skirmishers" and that there even were instances, reported by their own officers, of them "chasing an individual enemy throwing grenades at him instead of using the rifle."[23] The Allies, he also felt, were far too dependent on extensive planning. As an example he cites a French battle plan that ran 150 pages each for the offense and defense, while his own plan for the same battle was just six pages for the offense and eight for the defense. This demonstrates, he concludes, "the difference between planning for trench warfare... and open warfare."[24]

In the most fundamental sense, there were few who disagreed with Pershing. It was not a matter of him possessing brilliant tactical insight while his Allied colleagues remained inexplicably dense (or stupid). British and French generals also readily recognized the huge payoff of breaking through into open ground and engaging and then pursuing and eventually enveloping a fleeing enemy. Mark Grotelueschen, a U.S. Air Force officer and professor at the Air Force Academy, points out that with the exception of Germany's 1916 attack at Verdun, every major Western Front offensive had sought to drive the enemy into the open. The Allied and German generals' mistake had not been to choose deliberately to fight from trenches; it was not their choice. It was imposed on them by technological circumstances, such as the widespread deployment of machine guns and barbed wire on the Great War's western battlefield.

Their mistake, rather, was to continue ordering their huge armies over that battlefield, suffering insufferable losses for miniscule gains. Given a choice, these Allied generals surely would have fought open warfare. Indeed, they did just that in the war's opening weeks and, in fact, were advocating it even earlier. Typical was the 1913 memo cited by John Ellis' history of the machine gun. In it, Chief of the French General Staff Joseph Joffre, later one of France's wartime commanders in chief, wrote that the only law the French Army knows is "the offensive… All attacks are to be pushed to the extreme with the firm resolution to charge the enemy with the bayonet." And troops must do so, an 1899 French Infantry Regulation had decreed, "with a cheer." By mid-autumn 1914, however, bayonet charges and cheers were nullified by the harsh trench reality. And after three years of that, Allied generals could say to Pershing that "we painfully have learned something about fighting this ugly trench war and the AEF would do well to heed these lessons." Pershing disagreed, firing back that the Allies had learned the wrong lessons, as the catastrophically costly failures of their massive offensives testified. As bad, Pershing would add, Allied generalship had become far too cautious.

In many respects Pershing was right; the Allies had grown pessimistic and lost their enthusiasm. Yet, Pershing also was wrong. Trenches, in truth, very much had trumped open warfare and, as will be seen below, generally would continue to trump it. This the doughboys painfully and tragically were to learn in their early battles, charging German lines Pershing-style only to be naked to machine gun fire—as German officers looked on in disbelief. "Both the Germans and the Allies watched the American military intervention with amazement," writes Dutch Historian Hans Binneveld in his 1997 analysis of battlefield dynamics. "The Americans perished in the same way that all the parties involved had perished during the first three years of the war: side by side and wave after wave... The army of the United States set off to battle in 1918 as if the Great War had just begun, and had to discover the hard reality of trench warfare all over again."[25] And that was to remain the hard reality until mid-summer 1918 when German forces were so severely spent by their abortive offensives that they began buckling from Allied and AEF assaults. Only then could open warfare be waged. And it was, successfully. Ultimately, the battlefield was ready for Pershing's tactics.

Ultimately, too, were the Allies ready for Pershing to create and command a full-blown American Army. But, as his memoirs and other accounts of the war testify, he unceasingly had to battle to achieve this, prompting some historians to note that he spent as much time fighting the Allies as the Germans. The British and French subjected him nearly nonstop to what Gary Mead trenchantly calls "a guerrilla campaign" to grab control of the AEF. Even Britain's monarch, George V, was enlisted to pressure the AEF commander. What's more, writes Mead, Allied "military and political leaders did their utmost to ignore, belittle and undermine Pershing."[26] For good reason did Pershing complain of the Allies wanting to "dictate" where American troops would be used and of wanting doughboys "to serve under an alien flag." At times, in icy and even ugly confrontations with British and French government leaders and senior commanders, Pershing had to dig in his heels and seem impervious to Allied pleas that his cooperation and his troops desperately were needed to blunt German advances. At a May 1, 1918 meeting, for instance, he even had to acknowledge his readiness to see German battlefield gains rather than send doughboys to the front to fight under Allied officers.

Startled, France's Foch asked pointedly: "You are willing to risk our being driven back to the Loire?" To which Pershing answered as the other top commanders plus British Prime Minister Lloyd George and French Premier Clemenceau looked on in disbelief: "Yes, I am willing to take the risk." Then, recounts Pershing in his memoirs, they "attacked me with all the force and prestige of their high positions...whereupon I said with the greatest possible emphasis, 'Gentlemen, I have thought this program over very deliberately and I will not be coerced.'"[27] With that, he banged his fist on the table and stamped out of the room.

Four months later he again refused to be coerced. On August 30, Foch demanded that four to six AEF divisions be assigned to the French Army, under French command, in a push against the Germans who had begun retreating. Because losing control of these divisions would undercut Pershing's plans for his own long-scheduled AEF offensive and, worse, seriously fragment his newly created First American Army, he balked. Then, in what military historian Thomas Fleming calls "the ultimate insult one general could throw at another," Foch asked searingly: "Do you wish to partake in the battle?" Pershing shot back: "Most assuredly, but as an American Army and in no other way... You have no authority... to call upon me to yield up my command of the American Army and have it scattered among the Allied forces where it will not be an American Army at all." To this, recounts Pershing, Foch "was apparently surprised at my remark, and said, 'I must insist on the arrangement.' To which I replied as we both rose from the table where we sat, 'Marshal Foch, you may insist all you please, but I decline absolutely to agree to your plan. While our army will fight wherever you may decide, it will not fight except as an independent American

Army.'"[28] Later Pershing added: "The morale of our soldiers depends upon their fighting under our flag."[29] The bitterness and even anger with which Pershing recalls these and similar exchanges in his two-volume, Pulitzer Prize-winning *My Experiences in the World War*, published a full thirteen years after the war's end, testify that for him the wounds of such clashes with the Allies long remained raw.

In these Allied-Pershing disputes, history can muster some sympathy for the Allied generals. To them America was plainly and simply a deep manpower reservoir into which they could dip endlessly for replacements for their denuded units. So great, in fact, had been Allied losses that Allied divisions, regiments and even battalions had shrunk dramatically. France's Petain in May 1918 told Pershing that France soon would slash twenty-five divisions to half their size; Britain too was shrinking its battlefield units, cutting, for example, each division from twelve battalions to nine. What the Allies needed was clear; it was not American tactics or American morale; it was fresh flesh; it was American bodies. More specifically, it was the bodies of infantrymen and machine-gunners, the combat troops who bore the brunt of the fighting and the brunt of the casualties. These, implored and then demanded Allied commanders and government leaders, had to be—as they called it—"amalgamated" into the Allied ranks. They had to be folded into the battalions, even the companies, of the British and French armies, issued British and French uniforms and made ready for and then ordered into battle. Without amalgamation, warned the Allies, they would not be able to fight much longer.

But more of history's sympathy must go to Pershing. America had not entered the Great War to amalgamate into the Allies or to follow Allied generals into battle or, as Pershing put it sarcastically, to become "a recruiting agency for either the French or British."[30] Woodrow Wilson, after all, explicitly had assured the American people that their nation was not joining Britain and

France as a fellow "ally," but instead as an "Associate Power," thus preserving independence of action and command. Anything else, rightly, would have been unacceptable to the Congress and the nation. And these were Pershing's specific, crystal clear instructions from both the White House and the War Department. "The forces of the United States are a separate and distinct component of the combined forces, the identity of which must be preserved," read the secret instructions Pershing received on May 26, 1917 from War Secretary Baker. Publicly Baker said: The AEF "could never be anything but an instrument of the policy of the United States."[31] Thus it was official U.S. policy that Pershing continually was echoing to the British and French when he refused amalgamation and when he reminded them, as he did in May 1918, that "America declared war independently of the Allies" and that "there is no agreement between my Government and anybody else that a single American soldier shall be sent to either the British or the French."[32]

To this Pershing reasonably allowed some exceptions. Since his troops had to go to Allied units for training, for example, he agreed that they could be ordered into battle under British or French flags if those units came under attack. In addition, as described in the next chapter, he dispatched AEF divisions to fight under Allied command to counter the German offensives; a few of these divisions never returned to Pershing, remaining with the Allied armies until war's end, their men even donning Allied uniforms.

Moreover, reflecting American society's still harsh racial segregation, four all African-American AEF regiments permanently served with the French Army; neither the AEF nor the British was comfortable with them. Beyond these exceptions, Pershing remained adamantly opposed to amalgamation, greatly upsetting Allied generals and government leaders. Not giving up, London and Paris went behind Pershing's back to lobby the White House and War Department, attempting to undercut his authority. Yet Wilson and Baker, to their great credit, fully supported their AEF commander. "You have the president's entire confidence as you have my own," Baker wrote Pershing, adding, "We will back you in every possible way."[33]

Then the Allies tried blackmailing Pershing by holding back British shipping, declaring their vessels would carry to France only American infantrymen and machine-gunners. There would be no tonnage, they said, for AEF artillery, staff, supply services and other troops essential to create not only the full-fledged American Army that Pershing sought, but even a full-fledged American division. So miserly into mid-1918 was Britain with its shipping tonnage that American forces, until war's end, suffered serious deficiencies in artillery pieces, motor vehicles and other battlefield equipment— including horses and mules.

The animals supply saga typified the obstacles Pershing was encountering as he continued to try to build from scratch his American Army. He needed huge quantities of horses and mules, for they remained the backbone of battlefield transport. A typical AEF division required at least 350 horses and 1,650 mules. They hauled artillery into place, they lugged ammunition, food and other supplies to units in combat, they evacuated the wounded. Animals pulling wagons were almost as ubiquitous on the battlefield as soldiers, as photographs from the front testify. For good reason did horse casualties worry commanders nearly as much as (some would say more than) human casualties. And America had plenty of horses and mules to send Pershing.

The problem was that they took up lots of room on ships. In what he thought was a tradeoff, he agreed to forego tonnage for animals, as essential as they were to his plans, so that more space on ships could be devoted to the infantrymen sought by the Allies. In exchange, Pershing was assured that he could obtain animals locally. French officials promised that every month he could buy 15,000 horses from French farmers. But the farmers, for whom horses understandably were also essential, refused to sell their animals, even for the inflated prices offered by the AEF. As a result, the horse and mule shortage remained of great concern to Pershing throughout the war. "A crippled state as to horses," is how he later described it, explaining that "a considerable portion of our forces" were immobilized by "the French failure to supply animals."[34]

Pershing's rejection of amalgamation and his determination to control his troops were hardly unreasonable or unprecedented. Research by John Terraine, for example, cites the instructions from French King Louis XVI when he sent his soldiers to help the thirteen American colonies revolt against England. The king ordered that "the French troops shall not be dispersed in any manner and they shall serve at all times…under French generals."[35] In the Great War itself, notes Donald Smythe in his study of Pershing, the British never pushed amalgamation on the Australians, Canadians or Indians, nor did the French with their Moroccans, Senegalese or other troops from their colonies. Those troops all went into battle commanded by their own officers.

Motivating Pershing's unyielding resistance to amalgamation was, probably, a bit of personal pride. He surely did not want to be a commander in chief who in fact was not truly "in chief," not totally in command of his men. At work too may have been a bit of Pershing's renowned stubborn streak (what French Premier Clemenceau snidely described as "invincible obstinacy" and "Pershing, with his tight-lipped smile"). But these factors would have been minor; much more was in play. There was, for instance, the serious matter of national pride. Pershing knew, surely correctly, that with American patriotism and frenzied support for the war being whipped up at home by the Creel Committee, Liberty Bond drives and near nonstop pep talks by the Four Minute Men, Americans deserved to hear of and celebrate the battlefield triumphs of their own troops serving in recognizably-named American battalions and regiments and divisions. The satisfaction from this, a reward for having put their sons and husbands at risk, would be diluted enormously were their doughboys to be faceless cogs in victories won by British and French units. Writes Pershing in his memoirs: "No people with a grain of national pride would consent to furnish men to build up the army of another nation."[36]

Important too was Pershing's suspicion, shared by all of Washington, that London and Paris sought to minimize America's independent role on the battlefield as a way of minimizing America's eventual role at a peace conference. A confidential April 6, 1918 AEF memo warned that "America...will have no voice [at the peace councils] if her forces are used up by putting her battalions in French and British units."[37] Most important, without question, in pitting Pershing against amalgamation was his conviction, also felt by Washington, that it would undermine creation of a full-scale American Army. Every soldier, every company, pulled away from him would delay that, as would every ship that failed to bring enough of the auxiliary troops and labor required to field and supply an independent force. That the Allies deliberately were preventing such auxiliary forces from arriving in France was suspected in Washington. American historian David Kennedy writes that Army Chief of Staff Tasker Bliss complained that the Allies wanted "a million [American] men there and yet no American army and commander." It was even believed by U.S. military planners that London was understating its shipping tonnage availability to stop fully composed AEF divisions from arriving in Europe.[38]

Whatever the reasons for Pershing's stubbornness, it ultimately paid off. In the war's crucial final months, America did indeed field an independent army. The American First Army, fourteen divisions strong, was deployed on August 10, 1918, followed on October 12 by the American Second Army. America had moved far beyond casting its shadow over Europe's battlefield. Now the AEF was on the ground in great numbers, nearly 900,000 by the end of June 1918 and growing rapidly, with some 10,000 doughboys arriving each day, shipload after shipload. America had opened a spigot flooding doughboys onto a battlefield on which manpower on all sides had grown scarce. These arriving doughboys, anticipated and actual, were the first new factor introduced on the Western Front since that battlefield had frozen in the late months of 1914. They changed everything. And so doing, they changed the course of the century.

CHAPTER 6

AMERICA BREAKS THE STALEMATE

B Y THE TIME THAT THE GREAT WAR's guns fell silent on the late morning of November 11, 1918, Americans had seen Western Front action for about a year, in thirteen battles, great and small. They suffered 114,000 killed and 205,690 wounded, many very critically, with limbs amputated, bodies and faces disfigured, hearing and eyesight ruined. After tallying the toll, history can ask: Did they make a difference?

And history's answer is: Yes, they clearly did.

In shorthand, the difference made by the American Expeditionary Force can be encapsulated in a single large number: "One Million." This was the staggering combined British and French losses as their armies in spring 1918 were pulverized by, reeled from, regrouped and then began throwing back five massive, blitzkrieg-like German offensives. This also was the number of German losses. And, most relevant, this too was the number of American doughboys who had landed in France by mid-July 1918, when the last of the German thrusts had been halted. This number dramatizes how decisively the Americans transformed the Western Front's arithmetic by making up in full the horrendous Allied losses. For Germany, there was nothing to make up its losses, no prospects of manpower replenishment, no way to rebound. "America became the deciding factor in the war," later said General Erich Ludendorff, Germany's most important commander and architect of German battlefield strategy.[1]

And the million doughboys were just the start. They were to keep coming and keep coming, pouring from America's seemingly bottomless manpower reservoir at the very moment when Britain, France and Germany were running out of men and had begun calling up fifty-year-olds and even sixty-year-olds. In short, the AEF's arrival sharply tipped the Western Front's balance of forces and ensured Germany's defeat. "Rare are the times in a great war," writes World War One historian John Keegan, "when the fortunes of one side or the other are transformed by the sudden accretion of a disequilibrating reinforcement." The year 1918 was such a time.

By transforming the fortunes of the Allied side, America wrote the last chapter of the Great War, giving it an unexpected ending. It turned conventional analysis and expectations upside down. When the AEF began arriving in Europe in force in late 1917, Allied commanders anticipated no major offensive against the Germans until 1919 and no breakthrough likely until 1920. This also was American Commander in Chief John Pershing's timetable. But the enormous and accelerating U.S. troop mobilization, with the prospective gusher of 300,000 fresh doughboys arriving in France each month, changed everyone's calculations—and then their actions.

It sharply changed Germany's calculations, prompting its High Command to gamble desperately and rush to launch the five offensives it hoped could bring victory before even more Americans arrived at the front. These offensives, after initial impressive and (for the Allies) frightening gains, ultimately so drained German resources, manpower and morale that the German Army was weakened fatally and began pulling back. The AEF buildup similarly changed the

Allies' calculations, bolstering their shaky confidence and boosting their morale. Above all, it gave them the manpower advantage to pursue vigorously and massively the retreating Germans and to withstand the deadly German counterattacks which had, throughout the war, always stymied sustained Allied advances. This achieved what British and French generals had sought from the war's earliest months, a breakout from static trench combat to the mobility of open warfare, sending waves of Allied troops crashing across the landscape, using sweeping and enveloping tactics as old as Napoleon and Grant but now augmented and multiplied spectacularly by those new weapons of movement and momentum—tanks and war planes.

This Allied and American breakout did not by any means destroy the German Army, which remained powerful and still fully in control of huge swaths of Belgian and French soil. But it destroyed that army's will to fight. German infantrymen, having been assured that their punishing spring offensive sacrifices would end the war and bring, at last, a peace allowing them to go home, now grew so demoralized that they uncharacteristically began balking at fighting, disrespecting officers, breaking rules, getting drunk and even deserting (in what became increasing numbers). As significant, if not more so, it demoralized the German military command; the towering, imperious and reflexively smug Ludendorff was a broken man.

For all of this, America's role was critical. It was the AEF buildup which, without question, drove the Germans to gamble and take the risks which then so weakened their forces. Without this gamble and its devastating consequences, the Western Front would have remained stalemated. Without the arrival of doughboys by the shipload, there would have been no new troops to replenish the staggering losses the British and French had suffered in the German offensives and no Allied manpower superiority. Without the AEF divisions, now formed into the million-man-plus American First Army, the Allied/American pursuit of the falling-back Germans could not have accelerated to a galloping and ultimately victorious counteroffensive. Instead, the Germans would have retired, as they had assumed they would, to shorter, more defensible lines and then dug in, as had happened over and over again in that war of trenches and machine guns, and held back the advancing Allies.

Perhaps nothing more graphically testifies to America's game-changing role in the war than a snapshot of the Western Front on the war's last day. The Americans, formally in the war for only nineteen months and actually on the battlefield for only thirteen, nonetheless on the final day of the Great War manned positions stretching eighty-three miles along the front; this was longer than the British Army's seventy miles. And those doughboys were fresh and itching to fight ("straight and tall and vigorous," in the words of *New York Times* military editor Hanson Baldwin), while the British and French soldiers were tired and worn down.

It was the AEF's continued streaming onto the battlefield and its combat successes that propelled the Germans in October 1918 to seek an armistice. And it was the mounting masses of doughboys that emboldened the British and French, in the three-week-long armistice negotiations, to turn the screws ever tighter on the Germans. It thus is near impossible to posit a German defeat without the AEF on the battlefield. The Germans, of course, still would have been exhausted and their ranks depleted, but so would the British and French. And exhausted, it takes but little speculation to envision, they all eventually would have trudged reluctantly to a negotiating table for the kind of compromise peace that had ended every Europe-wide war for the previous three centuries. Instead, exploiting the AEF, London and Paris imposed a Carthaginian armistice on Berlin.

Strangely, to acknowledge America's central and decisive role in defeating Germany is not to recognize an obvious truism but to wade into a century-old controversy. No sooner had an armistice been declared than did erupt the debate over how much the AEF actually contributed to victory over Germany. The British and the French, who for so long had been begging America to come to their aid in the war, almost immediately began dismissing ("dissing," in today's argot) the AEF and Pershing. Since then, five generations of military historians and analysts of warfare have picked apart and dissected every aspect of the AEF's training, organization, weaponry and performance in battle. Often analysts have focused on AEF failings: flawed tactics, fumbling green officers, raw doughboys, shortage of American-produced tanks, artillery and planes and Pershing's stubbornness. There are strong whiffs of truth in all of the fault-findings, as will be seen below. But in the end, in the final analysis, the analysis that history counts most, the AEF did far more right than wrong, succeeded far more than failed. In the end, America transformed the Western Front and so doing won the war against Germany.

Germany's Generals Roll the Dice

The approaching gusher of arriving Americans riveted Germany's attention. Its generals needn't be an Einstein (then a thirty-eight-year-old physics professor in Berlin) to do the math. To the German High Command it made little difference under what flag the arriving doughboys fought, what uniforms they wore or who commanded them. The searing Allied arguments over doughboy amalgamation were of no concern to the Germans. Only one thing counted: the numbers. And they were moving inexorably (in the purest meaning of that word) against Germany, shipload by shipload, something Allied propaganda aimed at Germany began trumpeting. There was creeping realization in the High Command that time had become Germany's main enemy. If its army ever expected to crush the Allies, march into Paris as it had in 1871 and impose a punitive peace, Germany must strike soon. Or, failing that, even if the German Army sought nothing more than the kind of offensive gains that would give Berlin leverage at a peace conference, then it also must strike soon, before a critical mass of AEF soldiers arrived, were trained and headed for the Western Front. At a crucial High Command meeting in November 1917, head of operations Major Georg Wetzell put it very bluntly: Germany had "to deliver an annihilating blow...before American aid [could] become effective."

Field Marshal Paul von Hindenburg and General Erich Ludendorff, Germany's pair of top commanders, agreed. They ordered work to begin on plans for what the German press later called *Kaiserschlacht,* or the Kaiser's battle, a series of offensives for spring 1918. It was a roll of the dice (in John Keegan's words) which would send into battle almost every last bit of their manpower reserves, playing what some of their staff said was Germany's "last card."[2] Writing thirteen years later, B.H. Liddell Hart called it "a race between the effect of Germany's blow and the arrival of American reinforcements."[3] And it became a race whose risk and consequences of failure were vastly greater than Hindenburg and Ludendorff ever could have reckoned. As history records, it was to be an all-or-nothing gamble.

On Germany's home front too, time seemed to be running out. Fast evaporating was any patience with the war. Food (including the unappetizing turnip, typically fodder for animals) was being rationed tighter and tighter; so were coal and wood for heating and cotton and wool for warm clothing. Goods grew so short they almost disappeared. Before the war, each week a German on average was eating 2.3 lbs of meat; in late 1917 it was but 0.3 lbs. Such skimpy diets were leading to malnutrition and, worse, to pneumonia and tuberculosis, pushing up the death rate among women and children more than fifty percent above pre-war levels. Laborers, because of the battlefield's enormous manpower demands, were growing so scarce that the government, in effect, drafted all German males age seventeen to sixty to work in factories and fields if they weren't already in the army. Women too were pulled into the workforce. These conditions, predictably, triggered labor discontent, strikes and even food riots.

Meanwhile, the Socialist majority in the Reichstag, the Imperial parliament, was growing bolder in criticizing the war. Such criticisms even could be heard from centrist parties. In July 1917, the Reichstag, though lacking any real say in military or foreign policy, passed a "peace resolution," calling on its government to end the war "without annexations of territory or forcible measures of political, economic or financial character." Having just watched worn-down, war-weary Russians, backed by many soldiers and sailors, bring down their Tsar and overthrow a centuries-old imperial regime, the German High Command for good reason feared the same thing happening to Germany if the war continued much longer.

Much of German home front suffering was being inflicted by the formidable British naval blockade, which for three years had been stopping neutral nations from trading with Germany. It was, after all, to break this blockade, or at least force London to loosen it, that Berlin in February 1917 had ordered its submarine commanders to attack all vessels entering the war zone that Germany had declared around Britain and its allies. Though Berlin had reckoned (correctly, as it turned out) that such unrestricted U-boat warfare could bring America into the war against Germany, it also calculated that its U-boats would cripple British commerce and hence greatly weaken Britain before American troops could affect the Western Front's balance of forces. It would take but a half year, confident German admirals had assured Kaiser Wilhelm II and Germany's civilian government, for Germany's 100 U-boats to bring Britain to its knees by sinking 600,000 tons of British shipping each month.

Initially, the admirals delivered their numbers. In 1917's first half, U-boats sank an average of 630,000 tons of shipping per month, destroying 1,505 freighters. That April, calculates Political Scientist Benjamin Fordham in his 2005 study, about one of every four merchant vessels leaving Britain failed to return.[4] The pain dealt Britain and France was horrifying, depriving their civilians of food and their factories of key materials for making weapons and munitions. Crisis mood, at times panic, was mounting in London and Paris; their frantic and increasingly desperate cables to Washington helped propel America into the war. Had losses to the U-boats continued at that initial pace, Germany's admirals may have triumphed. Britain well may have had to make concessions to Germany and relax the blockade, perhaps even sue for peace.

But the losses did not continue at that rate. In May 1917, after stubbornly resisting for months, Britain's Royal Navy, helped by the French and American navies, began deploying warships to accompany merchantmen on the North and South Atlantic and Mediterranean if those vessels would cluster and travel in convoys. There was nothing new about this, of course. In the age of sail, warships routinely guarded convoys against raiders. But Great War British admirals had regarded convoys as too complicated to organize and operate and, moreover, as a degrading, unmilitary-like baby-sitting assignment for an advanced warship. In endless discussions they offered endless reasons why convoys couldn't work.

Well, they were wrong. After the first convoy formed up on May 10, 1917, sinkings decreased almost immediately. At the same time, U-boat losses mounted as Allied and American destroyers, steaming at twice U-boat speed, perfected anti-submarine tactics using heavy guns and depth charges. As a result of the combination of fewer merchantmen losses and greater U-boat losses, American and British shipyards found themselves turning out new ships faster than the Germans could sink them, while U-boats were being sunk faster than German shipyards could replace them. This meant, concludes naval historian Paul Halpern, that "submarines could not win the war for Germany."[5] That too was the conclusion of Hindenburg and Ludendorff. They had played their submarine card to no avail. The sole trump now seemingly left in their hands was one final Western Front push, promising Germany a victory jackpot. Or, if not victory, then an advantageous peace.

That such a push, a series of massive offensives, could succeed in 1918 where earlier Western Front offensives all had failed seemed plausible to the High Command for two reasons. First, it would have dozens of extra divisions to field, freed up from the Eastern Front where Russia had just collapsed. Though Russia, allied with Britain and France, had continued to fight Germany and Austria-Hungary in the immediate months after Tsar Nicholas II had been dethroned and arrested in February 1917, that changed dramatically when Russia suffered huge losses at German hands at the September 1917 battle of Riga and, more important, when Vladimir Lenin's Bolsheviks seized power the following month. Concerned solely about imposing their rule upon Russia, the Bolsheviks had no desire or reason to stay at war; in exchange for peace, they accepted extraordinarily harsh and humiliating German demands.

For the Bolsheviks, as history later confirmed, it was the right move. And for Germany, it meant that its two-front war by and large was over. At least a million of its soldiers now could be transferred from the Eastern Front to the Western, giving Germany (until the AEF began arriving in force) a ten percent manpower advantage over the Allies. Though it was not a huge advantage, since typically the attacker needs a two-to-one edge over the defender, it was the best Germany ever had in the west. And it was good enough to improve the odds when the dice were to be rolled.

A second factor giving Hindenburg and Ludendorff confidence in an offensive was the promise that newly crafted tactics at last would drive the British and French from their trenches into the open. There they would be hunted down and crushed by new fast-moving specially trained German units called storm troopers. Developed by German General Oskar von Hutier and used by him with extraordinary success against the Russians at Riga and later by Germans assisting the Austro-Hungarian Army in their devastating autumn 1917 defeat of Italian armies at Caporetto, the new tactics discarded what had been staple elements of the war's massive attacks.

In the typical Western Front offensive, honed over three years, heavy artillery first would bombard the enemy for days, even weeks, seeking to destroy trenches, machine-gun emplacements, bunkers and barbed wire to reduce resistance to the coming assault. When the barrage ended, masses of attacking infantry would pile out of their trenches and push across the field which, ostensibly, had been cleared for them. In moving forward, these attackers had been drilled to keep their lines straight and tight to prevent gaps from opening which the enemy could exploit. If the attackers did encounter resistance (as they always did) and suffer losses (as they also always did), reserves were rushed onto the field to replenish the ranks. And then the attempt to push forward continued.

That was the plan and, except for tiny variations, that also was the execution—always, as discussed earlier, with disastrous results. Since many defenders survived the artillery shelling, the attackers invariably ran into a wall of machine gun fire. Even in the opening moments, when those on attack have an advantage over those on defense, advances were tiny. And then always came the brutal counterattack, rolling back most of the initial gains. Such was the typical script of a Western Front offensive, acted and reenacted over and again.

It was this script that Hindenburg and Ludendorff were determined to tear up by using General von Hutier's ideas, what they called "maneuver of rupture." Its aim: to rupture Allied trench defenses. Surprise and speed were its main elements. In some respects, and certainly in spirit, this foreshadowed Nazi Germany's astoundingly successful "blitzkrieg" assaults of World War Two, which added the crucial ingredients of tanks and war planes. It also contained aspects of open warfare, prompting Pershing smugly to point to Hutier tactics as vindication of what he long had been advocating. In the new German script, explains Rod Paschall, "set-piece plans were out, and infantry, not artillery, would determine the pace and often even the point of attack. Leadership would have to be exercised on the battlefield, not in rear area headquarters."[6]

These are the tactics still dominant on today's battlefields.

To achieve surprise, the Germans abandoned the long preliminary artillery barrages, which (predictably) always had tipped off the enemy to the looming attack. Instead, in shellings lasting hours rather than days, German guns mainly sought not to obliterate enemy positions but, through an extremely powerful pounding which included gas and smoke, to unleash chaos by disrupting and confusing the enemy. To achieve speed, the barrage was followed not by masses of infantry in tight linear formation heading into battle according to a detailed plan, but by scores of nimble small units. Trained, writes Pershing biographer Donald Smythe, "to great audacity and boldness" and armed with light machine guns, light mortars, flamethrowers and grenades, these storm troopers sped over no man's land. Ordered to improvise and exploit opportunities, they probed for weak spots to destroy, poking holes in the defender's lines. Refusing to be stalled, they bypassed strong-points, flowing around them, says Smythe, "like water running downhill."[7]

Waiting behind in readiness was the great mass of German infantry. In the traditional offensive they would have been held in reserve to replace fallen attackers, to keep the advancing line intact. Now they prepared to pour through the gaps opened by the storm troopers and then fan out to consolidate gains. They also pivoted back to attack the bypassed and isolated enemy strong-points from the rear and the flanks rather than, as in the traditional offensive, head on. Meanwhile the storm troopers kept leaping ahead (some experts call them "leapfrog" tactics), probing for further weak spots to begin the procedure all over.

This is how Hindenburg and Ludendorff expected to break the Western Front stalemate in spring 1918. Using their extra manpower and these tactics they prepared to unleash a series of shattering offensives, one following on the heels of the other to keep the Allies off balance and on the run. Their aim: first crush the British and then turn against the French, all before AEF masses arrived.

And their planning was sound. The new tactics worked marvelously—initially. When launched, the German attacks thoroughly breached Allied lines for the first time since autumn 1914. It seemed a replay of Riga, of Caporetto. Completely surprising their enemies, the storm troopers, as trained, punched holes in Allied trench lines, allowing the German infantry mass, also as trained, to exploit and consolidate the gains. Allied divisions, whole armies of them, were sent reeling. Allied command structure broke down. Driven from their frontline and fallback trenches, Allied soldiers turned heel and retreated, suffering enormous casualties (as did the Germans).

To stunned Allied generals and their governments in London and Paris, it unbelievably seemed like August and September 1914 all over again, with German armies threatening to drive the British into the sea and the French from Paris. Indeed, the French government prepared to flee to Bordeaux (as it had in 1914) and the U.S. Embassy readied trucks to evacuate its staff from Paris. Allied commanders visibly and uncontrollably panicked, with Britain's Douglas Haig despairing that "our backs [are] to the wall" and France's Henri-Philippe Petain telling his troops that "the fate of France hangs in the balance." Pershing too was unsettled, later writing that it was "the greatest crisis of the war."[8] Shockingly, a German victory, after nearly four years of deadlock, seemed possible.

But that, as history knows, did not happen. Allied generals and Pershing overreacted. The Germans in 1918 ultimately failed just as they had failed four years earlier, and for nearly the same reasons. Despite the chaos and palpable panic, Allied lines only bent; they didn't break. Instead, the British and French rallied, stemmed the German onslaught and began pushing back. By early August, it was Germany's generals who were stunned and panicked, with a shaken Ludendorff muttering about Germany's "darkest day in the war." Within weeks, he and Hindenburg had to accept the undeniable: Their great gamble had failed.

"The Greatest Onslaught in the History of the World"

That, however, was not at all how it looked on March 21, 1918 when the first German offensive began. On that day and those immediately following, the Germans appeared unstoppable, as Hindenburg and Ludendorff hurled seventy-six divisions against the twenty-eight British divisions holding a key western sector of the front. After the short five-hour, 6,000-gun artillery barrage of unprecedented ferocity ("a hurricane of fire and thunder" in Holger Herwig's accounting), storm troopers, commanded by Hutier himself and using his tactics, swarmed across no man's land. Their speed, firepower and numbers took the British troops by complete surprise. The German assault quickly shifted to pursuit. Fleeing the attacking Germans, the dazed Tommies abandoned one trench line after the other; it was complete chaos as some of their battalions just disappeared. "The front crumbled like plaster," writes British military historian John Terraine in his 1978 study of the war's final year. To Winston Churchill, then Britain's Minister of Munitions and already a master of hyperbole, it was "the greatest onslaught in the history of the world."[9]

For the first time in the Great War, one side had penetrated the other's trenches and forced the battle into the open. Accustomed only to a static battlefield, the British soldiers and their officers were in visible disarray, unsure how to cope with open, fluid combat. In his memoirs Pershing almost gloats, writing that the British troops were "seriously handicapped" by their "long adherence" to trench warfare and were puzzled that, upon leaving their trenches, "there was not another trench somewhere for them to get into."[10] Discipline began cracking; in some areas British officers only by brandishing pistols were able to keep their troops together in their units.

By the end of the offensive's first day, Germany had taken 140 square miles from the British. Two years earlier, on that same battlefield near the Somme River, Allied troops had fought twenty weeks and suffered a half-million casualties to capture but ninety-eight square miles. Writes Keegan: The British Army "suffered its first true defeat since trench warfare had begun."[11]

It was for the Germans, seemingly, a romp. But only seemingly. After falling back, the British forces rallied and began resisting stubbornly, slowing, ultimately stopping, the German thrust. This earned Ludendorff's respect. After the war he admitted, most likely self-servingly, that "the enemy's resistance was beyond our powers." He also would admit that for all of its gains, his offensive fell seriously short of his main goal, capturing the vital Amiens railway junction. Worse, the attack had revealed significant flaws in the Hutier formula. While the storm troopers and follow-up infantry did, indeed, speed forward and devastate the enemy, the German supply line could not keep pace. Soon, the attackers began running low on ammunition, trucks, artillery cover for further advances and food for themselves and for their starving horses.

So hungry were German soldiers that units, sometimes whole divisions, stopped pushing the attack forward so that they could plunder the well-stocked warehouses they found in British rear areas, gorging themselves on food and becoming drunk on wine. One German captain reported that he could not get his men out of the wine cellars in the overrun areas. Another told Ludendorff that his men were not adequately dealing with British machine-gun nests because "they were too busy searching for food." By April 5, unable to deny that his forces had run out of steam, Ludendorff halted this first of the spring offensives.[12]

Four days later, on April 9, before the Allies could catch their breath, Ludendorff struck again, launching his second offensive, as before against the British (and a Portuguese division). And again the Germans romped to astounding, frightening, initial gains only again to falter as British resistance firmed and German divisions outran their supply lines and their artillery's ability to keep up with their rapid advance. As in the first offensive, hungry German soldiers delayed pushing forward as they pillaged British supply dumps, feasting on food and alcohol. "The troops will not attack, despite orders," reported a German officer to his superiors. On April 27, Ludendorff ended this offensive. He once again had captured considerable territory, but also once again had failed to destroy his enemies. This meant he was worse off strategically than when he had begun, for he now would have to commit extra divisions simply to defend his newly won land or abandon it.

One month later, on May 27, Ludendorff turned to the front's French sector, in a bold attempt to capture Paris and break the French will to continue fighting. Known as the battle of Chemin de Dames, this third offensive began with a four-hour artillery barrage of even greater ferocity than in the two earlier offensives and deployed the massive Krupp-made eighty-one-mile-range naval gun, mounted on rails, to bring Paris under fire. This was the famous "Paris Gun," (sometimes confused with the "Big Bertha" giant howitzer) whose barrel length equaled a twenty-story building and whose twenty-mile trajectory arch was so high that it became the first device ever to put a man-made projectile into the stratosphere. By war's end, versions of this gun could fire their shells 100 miles, a distance not exceeded until the 1960s. Since the Germans were not able to aim the gun accurately, it was mainly a harassment and terror weapon, landing some 367 shells randomly in Paris, killing 256 in its three-month deployment.

In this offensive's opening week, France's first encounter with Hutier tactics, German gains again were astounding. Paschall calls it "the greatest offensive of the war."[13] Ludendorff's armies captured huge swaths of the front and drove within fifty-six miles of Paris. French generals cried as they ordered their troops to retreat, watching them abandon towns for which so much French blood had been spilled in the previous three-and-one-half years. The French Army seemed broken and Commander in Chief Petain ordered it to: "Hold your ground! Stand firm! Our [American] comrades are arriving."

When AEF units were sped to reinforce the French, they witnessed extensive French soldier looting of deserted farms and villages. "French troops, some of them drunk from despoiled wine cellars," writes Smythe, "had looted everything not nailed down." The doughboys found farm animals slaughtered by the retreating French troops and, in the houses, dresser drawers and closets stripped of their contents and dumped on the floor. So rapidly were the Germans advancing that Pershing cabled the War Department that "the possibility of losing Paris has become apparent." Frenchmen obviously felt the same way; up to one million Parisians fled their capital. Once again, a frightening German victory seemed conceivable. After having dinner with France's top commanders, Pershing wrote in his diary: "It would be difficult to imagine a more depressed group of officers. They sat through the meal scarcely speaking a word as they contemplated what was probably the most serious situation of the war."[14]

They were wrong, as was Pershing. Ultimately, this German third offensive was no more effective than the first two. It may have conquered huge sections of the front but was halted on June 4 when, writes military historian David Trask, "German divisions soon outran both their artillery and their supplies and fell victim to exhaustion."[15]

Ditto for the fourth offensive, launched June 9 and waged but six days before Ludendorff recognized it too would fall short of its goals and called it off. No different was the story for the fifth offensive, unleashed on July 15, intending to resume the third offensive's drive to capture Paris. Ludendorff threw at French lines almost all of his remaining forces in the west. But this attack, as ferocious as it was and as much as it scared the French, too was over almost as soon as it had begun. So fatigued were Germany's troops that they could push forward for just four days before Ludendorff pulled them back. Neither he nor the Allied and American commanders could know it at the time, but this was to be

Germany's last offensive action; it no longer could attack. Germany now would be permanently on the defensive.

That was not then at all obvious. Tactically, on paper, as depicted by a Western Front map, Germany's spring offensives were impressively, even astoundingly, successful. The new Hutier tactics repeatedly had punctured the West's trench defenses. As a result, all along the front Allied troops had been thrown back farther than at any time since the war's inaugural weeks. Shells had rained on Paris, igniting panic. And panic too reigned in Allied command headquarters. Looking about Europe in July 1918, it was impossible not to be impressed, even intimidated, by Imperial Germany's new sway, surely its greatest in its history. In the east it had defeated Russia and was dominating the Baltic lands, controlling the Ukraine's breadbasket and was within reach of Baku's oil fields. In the west, Germany was occupying vast and industrially rich sectors of Belgium and France, had forced the British to abandon much of their hard-won gains of previous years and seemingly was within strike of Paris.

But the map was misleading. Germany may have gobbled up territory, but it lost leverage. It occupied more of France than ever before, but to no advantage (except, perhaps, as potential bargaining power at an eventual peace conference). To be sure, from late March to the end of June 1918, Ludendorff had carved out huge new salients poking deeply into France. But this was a costly gain, calculates World War One expert Hew Strachan, adding at least seventy miles to the Western Front that Germany had to defend.[16] And while Germany had badly bloodied Allied armies and commanders, it had not destroyed them. In fact, it had been bloodied every bit as badly as had the British and French.

The raw numbers dispassionately tell much of the story. The Germans inflicted some 450,000 casualties (dead, seriously wounded, missing and captured) on the British and 490,000 on the French. This was an astounding number, even by that war's standards. But the Germans paid dearly for this, sacrificing towering numbers of its best men and junior officers (and horses); their own casualties of 963,000 exceeded the combined Allied losses. And those Germans who survived—who were neither dead nor wounded nor captured—were exhausted and demoralized. For the German soldier, writes military historian O'Brien Browne, the offensives' failure to end the war "bred cynicism, frustration and disillusionment… These men no longer believed the propaganda of their own government." This meant, Browne continues, in a judgment universally supported by other historians, that the Hindenburg/Ludendorff offensives were the "most ironic of battles… The winner was the loser and the loser the ultimate winner [and] the Allies emerged stronger and more unified than ever."[17]

Thus the results of Germany's spring offensive gamble were in: Germany had lost it. The German Army never recovered from its 1918 offensives.

In the riveting drama of those offensives, history must ask: What was the role of the American Expeditionary Force? The shorthand answer is that the AEF played both a central and a marginal role. It was central because absent the looming presence of the AEF itself, absent the specter of shiploads of arriving doughboys, the Germans would not have rolled the dice; there would have been no do-or-die spring offensives. Unambiguously straightforward on this are Hindenburg's memoirs, recalling that "we had to keep the prospects of American intervention steadily before our eyes."[18] It thus was, history records, the AEF which prompted Germany to launch the operations which fatally weakened the German Army. But once the fighting actually began on March 21, the AEF role was marginal, with the doughboys contributing barely at all to the Allied resistance to the attacking Germans. Here, again, the raw numbers tell a story: AEF dead and wounded in the offensives' four months were 9,685, a tiny fraction of the two million combined

Allied and German losses.

That the AEF role was so marginal in the spring 1918 combat is a matter of extraordinary historical importance. It means that America was not needed to prevent a German victory. It refutes any argument that without the AEF, Germany's spring 1918 offensives would have succeeded, that Britain would have been driven from the battlefield, that Paris would have been captured and that Germany would have won the war and then imposed a crippling peace on the Allies. Such a triumphant Imperial Germany, continues this flawed argument, then would have emerged as Europe's controlling power and a serious geostrategic and economic threat to America. According to this reasoning, America's declaring war on Germany thus greatly served America's interests because the AEF was absolutely necessary to prevent such a German triumph.

Were this true, it indeed would validate and vindicate America's entry into the Great War. The trouble is, this argument collapses under history's weight of facts, under what actually happened on the battlefield. In responding to the ferocious German attacks, to the unprecedented violence unleashed by Hindenburg and Ludendorff, the British and French generals and their forces ultimately demonstrated that they did not need Americans to save them from defeat. They were capable of saving themselves. And that they did—without the AEF. The record of this is beyond dispute. Until the final weeks of the offensives, the British and French fought the Germans with almost no doughboy help.

Some AEF troops, of course, did clash with Germans in the first offensive. But they could hardly be called reinforcements. They were simply a handful of AEF engineer companies that happened to find themselves repairing railways and building roads in the British sector when the Germans overran British lines. Hastily issued arms, the American engineers were thrown into battle. By all accounts, they fought well, suffering seventy-eight casualties. Their pale numbers, however, had no impact on the battle's outcome. Even so, they made history. These engineers, writes S.L.A. Marshall, were "the first American troops to know full-scale battle since the Civil War."[19]

The AEF story was the same in the second German offensive, launched April 9. Some 280 doughboys (again, mainly engineers working in the British sector) hurriedly were pulled into combat but added little to Britain's eventual success in halting the German advance. The situation began changing by late May and the third German offensive. As AEF numbers in Europe mounted, the AEF's 2nd Division (which included a Marine brigade) and 3rd Division were dispatched by Pershing to reinforce French efforts to block the German march on Paris. The Americans fought hard and heroically. From this battle sprang one of those episodes that rooted itself in U.S. wartime lore, repeated across the decades and, in this instance, more likely to be true than apocryphal. In John Keegan's telling, a demoralized French officer, leading his troops in retreat, encountered U.S. Marine Corps Captain Lloyd Williams and told him that he too should consider retreat. To which the Marine, exhibiting what became celebrated as endearing American "can do" bravado, exploded: "Retreat? Hell no, we just got here."[20]

Captain Williams was right. The AEF was just getting to France—and now in rapidly accelerating numbers. By Ludendorff's fifth and final offensive, in mid-July 1918, about 10,000 doughboys every day were landing in France. It was at this moment that the AEF began to register its vast difference on the Western Front, the kind of difference that the German High Command had dreaded and that had led it to gamble on the offensives. By this fifth offensive, however, with German troops obviously an exhausted, spent force, the doughboys were not needed to blunt a German advance. The Allies already had done that. But this left them nearly as exhausted and spent as the Germans. By visible contrast, the now million-strong doughboys were fresh and eager for combat. Their swelling ranks conclusively shaped the decisions and actions of the next (and what was to be the final) 100 days of war. They inspired the

Allied commanders, as the Germans faltered in their fifth offensive, to risk deploying Allied reserves in a counterattack. And then AEF manpower enabled the counterattack to become the full-blown counteroffensive which defeated Germany.

Though not needed to save Britain and France from defeat in 1918, the AEF was needed to transform what began as an Allied push-back into an all-out offensive. Without the AEF, the Allies and Germans, each staggering from the one million casualties that each had suffered in the offensives, almost assuredly would have collapsed back into stalemated Western Front warfare. Instead, the AEF was a transfusion bringing sustenance and energy to the exhausted Allied ranks. There was no transfusion for the Germans.

Counterattack Surges into Counteroffensive

The Allied counterattack began carefully and methodically. It drew on reserves that France's Ferdinand Foch, having been made the most senior commander (an actual generalissimo) of all Allied and AEF troops in late March, had been saving just in case an opportunity offered itself to exploit German weakness. Holding back these reserves, refusing to rush them to bolster the British and French armies being hammered by the German offensives, was a gamble, perhaps no less so than Ludendorff's. But this was a gamble that paid off big, making it one of the conflict's most important and consequential strategic decisions. And this winning gamble and its skillful execution deservedly have won, through the decades, respect for Foch as the war's most successful strategist.

Throughout the stressful weeks of German advances, Foch remained unshakeable. Though the offensives were bringing German troops within striking distance of Paris or seemingly were about to crush the British Army, he resisted mounting and urgent pleas from his generals for reinforcements. Repeatedly (and stubbornly) he declared that the British and French forces on the line could hold back the Germans. His message to British Commander in Chief Haig and French Commander in Chief Petain in effect was: "You are stronger than you think; the Germans are weaker than you think." They were not convinced. But Foch was certain that his reserve divisions ultimately could be much better deployed against what he bet would be Ludendorff's exhausted armies than as reinforcements for Haig and Petain. He was right. But even he did not realize just how weak had become Germany's forces, how much they were suffering from their huge losses of men, of junior officers, of horses. Or how their territory gains (their ostensible victories) had left them in precarious positions, protected only by lightly fortified trenches, with extended and hard-to-defend lines of supply.

That weakness became clear almost as soon as Foch on July 18 ordered a counterattack against the now stalled and faltering German armies closest to Paris, in the Marne River area. History calls this the Second Battle of the Marne. The first had been the great French victory (remembered reverently in France to this day as the Miracle of the Marne) nearly four years earlier, in September 1914. Then the advancing German armies, which had been barreling through Belgium and France nearly nonstop from the day the war began, finally were blocked by five French armies and one British Army, quashing Berlin's plans for a quick victory. It was this French success that had forced the Germans to pull back and dig in, shifting to the static trench warfare which then defined the Western Front.

The Second Battle of the Marne, though not as celebrated in the public mind as the First, is just as important. It not only stopped the German offensive but set the Germans on what became their permanent retreat. For his attack Foch was able to assemble huge numbers of British, French and Italian troops plus, importantly, six AEF divisions, organized into the U.S. First Corps and Third Corps. With an AEF division numbering 26,000 to 28,000 men, more than twice as large as French, British and German divisions, America for the first time was making its presence felt on the battlefield. With each American division, in effect, equaling at least two Allied or German divisions, the doughboys impressively comprised about a quarter of Foch's force. This AEF readiness to join Foch's campaign was a hint at and confirmation of how the doughboys decisively would change the Western Front's arithmetic.

For two days, Allied and AEF troops pummeled the Germans, inflicting enormous casualties. Bending under the beating, Ludendorff on July 20 ordered a retreat. Within two weeks his armies had fallen all the way back to where they had begun in spring, yielding every square yard of territory that their offensives had purchased at such enormous cost to Germany. Only when they had reached their well-fortified original lines were they at last able to halt the Allied and AEF advance. The Second Battle of the Marne was over and, as the First, a huge victory for France. The victory had enormous consequences. It "was decisive," writes Canadian World War One expert Timothy Travers, "in shifting the balance of the war against the German army."[21]

This solidly was confirmed almost immediately. No sooner had the Germans been pushed back from the Marne than Foch struck elsewhere. The tipping point, the moment the Allied and AEF counterattack accelerated into an all-out counteroffensive, was the second week of August, in the British sector. There Haig's British Expeditionary Force, reinforced by Australian, Canadian and New Zealand divisions, crushed and sent into flight the German armies just outside the key rail hub at Amiens, the important prize that Ludendorff had failed to capture in April. It is a battle loved to be recounted by military historians; so much that Haig and his troops did turned out right and proved effective. For the first time in the war, indeed in history, war planes, tanks and artillery were coordinated to support infantry advances, what experts now call "combined-arms assault." It also marked the end of static trench warfare.

It began on August 8 when Haig hurled some 1,900 planes, nearly 600 tanks and ten divisions (with another fifteen in reserve) against the twenty-nine tired German divisions holding their lines outside Amiens. On the first day, his forces gained an average of seven miles along the ten-mile front, a huge advance by Western Front experience. Mimicking, in many ways, Germany's Hutier tactics of the spring, Haig's was a surprise assault of overwhelming force. To ensure that surprise, Haig, like Hutier, abandoned the long preparatory artillery barrages, designed to destroy enemy defenses (though often failing at that) but which gave the enemy a clear signal of an attack's imminence. For Haig and his generals now, as for Hutier earlier, artillery no longer was intended to destroy but rather to disrupt and confuse, forcing the opposing Germans to hunker down as British troops, with their artillery cover creeping about a football field-length ahead of them, quickly crossed the field in attack.

It worked stunningly well, tearing a huge hole in the German lines. In just a few hours, six German divisions had collapsed and units began surrendering en masse. So rapid was the British advance that a group of German officers were captured while at breakfast. After two days' fierce fighting, 20,000 Germans were dead and 30,000 had surrendered. More telling, more prophetic, according to Germany specialist Roger Chickering, tens of thousands of German soldiers avoided battle, fleeing to the rear, feigning illness, hiding. In the following weeks, the number eluding combat surged to 750,000 or even to 1,000,000, amounting to what some call a "covert strike."[22]

The crushing defeat at Amiens and the wilting behavior of the once disciplined and steadfast German soldier overwhelmed Ludendorff personally, driving him into a funk obvious to those around him. In a despairing statement universally cited in accounts of the war, he reviled August 8 as "the black day of the German Army." Years later this too was the verdict of the authors of postwar Germany's official history of the war; they judged Amiens "the greatest defeat which the Germany Army had suffered." For the Allies it was the opposite. It was a clear victory, spiking their morale and visibly raising their spirits. Reported British War Correspondent Philip Gibbs in his dispatches from the battlefield to *The Daily Telegraph* and *Daily Chronicle*: "The change has been greater in the minds of men than in the taking of territory."[23]

The Amiens victory by Haig and his armies was the opening narrative of the final chapter of the war, what John Terraine terms the "spearhead of victory," the start of "practically unceasing successful attacks."[24] The Germans repeatedly were forced to abandon one defensive line after another, falling back almost nonstop, until, in late August, they reached their extremely well fortified Siegfried Line (what the Allies and Americans called the Hindenburg Line). It was here that Ludendorff was determined to make his stand. Victory, he now realized, had slipped beyond Germany's grasp. "Our only course," he conceded, "was to hold on" and keep occupying enough Belgian and French territory to gain concessions at peace negotiations. This was, dismissively judges military historian and World War One veteran Liddell Hart, no strategy at all, but "mere passive resistance to the enemy's kicks."[25]

Still, Ludendorff had some reason to be confident. The Siegfried/Hindenburg Line ambitiously had been constructed starting in mid-1917 as an impregnable defense against anticipated British and French offensives. It was more than three miles deep, with six separate defensive lines of trenches and machine-gun bunkers with deadly interlocking fields of fire. In front of it was a massive cleared zone created also in mid-1917 when the Germans pulled back to consolidate and shorten their lines, ceding to the Allies about 1,000 square miles of the front. As the Germans did so, in what they called Operation Alberich (named after a destructive dwarf in Teutonic mythology), they systematically laid waste to the abandoned territory to make it useless to the British and French. This opened a vast killing field for German artillery and machine-gunners. They poisoned wells in French villages, ripped up railway tracks, felled trees, demolished just about every bit of housing, dynamited bridges and laced the area with booby traps. It was a genuine atrocity, giving new, sinister meaning to the term no man's land.

And it forged a very strong and very deep defense from which German armies expected to resist Allied assaults. They may well have done so if not for Ludendorff's spring gamble. To sit securely on the Siegfried/Hindenburg line could have allowed Berlin to wait for the exhausted British and French ultimately to sue for peace or, alternatively, to consider a German peace proposal. But that calculus was all changed by Ludendorff's spring offensives. Now, as he soon would learn, with his troops every bit as exhausted as the Allies (if not more so), the Siegfried/Hindenburg line could not shield the Germans.

While Ludendorff was wrestling with defensive strategies, Foch was thinking of nothing but offense. Elated and emboldened by his victories on the Marne and at Amiens, he declared that the Allies and Americans must keep pressing forward rather than regroup and rest. The Germans, he insisted, were on the brink of collapse. To push them over that brink he had devised a grand plan, though it was not at all "grand" by World War One precedents. Rather than unleash a single, elaborately prepared massive attack designed to blast a devastating hole in enemy lines and bring enemy armies to their knees, as prior Allied and German offensives had intended, Foch now called for more limited attacks—the kind of "kicks" to which Liddell Hart refers.

In aggregate, of course, there was to be nothing limited about them. Huge numbers of infantry, artillery and aircraft powerfully would punch the Germans over and over along the entire front, denying Ludendorff any chance of resting, of realigning his units or of bringing up reserves to plug gaps. Foch's offensive would be a relentless series of almost nonstop assaults to wear down the Germans until they begged for peace. It was a flashback to General

U.S. Grant's recipe for victory in America's Civil War a half-century earlier. Rather than seek "decisive results in any single battle," explains Russell Weigley in his history of American military strategy, Grant had won "a peace of exhaustion." And, "like Grant facing Lee," adds Smythe in his study of Pershing, Foch applied "pressure on all points simultaneously until the German war machine came crashing down."[26]

Crash down it did. The Allies, now with enormous and growing AEF contribution, became a steamroller, whose force and momentum took even Foch and his fellow American, British and French commanders by surprise. To them the inconceivable was becoming gradually conceivable and then likely: 1918 could be the year of victory. And they were right, something that they would not remotely have guessed just two months earlier. Nor would they then have guessed that they would achieve their victory not by a final Napoleonic-style massing of troops for a sharply focused attack, not by a dramatic and crushing singular blow to the enemy. There was to be no Yorktown, no Austerlitz, no Waterloo, no fall of Berlin to the Red Army, no Hiroshima, but rather a Grant-like crippling exhaustion of a German Army and nation which desperately wanted the war's agony to end.

AEF Steam for the Steamroller

In the surprising lightning-fast action of the war's final months, what historians marvel at as "the last 100 days," the AEF contribution was decisive and game-changing. Without the doughboys, 1918 would not have denied the war a fifth year. To be sure, some analysts, essayists and historians over the decades have disagreed with this assessment, relegating the AEF at best to a supporting role in the victory drama. Such voices are likely to be heard once again as the war's centenary focuses new attention on the great conflict. But no fair reading of the facts and the events can ignore the compelling likelihood, the almost certainty, that without the AEF the year 1918 and beyond would have remained years of Western Front stalemate.

It was not, as sketched below, that the AEF won spectacular battles that changed the front's map, though they logged impressive victories that remain deservedly treasured in American history. It was also not that the AEF brought new technologies, techniques and tactics to the battlefield. They did not. Their officers were inexperienced (none, including Pershing, ever had led even a division in combat) and they lagged behind the British, French and Germans in using tanks and airplanes, the new weapons that helped advancing forces puncture trench lines and break combat out into the open.

What the United States did, and what no other combatant could do, was to dispatch by mid-1918 such huge numbers of new, eager troops to the Western Front that Foch's risky counterattack against the exhausted Germans by the equally exhausted Allies was conceivable and then, more important, that it could accelerate and explode into the counteroffensive that quickly ended the war. The arriving doughboys were, writes John Keegan (correctly, though a bit floridly), "an army whose soldiers sprang, in uncountable numbers, as if from soil sown with dragons teeth." A senior German officer, whose troops had just fought the doughboys, ranked their enthusiasm equal that of 1914's exuberant German volunteers. Ludendorff would agree, marveling (after the war) at the doughboys' "tremendous superabundance of pent-up, untapped nervous energy." And to a British nurse at the front, quoted by Hew Strachan, the young Americans were "so god-like, so magnificent, so splendidly unimpaired in comparison with the tired, nerve-racked men of the British Army."[27]

Such assessments were no exaggerations; they were true. If during the war's last 100 days German armies were smashed by a steamroller, as they were, it was the AEF that was the steam powering the machine and keeping it rolling. And this exactly was how Ludendorff saw it. To a September query from Berlin about why his armies were faltering, he answered: "The sheer number of Americans arriving daily at the front."

It took some time, understandably, for the AEF to build up its steam. At first, in early 1918, AEF units were sent to the front's quiet sectors, areas of almost no fighting; some had been quiet for years. This was, however, no small matter. The arriving doughboys relieved experienced French units which then shifted to hotter sectors. Thus even though the doughboys were not yet directly fighting Germans, they still began transforming the front's arithmetic by increasing the Allied forces available for combat. This AEF role changed in May. As the German attacks intensified, whole AEF divisions were rushed onto the fighting line to help the Allies, serving under British and French overall command (with some even wearing Allied uniforms). The doughboys now found themselves deep in major battles, including what became their fabled encounters at Cantigny and Belleau Wood and at the banks of the Marne River. And, for the first time since the Civil War, America's towns and cities began receiving steady casualty reports of their sons. Then the AEF role changed again after a true American Army began fighting independently, under the American flag, in its own important sector and under American commanders.

In each of its battles, AEF performance was closely watched. At home, Americans were eagerly awaiting accounts of victories and heroics. In Allied and German headquarters, commanders were assessing doughboy competence. At AEF headquarters in Chaumont, Pershing nervously was looking for evidence that his training and tactics were working, that his troops need not be "amalgamated" into British and French units and that, at last, America had joined the war and was making a difference.

In their first true clash with the Germans, beyond the few, small initial skirmishes or the times when the British tossed

AEF engineers rifles and grenades to help stop a German attack, the doughboys demonstrated both their main strengths (energy, enthusiasm and skilled marksmanship) and distressing weaknesses (limited training and Western Front inexperience). These weaknesses were to impose heavy costs and raise howls of criticism from the Allies and from Washington. This was true of the April 20, 1918 battle at Seicheprey, ranked by historians as the AEF's World War One baptism. At 5 o'clock that morning, while the gargantuan second German offensive was raging elsewhere, about 3,000 Germans (including several hundred elite troops) hit the AEF 26th Division, which had been moved into the normally quiet Seicheprey sector. The attack was, admitted Pershing, "a complete surprise."[28] It also was a complete rout. In the one-day battle, the Germans drove the doughboys from their positions, killing eighty of them and taking 130 prisoners; 424 were wounded or missing. Three AEF companies had lost half of their men.

Though such casualties obviously were not were huge by Western Front standards, they loomed large in America and had deadly long-term consequences. Lots of American blood now had been spilled. American sons and husbands now had been killed and battered—and marched into prison camps. The assailants, the cause of American families' losses and agonies, were Germans. For the first time, the popular American mind legitimately could see the German and Germany as the enemy. Though America at the war's start had no true quarrel with Germany, though America in the war's early years had been injured vastly more by British violation of America's freedom of the seas than by German actions, though Germany had not attacked America nor posed any threat to its interests and though it was America (not Germany) which had declared war, once Germans started shooting at and killing Americans, Germans became the enemy.

On the battlefield, doughboys would deal with this by killing Germans. At home, as future Western Front battles multiplied the losses, grieving and angry Americans and their elected representatives would deal with this by demanding that their fallen sons and husbands be avenged, that Germans be punished and that Germany be made to bleed. This, after all, was the quickening drumbeat in America of the powerful Creel Committee's propaganda operations, of the Four Minute Men's pitches, of Liberty Bond rallies and of the gruesome pamphlets, posters and war movies. Thus hardly surprising would it be that when the time would come to deal with a defeated Germany, America—once so steadfast in neutrality, so ambivalent about the war, so dedicated to a "peace without victory" and a "peace between equals"—would demand that the German be shown no mercy.

Seicheprey, obviously, was not a good start for the AEF and Pershing was angry. He knew, as he later wrote, that the first AEF battle with the enemy had to "be a victory for the Americans... [which would] raise the morale of our allies and correspondingly depress the enemy."[29] Seicheprey certainly was not that. The Germans deliberately had wanted to humiliate the AEF and bloody its nose; and they succeeded. Meirion and Susie Harries' history of America during the war relates that Berlin radio stations broadcasted details of the German victory worldwide, while German planes dropped, on neutral countries, photos of the successful raid.[30] And in London, Prime Minister David Lloyd George was quick to opine, snidely, that the AEF's defeat had unmasked it as an "amateur" army; what it needed, he declared, was the "guidance of more experienced General Officers." His thinly veiled meaning: The AEF should be amalgamated into British and French units and serve under British and French officers.

Yet, too much was made of the Seicheprey setback. It was, without doubt, a genuine embarrassment to Pershing and the AEF. All it did, however, was show that the AEF was under-trained and its officers inexperienced. S.L.A. Marshall gets it right when he writes that Seicheprey proved that the AEF unit "had a plethora of fight spirit and a dearth of know-how." Yet how could it have been any different? Almost all of the AEF, including officers, had been civilians just a year earlier. Unlike the Germans who attacked them and the British and French who criticized them, the doughboys had not been on the Western Front for years. They had just arrived and were untutored in the lessons of the long war. Some even were being rushed into battle without actually ever having fired a weapon.

But they were to prove very fast learners, faster, in fact, than had the British or French, whose infantrymen were so ill-prepared and ill-equipped for combat that great numbers of them surrendered in the war's opening months. Even the much-celebrated enthusiastic British volunteers of 1914 and 1915, the so-called New Army (or Kitchener's Army), many of whom trained with mock-up wooden weapons and wore their own boots and civilian clothes, were not battle-ready for a year. The true wonder, say military experts such as Canada's Tim Travers, is that the doughboys adapted so well in so short a time.[31]

In many respects, the education of the AEF was the story of its next two main battles: Cantigny and Belleau Wood. These names, today still important in U.S. military annals and still triggering debates and analyses which have raged for a century, were signposts on the AEF's road to mastering the Western Front. In both, doughboys fought under Allied overall command and thus, in a sense, were "amalgamated" into Allied armies. Feeling he had little choice, Pershing reluctantly (and unhappily) agreed to assign some of his divisions to help the reeling British and French hold back the German offensive onslaught. Unlike the Seicheprey baptism, these two subsequent battles were clear AEF victories, demonstrating that the doughboys indeed could fight and that its junior officers indeed could lead. This thus strengthened the U.S. case that AEF divisions should go to battle under American command.

The two battles also exposed AEF problems. One was the AEF's limited experience working with artillery, the battlefield's dominant weapon whose precisely-timed rolling barrages, moving forward about 100 yards every two minutes to lob shells just ahead of advancing units, were essential for successful infantry assaults. This AEF failing in great part was the legacy of the Allies' incessant insistence that the U.S. use almost all available trans-Atlantic shipping "tonnage" to transport combat infantrymen, leaving little room on the ships for artillery, other heavy weapons and trucks. As a result, though doughboys had landed in France in huge numbers, artillery pieces had not. AEF units thus had little opportunity to train with the big guns; in combat they were almost fully dependent on the Allies, primarily the French (few of whom spoke English), to furnish and fire artillery. Similarly, doughboys had almost no practice in tank-infantry operations, an increasingly critical element in successful attacks. David Trask, an expert in U.S.-Allied relations during the war, writes that the AEF, in its entire service in France, never fired an American-made cannon or shell nor ever went into battle in an American tank.[32]

A second problem was poor reconnaissance and coordination, with attacking units failing to support each other sufficiently. Contributing to this, of course, was AEF officers' inexperience; for instance, many had difficulty reading maps and recognizing terrain features. A problem too was doughboy exuberance and daring-do enthusiasm. Though undeniably an extremely valuable attribute, it had its dark side. It prompted the doughboys to dash incautiously across open fields, with little regard for enemy machine guns. "They don't take sufficient care; they're too apt to get themselves killed," observed French philosopher Pierre Teilhard de Chardin, a stretcher-bearer in the war. This took a high toll, causing what experts have judged as unusually excessive doughboy casualties. In some battles, for instance, where AEF and French units were fighting side-by-side, French casualties were one-third of the American.

Then there was the problem of AEF combat tactics. The doughboys found, particularly at Belleau Wood, as described below, that when they executed Pershing's cherished "open warfare" tactics, calling for marksmen to charge the enemy over open fields, they bunched together and exposed themselves dangerously. Too often were they felled quickly, almost crumpling, by enemy fire.

Cantigny is celebrated as the AEF's first offensive operation. In their sporadic previous clashes with the Germans, the doughboys had been reacting to attacks. Now, at Cantigny, a tiny, German-held, war-battered French hamlet of about 100 people seventy-five miles north of Paris, it would be the AEF on the attack. Its goal: to capture and, more importantly, hold the tactically valuable plateau on which the hamlet sat. Twice in recent weeks French forces had managed to capture Cantigny, but each time lost it quickly to German counterattacks. Now it was the AEF's turn. For this, Pershing had chosen a regiment (about 4,000 men) of the 1st Division, his best-trained and most experienced unit, and the first to have arrived in France. They rehearsed the assault on similar terrain, including attacking mock trenches resembling those they would encounter; they studied models of the village; and they were well armed. Their rifles and bayonets were American-made, but their other weapons— mortars, artillery, tanks, flamethrowers—were all French.

In the early morning of May 28, the AEF regiment, bayonets fixed, hit the Germans hard. Within just two hours the doughboys had taken Cantigny and the key area beyond it. But that, of course, was just the opening act. The fury was still to come, AEF officers knew, with the German counterattack. And it did, with uncommon ferociousness and brutality, perhaps, reason historians, because Ludendorff wanted to puncture American cockiness and morale. The Germans sought to show "the world that the American soldier was of poorer stuff than the German," wrote one of the AEF attack planners, Lt. Colonel George C. Marshall, the future World War Two Army Chief of Staff and later Secretary of Defense and Secretary of State.[33] For seventy-two hours nonstop, German artillery bombarded the 1st Division units, which barely had time to dig in. Impressively and courageously, the doughboys held their ground, repelling six successive German attack waves. At the end of four days, the Germans gave up and pulled back. In its first offensive act, the AEF had won. It had killed or wounded an estimated 1,400 Germans and captured 225. But AEF's casualties also were high, too high critics over the decades have judged: 1,603 casualties, of which 199 were killed.

Admittedly, Cantigny was not a major battle in a major sector at the front. It was merely a skirmish, changing almost nothing. George Marshall deemed it "of no strategic importance and of small tactical value." Merely "a gesture," is how Gary Mead ranks it in his doughboy study. Still, undeniably, it was a victory. American newspapers and politicians were jubilant. And Pershing was pleased. He had demonstrated that his troops could plan and execute an attack and thus need not be "amalgamated." It proved, as 1st Division Commander Robert Bullard later put it, that "Americans will both fight and stick."[34] And it was a rare bright spot at a time when, elsewhere on the front, the German offensive was crashing through French lines. Today the town of Cantigny remembers this bright spot by a monument in its public square, erected by the U.S., commemorating "the first attack by an American division in the world war."

Just days after the 1st Division's Cantigny victory, the AEF 2nd Division, which included a U.S. Marine Corps brigade of about 10,000 men, was on the attack eastward, at Belleau Wood. A one-square-mile forested plateau, with huge boulders offering defenders extraordinary cover, the woods were near the tip of the German third offensive's furthest thrust into France. The AEF's ferocious twenty-day battle there became of the stuff of legends and lessons. For one thing, it was an important and still honored Marine Corps and Army victory (though the Marines, for reasons still sparking controversy, garnered most of the publicity). For another, it was at Belleau Wood where that Marine captain, cited above, issued that well-quoted rejoinder to the French officers urging him to join their retreat: "Retreat? Hell no; we just got here."

At Belleau Wood, too, the bravery and tenacity of the AEF's Army and Marine units earned Allied and German respect, showing for the first time that the doughboys just perhaps were as good as the Germans. In fact, a German Army post-battle intelligence report describes the doughboys as "very good" soldiers, "healthy, vigorous and well-developed," who carry out attacks "with dash and recklessness" and whose nerves "are still unshaken." Military historian John Terraine describes the Marines as "tall men, strong and fit, relaxed but disciplined, mostly good shots, good marchers," while a German intelligence officer marveled at doughboy spirit, admiringly quoting a captured doughboy as proclaiming, "We kill or get killed."[35]

But it also was at Belleau Wood where Marines demonstrated how much the AEF still had to learn and appreciate about the special deadly nature of Western Front combat. At the woods, the "inexperience [that] dogged the Americans" (as David Trask puts it) was all too painfully on display, leading to towering casualties.[36] Typifying this hands-on experience deficit was Brig. General James Harbord who led the Marines in that battle; he admitted that before he took command of the Marine brigade he "had never commanded more than a squadron of cavalry."

Initially the 2nd Division, along with the 3rd Division, hastily had been dispatched to the Chateau Thierry area, of which Belleau Wood is part, to help the French blunt the German advance. (The Marines were hurried to the front in trucks of a French colonial transportation unit driven by Vietnamese from, among other places, Danang and Hue in Viet Nam. In and around these cities a half-century later, in one of history's moving moments of poignancy, the descendants of the drivers were to be defended from communist attack by the descendants of the Marines.) The AEF units arriving at Chateau Thierry immediately ran into French troops heading the opposite direction, fleeing the front, shouting, "The war is over." Clearly, of course, it was not. The AEF's arrival greatly bolstered French resistance. So much so that by June 6, the 2nd Division's mission changed from defense to offense: to drive the Germans from Belleau Wood. At dawn that day and again that evening, waves of Marines attacked. Drilled in Pershing's open warfare tactics, they marched determinedly toward the dense woods in disciplined ranks in an open field waist-high with wheat and bright poppies.

The results, after the years of Western Front combat, should have been anticipated. Huge numbers of doughboys were mowed down, slaughtered in neat, ordered rows by German machine guns firing 1,000 bullets a minute. American military historian Edward Coffman describes the advance as "lines of infantry, dressing right as if on parade." To Rod Paschall, the attacking Marines "in waves of four ranks" was "little different from an American Civil War assault." And to German machine-gunners, startled (though surely appreciative) by the easy targets the Marines were making of themselves, it seemed a flashback to the war's early years, when they easily had obliterated similarly-advancing well-ordered British infantry. Some Germans even pitied the doughboys, horrified, as Paschall writes, "by their careless confidence and the lack of tactical proficiency…of their officers." It was to World War One chronicler Laurence Stallings, himself a Marine severely wounded at Belleau Wood, "the hardest day in American military history since the Civil War."

The outcome was ugly. "Nearly everywhere men crumpled and sprawled," Coffman writes, "when the enemy machine guns crisscrossed the formation." Whole AEF platoons were isolated and wiped out. One battalion lost two-thirds of its men. Marine Maj. General John Lejeune, 2nd Division commander, acknowledged that "the reckless courage of the foot soldier with rifle and bayonet could not overcome machine guns well-protected in rocky nests."[37]

Yet the doughboys kept pushing forward, often fighting the German defenders hand-to-hand. And by day's end, their tenacity had managed to seize a tiny foothold in the woods. For nineteen days more the battle raged, with the Marines attacking the woods six times, fighting parts of four German divisions, gaining yard after yard at great cost. It was agony, with officers at times informing headquarters that "the situation is intolerable." Some AEF units suffered sixty percent casualties. But they didn't stop fighting. Finally, on June 26, Belleau Wood was cleared of the enemy, giving the AEF its second victory in a month. The cost was huge; doughboy casualties totaled 9,777, of which 1,811 were dead. On June 6 alone, the battle's opening day, 1,087 Marines were killed or wounded, making it the worst day in U.S. Marine Corps history, a grim marker which stood until November 1943 when Marines attacked the Japanese on the Pacific's Tarawa Island.

Big battles, however, always inflict high costs; it rests with the military historians to rule whether such battles' gains merit the lost lives and lasting injuries. While such a debate over Belleau Wood continues, what is beyond dispute is that the 2nd Division victory, on an admittedly strategically marginal piece of the Western Front, boosted Allied and AEF spirits enormously and dented German morale. Ludendorff personally had made defeating the AEF at Belleau Wood a high priority, to stall, he had hoped, the creation of an actual American Army. He had failed.

More important, for many experts Belleau Wood was a game-changer. Its message was that America now was assuming a big part of the fighting—a role certain to grow. John Mosier sees it as "the turning point of the war," while S.L.A. Marshall compares it to Lexington and the Alamo in changing "the face of history." Characteristically sweeping in his style, Marshall adds that "within a few fleeting days, morally and numerically, the whole situation had been reversed." Hyperbole aside, he is close to correct. Just ten weeks earlier, having reckoned that time was running out for his armies, Ludendorff had launched his risky offensives. Against the doughboys at Cantigny and Belleau Wood, Ludendorff and Germany, concludes John Terraine, "lost their race against time." The Americans had begun fighting, while the British and French had remained undefeated.[38]

The AEF's rapidly improving proficiency was confirmed just three weeks later, in mid-July, at a crucial battle on the Marne River, that barrier which for ages has protected Paris from invaders. There, stubborn, rock-solid doughboys' refusal to buckle under German pounding helped set the stage for Foch's Second Battle of the Marne, that risky counterattack which truly was the war's turning point. Pershing had sped his 3rd Division to the Marne, placing it under French command, when it became clear that Ludendorff was about to launch yet another offensive, his fifth of that spring. As with the prior four offensives, the opening days saw the attacking Germans trouncing Allied troops and panicking Allied commanders. French lines once again collapsed. And once again too it appeared that Paris could fall— if Ludendorff's armies could cross the Marne. By the morning of July 15 that seemed increasingly likely as the German juggernaut, under fog and smokescreen cover, prepared to traverse the fifty-yard-wide river in boats and over pontoon bridges. To prevent this, French units earlier had been deployed on the left and right of the far side of the river, with the AEF 3rd Division holding the center. But the French defense quickly dissolved, dangerously exposing the 3rd Division on three flanks. Though the doughboys came under predictably ferocious attack, they held fast, blowing up pontoon bridges as soon as the Germans tried to place them. When the French suggested that the Americans too may want to fall back, 3rd Division commander Joseph Dickman, speaking French, retorted *"Nous resterons la"*—"We Shall Remain Here" (a phrase still emblazoned on 3rd Division arm patches).

He meant it. The doughboys battled almost nonstop for fourteen grueling hours, firing in three directions, at times fighting the Germans with their fists. And they won. German officers, in their after-battle reports, talked of their opponent's "savage roughness." A German lieutenant pronounced the doughboys "coldhearted" and possessed of "bestial brutality," adding that "'the Americans kill everyone' was the cry of fear on July 15 and for a long time caused our men to tremble."

Whether Ludendorff too trembled is unknown, but he certainly blinked. With his armies once again stopped by the Marne, he shut down the offensive on July 16, giving Foch his chance for the sharp response that became the Second Battle of the Marne. Soon, Germany would be on permanent retreat. The German command even tacitly acknowledged this, changing its measure of "success," according to Coffman, from how much ground it had gained in attack to how well it had conducted a retreat. As for the AEF, its extraordinary performance, its rock-solid stand on the river's banks, won exuberant cheers from Allied generals and politicians, admiration from the Germans and honor for the 3rd Division, earning it the nickname, "Rock of the Marne." To this day, the unit is called the Marne Division, even though it went on to fight in World War Two, Korea and Iraq, winning scores of battles, including capturing Rome.

After this, with doughboys continuing to pour into France, the AEF remained on the attack, ultimately allowing Pershing to achieve what he had sought from that June 1917 day when he had arrived at the war: an AEF-led offensive of its own, on a strategically decisive sector of the front. He at last would have his American Army, wearing American uniforms, fighting under the American flag, commanded by American officers. On August 10, 1918, the American First Army officially was organized, complete with fourteen combat divisions and support units (though all of its tanks and nearly all of its artillery and aircraft were British or French). Greeting the First Army's birth was a buoyant French Premier Georges Clemenceau, wiring Pershing: "History awaits you. You will not fail."

Pershing Fields His American Army

Pershing did not fail—ultimately. But his road to success was to be infuriatingly rocky. It was to take him and his new First Army through the hellfire of the gigantic Meuse-Argonne Offensive, the war's iconic American battle. This late September assault, on a twenty-mile front running from the Meuse River westward to the Argonne Forest, became the AEF's signature, its Yorktown, Gettysburg, Iwo Jima, Battle of the Bulge, Pork Chop Hill. It was for the doughboys what Passchendaele was for Britain's Tommies and Verdun for France's poilus, a searing experience whose name for decades symbolized America at war, stirring memories, prompting sighs and tears and stoking hard-earned pride. It was in the Argonne Valley that the AEF proved itself, won its greatest victory, captured its greatest ground and killed and wounded the most Germans—and suffered its greatest losses, revealing how much it still had to learn. Of the war's total 114,000 AEF dead and 205,690 AEF wounded, 26,277 were killed and 95,786 were wounded there. That averages 2,600 doughboys killed or wounded each day of the campaign, a grim number recalling Passchendaele's carnage.[39]

Yet in the chronicle of the Great War, for all its importance to the AEF and its hallowed place in the American military memory, Meuse-Argonne does not rank among the war's biggest nor longest nor most critical battles. Nor was it, in those astounding last 100 days, the definitive offensive stroke felling the Germans; that was delivered, splendidly, by the British Expeditionary Force which, after four costly years, at last had learned how to win on the Western Front. Nor too was Meuse-Argonne the fulfillment of Pershing's and America's plans for the AEF to drive deep into Germany and thus give America and Woodrow Wilson the dominant seat at the eventual peace negotiations. The AEF offensive never got beyond French soil.

Nonetheless, without question, Meuse-Argonne, as described below, was a massive and consequential battle. It was fought on what many historians rate as the Western Front's most important strategic sector; it engaged, tied down and ultimately was poised to defeat thirty-three German divisions which otherwise would have been fighting the British and the French, and, after a disturbingly and (for Pershing) embarrassingly shaky and horribly muddled start, it confirmed that the doughboys and their officers had come of age and soon would assume the brunt of Western Front fighting.

That, of course, did not happen. German armies began collapsing so surprisingly fast in October that what actually ended Meuse-Argonne fighting was not a stunningly conclusive AEF victory but the November 11 armistice silencing the guns. Just as the doughboys were hitting stride, the fighting stopped, the clock ran out. Just as the American Army reached four million strong, with half of its forces already in Europe, and just as American industry was beginning to turn out large numbers of rifles, machine guns, artillery, trucks, tanks and airplanes, the Western Front went all quiet.

Before the doughboys were to fight in the Argonne Valley, however, they found themselves embattled further east, against what was called the St. Mihiel salient. That, in fact, originally was to have been Pershing's great (and decisive) offensive, aimed at crippling the German armies. For more than a year he elaborately had been preparing to strike the salient, a fat wedge-like 200-sq.mi. area poking sixteen miles into Allied lines about twenty miles southeast of Verdun and 150 miles east of Paris. Repelling two French attempts to capture it, German troops had held the strategically valuable protrusion for four years, settling in comfortably, even bringing electricity and running water into their trenches, some of which were paneled. (The Germans also fathered some 200 children with village Frenchwomen). The salient was known to be well fortified, strewn with rows upon rows of coiled barbed wire, with machine-gun nests occupying the high ground. Pershing's aim was to succeed where the French had failed, to drive the Germans from the salient and then to continue pushing relentlessly forward, capturing important rail and road junctions and fortifications and then advancing into Germany itself, at long last and for the first time bringing the war and the fighting and the destruction onto the German homeland.

Strategically, Pershing's St. Mihiel blueprint was solid. Were it to succeed, and odds of that were excellent, it likely would give the AEF the central role in defeating Germany. This, of course, did not happen. New Western Front realities intruded, transforming the AEF's St. Mihiel attack into something of a sideshow, with little strategic value. As the Allied mid-July counterattacks continued their surprising gains and as German retreats just as surprisingly accelerated, Supreme Commander Foch decided to go for the kill with a series of four great attacks west and north of St. Mihiel. This, he told Pershing forcefully on August 30, made the AEF's St. Mihiel Offensive rather superfluous. Cancel it, ordered Foch, and instead send the just-created American First Army west to join the new offensive against the Germans. Reluctantly (and very unhappily) Pershing accepted this argument, but only if he still could launch a kind of mini-St. Mihiel operation. Foch acquiesced.

Pershing now would have to revise and truncate drastically the long and extensively planned offensive, for which some of his divisions had been training for months. Though the AEF still would clear the Germans from the salient (thus removing a threat to France and to the AEF rear), it would push no further. Instead, the First Army, though sure to be exhausted from St. Mihiel battling, would wheel and rush at breakneck and tiring speed sixty miles westward to the Argonne Valley to join Foch's massive and (as it turned out) final push against the Germans. Doing so would extend the AEF's area of responsibility to ninety-four miles, giving it an impressive one-third of the active Western Front.

First, however, Pershing would attack St. Mihiel. He did so at 1:00 a.m. on September 12, starting with a thundering four-hour artillery barrage, followed by an infantry and tank charge. "Exultation," is how Pershing describes it in his memoirs, adding that "at last, after seventeen months of effort, an American Army was fighting under its own flag."[40] He sent into battle more than a half-million doughboys, supported by 110,000 French colonial troops. It was history's greatest American military aggregation to that time, more than the combined Union and Confederate armies at Gettysburg and about four times Grant's Army of the Potomac. It also deployed a massive air armada: 1,476 observation planes, day bombers, night bombers and fighter-pursuit planes. Not one of them, however, was U.S.-made. They were flown by pilots from Britain, France, Italy and Portugal and, of course, by the fast-growing AEF Air Service commanded by Colonel Billy Mitchell, rightly lionized by history as the founder of the United States Air Force. In addition to Mitchell, among First Army officers at St. Mihiel were other stellar lights of future American wars: Brig. General Douglas MacArthur, Colonel George Marshall and Lt. Colonel George Patton.

Pershing's huge, formidable attack-machine, of course, had been assembled not simply to capture the salient, but to drive far beyond it. But those plans now had been dropped. Confronting Pershing in the salient was a meager defending-force, barely one-fifth the size of his army—nine mediocre German divisions (three of them militia and others still very tired from their recent repositioning from the Russian front) plus one Austrian division whose soldiers, it was no secret, long before had lost their stomachs for continued fighting. These German and Austrian units, in fact, were rated second class by the German High Command.

Unsurprisingly, the AEF found only light resistance; in some areas there was no resistance at all. Often doughboys advanced carrying their rifles slung. Unknown to Pershing, two days before the attack German forces had begun pulling out of the salient as part of Ludendorff's efforts to shorten his lines, to make them easier to defend. Advancing doughboys thus found many trenches abandoned, while much of the putatively formidable barbed wire had been neglected, becoming rusty and brittle. Some German divisions, writes historian James Hallas, "crumbled like rotten wood." To be sure, there were pockets of stiff resistance, against which AEF units had to fight fiercely, suffering casualties.

By afternoon of the offensive's opening day, however, Pershing knew his AEF had won a great victory. The following afternoon, on September 13, the town of St. Mihiel was captured, ending the battle for the salient. AEF casualties were relatively light, some 7,000 killed and wounded; the Germans lost 17,000, of which over 14,000 were prisoners captured by the doughboys. "A remarkably quick and easy victory" is how Laurence Stallings describes it, though it also was, in Gary Mead's view, "something of an anti-climax."

Nonetheless, it was a victory that counted greatly. As any victory, it fired AEF morale and, vastly more important, proved Pershing and his staff capable of planning a huge, independent offensive and his officers and doughboys capable of executing it. Liddell Hart calls it a "vindication" of the AEF and "especially of Pershing." Though still not a seasoned Western Front army, the AEF was quickly climbing the learning curve. There thus was well-earned back-slapping and broad smiles at Pershing's field headquarters as dignitaries came calling to congratulate him, among them France's Clemenceau, Foch and Petain. To this day, "St. Mihiel" is a name honored by the U.S. armed forces and military experts as a proud milestone in American battlefield achievement.

The congratulations and accolades ended quickly. The AEF had no time to relish victory. Foch had scheduled his great offensive for September 26, giving 400,000 doughboys and their officers, along with their weapons, equipment, horses and mules, trucks, field kitchens, hospitals and other facilities less than two weeks of mainly night travel (to avoid German detection) to reach the Meuse-Argonne sector. In World War One time, this was the blink of an eye and what Stallings calls "one of the most difficult undertakings in the history of war."[41] Offensives typically took many months to plan; now Pershing's staffers would have mere days to prepare for their greatest, most complex operation. They knew that Meuse-Argonne would be a grueling test and certainly no replay of St. Mihiel.

It would be hard to find a Western Front area more difficult to attack and better to defend; the Argonne Valley was a natural fortress, a defender's dream, an attacker's nightmare. Historian Laurence Moyer rates it "the strongest point" in the "German defense system."[42] Its steep ravines, numerous streams and jagged ridges dared an attacker to try, while its bluffs and hills gave both protective cover and advantageous fields of fire to a defender. "The terrain was so repellant," says S.L.A. Marshall, "as to suggest that nature had designed it to serve as a barrier."[43] To this landscape's natural unfriendliness, the Germans had added lethality. For four years they had improved and hardened its defenses, constructing four solid, seemingly impenetrable, fortified lines. Writes Stallings: "Every road and bridge, every possible avenue of attack had been studied [by the Germans], its distance and range recorded in advance for artillery fire from three directions."

The Germans had very good reason to defend the Argonne. It was the key strategic area on the Western Front, the gateway to Sedan, the German-occupied French city through which ran the railways and roads supplying German operations throughout France. Without Sedan, without these supply lines, Ludendorff's armies no longer would be able to fight in France; they would have to retreat to Germany. To lose control of it was unthinkable for Ludendorff. Now it was up to the doughboys, 1.2 million of them, to drive the Germans from the Argonne Forest and to capture Sedan.

The obstacles in a Meuse-Argonne campaign would have been daunting even without the area's unwelcoming terrain, the determination of the Germans to hold it and Pershing's sharply abbreviated preparation time. For one thing, the haste with which the doughboys had to redeploy from St. Mihiel via inadequate and narrow roads to the Argonne Valley guaranteed that they would arrive at the offensive's launch line exhausted at the very moment when they needed to be fresh and alert. For another, the attack's large number of divisions required Pershing to throw green and raw troops and officers into battle. Some had never fired a rifle; some had arrived in France just weeks earlier and had only three or four months of U.S.-based training; and some actually had been drafted as recently as July.

A huge problem too was the AEF's woeful shortage of the field guns absolutely essential to give protective cover to troops attempting to advance through the valley and forest. Not only had American factories only recently started manufacturing in great numbers artillery pieces suitable for the Western Front, but the U.S. Army's own artillery stocks, by and large, had been left at home, since the trans-Atlantic shipping had been devoted almost entirely to transporting men. Historians conclude that Allied shipping policies inflicted a steep price on every AEF division, hampering their operations and raising their casualties. Pershing's memoirs frustratingly note that four of the nine divisions leading the Meuse-Argonne attack lacked their own artillery. As a result, he was reduced to asking (some historians use the word "begging") the Allies for both artillery and their gunners. Indeed, he later admitted "we were literally beggars as to every important weapon, except the rifle."[44] He seldom got as much as he requested. And when the guns were delivered, most doughboys were unfamiliar with them, while his junior officers, including an artillery battery commander and future commander in chief named Harry Truman, had only very limited practice in coordinating infantry advances with artillery barrages.

Compounding the difficulties was, once again, the horse shortage. Lacking enough of the animals to haul artillery to the front, doughboys had to hitch themselves to wagons and strain forward. Another problem, regrettably, was the legacy of Pershing's insistence on "open warfare" battlefield tactics, discounting the lethality of the machine gun. Adhering to these tactics at Meuse-Argonne, doughboys too often attacked upright in bunches across open fields and then were cut down wholesale by German machine-gunners.

All these problems tormented the AEF in the dismal opening weeks of the forty-seven-day campaign. With some AEF units still scrambling to get to the launch line, the battle began just before midnight September 25, with 4,000 artillery guns pounding the 200,000 German soldiers in the valley. Initially, the fighting went well for the AEF; the barrage, as intended, scattered the German units and disrupted their defenses. As a result, when the fifteen super-size AEF divisions (about 26,000 men each) went on the attack along the twenty-mile front at 5:30 a.m. on September 26, they advanced quickly, seizing important ground. But then they suddenly slowed, in part because their artillery could not keep pace with their brisk advance (they lacked sufficient horses to pull forward the field guns) and in part to allow the many lost and scattered units to organize and form up. This delay, putting on the "brake… prematurely" (in Liddell Hart's words), was fateful. It enabled the Germans to regroup, call in heavy and high-quality reinforcements and organize what became a staggering resistance.

Now the AEF barely could crawl forward. Whenever doughboys tried to advance, they ran up against Germans fighting doggedly to defend every yard of the strategically vital valley. And when they did capture some ground or a village, too often they would be pushed back by a fierce counterattack, suffering mounting and, for the AEF, unprecedented casualties. Losses climbed even further as the doughboys, in massed and bunched-up formations, frontally charged German machine-gun nests. Germans mused that the Americans seemed not to care about taking heavy losses. Making matters worse, the attacks frequently were sloppily coordinated, with units not only failing to work with artillery but even with each other. Many companies and battalions, says Coffman, "virtually ceased to exist."[45]

Without doubt, of course, individual doughboys fought well and books, published over the decades, are crammed with many hundreds of stirring heroic accounts. Most famous, of course, is the tale of Corporal (later Sergeant) Alvin York, a draftee whose bravery and skills thrilled Americans and inspired books and a 1940 movie (with Gary Cooper playing York). This log cabin-born marksman (and pacifist), his sharpshooting skills honed hunting in the east Tennessee backwoods, in a single October 8, 1918 encounter at the edge of the Argonne Forest silenced three dozen German machine guns, killed twenty-five machine-gunners, and took 132 prisoners.[46]

But individual heroism could not rescue the AEF from an Argonne Valley catastrophe. The unrelentingly dismal performance drenched the Americans in gloom and confusion. "Even the greenest soldiers were aware that this battle was frightfully mismanaged," concludes S.L.A. Marshall.[47] To some observers, the doughboy bloodletting recalled the earlier agonizing and hapless British and French offensives. Like them, progress definitely was being made and enemy ground captured, but very slowly and at extreme cost. "The attacks were not going well and the whole world knew it," says Smythe.[48]

Logistics became a true nightmare—recounted for generations. "Everything imaginable proceeded to go wrong," according to military historian Thomas Fleming.[49] The three narrow, heavily-shelled roads leading into and through the Argonne, at times badly muddied by autumn rains, simply could not handle the masses of ammunition, supplies, trucks, tractors, horse-drawn wagons and caissons, reinforcements and forage (for 90,000 mules and horses) daily sent to the front and the masses of wounded doughboys and relieved units sent back from the front. Just to keep the doughboys supplied with ammunition required fourteen trainloads of shells every day.

At times everything on the roads simply halted, frozen by a genuine gridlock a half-century before that term emerged in general use. Traffic jams extended to seven miles. For long stretches, nothing moved, not even a horseman or cyclist. Food and supplies were not getting to the front; wounded were not being evacuated.

Adding to the congestion, thousands of horses died, dropping to the roadway. It was a mess, a huge mess, and immediately came to be the metaphor for the whole dreadful start of the greatest AEF offensive. These first two weeks of October, writes Mead, were "undoubtedly the most difficult in the brief history of the AEF."[50]

Pershing struggled to get the attack on track. He dashed about the battlefield, visiting each of his divisions, shuffling units, sending poorly performing green troops to the rear and bringing up those with at least a whiff of combat experience. He dressed-down and relieved regiment, brigade and even division and corps commanders of their posts; among Meuse-Argonne's casualties were many generals' careers. Pershing even, to the horror of the British and French, halted his entire massive operation several times, to untangle the logistics mess, to realign and reinforce his battered divisions and to give his doughboys rest.

What the Argonne was doing to his new First Army truly and profoundly humiliated him. Adding to his pain was the contrast with the British and French; their armies were smashing the Germans and making quick and impressive gains. So much so that Ludendorff, on September 28, seemed to crack in front of his staff. In S.L.A. Marshall's accounting, Ludendorff's words blurred, his fists tightened and his face grew livid as he unleashed a tirade against everyone, accusing his staff of disloyalty, the Kaiser of weakness and the German people of cowardice. Then, according to Marshall, he toppled and fell to the floor.

Clearly, the British and French, but not the AEF, had the Germans on the run. It would take Pershing's First Army a long three weeks to reach what had been its Day One Meuse-Argonne goal. Such repeated AEF delays were driving Foch "violent," French Commander in Chief Petain warned Pershing. This became clear in Foch's tense October 13 meeting with Pershing when the Frenchman bluntly pointed out that everyone rapidly was pushing back the Germans "on all fronts except the Americans." He then ordered Pershing to advance, declaring, I want "no more promises! Results!" At one point he even threatened to take a half-dozen AEF divisions away from Pershing and reassign them to French armies where, he said, they better could be used to fuel the successful attacks against the Germans rather than remain mired and barely mobile in the Argonne Valley. When Pershing objected, Foch backed down but ordered the AEF to resume its attacks "without delay" and to continue "without any interruptions."[51]

Foch's irritation and dismay were mirrored, even amplified, in London and Paris. British Prime Minister Lloyd George instructed his ambassador to the U.S. to advise Woodrow Wilson that the AEF has been "quite ineffective." The British cabinet privately was told that the AEF "has suffered severely through ignorance of modern war and it must take at least a year before it becomes a serious fighting force." French Premier Clemenceau, meanwhile, seemed not to care who heard his views. Living up to his nickname "The Tiger," earned over an embattled half-century French political career, he growled that Pershing suffered from unbending stubbornness and that his performance in battle "was inferior to what was permissible to expect." Pershing, continued Clemenceau, must accelerate his attack, fix the logistics, clear the Germans from the Argonne—and do all of that at once. He even vowed to wire Wilson to demand that Pershing be fired.[52]

Pershing, of course, was not unaware of Clemenceau's nasty words and was pained by them. They typified, he believed, France's insulting attitudes toward America and the AEF. He bemoaned the "bad treatment" that his troops "had received from the French" and fumed, according to his biographer Donald Smythe, that the French "had never once said a word of thanks or complimented the American troops on what they had done." He added that "it was difficult to exaggerate the feeling of dislike for the French which existed in the American Army."[53]

Yet, for all the AEF's dismal initial Meuse-Argonne showing, the criticism of it was excessive; not completely undeserved, of course, but overblown. The reality was that its successes at Cantigny, Belleau Wood and St. Mihiel, welcome and even impressive as they were, did not prepare it for the Argonne Valley. It too much remained a green, inexperienced army. And it knew it; AEF officers and troops actually nicknamed the divisions leading the Meuse-Argonne assault "the thin green line."

Pershing knew it too; he well understood his AEF's shortcomings. Still, admirably and bravely, he had agreed to launch, at very short notice and with almost zero preparation, one of the entire war's most challenging offensives. He did not even mildly protest Foch's ordering the AEF to the Argonne Valley, something that puzzles S.L.A. Marshall.[54] And though the early Meuse-Argonne weeks undeniably and deservedly were painfully embarrassing, they mainly proved not AEF incompetence but merely that—despite its enthusiasm and courage, despite all of the talk (and boasting) that Americans were profoundly different—it still needed the tempering offered only by actual combat on an actual Western Front battlefield. This, in fact, in almost so many words, was Foch's response to Clemenceau's griping about the Americans. He told his Premier and nominal superior: "The Americans have got to learn sometime. They are learning now, rapidly." And this too is the view of British historian John Terraine whose histories typically (possibly reflexively) are tough on the AEF. Of Pershing and his troops during the Meuse-Argonne early phase, Terraine states: "They were simply learning how difficult the war could be…just as every other army had to learn."[55]

And learn the AEF did. By the start of November, after halting for several weeks, it was as if a new AEF had taken to the field. Its commanders and junior officers had gained some experience and its infantrymen had new tactics, fresh reinforcements and, at last, stockpiles of ammunition regularly replenished as a steady infusion of supplies finally started flowing from America. The doughboys began punching the Germans, advancing impressively, absorbing counterattacks, punching once again and again advancing impressively, speeding ahead. Helping too was the more friendly landscape, for they now had moved beyond the Argonne's worst terrain and were attacking in fields more open and thus less accommodating to the German defenders. To Smythe, often viewed by fellow historians as decidedly critical of the AEF and Pershing, the AEF "had reached the point where it could keep going... The First Army was running off the map."[56]

The Unknown Final Days

"Running off the map" was no exaggeration. The American First Army so steadily was advancing and the Germans so steadily retreating that AEF intelligence officers kept losing track of their own and enemy unit positions. If the first four years of Western Front warfare had been frustrating stasis and snail-like gains, the first ten days of November 1918 were a dynamic rush of jack rabbit-like leaps. By now the AEF had mushroomed to 1,790,823 men plus 76,800 officers, with thousands more arriving daily. Huge numbers of these were assembled for Pershing's re-launch of his Meuse-Argonne Offensive. He kicked this off early November 1 and by night his forces had reached their Day One objectives. The following morning, their assault and gains continued, supported by vastly improved AEF logistics and communication. Three days later, on November 5, the AEF crossed the once-formidable Meuse River barrier. Opportunity after opportunity offered itself for doughboy exploitation. When, for instance, AEF commanders sent out units on routine reconnaissance missions to gauge enemy strength, they often encountered such flaccid resistance that what had started as cautious patrols morphed into full-scale advances. Says Rod Paschall: "This was not the German Army that they had known."[57]

By November 6, Pershing's First Army was just ten miles from Sedan and its rail hub essential for German operations in France. Two days later, the army had captured the heights overlooking, and thus controlling, that key city; AEF artillery then moved up, opened fire and started pulverizing the rail facilities and tracks. Two days after that, on November 10, the newly created American Second Army launched its own offensive, east of the Meuse-Argonne campaign, to drive into Lorraine and then into Germany itself. Thus, by dawn November 11, just hours before the fighting was to cease, two full American armies were deep in combat, ready to carry the war onto German soil.

Action was moving swiftly too in the British sector, to the AEF's right, and in the French sector both to the right and left. Foch's relentless pounding of the Germans along a 250-mile front was succeeding. The British and their Australian, Canadian and New Zealander divisions had smashed through the Siegfried/Hindenburg Line's heavy fortifications and now rapidly were advancing into open country. Similarly pushing ahead, though quite a bit slower, were the French. A new Western Front script was being written: The Allies and Americans in their sectors attacked the Germans; initially the Germans lightly resisted but ultimately scrambled back several thousand yards, there establishing a new defensive line of powerful artillery and machine guns; and then the Allies and Americans repeated the process, attacking the new German positions.

This was the script that defeated Germany. Yet, muses John Terraine, it is a "virtually unknown story."[58] He is correct. Though Verdun, Passchendaele, Gallipoli, the Somme and the war's other epic battles are burned deeply into the popular mind, chronicled by whole books (and even movies), this final stage is covered in hurried paragraphs. But this is understandable. Little was dramatic about each of the last 100 days' individual clashes. Foch, after all, deliberately rejected an attempt to defeat the Germans in a single shattering blow. Instead, he gradually drained the German armies of their weapons and manpower through incessant attacks along the whole front. And it worked.

But there was nothing easy about it. Despite the new script's seeming simplicity, the Allied/American advance was no romp. The Germans may have been put on the run, but they were not fleeing; there was no rout, no panicked stampede to the rear. Few German soldiers were dropping weapons, tossing backpacks, shucking heavy boots to speed faster from battle. Rather, their withdrawal almost everywhere was orderly. In fact, as they retreated and turned on their attackers, often at canals and rivers, they ignited some of the entire war's heaviest fighting and inflicted some of its heaviest casualties. Laurence Stallings calls this last-ditch German fighting "savage" and full of "sagacious fury," while British historian Niall Ferguson emphasizes that "the Germans continued to be highly effective at killing the enemy." Indeed, in some respects autumn 1918's human losses rivaled those at the mammoth Somme and Passchendaele battles.[59]

On the brink of defeat the German Army may have been, but it was not crushed. Concludes Gary Mead in his chronicle of the doughboys: "The conflict remained astonishingly close, right up to the final hurdle." And by withdrawing, the Germans continually were shortening their lines, making them easier to defend. And this worried Allied and American commanders. Similarly worrisome was the looming prospect that the Germans soon would be driven back onto German soil. This cut both ways. Bringing the war and its devastation at last to the German people certainly would be an astounding achievement and dramatize Allied/American success. But it also meant that German soldiers, whatever their flagging morale, should be expected to fight with renewed vigor and tenacity to defend their homeland.[60] This precisely was the concern of British Commander in Chief Douglas Haig. In mid-October he warned the British cabinet that "any attempt to touch the honour of the German people would make them fight with the courage of despair."

The Allied and American worries were unnecessary. As it happened, the attackers never had to face desperate and dangerous Germans protecting their homes and families. Germany threw in the towel before its troops could cross back into their country, unable to resist the incessant and mounting pounding from the Allied/American armies, particularly from the British and the Americans. In classic open warfare pursuit, the attackers were giving Ludendorff's forces no respite, no chance to regroup, no chance to forge a defensive line. And though both sides were hemorrhaging infantrymen by running up some of the war's highest casualty ratios and though the British, French and German manpower wells were close to running dry and thus could offer little chance of fully replacing battlefield losses, the American manpower reservoir was as deep as ever. Shiploads of doughboys continued to land at French docks every day, while Pershing began talking about a three million and even four million-strong AEF. When the German socialist newspaper *Arbeiter Zeitung* reported in its October 24 edition on the gusher of arriving Americans, it asked its readers: "Do the people wish to continue the war under such circumstances?"

The Western Front thus had become precisely what had terrified Ludendorff the previous year, when he began planning to gamble on launching sledgehammer-style offensives before the AEF could arrive in great numbers. He had concluded that time had become his enemy. And, indeed, he was right; time now had run out for Germany. While there were no conclusive, war-ending battles in the war's last months, no knock-out punches, no Waterloos or Hiroshimas, the endless punching brought the German Army to its knees. "At the end," concludes David Trask, "[German] resistance simply melted away." Though the end thus lacked drama, in the end Germany was defeated and forced to seek a ceasefire, an armistice.

By November 8, everyone knew peace talks were underway and a ceasefire imminent. Three days later, at precisely 11 in the morning Western Front time, the guns went silent. All now was as quiet on the Western Front as on the Eastern and in the Great War's other theaters. The toll, by any historical standard, was unfathomably high and took years to tally; even today, authoritative sources disagree on precise numbers. Total World War One dead, wounded and taken prisoner on all sides and on all fronts were 32,779,826. Of that 9,450,000 were killed in battle or died of injuries and other combat-related afflictions. British dead totaled 723,000, with another 1,662,625 wounded; French losses were 1,398,000 dead and 2,000,000 wounded; German were 2,037,000 dead and 4,207,028 wounded; and Russian were 1,811,000 dead and 1,450,000 wounded.

America, despite its brief time in combat, still lost 114,000 dead, 205,690 wounded and 4,480 held as prisoners at war's end, amounting to 324,170 total casualties. Those doughboys who had been killed left some 40,000 widows back home. According to Ferguson's calculations in *The Pity of War,* his 1998 analysis of the comparative strengths of World War One's combatants, 2.7 percent of all Americans mobilized were killed, compared to Britain's (including Ireland's) 11.8 percent, France's 16.8 percent, Germany's 15.4 percent and Russia's 11.5 percent.[61]

Battlefield casualty statistics, however, do not in themselves measure the toll. For Britain, France, Germany and Russia, a whole generation was more than decimated; it was shredded. And of that generation, its best-educated and best-bred, those who thus had been the war's junior officers and most exposed on the battlefield, were almost wiped out. The effects subsequently were all too visible in Europe's troubled and dismal postwar years; its legions of limping or blind or wheelchair-bound veterans, its masses of widows and women with little chance of ever finding a husband among the grimly-diminished male population, its leadership vacuum, its cynicism and loss of optimism, its determination never—ever— to subject itself again to such agony and devastation and hence its 1930s' appetite for appeasement.

America, of course, in neither the short nor long term, had suffered or would suffer anywhere as much as had and would Britain, France, Germany and Russia. The Great War—what was coming to be called the World War and then, a generation later, World War One—did not devastate America or crush a generation. In fact, in many respects, certainly geopolitically and arguably economically, America exited the war stronger than it had entered. But in one crucial arena America did not exit strong enough: on the battlefield. There, it can be argued, the war ended too soon. "Among the AEF," reports Mead, "there was a widespread sense of having been cheated of real triumph."[62] Pershing himself said as much. As the clock at his headquarters ticked towards the moment of armistice, he glanced at the map of his ongoing offensive and remarked to his staff: "I suppose our campaigns are ended, but what an enormous difference a few days more would have made." At that moment, he had under his command forty-two huge AEF divisions, totaling some two million men, outnumbering both the British forces (including all the empire's units) and the French. Another two million prospective doughboys had been drafted and were training at home, preparing to be shipped to France. This massive American Army was just hitting stride, poised to push into Germany itself. That it did not get the chance had significant consequences.

For all of America's decisive contribution to victory, for all of the crucial difference it made in the defeat of Germany, when the war ended the AEF was not holding enough land to give America a powerful voice in setting the terms of the armistice or in setting the course at the subsequent peace conference at Versailles. The British and French commanders, as described in the following chapter, did not even include Pershing at the solemn meeting where the German generals surrendered. Ironically—and, as it turned out, tragically—the armistice meant that America merely had brought enough forces into the war to end the stalemate and to give victory to Britain and France but not enough to restrain them in that victory and prevent them from imposing a punishing defeat on what by then had become a German Republic.

Crassly put, America simply had not bled sufficiently to gain a commanding seat at the peace table. This plainly was not what Woodrow Wilson on April 6, 1917 had intended when he led his nation into war; it was, in fact, everything he had dreaded and sought to avoid. From a hundred-year vantage it can be said that it would have been far better, for America and Europe and history, for Wilson to have kept his nation out of the war and allow a Western Front stalemate to drive the exhausted combatants to a negotiated peace. This could have spared the 20th Century much of its agony.

CHAPTER 7

CULMINATION: ARMISTICE AND VERSAILLES

"Everything for which America fought has been accomplished."

T HUS DID WOODROW WILSON ANNOUNCE to his countrymen the November 11, 1918 armistice ending the Great War's fighting. It is a statement that history turns upside down. Little for which America had fought had been accomplished. America, to be sure, had wanted the Allies to win, and win they did. But just about nothing else came out the way Wilson or America had intended. The first proof of this emerged in the armistice, when the British and French treated Germany as a soundly defeated enemy for whom every shred of honor would be withheld. This was followed a few months later at the Paris Peace Conference and in the peace treaty. They were to be the culmination of the transforming actions taken by America since it entered the war in spring 1917. That, as earlier chapters relate, dramatically altered the dynamics and balance of the Western Front, giving Britain and France a victory otherwise almost certainly unachievable. It consequently gave them the opportunity, which they seized, to punish, strip and humiliate Germany. This clearly was not why America had fought and, in fact, was everything Wilson had said he opposed.

If it was a fateful mistake for America to have entered the Great War, it was still a mistake which could have been rectified by ending the conflict with genuine negotiations and compromise. At the armistice and peace talks, America had a last chance to blunt the long-term, history-changing tragic effects of its having taken sides in the war.

But that Wilson and America failed to do. Instead, the armistice dissolved any possibility of fulfilling Wilson's repeated vow of a peace without victory, while the Versailles Treaty, as the peace terms came to be known, confirmed that the Allied and American victors would punish Germany unmercifully. So brutal was this punishment that it shocked even those who had authored it. "Immeasurably harsh and humiliating," said U.S. Secretary of State Robert Lansing of the treaty. "All a great pity," was how British Prime Minister David Lloyd George assessed it, adding, "We shall have to do the same thing all over again in twenty-five years at three times the cost." And Wilson's press chief admitted, "If I were a German, I think I should never sign it."[1]

America would have good reason to not sign. The reality of the treaty shattered Wilson's vision of a compromise peace allowing Germany to emerge from the war healthy and strong enough to be a major player among Europe's nations (and an essential check on what Wilson feared were France's aggrandizing ambitions). The reality of the treaty fulfilled the fears Wilson had confided to aides sailing with him to Europe for the peace conference: that "our greatest error would be to give [Germany] powerful reasons for wishing one day to take revenge." Yet when Wilson and other American negotiators at the peace conference were to try to temper the treaty's harshest points, they were to be rebuffed by the British and French who openly trivialized the American Expeditionary Force role in winning the war. The U.S. had not earned on the battlefield a right to determine the peace, Wilson and other Americans were to hear in dozens of indirect ways. And not only was Wilson unable to determine the peace, he could barely influence it.

Wilson's Road Map to Peace

Throughout the war there had been periodic attempts at peacemaking, including those by Wilson and the Vatican. They had gone nowhere. There also had been occasional offers by the various belligerents to start ceasefire talks. They too had gone nowhere, mainly because they were scarcely genuine, little more than thinly disguised gambits to win diplomatic points and gain favor among the neutral states. In this process, only Wilson's efforts ultimately carried any weight. For one thing, Britain and France could not readily dismiss (as much as they very much would have preferred) efforts by their increasingly essential benefactor. For another, Germany and Germans, even after America entered the war, regarded Wilson favorably, seeing him as a fair-minded broker. The significance was not lost on Berlin, for example, that Wilson had brought America into the war not as an "ally" of Germany's enemies, but merely as an "associate," explicitly retaining an arms-length ability to act independently. It thus was possible, and occasionally hinted at by Washington and greatly feared by London and Paris, that America would make its own, separate peace with Germany. Therefore when Wilson talked peace, the combatants paid some attention.

Wilson's road map for peace began taking shape in a January 22, 1917 address to the Senate, just six weeks before he was to ask Congress to declare war. Its most important message, points out George Kennan's study of American diplomacy, was its repudiation of total victory. On this Wilson was unambiguous. He hardly could have been more explicit, more clear, than when he called for a "peace without victory." Victory would be catastrophic, he explained to the Senators, because a victor's terms "imposed upon the vanquished would be accepted in humiliation...would leave a sting, a resentment, a bitter memory upon which terms of peace would rest, not permanently, but only as upon quicksand." Prophetically he warned, "only a peace among equals can last."[2]

From this sensible view, rooted firmly in the lessons of

history, Wilson barely wavered. In August, he said that the U.S. sought no "punitive damages" and no "dismemberment of empires," including the German Empire. And in December, he assured that the U.S. intended "no wrong against the German Empire, no interference with her internal affairs." While he stressed that Germany certainly would have to right the wrongs that it had committed, he quickly added that "they cannot and must not be righted by the commission of similar wrongs against Germany." It says much for Wilson and the strength of his belief in a compromise peace that he made these statements, offering what Wilson scholar Arthur Link calls "generous terms," when America already was in the war, when George Creel's Committee of Public Information and the platoons of Four Minute Men were whipping up anti-German sentiment across the U.S. and when doughboys were starting to be killed by Germans.[3]

A month later, in a January 8, 1918 address to a Joint Session of Congress, Wilson laid out his most detailed vision, listing fourteen specific elements of a peace, an important statement instantly termed (and remembered to this day as) the "Fourteen Points." More points were added in subsequent statements—the "Four Principles," "Four Ends" and "Five Particulars"—so that by fall 1918 there were twenty-seven of them. History generally lauds Wilson's propositions. Gary Sheffield in his 2001 account of the war, for instance, calls the Fourteen Points "some of the most extraordinary proposals ever to be introduced in the arena of international relations." Diplomatic history specialist Harry Rudin concurs, praising Wilson for going "far to meet the demands of war-weary peoples everywhere for a peace of reconciliation and understanding."[4] Indeed, brimming with promise the Fourteen Points well may have been. But they turned out to be promises unfulfilled.

Though the Fourteen Points addressed issues related to all the war's belligerents, most important was what Wilson said about Germany. Points six, seven and eight required that German troops withdraw from all of the land they had seized and occupied in

Belgium, France and Russia and that Germany return to France the regions of Alsace and Lorraine taken from France after its 1871 defeat. But Wilson's demands on Germany stopped there. As significant as what he said was what he did not. His points importantly did not call for Germany's unconditional surrender, or its unilateral disarmament or its forfeiture of colonies. And on such critical (and, later, highly inflammatory) matters as whether Germany should pay financial reparations or confess guilt for starting the war, the points again were silent. In short, Wilson wagged no accusatory finger at Germany. Nor did he attempt to isolate Germany or make it a pariah state. To the contrary. "We have no jealousy of German greatness," he told Congress. "We do not wish to injure her or to block in any way her legitimate influence or power… We wish her only to accept a place of equality among the peoples of the world."[5]

These sentiments were reinforced by other Wilson statements throughout 1918, culminating in his September 27 "Five Particulars" speech in New York City. In it he reassured Germany that it would be treated fairly in a peace arrangement, calling for "impartial justice" among nations. In their aggregate, Wilson's proposals truly were a road map to a peace without victory. Had the map been followed, the Great War's fighting would have been stopped by compromises, surely setting Europe on a path to stability and peace instead of what actually followed—three-quarters century of convulsions.

Wilson's words immediately resonated in Germany, first among the leftist political parties and then gradually the center. As home front suffering continued to deepen, much of it from Britain's naval blockade, so did German desire for peace, though tight censorship (as in Britain and France) allowed no public criticism of the war. The censors, however, could not hide from Germans their exhausting lengthening workweeks, the conscripting of ever younger and older males and the painful and mounting daily deprivation. There were severe shortages (or total absence) of almost all food, including milk as cows could not be fed enough to produce it; of metal, prompting the government to confiscate metallic objects and structures from German homes (and to melt some of Berlin's monuments); and of cloth, requiring restaurants and hotels to turn in their table linens. "Wherever Germans turned," writes Harry Rudin, "they found nothing to give them cheer or hope."[6] The deteriorating living standards helped spark a January 1918 wave of angry strikes, spreading to one million workers in Berlin, Hamburg and other major cities.

In the following months, home front despair plunged further as Germans everywhere and of all stations began suffering the consequences of Ludendorff's spring offensives. Newspapers may not have been allowed to print (nor even were told) that in those offensives a half-million German soldiers had been killed and that many more had been injured, but no village or town needed to be informed formally of its losses. Their own eyes and ears and family experience told them that the offensives' bloodletting had been catastrophic and seemed to bring the country no closer to peace. This too was felt in Berlin by the deputies in the Reichstag, Germany's parliament. Though they had little say on war or military policy, they began reflecting their constituents' war-weariness. For them, therefore, Wilson's statements, particularly his Fourteen Points, offered hope.

No movement towards peace, of course, was possible so long as Germany's two top military commanders, Generals Paul von Hindenburg and Erich Ludendorff, kept assuring Kaiser Wilhelm and the civilian government that the German Army was doing very well and that its battlefield gains soon would force the British and French to sue for peace. In the spring offensives' early weeks, such assurances could ring true. But by summer 1918, they were hollow; all air had leaked from them.

Ludendorff's massive attacks, whatever their startling initial tactical successes and impressive conquests of land, had been a strategic catastrophe. They merely had bloodied (very badly) but had not destroyed the British and French armies, which now were counterattacking effectively. His great battlefield gamble had failed. Having risked just about all of his reserves to change Western Front dynamics before masses of Americans would arrive, he now found himself crippled by manpower shortages and diminished options. He and Hindenburg could not ignore the battlefield's verdict: that victory had slipped permanently beyond Germany's grasp. Germany's only good move, they then decided, was to seek a peace based on Wilson's Fourteen Points. And that, in a startling meeting on September 29, is what they told a shocked Kaiser and the country's political leaders. Declared Hindenburg: "There is no longer any possible hope of forcing peace on the enemy. The situation grows more desperate every day."

Even more startling was the meeting several days later at the Reichstag, when a military delegation representing Hindenburg and Ludendorff briefed party leaders. Until that moment the politicians had believed, having been repeatedly told, that their soldiers were winning the war, that their losses were heavy, but the enemy's were worse and that an eventual peace favorable to Germany was within reach. They thus were completely unprepared to hear that the generals now wanted to stop fighting, now wanted (as they admitted) "to end the struggle in order to spare the German people and their allies further sacrifices" and now saw "further prosecution of the war as hopeless." The aghast political leaders were warned that Germany's "reserves are coming to an end," while the "enemy, by virtue of American help, is in a position to replace its losses." As a result, concluded the military delegation, "according to human calculation, there is no longer any prospect of forcing the enemy to seek peace."

These words were a thunderbolt and "shocked all who heard them," writes Rudin. "Now there was panic in Berlin." Accounts recall that the incredulous politicians turned "white at the news." So shocked and furious, for instance, was the strongly pro-monarchist, pro-military head of the Conservative Party that he literally ran up and down, shouting: "We have been deceived and cheated."[7]

From this moment, any German rationale for continued fighting dissolved. Within days Berlin sent a message to Washington, delivered on October 7 by Swiss diplomats, stating its readiness to agree to a peace shaped by the Fourteen Points and the subsequent Wilson statements. Bypassing the British and French, Germany's officials sought to deal initially only with the Americans whom they felt would treat them fairly. In the following two weeks, Wilson and the Germans exchanged a number of notes, sketching the principles of an armistice and of what Wilson and the Germans expected would be a peace treaty.

Meantime, London and Paris predictably were horrified by the spectacle of Wilson negotiating the end of the war. As Bullitt Lowry writes in his detailed 1996 analysis of the Armistice, they "groused about Wilson's monopolizing the negotiations."[8] The British and French dismissed and, worse, derided the Fourteen Points and its author, belittling the American president as a fuzzy-minded dreamer likely to be much too lenient on Germany. From their perspective, having fought more than four years, they had a point. Their nations had bled and suffered vastly more at German hands than had America. Understandably (though not necessarily wisely) their people and politicians sought full-bore revenge. For the moment, however, London and Paris had to be frustrated bystanders as Wilson hammered out an armistice structure, which he then would present to them for review.

The American-German exchanges dealt with issues on two fronts. On the military, Wilson demanded that German forces be so disarmed that they could not resume battle. In a cable to U.S. Commander in Chief John Pershing, Wilson stated that "the terms of the armistice should be rigid enough to secure us against renewal of hostilities by Germany." But he pointedly added that the Germans must not be weakened too much; they must not be humiliated, he told Pershing, "beyond the necessity." Indeed, according to Arthur Link, Wilson "was eager to maintain sufficient German military power" as a "counterweight to French and British power" at the eventual peace conference. In that, of course, Wilson ultimately failed.[9] By late October, Berlin accepted Wilson's military terms, agreeing to withdraw German troops "everywhere from invaded territory," to give up enough arms to ensure Allied and American battlefield supremacy and to end submarine attacks.

On the political front, Berlin also agreed to Wilson's terms. Acknowledging his declaration that he would not deal with "military masters and monarchical autocrats," the Germans pledged substantial steps towards democracy, towards what a much later generation would call "regime change." In fact, these steps already had begun. The socialists (the majority party) had just been brought into the government by the new chancellor, Prince Max von Baden. Though a cousin of the Kaiser and heir to the throne of the Grand Duchy of Baden, Max had earned a reputation as a reformer and advocate of a negotiated peace. His new cabinet, significantly, excluded the most pro-military factions. Even more important, he had won key powers for the Reichstag that had been the Kaiser's sole prerogative, including the right to appoint the minister of war, to declare war and to make peace.

These measures, in part, were to convince Wilson that when he would treat with Germany it would be a new Germany. And this was just the start, said Max in a note to the American president, promising that German suffrage was soon to be expanded. Germany, in fact, now was moving swiftly down the path to parliamentary government and a constitutional monarchy; German newspapers even began running regular features on the galloping political reforms.

These military and political concessions by Germany's new government infuriated Ludendorff, who by now had rebounded from his pessimistic funk and had regained his spirit. In this new mood he asserted (very probably correctly) that his armies were still powerful enough to stand at and defend Germany's borders. To bolster his argument he pointed out that the advancing French and British forces were showing fatigue and running short of reserves (something acknowledged privately by British Commander in Chief Douglas Haig), while America's Meuse-Argonne Offensive had bogged down (also true). An Allied/American breakthrough, the now feisty Ludendorff told the cabinet on October 17, no longer was imminent. This, he insisted, gives Germany leverage to win much better armistice terms from Wilson than those being obtained by Prince Max.

But Ludendorff's words fell flat; events had swept past him. For one thing, Germany was becoming isolated as its Central Power allies began quitting the war; Bulgaria signed an armistice on September 29 while Turkey and Austria-Hungary clearly were about to do so. There were even rumors that Bavaria's king wanted a separate peace. For another thing, Berlin's negotiations with Washington had moved too far to turn back. Most significantly, Ludendorff's earlier defeatism and the gloomy briefings his lieutenants had given Reichstag deputies had seeped out to the public. They had fueled a German longing for and expectation of peace. German soldiers began asking themselves why they should continue fighting if peace were being sought. These feelings could not now be extinguished. Writes William Mulligan in the journal *War in History*: "Nobody wanted to be the last to die in a lost war."[10]

If the peace genie thus had been let out of the German bottle, it was Ludendorff who did it. Increasingly seen as a huge obstacle to peace, serious moves to oust him had begun in the now more muscular and assertive Reichstag. Upon learning that the new cabinet was demanding his dismissal, he insisted on an audience with the Kaiser. In their stormy October 26 meeting, Ludendorff quit, just moments before he was to be fired. A few weeks later he fled to Sweden, disguised with a false beard and dark glasses. The Kaiser was not to last much longer than Ludendorff. By the time the armistice was signed, Wilhelm II and the Hohenzollern monarchy were to be gone, as would be the ruling royalty of other German states, victims of a swift, surprising (though brief) revolution that began sweeping the country.

Dismantling Wilson's Peace, Piece by Piece

Satisfied that the terms he had imposed on Berlin were both a step towards fulfilling his Fourteen Points and a guarantee that the German Army would be too weakened to fight, Wilson sent the armistice draft to the British and French. He also sent his most trusted adviser, Colonel Edward House. Wilson and House anticipated wielding considerable leverage over the Allies in hammering out final armistice details. After all, they reasoned, Britain and France had grown dramatically dependent on the U.S. As Wilson put it in a cable to House, they are "financially in our hands." There was great truth to this. Britain, for instance, since the start of 1918 had been relying almost totally on America for food and supplies for its army and civilians.

But Wilson and House miscalculated. British and French leaders were in no mood to rubberstamp America. Stubborn and dismissive of House, they insisted on an armistice much tougher on Germany than Wilson had negotiated. Though House, in some contentious exchanges with the Allies, threatened that America would go its own way and "withdraw its army from the war" if armistice terms strayed seriously from the Wilson draft, ultimately and repeatedly he gave in on key issues. What most mattered to House was winning British and French endorsement of the Fourteen Points. But Allied leaders did little to hide their contempt for Wilson's idealistic proposals or their anger at not having been consulted earlier by him. For example, at a meeting shortly after House arrived in France, French Premier Georges Clemenceau turned to British Prime Minister David Lloyd George and queried theatrically: "Have you ever been asked by President Wilson whether you accept the Fourteen Points? I never have."[11]

In the end, to win even just lip service endorsement of the Fourteen Points, House caved in on almost everything else, including crucial details affecting how the Points later would be interpreted and applied. In these negotiating sessions, the Allies uncannily seemed to know that they could push House quite far. For good reason. The British not only long before had broken the State Department code Wilson was using to cable U.S. diplomats in Britain and France, they also just had broken the special ciphers devised for Wilson's cables to and from House. London knew nearly everything Wilson and House were saying to each other. Because of House's many concessions, says Thomas Knock in his 1995 analysis of Wilson's diplomacy, the "Allies gained a stranglehold on Germany that weakened Wilson's future bargaining position."[12] Just how extraordinarily weakened would become frustratingly clear just a few months later at the peace conference.

Piece by piece, Clemenceau, Lloyd George and their staffs shaved and twisted Wilson's draft armistice. Then they handed over the process to their army commanders, saying that a ceasefire, after all, is really a military matter requiring military decisions. Surprisingly, at this level there were calls for restraint. British Commander in Chief Haig, for one, pressed for more lenient treatment of Germany. It was not that he, architect of those massive offensives in which many tens of thousands of his Tommies had been killed by Germans, had grown soft. Rather, he feared that terms too tough could prompt Berlin to reject the deal and thus continue the war.

Haig well knew that his forces and France's were in poor shape—tired, supply lines stretched much too far and reserves much too thin. He already had advised Supreme Commander Ferdinand Foch that deepening manpower shortages would force British divisions in 1919 to shrink their size. By contrast, as Haig had told Britain's War Cabinet, the Germans were in relatively decent shape, retreating to shorter, tighter, easier-to-defend lines, from which they could fight for months, even longer. Whether his own army could stay on the attack for that long Haig was unsure. After all, as impressive as Allied and American battlefield gains had been since August, everywhere they still faced stiff, disciplined German opposition. Haig's views were reinforced by his lieutenants. When he asked his four top commanders on October 31 to assess the battlefield, they told him, as he later wrote (the italics emphasis is his): "The enemy is fighting very good rear-guard action and *all are agreed* that from a military standpoint, *the enemy has not yet been sufficiently beaten as to cause him to accept an ignominious peace.*" This judgment was seconded by French Commander in Chief Henri Philippe Petain who similarly worried greatly about the state of his armies.[13]

Strongly disagreeing with them were Pershing and, much more important, Foch, who demanded terms far tougher than anything Wilson had imposed on the Germans. With Foch steadfastly supported by Clemenceau, Haig and Petain backed down. In the end, Foch's determination to cripple and humiliate Germany shaped the armistice to be proposed to Berlin, just as it was to shape much of the final peace. Quipped Clemenceau, the terms may not have "asked for the Kaiser's trousers, but that is about all." Scrapped were Wilson's vows and negotiated promises of a fair ceasefire. General Tasker Bliss, America's top political envoy to the Allies and onetime U.S. Army Chief of Staff, acknowledged that the Foch armistice was not an armistice at all but a "demand for a complete surrender." Equally despairing was Haig, admitting in a letter to his wife that were he a German officer "in similar situation," he would "rather die than accept such [armistice] conditions." In another letter he prophetically told his wife that "[we should] not attempt to so humiliate Germany as to produce a desire for revenge."[14]

In the Allied/American negotiations crafting armistice terms, Pershing played a disquieting role: he pushed for Germany's unconditional surrender even though he knew full well that he was contradicting and thus undermining Wilson. On October 30, for instance, Pershing called on his fellow commanders in chief to "continue the offensive until we compel [Germany's] unconditional surrender." He even openly went around Wilson. Without informing Washington he communicated his views directly to Clemenceau and Lloyd George, telling them that he believed that "the complete victory can only be achieved by continuing the war until we force unconditional surrender from Germany."

Pershing's memoirs reveal just how adamantly he felt; what he wanted, he writes, was "no peace until Germany is completely crushed." That would result, he adds strongly, in a "dictated peace" rather than a "negotiated peace."[15] His use of the word "dictated" was an eerie and unfortunate foreshadowing of how that word was to be deployed during Germany's postwar turmoil. German extremists and ultra-nationalists, including Adolf Hitler's National Socialists, were to mobilize mass support to undermine the legitimacy of Germany's new democracy by thundering repeatedly that the peace the government had signed was a humiliating "*diktat,*" imposed unfairly on Germany.

By his words and actions opposing Wilson's policies, Pershing undoubtedly had crossed the line of insubordination. Though he survived, later generations of senior American commanders who similarly were to ignore or contradict their presidents would lose their jobs. Most dramatic, of course, was General Douglas MacArthur's April 1951 dismissal by Harry Truman as commander of U.S. forces in the Korean War. More recently, General Stanley McChrystal in June 2010 was sacked as commander of U.S. operations in Afghanistan by Barack Obama for disparaging Administration officials and policy.

History, of course, can understand Pershing's strong feelings and his urge to express them. His American Expeditionary Force, after eighteen long months of preparation and training, had just reached its stride and had begun to flex its muscle on the battlefield.

His headquarters' file cabinets were overflowing with fresh plans and strategies for an AEF push deep into Germany, for defeating the German Army, for winning the war. This was no time, he could think, to stop. Haig's and Petain's soldiers may be tired, he could say sympathetically, but his were not; British and French manpower reserves may be depleted, but his certainly were not—indeed, thousands of doughboys were continuing to land in France every day. For Pershing, as he candidly was to remark at the exact moment when the armistice took effect, the war was ending too soon.

Pershing's hawkishness on the armistice was mirrored at home. This too history can understand. Though the American public by no means had greeted war with Germany enthusiastically and though Germany had neither attacked America nor was even accused by Wilson as threatening America, once war was declared the popular mood abruptly changed. The U.S. government's massive propaganda campaign orchestrated by George Creel's Committee on Public Information plus the hyper-energetic war bond rallies, popular songs, orators on lecture circuits, patriotic and sensationalist newspaper reporting from the battlefield and the newly introduced motion picture all relentlessly portrayed Germany as the incarnation of evil and as America's dangerous, barbaric and bloodthirsty enemy. This portrayal forcefully started ringing true once German soldiers began shooting at, and killing, doughboys. At that moment, with blood spilled, Germany indeed did become America's enemy. It is no surprise, therefore, that Americans would want revenge and feel cheated were a defeated Germany treated lightly. "War mad," is how Wilson adviser House described the American public.

There was plenty evidence of that. Around the country, self-proclaimed patriotic organizations, such as the Connecticut Council of Defense, adopted resolutions opposing any ceasefire not based on Germany's unconditional surrender. Loudly echoing such sentiments were both Republican and Democrat newspaper editorial pages. The *Baltimore Sun*, for example, demanded absolute surrender; the *New York Tribune* insisted on a "crushing military defeat" of Germany; and the *New York Times* blasted the notion of "peace without victory," declaring in an October 7 headline that there should be "No Peace with the Hohenzollern."

Ratcheting up the rhetoric, Syracuse University's Rector proclaimed that "it is religious to hate the Kaiser because the Bible teaches us to hate the devil and all his works." And the *Chicago Daily News* called for a firing squad to execute the Kaiser. Thus, while Wilson's visions for an armistice and subsequent peace may have been sound and wise policy, they were out of step with what fast was becoming masses of the American people. He may have been able to bring his nation into the war, but doing so fueled and sparked forces he could not control. America's entry into the Great War may have launched Wilson's war, but the peace was not at all to be Wilson's peace.

Undermining Wilson further and stoking public rage were his political opponents. Teddy Roosevelt, who already had lost one son on the Western Front and saw another wounded, traveled the nation, letting loose his extraordinary oratorical firepower to vilify Germany and demand its punishment. "The thing to do is lick Germany and tell her what arrangements we are going to make," he boomed to a New Hampshire crowd. In Maine he demanded that America "beat Germany to her knees." Repeatedly he declared that America must not pursue Wilson's "quack peace" but force Germany to surrender unconditionally. Republicans, he vowed, would push the "war to the hilt." Inspired by Roosevelt, GOP Senators introduced a resolution to bar Wilson even from negotiating with the Germans until they had surrendered. Putting it most bluntly was Henry Cabot Lodge, the Senate's leading Republican and a long-time Wilson foe; he thundered in the Senate that: "No peace that satisfies Germany in any degree can ever satisfy us."[16]

In the end, American and Allied advocates of a tough, crippling peace swamped Wilson's compromise "peace without victory." A dispirited House wrote in his diary: "Neither the President nor I desired to make a vengeful peace. Neither did he desire to have the Allied armies ravage Germany... I am sorry [the President] is hampered in any way by the Allies and the vociferous outcry" in America.

Germans "Entrapped to Their Doom"

Tough, very tough, terms therefore were to greet the German armistice negotiators when they met the Allies on November 8, 1918. Representing the new largely democratic German government, they were a rumpled, tired, demoralized band. They first had traveled in a Mercedes caravan under a billowing white flag through German lines into no man's land over bumpy, gutted roads and trails, and then, after meeting French Army escorts, crossed behind French lines, ultimately transferring to a three-coach train taking them to a rail siding at Rethondes, a village in the Compiègne Forest. There they parked opposite Foch's private train.

Leading the delegation was not a military man (as would have been traditional for armistice talks), but a Württemberg-born politician and former teacher and journalist, Matthias Erzberger, head of Germany's third largest party, the Catholic Center Party. Though he specialized in finance issues, he had begun criticizing the war in 1917 and sponsored the Reichstag's July 1917 peace resolution. He also had lost a son in the war. Berlin was hoping that these credentials and the fact that he was not a Prussian would win sympathy from the Allies. They did not. The German delegation's military members, who were to face an imposing Foch, majestic as the supreme Allied/American commander and a Marshal of France, were pygmies: an elderly army major general and an obscure navy captain. Glaringly absent were any of Germany's top military commanders.

These German emissaries, tired from little sleep and still wearing the clothes in which they had started, had come fully prepared to surrender. But they also had come fully expecting to negotiate key surrender and ceasefire details along the lines painstakingly drafted by Wilson and Berlin. Soon, to their shock and horror, they discovered how wrong they were. Totally unaware were they of how the Wilson armistice had been mutilated by the French and British. Equally unaware were they that there would be no opportunity for real negotiations. Instead, they were to be handed, in effect, what Pershing had desired, a "dictated peace."

At 9 a.m., November 8, the Germans formally presented themselves to Foch and his associates. Representing Britain was First Sea Lord Rosslyn Wemyss. Missing, significantly—and strangely—and as what the Germans could view only as a very ill omen, was any sign of an American. Astoundingly, at this crucial final stage of crafting the armistice for a war that could not have been won without America, a war that, in truth, America had won, America was excluded. Pershing was not at Compiègne nor were any of his lieutenants. For these missing Americans historians have found a dozen explanations and rationalizations, all of which may be slightly plausible. Yet none can justify the staggering insult to America and, much more important, the enormous strategic mistake by America of its failure to be present to accept Germany's surrender and to establish the final terms of that surrender.

Foch immediately set the meeting's tone. He was brusque, curt, unyielding. The Germans, he quickly made clear, were expected to grovel submissively. After Erzberger and his colleagues entered a conference car in Foch's train and took their seats at the narrow table, both sides were silent. Foch asked Erzberger why he had come, to which the German replied that he was there to listen to Allied armistice proposals. Foch cut him short, snapping that he had no proposals. Then Erzberger said that he was there to ask what armistice conditions the Allies were seeking. Again he was cut short, with Foch saying that he had no conditions to offer. But, explained a puzzled and visibly rattled Erzberger, the Germans had come because Wilson's November 5 note to Berlin explicitly had instructed them to go to Foch to learn the conditions. Foch again dismissed this. Germany, he intimated, must first request the armistice and only then would he present conditions.

This was alarming; there was nothing subtle about the enormously significant principle Foch was establishing. It shocked the Germans and would have infuriated Wilson. Foch was mandating that the armistice was not being requested mutually by both sides but solely by Germany. This ignored the entire substance of the weeks-long Wilson-Berlin exchange which had rested on the premise that both sides wanted the fighting to stop, that both sides were seeking an armistice. This notion Foch now scuttled. Getting the message, Erzberger, the former school teacher, meekly said that yes, he had come to request an armistice.

A Foch aide then read the conditions. Going far beyond anything Wilson had approved, making a mockery of any notion of a peace without victory that would not humiliate or cripple Germany, the armistice demanded almost total German demilitarization. What the Germans in essence discovered at Compiègne was that, as B.H. Liddell Hart wrote in 1930, they "had been entrapped to their doom by [Wilson's] promises."[17] More than a half-century later, British historian Niall Ferguson concurs, speculating in his 1998 study of the war that had Germans really known what they would encounter they well may have not gone to Compiègne. Instead, Ferguson writes, German "morale both at home and at the Front would almost certainly have been fortified" by the French torpedoing of the Wilson peace.[18]

The Foch ceasefire contained thirty-four terms. Among them, Germany would have to evacuate within two weeks all of the territory it had occupied, including Alsace-Lorraine (which had been German since 1871); it would lose all holdings on the west bank of the Rhine; it would give to America, Britain and France east bank Rhine military enclaves at the important cities of Koblenz, Cologne and Mainz; it would surrender almost all of its machine guns, artillery and airplanes; it would turn over to Britain and France almost the entire German Navy; it would hand over 5,000 locomotives, 150,000 railway cars and 5,000 trucks; and it would pay the victor nations reparations for war damage. There was more. Even though the fighting was to stop, the British naval blockade would not. German civilians for the foreseeable future thus would continue being deprived of food and other basic goods. And they were, well into 1919.

During the reading of the terms, according to historical reports, Erzberger sat impassively. His associates were more expressive. At hearing how many weapons Germany was to surrender, one German cried out: "But then we are lost! How are we going to defend ourselves against Bolshevism?" Another quietly wept. Understandably. Writes British military historian John Terraine: This "was nothing less than unconditional surrender."[19] And though this definitely was not the armistice that Wilson had led Berlin to expect, the German delegation could find no Americans at Compiègne to which to appeal.

Erzberger was given seventy-two hours to consider the terms. Until then, the Germans were told, the war would go on, with the Allied and American armies continuing to press forward towards German soil. Erzberger pleaded for an immediate temporary ceasefire, for the killing to stop, but was summarily refused. He begged that the British blockade be lifted, to prevent German cities from starving. Again, he was refused.

With that, the Germans left for their quarters to begin analyzing the terms and drafting responses. By couriers, they sent the proposed armistice to the German High Command at its Spa, Belgium headquarters and to the government in Berlin, asking for instructions. To each of the thirty-four points, Erzberger drafted counter-proposals, seeking to soften conditions. In this, he was encouraged by both Berlin and the High Command. But he also was instructed, unambiguously, that whatever the results of his efforts to modify the armistice, he must sign it. Years later, German ultra-nationalists would accuse the civilians in the new government and at the armistice table of selling-out Germany, of (as they put it) "stabbing Germany in the back." It was an accusation which, to history's misfortune, resonated widely in Germany and stuck. Yet the accusation had (and has) no basis in fact. It was Ludendorff who first asked for an armistice and it was Hindenburg who explicitly instructed Erzberger to sign.

Little was to come of the Germans' attempts to salvage the Wilson armistice. In the end, at about 5 a.m. on November 11, with Foch having rejected just about every one of Erzberger's modifications, Germany accepted the terms. Erzberger signed the armistice. Foch did so for France followed by Admiral Wemyss for Britain. (There was no one, obviously, to sign for America.) Foch then declared that the ceasefire would take effect six hours hence, at 11 a.m. Erzberger rose, extending his hand to Foch; it was rebuffed. Erzberger then said (or perhaps warned): "A nation of seventy million suffers but does not die." As soon as the Germans left, Foch by radio and telephone sent the order to his commanders in chief: "Hostilities will cease on the entire front on November 11, at 11 a.m. French time."

Erzberger and his delegation immediately headed home. There they were to find a Germany in absolute upheaval. In the few days that they had been away, revolutions had erupted across the land. Events were moving so rapidly, in fact, that when Erzberger signed the armistice he did so on behalf of a still newer German government, this one a genuine republic. Gone was Kaiser Wilhelm II, forced to abdicate and seek refuge in Holland (where he lived until his death in 1941 at age eighty-two). Gone were the kings of Bavaria, Saxony and Württemberg and gone were a host of ruling dukes.

Gone too was Prince Max. With sailors revolting in every German seaport, demanding peace and the Kaiser's removal, and with workers igniting general strikes in main cities, Max had stepped down as chancellor, asking Socialist Party leader Friedrich Ebert to take his place in the hopes of preventing communists from seizing control of the protests as the Bolsheviks had a year earlier in Russia. Ebert accepted and hours later a socialist colleague proclaimed Germany a republic. Though the German Army at the front remained well disciplined and under command of its officers, with its units still fighting very competently (so much so that Haig questioned whether his British forces would be able to drive through German defenses), the story was very different in the German rear and in the garrisons. There mutinies were multiplying, with soldiers hoisting red flags, refusing to salute officers and forming "barracks councils" modeled on Russia's "soviets."

This revolt, however, though extremely radical and bloody in Munich and a few other cities, was short-lived. Order was restored within days when key and reliable army regiments and nationalistic paramilitary bands threw their support behind the new republic and its government. Though relatively brief, the violence and bloodletting were to scar permanently the emerging democratic order. Emerge, however, that order managed to do. Less than a half-year after the uprisings, in summer 1919, a constitution establishing a very liberal parliamentary democracy was written by a constituent assembly meeting in the central German city of Weimar, giving birth to what history remembers as the Weimar Republic.

With just six hours to go after Foch's announcement of the 11 a.m. armistice, Western Front combat began winding down. Nearly all French units, for instance, immediately stopped fighting. But not Pershing's AEF. On November 9, anticipating ceasefire, he had ordered his commanders to keep pushing ahead, imploring: "I appeal to the energy and initiative of the commanders and their armies to secure decisive results." And they followed his orders. At the AEF 79th Division, for instance, at 8:56 a.m. on November 11, the commanding general radioed his brigade commanders to remind them that until the final minute of the war "the operations previously ordered will be pressed with vigor." In parts of the front's AEF sector, even as late as 10:30 a.m. doughboys were still leaping out of trenches and assaulting German positions. For some it was actually their first day of combat. Writes Joseph Persico in his history of the armistice: "The American advance struck the [German] gunners as madness... They had only to wait out the next half hour and they could all go home alive."[20]

But they didn't wait and thus not all went home. Casualties were inflicted and injuries suffered. In the Western Front's final six hours, Persico calculates, 2,738 men on all sides were killed and nearly three times that number wounded.[21] Memorials to fallen soldiers can be found scattered around America, poignantly listing the time of death as some moment in the morning of November 11, 1918. After the war, Pershing was widely criticized for sending his doughboys into harm's way and sacrificing lives for apparently no purpose with the conflict about to end. This was the question an angry Congress was asking, in January 1920, when it began investigating why so many doughboys had been killed in the war's final hours.

On the dot, at 11 a.m., the war finally was over. On the Western Front all at last was calm. Germans began pulling back to their country, while the Allies and the AEF moved to take over German positions. In the following days, Belgian and French areas ruled by Germany for more than four years began being liberated, with scenes of joy and relief captured by movie cameras. Many military experts had thought that the couple weeks' requirement for complete German withdrawal was much too short, that the logistics of moving more than two million soldiers over a great distance needed more time and more trucks and railway cars than Germany had. In fact, speculates Bullitt Lowry in his armistice study, Foch had insisted on a rapid German withdrawal because he was assuming that it would trigger chaos.[22]

Yet Germany kept to the timetable. Mainly on foot, German soldiers covered a set distance each day, camping out in the open at night. Vividly describing the scene is Richard Watt's *The Kings Depart*, an acclaimed chronicle of the war's last year: "Every road heading east was suddenly filled with unending gray-clad columns trudging back toward the Rhine… The field army was no disorganized mob. The troops marched in strict order, perfectly under the control of their officers… Such Allied officers as were able to witness the evacuation were frankly impressed… The German field army did not look like a defeated force; the regiments…were in good order, singing, their bands playing."[23] American intelligence officers who observed retreating Germans add: "The discipline and morale were perfect… There was an almost unbroken column… There was not a straggler nor a symptom of disorder."[24] By November 25, just two weeks after the armistice began and on schedule, almost all German soldiers were out of Belgium and France.

Since the retreating Germans in no way behaved like a defeated, broken army, history can ask: And what if Erzberger had not signed? In most respects, such speculation may be fully moot. He had no choice. He had been ordered to end the fighting. Though Germany was in near complete chaos, with powerful forces arrayed against each other plotting or fearing revolution, the one matter upon which all sides and factions in November 1918 agreed was that their nation immediately must stop the war, must stop its soldiers from being killed, must bring its sons home. Yet, in some respects it may be acceptable to speculate about a different outcome of Erzberger's meeting with Foch, though it is pure, even fanciful, speculation. Perhaps Niall Ferguson is correct in supposing that German leaders, politicians and civilians would have felt very differently about asking for peace had they known that its terms were to be but a whisper of what Wilson had offered. Were they to know what they would encounter at Compiègne, he writes, German morale at home and at the front could have been "fortified." Maybe even fortified enough to reject Foch's proffer.

If so, then what? A plausible answer is that the Great War would have continued. With their morale strengthened, the German armies slowly and orderly would fall back towards their nation's frontiers and a more defensible line. This, after all, had been Haig's great fear. He rightly worried, as explained above, that his and France's troops were too exhausted and too short of supplies and fresh manpower to keep attacking at the pace and with the ferocity they had set since August. They lacked, as his top commanders told him, the strength to force an "ignominious peace" on Germany.

This in no way, of course, means that there was a possibility of German victory or even a return to Western Front standoff. Ruling that out completely was America's AEF. It already was huge and still building steam. With every passing day, it was gaining advantage, not only over the Germans but also over the British and French. Soon the doughboys would be the Western Front's undeniably dominant force. Pershing then could execute his grand strategy, driving deep into Germany and winning the war. Were that to happen, to speculate further, Wilson's war had the chance of becoming Wilson's peace. The American president would wield enormous, probably decisive, influence in setting the terms of an armistice and a subsequent peace. The mistake of America entering the war then could be rectified by a peace of compromise. If this speculative script can claim any plausibility then, probably, Pershing was right. The war was ending too quickly—too quickly not only for him and his exquisitely planned strategies but too quickly also for Wilson and his vision of peace. But history does not allow rewrites. Erzberger did sign Foch's armistice and Germany did accept terms that Wilson had always deplored.

One Last Chance

With the armistice in force, just one last chance remained for America to reverse its mistake of declaring war. It was at the Paris Peace Conference, convened January 18, 1919 at the French Foreign Ministry, where a treaty ending the war with Germany was to be negotiated. There, personally representing his nation, Woodrow Wilson would be able to push for the measured peace he had been advocating for two years. But by then, as scores of books and academic papers over the past century (sometimes accusingly and angrily) explain, it was too late. The peace conference deck was stacked against Wilson and America. For one thing, as the Allies repeatedly needled Wilson, his army had neither fought nor bled enough to earn America the dominant negotiating voice. For another, and more important, the armistice had so weakened Germany that Britain and France, along with other victor nations, felt little restraint in grabbing as much as they could from the new German Republic. Making matters worse, with the fighting over and Germany humbled, Britain and France painlessly could dismiss Wilson's views; no longer did they need America's soldiers or resources.

Escorted by U.S. Navy destroyers and a battleship, Wilson set sail for the peace conference from Hoboken on December 4, 1918, aboard the USS *George Washington*, a former German ocean liner captured in the war and renamed by America. Ten days later he arrived in Paris. This first president ever to visit Europe while in office took the Continent by storm. Two million Parisians are said to have jammed their city's boulevards to celebrate him, raining flowers upon him and waving banners proclaiming: "Hail the Champion of the Rights of Man" and "Wilson the Just." Rome greeted him in the ancient manner of welcoming victorious generals, sprinkling its streets with gold-colored sand, while Milan's near-hysterical crowds unfurled banners declaring, "The Saviour of Humanity" and "The Moses from Across the Atlantic."

He was esteemed as much more than a mere politician or national leader. Rather, he was nearly deified as the towering symbol and prophet of vast new social and political changes, of an emerging 20th Century in which the vote was to be expanded, the workingman's lot to be improved and international conflict to be abolished. Herbert Hoover, in his 1958 book about Wilson, may go a bit over the top in describing the adulation, even rapture, generated by the president's arrival in Paris (which Hoover witnessed), but he surely captures the moment's intensity. To Parisians, Hoover writes, "no such man of moral and political power and no such an evangel of peace had appeared since Christ preached the Sermon on the Mount. Everywhere men believed that a new era had come to all mankind."[25]

All of this enormously worried France's Clemenceau and Britain's Lloyd George—understandably. Wilson's triumphal tour, with the popular passion and affection he ignited, truly was, as Thomas Knock points out, "the stuff the Allied prime ministers' nightmares were made of."[26] They feared that Wilson's capturing their publics' imaginations could be wielded at the conference table to America's considerable advantage. In fact, this is exactly what Wilson sought; he assumed that his superstar-like popularity would strengthen his voice and increase his negotiating leverage. The other national leaders, he reasoned, would not dare oppose someone so acclaimed by their peoples.

In this, alas, Wilson was to be gravely disappointed. His limitations were most painfully obvious in April 1919 when he tried to pressure Italy's prime minister on a key issue by going over his head and speaking directly to the Italian people. Via a letter sent to and published in Italy's newspapers, Wilson asked Italians to back the principles for which he stood and for which they so exuberantly had cheered when he had visited Rome and Milan. His appeal flopped. Italians ignored him, rallying instead around their prime minister and loudly backing his demands that the newly created Yugoslavia cede key territory to Italy. This episode was typical. At no time in the peace conference could Wilson transform personal, street popularity into negotiating muscle.

Joining Clemenceau, Lloyd George and Wilson in Paris and spreading out into dozens of buildings were delegations from twenty-four other nations plus five British dominions, all of which, in one way or another, had opposed the defeated Central Powers. On the agenda, therefore, was not just a treaty with Germany but also with Austria, Bulgaria, Hungary and the Ottoman Empire. As such, the Paris Conference attracted a cast, literally, of thousands. Typically led by kings, presidents or prime ministers, the delegations all had shopping lists firmly in hand and expected to come away with bounty. To them Paris was a kind of bazaar for haggling over shares of the spoils. A "free for all" is what Henry Kissinger calls it in his history of diplomacy. He calculates that it set up fifty-eight committees which met an aggregate 1,646 times.[27] Counting most was the "committee" dealing with Germany. An informal and select group, its members ultimately numbered just three: Clemenceau, Lloyd George and Wilson. Unsurprisingly, it began being called, to the dismay of other large nations' leaders, the Big Three.

Absent from this grand conference, unable to partake in negotiations, was the German Republic. It had not been invited and was barred even from peeking in as observers. Only near the very end were the Germans summoned—not to negotiate but, as they were harshly instructed, to "receive" a treaty. These missing Germans were extraordinarily bad news for Wilson. Their absence deprived him of the crucial negotiating leverage on which he had counted. All along he had assumed that Germany would sit at the peace table as a great power, weakened to be sure, but still a considerable counterweight to Britain and France. America then would be the indispensable balance wheel, the swing vote shaping the talks' outcome. This leverage Wilson now was to lack, confirming his fears. In a cable to Colonel House during the armistice talks, he had warned that were Germany weakened too much it would "make a genuine peace settlement difficult if not impossible." His fears were to be realized.

It was at the Big Three's morning and afternoon sessions, usually hosted by Wilson in the study at the grand Parisian residence made available to him by the French, where Wilson's skills were tested. By almost all accounts, he failed. His negotiating efforts repeatedly were blunted and outmaneuvered by the British and French. This shocked William Allen White, the renowned editor and Progressive leader who was in Paris. Writing later in the *Saturday Evening Post*, he told readers that Wilson's Paris performance "was as if a man sat down at a card-table with players he scarcely knew, with cards he could not comprehend, playing a game whose rules were beyond him and who was playing for different stakes from the others."[28]

It was not just that Wilson's health began flagging, as it did, or that he was weakened politically, as he was, by recent U.S. elections. Nor was it simply that America's aims in entering the war had never been articulated, as they weren't. In sharp contrast to Italy, Japan and other nations that had allied with Britain and France only after being wooed and promised rich rewards in the event of victory, Washington had set no conditions on the Allies for its entry. And Wilson's speech asking Congress for war was silent on what America expected from victory.

Those factors undoubtedly limited Wilson's clout. But much more important a handicap was his inflated confidence in his own intellectual and negotiating abilities. Seldom did he look to others for advice, even though it was plentiful and well prepared. America, in fact, intensively had been getting ready for a peace conference. In September 1917, House had recruited some 150 experts, whom he set working in rooms first at the New York Public Library and then at the American Geographical Society building in New York City, to research economics, geography, history, political science and other topics relevant to issues certain to arise at talks. This group, likely America's first ever "think tank," quaintly was called "The Inquiry." The problem was that Wilson seldom used its rather impressive output, well over a thousand reports. Instead he relied primarily on what Wilson expert (and fan) Arthur Link calls his "remarkable conviction that he was an instrument of divine purpose."[29] This so rankled Secretary of State Robert Lansing, the second-ranking American at the conference, that he complained of Wilson ignoring "established facts…if they did not fit in with his intuitive sense."

Even aboard the *George Washington* en route to Europe, with ample opportunity for Inquiry experts to brief him and run crash courses on the issues, Wilson kept to himself. During the entire crossing he had but a lone meeting with advisers; and at it, according to participants, his remarks distressingly seemed "vague" and "impromptu." It was the same story at Big Three sessions where it frequently was obvious that, in sharp contrast to Clemenceau and Lloyd George, Wilson had not mastered enough detail to grasp the subtleties of many key issues.

What most impaired Wilson in Paris was his overwhelming (some historians say "obsessive") determination to create a "League of Nations," a kind of United Nations precursor whose power, he insisted, not only would assure world peace but also would remedy whatever flaws the peace treaty might contain. So fixated was he on winning backing for his League that he readily conceded almost every major point in exchange for it. Clemenceau and Lloyd George soon realized that in bargaining with Wilson they merely need hint at opposition to his League to reap one key American concession after another.

And it worked. To win support for the League, Wilson even sacrificed key elements of his Fourteen Points. For example, though he long had championed "self-determination" of nations, the term used to describe the right of peoples to vote to determine who would govern them and how they were to be governed, he abandoned the principle when it applied to the Germans. Thus to Clemenceau's demand that France be granted control of the thoroughly Germanic Rhineland, Saar and other territories, Wilson caved. Not daring to risk losing the Frenchman's support for the League, Wilson dropped his insistence that Germanic lands were entitled to self-determination.

Nor did he stand firm against Britain, France and others demanding possession of Germany's colonies, though that too would violate self-determination. In the final treaty, calculates Thomas Fleming, the British Empire gained more than eight million subjects and 862,000 square miles and the French Empire gained more than five million subjects and 238,000 square miles.[30] Wilson caved again on the guarantee of "freedom of the seas," one of the most important of the Fourteen Points and, of course, one of his most-stated reasons for taking America into the war. Faced with Lloyd George's absolute rejection of anything that could limit Britain's naval operations and maritime dominance, Wilson backed down, not willing to lose the British prime minister's vote for the League. And he bowed to Clemenceau's and Lloyd George's demands that Germany pay massive financial reparations.

Beyond these examples, the catalogue of Wilson capitulations in Paris runs on and on. In the opinion of Wilson expert Thomas Knock, "the Allied statesmen...had decided to take the League of Nations hostage. Throughout the spring, each of them would present a different ransom note." And each time, Wilson paid. Each time he retreated. These retreats from core U.S. positions enormously dismayed Lansing. "The League has become a veritable millstone around our necks," he complained. As a result, the eventual peace agreement actually went further than the armistice in pummeling Germany. In what was to be a sad truth, as Meirion and Susie Harries rightly point out, Germany "paid the price for Woodrow Wilson's dream."[31]

Just as Wilson focused intensely on establishing the League of Nations and obtaining a peace rooted in the Fourteen Points, Clemenceau and Lloyd George similarly had precise aims at the conference. For Clemenceau, the bottom line was restoration of the kind of continental hegemony France had enjoyed for nearly two centuries, until Germany's 1871 unification. This meant the treaty would have to transfer territory from Germany to France, keep Germany militarily puny and force Germany to pay to France (and others) as much reparations as possible. Lloyd George, meantime, wanted to eliminate Germany as a rival to Britain's Royal Navy as well as a competitor for colonies. Much of this, in fact, the British already had attained in the armistice. As Lloyd George remarked, "One of our chief competitors has been most seriously crippled... That is no small achievement." All that now remained was for Paris to enshrine Britain's gains in a formal treaty.

Not surprisingly, Big Three talks at times grew heated. Clemenceau, in particular, bristled at Wilson's ceaseless pressing that Germany be treated in accord with the Fourteen Points. The notoriously prickly and acid-tongued Frenchman accused Wilson, to his face, of being "pro-German" and of "seeking to destroy France." Picking up the theme, French newspapers began attacking the American president. Gone was his aura of savior from America bringing peace to Europe; gone was any chance of intimidating Clemenceau and Lloyd George.

Now Wilson was reduced to being simply just another politician. And he was, all were reminded, no longer even a very successful politician. While Lloyd George soundly had triumphed in Britain's December 1918 parliamentary elections and while Clemenceau just had won overwhelming four-to-one backing in France's Chamber of Deputies, Wilson had stumbled badly in America's November 1918 congressional elections, held just days before the armistice. Against much sound advice, he had made the voting a referendum on his conduct of the war and his peace policies. "Back Up Your President" was the appeal of Democrat ads and banners. Republicans gleefully took up the challenge, retorting endlessly that Wilson was neither competent to make the peace nor be tough enough on Germany. Typical was GOP Senator Harry

New of Indiana. Taking direct aim at the president, he warned that making peace "must not be left to the dreamers, the social uplifters."[32]

The election results humiliated Wilson. Voters yanked control of the House of Representatives and Senate away from the Democrats and gave it to the GOP. This made Wilson archenemy Henry Cabot Lodge of Massachusetts the new chairman of the Senate Foreign Relations Committee, the very panel whose support Wilson ultimately would need to win Senate approval of whatever treaty he would bring home. So emboldened were the Republicans by their election triumph that Teddy Roosevelt, in what today would be shockingly bad form (and unforgiveable), openly tried to undermine Wilson's standing in Paris. As the president was setting off for Europe, Roosevelt declared that "Mr. Wilson has no authority to speak for the American people at this time. His leadership has just been emphatically repudiated by them."[33]

By April, work on the German treaty was finished. Its 440 articles (plus many annexes) mainly were the product of Wilson's weakness and Clemenceau's and Lloyd George's stubbornness. Wilson got his League of Nations, with the peace treaty's first twenty-six articles, grandly called a "Covenant," spelling out the new organization's structure and function. But the League was just about all that survived of Wilson's Fourteen Points and of Wilson's many, many statements about the need for and shape of a balanced peace.

To be sure, a transcript of the Paris talks would record a good many squabbles won by Wilson in bargaining with his two counterparts, but they were minor. At best, almost always, they merely softened at the margins extremely harsh terms sought by the British or French. What filled the rest of the treaty, after those first twenty-six articles, was item after item punishing, humiliating and ultimately weakening Germany's emerging democracy. If all America sought from Germany's defeat was the chance to erect a League of Nations then America got what it wanted. But that is all it got. Wilson brought home almost nothing even remotely serving

America's interests—or, history records, serving peace.

For Wilson and America, in the end, the Paris Conference was a bust. And it was a bust that would spawn enormously horrid consequences. Yet, it would be tremendously unfair to declare Wilson's dismal Paris performance the culprit guilty of those consequences or even of the dreadful peace treaty. To do so exaggerates vastly the conference's importance. It was simply the final episode in an unfortunate saga beginning April 6, 1917 with America's declaration of war. It was not, after all, the conference itself that set the world on its tragic 20th Century course. Nor was it Wilson's failure to stand up enough to Clemenceau and Lloyd George, nor Wilson's fumbling some negotiating subtleties nor Wilson's obsession with his League of Nations. All of that, of course, happened and are grounds for indicting Wilson as a flawed diplomat; on that a near-century of histories agrees.

But there never would have been that kind of Paris Conference, a gathering of chest-thumping victors to the complete exclusion of the defeated, had America not gone to war, had America not rescued Britain and France from their hemorrhaging Western Front stalemate, had America not sent the troops and resources to hand to Britain and France their triumph over Germany. Those actions were the culprits. And because of those, there was little that Wilson could have won in Paris no matter how tough or shrewd (or healthy) he would have been.

Because of what the doughboys had achieved on the battlefield, Britain, France and the other nations could stream into Paris as ravenous victors demanding their pound of German and other Central Powers flesh. They were determined to get it and their peoples back home, huge numbers of whom had suffered horribly in the war, were demanding it. Hard it is to imagine convincingly how Wilson, single-handedly, could have stood up to them and forced a reasonable peace. The "sin," to invoke a word that would be felt deeply by Wilson the moralist, was not his performance at the Paris Peace Conference. The "sin"—indeed the "original sin"—was America's decision to enter the Great War. The final treaty merely codified the consequences of that.

Treaty Terms – Turning Wilson on His Head

Even what are regarded as the treaty's minor provisions testify to the harsh, non-Wilsonian treatment of Germany. Not only were they designed to punish the German economy and award the victors an economic competitive edge, they humiliated Germany. The treaty canceled all German prewar international patents, required all German prewar treaties and financial agreements to be submitted for review and approval, confiscated German ownership of underwater cables and profits from international copyrights of books, art, music and other creative products, took from Germany's control the major rivers Elbe, Oder and Rhine and proclaimed them international waterways and denied Germany the right to impose customs or other regulations on goods entering the victor-occupied Rhineland, thus opening the entire German market to foreign goods duty free.

And these were just the minor terms. Harsher were the treaty's hundreds of articles stripping Germany of almost all its military capabilities, seizing huge areas of German land, requiring Germany to pay unspecified, but threateningly high, reparations, forcing Germany to admit responsibility—"guilt"—for starting the war and, in one of the great ironies of a peace conference at which Wilson traded a great deal for his League of Nations, denying Germany membership in that world organization.

The military terms were drafted by Foch and fulfilled his and Clemenceau's dream of winning for France a commanding supremacy over Germany. The treaty slashed the German Army to a tiny force of 100,000, the Navy to a tinier 15,000 and the Air Force to an even tinier zero. In fact, a German Republic air force was completely banned. So were tanks, armored cars, heavy guns, submarines, a general staff, the training of cadets at high schools and universities and the import of weapons. Severely limited to a handful were factories for producing war materials. So obliterated were the German armed forces, writes Margaret MacMillan in her definitive history of the Paris Peace Conference, that even the Allies admitted that Germany was left "with something closer to a police force than an army."[34]

Equally harsh were the treaty's territorial terms, stripping Germany of thirteen percent of its prewar territory, more than 6.5 million of its inhabitants and ten percent of its prewar coal and iron. Belgium, Denmark and the newly created Czechoslovakia each picked up some German land, while the now independent Poland gained huge tracts, including most of Upper Silesia and a wide strip allowing access to the Baltic Sea. This so-called "Polish Corridor" cut off East Prussia from the rest of Germany. France claimed the most valuable territorial bounty: Alsace and Lorraine, which Germany had taken from France in 1871 as spoils for its Franco-Prussian War victory (though the German-speaking areas had been part of France only since 1552 at the earliest, and some parts only since 1798). Meanwhile, control of the coal and iron-rich Saar was given to an Allied/American body for fifteen years. For up to fifteen years too were the victors to administer the Rhineland, that sizeable area of historic Germany which then (and now) sits on the west bank of the Rhine. Continuing uncertainty about Rhineland and Saar status significantly impeded German postwar investment and economic growth, as did the loss of Upper Silesia.

In addition to stripping away territory from Germany's borders, the treaty confiscated all German colonies and handed them as spoils to the victors. Belgium walked away from Paris with what today are Rwanda and Burundi. Portugal got a sliver to attach to its Mozambique colony. South Africa, a British dominion, took today's Namibia; New Zealand, another dominion, took Samoa; and

Australia, yet another dominion, took today's Papua New Guinea. Britain profited most. It divided with France the German colonies that are today Cameroon, Togo and parts of Ghana and, much more consequential, took the lion's share of German East Africa (part of which is today's Tanzania). With that, London fulfilled its long fantasy of ruling an unending swatch running Africa's full length, from Cairo to the Cape of Good Hope.

Japan also did well. It got the Marshall Islands and all other German Pacific colonies above the Equator. It also took Germany's concessions in China. That, in particular, ignited a Paris Conference controversy reverberating even today. China's young republic had been promised that the valuable German enclave on China's Shandong Peninsula would be returned to China if it declared war on Germany. It did so in 1917, ultimately making what Macmillan calls "a substantial contribution to Allied victory." More than 100,000 Chinese (some sources put the number at 140,000 and more) labored on the Western Front, digging trenches, clearing minefields, working in hospitals and building roads, thus freeing Allied troops for combat. It was dangerous work and killed several thousand Chinese.

Then, to the horror of China's delegation in Paris, the victors handed Shandong to Japan, breaking their promise to China and openly mocking Wilson's central principle of self-determination. So furious were the Chinese that they walked out of the conference and China never signed the treaty. And so embarrassed (and angry) were some Americans that they too walked out, quitting the U.S. delegation in protest. To this day, American visitors to China at times encounter, from both old and young Chinese, bitter reprimands for America's and Wilson's betrayal in Paris. This betrayal and the Chinese delegation's failure to recover Shandong sparked huge Peking University student protests in Tiananmen Square on May 4, 1919.

The loss of so much territory and so many industrial and agricultural resources severely impeded Germany's postwar economic growth and stability, eventually undermining popular support for German democracy. So too did the victors' bill for reparations. To be sure, reparations paid by losers to winners were no strangers to European peace settlements; they had been typical through the centuries. When Germany defeated France in 1871, after all, Berlin had collected an indemnity amounting to twice its military outlays for the conflict. What was unusual and extraordinarily excessive about the reparations sought by the Great War's victors were their scope and size. "A fiasco from the beginning" is how Link describes the reparations.[35] Not only was Germany told, as could have been expected, that it must pay for damage done by its troops and occupying forces to Belgian and French farms, villages, factories and other civilian property. It also was told to pay vast sums for other ostensible war costs rarely if ever added to a reparations tab. These included, among other things, reimbursing the victors for interest they were paying on wartime loans, for the cost of demobilizing their armies and for future pensions for war widows, orphans and wounded soldiers. This pension provision, says Kissinger, "was unheard of; no previous European treaty had ever contained such a clause."[36] Much of the penalties imposed on Germany, in fact, were unheard of.

The potential reparations total to be paid by Germany was staggering. It violated Wilson's promise that the peace would bring "no annexations, no contributions, no punitive damages." These were words the Germans had believed and relied on when they accepted Wilson's armistice terms. And these words also guided the American members of the conference's Committee on Reparations who understandably were shocked by the British and French demands. Wilson too initially may have been shocked. Yet here, as at so many of the conference's other critical moments, he backed down under pressure from Clemenceau and Lloyd George who themselves were being pressed by their populaces to squeeze every last pfennig out of Germany. To make matters worse, ultimately much worse, disagreements among the Americans, British and French prevented a fixed reparations sum from being set in the treaty. That was not to be determined until 1921. This meant that Germany was being asked to sign a treaty obliging itself to pay an unspecified sum. Wilson's agreeing to this, writes Richard Watt, "filled the American delegation with horror."[37]

Economists and historians for the past century have analyzed and debated (and disagreed over) exactly how much Germany actually paid in reparations. In today's dollars it easily would be about $77 billion. But for history, the actual sum is less significant than the dark cloud that reparations hung over Europe for more than a decade after the war. Arguments over how much Germany should be paying and how much Germany could afford to pay dominated and poisoned relations between Germany and the victors. As important, it enormously constricted German growth and injected massive uncertainties into business and investment decisions on both sides of the Atlantic. Most dramatically damaging (as detailed in the following chapter), a reparations dispute triggered the cascade of events culminating in the astounding 1923 German hyperinflation. Wiping out savings, this catastrophe (the specter of which influences German economic and monetary policies to this day) impoverished and demoralized the once solid and respectable German middle class, launching it on the tragic descent into political despair and radicalization ultimately to be harnessed by Hitler's National Socialists.

No section of the peace treaty was to be more controversial—the word "notorious" would not exaggerate—than Article 231. It took no territory from Germany, did not punish Germany economically nor placed any military restrictions on Germany. Yet, more than any of the treaty's 439 other articles, it discredited the peace agreement (abroad as well as in Germany) and tainted the German democracy which had signed it. In this article, Germany was blamed for the war. And blamed solely. It was forced to accept "the responsibility...for causing all the loss and damage" suffered by the victors "as a consequence of the war imposed upon them by the aggression of Germany and her allies." Almost immediately Article 231 became known worldwide as the "war guilt clause" and the massive resentment of it by Germans was exploited with great success by the Nazis and other ultra-nationalists in their assault on the Weimar Republic.

To Germans then and later, it was infuriating and preposterous and, most of all, extraordinarily unfair to be blamed exclusively for the war. Surely no aspect of the war has been more extensively dissected than its outbreak. Scrutinized minutely by historians have been the words, treaties, cables, once-secret documents and actions of the war's key players—Austria-Hungary, Britain, France, Germany and Russia. From this research scholarly fingers, over the decades, have pointed accusingly first at one and then at another of the combatants. At times, for instance, Russia's mobilizing its army, the biggest in Europe, has been seen as the war's main trigger because it panicked Germany, which bordered Russia for some thousand-miles; at other times Austria-Hungary has been the primary culprit, for recklessly threatening war against Serbia (and hence, by proxy, against its protector Russia) after the June 28, 1914 assassination of Austrian Archduke Franz Ferdinand in Sarajevo. Germany has been indicted for its bombastically assertive pre-war global policies and for invading Luxemburg and Belgium, while France has been blamed for igniting the war by pressing Russia to rush and intensify its mobilization. Some historians even have accused Britain of tipping the continent into conflict by sending very confusing and contradictory signals to the major powers and for promising to back France militarily. British historian Ferguson, for one, makes a strong case that it was Britain's actions, not Germany's, that made a continental war more likely.[38]

Many World War One experts over the years, including some today, don't accuse any country at all. Instead, they argue that early 20th Century Europe's complex web of alliances and commitments, plus the rigorous and unforgivingly rigid national military mobilization schedules, kicked in as if on automatic pilot once the crisis between Austria-Hungary and Russia erupted following the Archduke's assassination. This "war by timetable," as it often is known, overpowered all efforts to control or derail a momentum that propelled Europe to a continent-wide war. To Lloyd George, reflecting on this in his memoirs, "the nations slithered over the brink to the boiling cauldron." More than a half-century later, John Keegan agrees, writing that "the states of Europe proceeded, as if in a dead march and a dialogue of the deaf, to the destruction of their continent."[39]

If one thing is definite about what is called "this most contentious of topics," it is that there has been no consensus about how the war started—except on one point. Just about everyone agrees that no single nation or single factor or single miscalculation or single stupid decision started the Great War.[40] This, after all, was not World War Two, with its smoking-gun culprits: Japan invading China and attacking Pearl Harbor and Germany invading Poland. In August 1914, guilt was not Russia's alone nor France's nor Austria-Hungary's. And it was not Germany's. "Most historians today believe that Germany did not deliberately plan to go to war," writes Hew Strachan in *Foreign Affairs*.[41] Even those very critical of the Germans at most argue, as does Britain's Gary Sheffield in his 2001 history *Forgotten War*, that Germany's "behavior in July 1914 was the most important single factor" igniting the conflict.[42] That is quite different from saying that it was the sole factor.

In truth and fairness, blame is shared, to varying extents, by all the Great War's principal belligerents. At one time, in fact, Wilson would have agreed; in 1916 he talked about "the obscure foundations" of the war and, according to George Kennan, stressed that the U.S. was "not concerned" about its causes.[43] That Article 231 thus branded Germany alone guilty reveals just how determined the victors had become to punish Germany severely. And that article came to typify just how much the treaty had turned Wilson on his head. In place of his "peace without victory," the peace conference crafted what in just a generation turned into a victory without peace.

"Where are our Fourteen Points?"

More than three months after the peace conference convened, Germany at last was permitted to send a delegation to Paris. Its 180 members—headed by the foreign minister and including senior diplomats, experts, academics, translators, secretaries, journalists— left Berlin on April 28, 1919, in two special trains, loaded with research papers, maps, what a later generation would call "talking points," demographic data and all else they felt would bolster their arguments in the tough negotiations they believed awaited them. Of the treaty's proposed terms or of the Big Three's intensive and contentious bargaining, they were almost completely in the dark. Having been barred from the conference's negotiating and drafting sessions (even from their environs), German knowledge of what had been happening in Paris was all second-hand, mainly from foreign and generally unreliable newspaper accounts or from the occasional intelligence source.

Still, Berlin allowed itself mild optimism as it dispatched its delegates. Though the Armistice had been unnervingly harsh, the Germans were expecting the peace agreement itself to be much different, much more lenient. After all, in Paris, in stark contrast to the Compiègne Forest armistice meeting, America would be at the table. And not simply America, but Woodrow Wilson himself. In him, Germans continued to place extraordinary trust. He would treat Germany fairly, they deeply believed, not only because of his Fourteen Points and other statements about and promises of a balanced peace, but also because when Germany had stopped fighting it had done so under conditions negotiated with him. Certainly, they reckoned, he would stay true to those conditions. "The Germans," explains

MacMillan, "clutched the Fourteen Points like a life raft."[44] Even more important, as German leaders kept reassuring themselves, they had been fulfilling one after another of Wilson's demands. They had deposed the Kaiser and overthrown the centuries-old Hohenzollern dynasty; they had become a republic; they had become a parliamentary democracy; they had expanded suffrage, enacted workers' and union rights and brought socialist parties into the government; they were abiding by the Armistice terms and in Weimar they were crafting a constitution of which Wilson, the political scientist and Progressive president, would be proud.

Would not all of this, Germans said to each other, prove to Wilson that the Germany he was dealing with in Paris was far different from the Imperial Germany whose "military masters and monarchical autocrats," as he had called them, had fought the war? Was this not, as Wilson had demanded, a Germany representing its people? And had he not, when declaring war on Germany, stated explicitly that Americans "have no quarrel with the German people. We have no feeling toward them except one of sympathy and friendship"? Had he not promised as recently as at an April 1918 Liberty Bond rally, with America already at war a full year, that America would "be just to the German people" and "deal fairly with the German power, as with all others"? This new Germany, this genuine German democracy, its leaders deeply believed, Wilson would not allow to be crippled.

They were, of course, to be astoundingly disappointed. From the first moment of the delegates' arrival in Paris the omens were bad. They were shepherded to a hotel where their luggage rudely was dumped in the courtyard. Their quarters were surrounded by barbed wire and patrolled by French soldiers, cutting them off from the contact with conference delegates, journalists and others that they had been promised. For a nervous, apprehensive week, they waited in isolation, hearing nothing and being told nothing. Finally, on the afternoon of May 7, as instructed, they headed for the Trianon Palace at Versailles, some twelve miles outside Paris. There, as MacMillan, Watt and other historians describe the scene, in an elegant room packed with delegates representing all the victors, the German Republic's delegation was led to seats facing Clemenceau, Lloyd George and Wilson. Gravely, the French Premier said: "The hour has struck for the weighty settlement of our account. You have asked us for peace. We are disposed to give it to you."

With that, the Germans were handed a single copy of a white-covered, 200-page book entitled (in English and French) "Conditions of Peace," containing 440 separate articles of what was called the preliminary treaty. They were given fifteen days (later extended to twenty-two) to review it and send their "observations" in writing. There would be, they learned horrifyingly, no face-to-face oral negotiations, no arguments and rebuttals and, most devastating of all, no chance directly to engage, to say nothing of appeal to, Wilson. After their "observations" were submitted in writing, the Germans were told, the victors would review them. Then the Germans would be summoned to "receive" the final terms.

It was not only the Germans who got their first look at the treaty on May 7; so did the victor delegations. Not until that moment had the treaty's scores of sections, crafted by separate committees with little contact with each other, been amalgamated and collated in a single volume. Thus not until that moment had anyone actually read the entire treaty text. "It came like a bombshell to many of them," says Watt. The U.S. delegation's press chief, for one, called it "a terrible document, a dispensation of retribution with scarcely a parallel in history." This verdict was echoed by Secretary of State Lansing, who called the terms "immeasurably harsh and humiliating." Many of the articles, he added presciently, "seem to me impossible of performance."[45]

This victor delegates' jolt was little compared to what would be the Germans'. As soon as the German delegates returned to their hotel, they ripped their single copy of the proposed treaty into sections, assigning each to a group for translation and review. As the work began, the magnitude of the disaster began sinking in. Nothing in their intensive preparations for the negotiations had readied them for what the translators were reading to them. Over the decades, historians have sought words to describe the German reaction: horror, incredulity, dismay, anger, shock, frustration, rage—and, of course, betrayal. It seemed as if every aspect of German sovereignty and future well-being had found its way into one or another punishing treaty article. "Nothing had been spared them," judges Watt.[46] And nothing would be spared them.

Within three days, thousands of translated treaty copies were in the hands of officials in Berlin. That city's shock and bitterness are hard to exaggerate. They were expressed in many ways. National mourning was declared for a week, government buildings flew flags at half-mast and the stock exchange was closed. Every political party denounced the treaty, including the extremely radical and revolutionary Independent Socialists. So did the pacifists, who had taken great personal risks in tirelessly opposing the war. That, they claimed, gave them a special moral right to speak out on the terms of peace. And they did so strongly, with one national pacifist leader declaring that the answer to the victors must be "No, and a second time, No, and a third time, No!"

Angry Berliners, meanwhile, gathered outside the American military mission and shouted accusingly: "Where are our Fourteen Points? Where is Wilson's peace?" And at a May 10 National Assembly meeting, Philipp Scheidemann, the moderate socialist who was now chancellor, dramatically gave voice to the national outrage and despair in a statement which was to echo through a century of German history and is cited by Germans still in our day. "What hand would not wither," he thundered, "that binds itself and us in these fetters?"[47] He ultimately resigned rather than put his hand to the final treaty.

Back in Paris, the German delegation, with its experts, was analyzing the treaty article by article, word by word. Carefully-argued, tightly-reasoned rebuttals were being drafted, citing treaty inconsistencies with the Fourteen Points and with the promises Berlin had received from Wilson in exchange for agreeing to a ceasefire. After all, it was stressed, Germany had not surrendered unconditionally. It had received assurances; promises had been made. But when the German delegation's rebuttals were sent to the conference requesting treaty revisions, almost without exception they were denied. At one point, a clearly irritated Wilson briskly rejected a German note by saying dismissively that "the time for discussion is past." In truth, of course, no discussion by the Germans ever had been permitted. And there was to be none.

On May 29, meeting the twenty-two-day deadline, the Germans formally sent 119 pages of counterproposals to the victors. Then they nervously awaited a response. During this time, unknown to them, their arguments actually were gaining a bit of traction. In particular, Britain's Lloyd George and many members of his delegation were growing increasingly uneasy with the proposed treaty's severity. So much so that he, on June 1, called the British cabinet to Paris to discuss the document and Germany's objections, many of which seemed sensible to the British. In an astounding two-day meeting, the cabinet, including Secretary of State for War Winston Churchill, reviewed article after article, deeming first one then another unreasonable or unfair—the sections on reparations, on the amount of land given to Poland, on the duration of the victors' Rhineland occupation and on dozens of others.

Upsetting the British too was Germany's exclusion from face-to-face negotiations. In the end, the cabinet unanimously told Lloyd George to seek broad and fundamental treaty changes. But when, later that day, he tried to do so, he failed. Clemenceau opposed any substantive revisions, snapping: "We do not have to beg pardon for our victory." And when Lloyd George turned to Wilson for what he expected would be support, the American president fully backed the Frenchman. By this time, as British historian David Stevenson chronicles in his study of World War One diplomacy, Wilson too had come to champion punitive treatment of the Germans, reversing what he previously and frequently had proclaimed. He even stated, according to MacMillan, that the Germans "should be shunned and avoided like lepers for generations to come."

There thus was to be no reconsideration of the treaty's terms. As such, two weeks later, on June 16, when the Germans received the answer to their counterproposals, just about all were rejected. In addition, the Germans would be allowed no further arguments. This was, the victors' response stated flatly, the "last word." Then, in an ultimatum, the Germans were told that they must accept the treaty within seven days or the Armistice would be terminated and Allied and American armies, it was hinted, would resume the war, attack Germany and march on Berlin.

After quickly examining the victors' statement, the German delegates concluded that there was nothing left for them to do in Paris. They headed back to Berlin where the government and National Assembly now would have to decide whether to accept the treaty. There, no one wanted to put his signature to the loathsome document; no party wanted the responsibility of imposing the humiliating and painful conditions on their countrymen. But they had no real choice. At the time of the ceasefire, of course, Germany had some muscle. As British commanders and others feared, Germany then could have mounted a powerful defense of its borders against an Allied/American offensive and inflicted great pain on the attackers.

But now there was little prospect that the tiny, remnant German Army could even slow an assault. The new reality dictated that the government's sole option was to accept the treaty. This it voted to do—but only after a chaotic week of political turmoil, violent National Assembly debates and the dramatic and unsettling resignation of the Scheidemann cabinet, hopelessly divided about whether to sign. With only hours remaining before expiration of the victors-imposed deadline for accepting the treaty, a new German government was organized. It immediately brought the treaty before the National Assembly, managed to stitch together a very reluctant and relatively slim majority and then, with the clock ticking toward the deadline, formally informed the peace conference that Germany would sign.

Five days later, on June 28, in the Palace of Versailles Hall of Mirrors, in a setting described by Colonel House "as humiliating to the enemy as it well could be," where, later recalled English diplomat and author Harold Nicolson who witnessed the event, "the Germans were conducted like prisoners from the dock," two representatives of the German Republic signed what history came to know as the Treaty of Versailles.[48] It was France's Foch, though author of some of the treaty's most punishing sections, who well recognized what he and his fellow victors had wrought. "This is not peace," he said, "it is an armistice for twenty years." He was prophetic almost to the day.

This flawed peace and the consequences flowing from it obviously were not the reasons why America had gone to war. But they were the consequences of America having done so. Without U.S. entry into the conflict, without the specter of millions of American troops heading for France and without the reality of two million doughboys actually marching onto the Western Front, there never would have been such a peace treaty. Unintended consequences were they for sure. But consequences nonetheless.

CHAPTER 8

LEGACY OF A VICTORS' PEACE

THE DELEGATIONS BEGAN LEAVING FRANCE right after signing the Versailles Treaty. Woodrow Wilson sailed home from Brest on July 2, 1919. His work and that of his team were finished. World War One was over. World War Two was to start but twenty years and two months later. Wilson had led America into war mainly to assure a seat at the peace table. That he had achieved. At that table, he had sought a League of Nations. That too he had achieved. And this accomplishment, which to the end of his life he valued above all else, cheered him immensely, prompting his staff to remark how relaxed, even buoyant, he appeared on shipboard after the months of grinding and physically-draining negotiations.

But his League was expensive. Its price tag was a Treaty of Versailles packing into its 440 articles almost everything he, over the previous four years, had warned would lead to disaster. And year after year of the following two decades proved him prophetic, though he could not wildly have guessed just how enormously destructive and enduring that disaster would be. What he also could not prophesize was that the first disaster would be Woodrow Wilson himself, brought low by the bitter, agonizing battle to win his nation's approval of the treaty. It destroyed him politically and destroyed his health.

"I Shall Consent to Nothing."

Much of Wilson's time at sea was spent crafting his speech to the Senate asking for approval of that treaty, which, of course, included as its first twenty-six articles the grandly named Covenant of the League of Nations. Wilson realized that securing the two-thirds majority needed for treaty ratification was no sure thing, particularly since Republicans had won Senate control in the 1918 elections and were led by Henry Cabot Lodge of Massachusetts who openly reviled the president, stating repeatedly that he neither trusted nor respected him and admitting that he had never hated "any one in politics with the hatred I feel towards Wilson."[1] To make matters more difficult for the president, Lodge also chaired the Senate's Foreign Relations Committee whose hearings on the treaty greatly would influence most senators. Still, Wilson was very upbeat, confident that the American public broadly supported the League and that his legendary oratorical skills would sway the Senate. He had good reason to be sanguine. Two months earlier the *Literary Digest*, in surveying 1,377 of the nation's newspapers, had found 718 absolutely supporting the League, 478 conditionally supporting it and just 181 completely opposed. League backers, significantly, included many Republican papers. Meanwhile, thirty-two state legislatures and thirty-three governors had endorsed the League.

On July 10, just two days after arriving back in Washington, Wilson personally carried the Versailles Treaty up Capitol Hill and delivered it to the Senate. To packed galleries, he extolled it and its Covenant of the League as "one of the great charters of human liberty" and "the only possible guarantee against war." He gravely warned the senators that rejecting the treaty and keeping America outside the League would be a mistake for which the nation eventually would have to repent. Though the Senate received him warmly (even enthusiastically), almost immediately there were problems. To deflate the seductive impact of Wilson's dramatic Senate appearance, with its aura of a triumphal leader returning home from foreign glory, Lodge ordered the entire treaty to be read, word by word, to the Senate. That consumed two weeks. Then he convened his committee to hold hearings; week after week they plodded along.

During this time, questions and doubts about the treaty mounted—from all political sides. Many influential liberals denounced the treaty as a "bad peace," with Progressive leader and renowned editor William Allen White calling it a "grand gesture of revenge and humiliation." Prominent reformer Amos Pinchot dismissed it as "the shameful peace of Versailles." Among other things, liberals objected to the treaty's harsh treatment of Germany. Pioneer muckraker Lincoln Steffens, for example, warned that "we cannot have both our vengeance and permanent peace." Liberals were also very bothered by the League's explicit recognition of imperialism, thus betraying, they argued angrily, the key Wilsonian principle of self-determination. They complained that the League allowed Britain, France and others to keep their colonies. Such concerns prompted the *New Republic* to apologize to its readers for having backed U.S. entry into the war and to demand rejection of the treaty, which its editor, the very influential Herbert Croly, dismissed as an "inhuman disaster." Agreeing was Walter Lippmann, already an iconic voice of liberalism; he damned the League as "fundamentally diseased."[2]

The most determined resistance to treaty ratification came from a dozen Republican senators so opposed to the League that they happily called themselves "irreconcilables." More consequential was a much larger Senate group, including Democrats, that said they would vote for the treaty—but only if parts, about which they had what they termed "reservations," were changed. What most troubled them were treaty clauses that they feared clipped American sovereignty and freedom of action. Some Republicans argued that the League could force the U.S. to intervene abroad militarily and thus would override Congress' exclusive right to declare war. America, they warned, likely would find itself perpetually in combat. They also complained that the League undermined the Monroe Doctrine, imposed huge barriers to quitting the organization, consigned America to a voting disadvantage since Britain's dominions each would have League seats and required the U.S. to submit to arbitration on foreign policy matters affecting national security. In their arguments, many League opponents in tone and substance echoed Lodge who early on had denounced the League for seeking to substitute "an international state for pure Americanism."

Any call for revising the League Covenant infuriated Wilson. But he could not deny that the Senate, through the "advice and consent" clause in Article II of the Constitution, had the right to demand changes in agreements negotiated by the Executive Branch. In modern times, it is a right the Senate frequently has exercised, as when it forced significant revisions in arms reductions treaties negotiated with the former Soviet Union and free trade agreements negotiated with a host of countries. Understandably, such Senate actions enormously frustrate the White House, which invests huge efforts in striking a deal with a foreign country. Frustrated too (and confused) are those foreign countries that think they have struck that deal with the U.S. and then find it unraveling.

America's treaty ratification procedures, without doubt, can be messy, particularly compared to those of parliamentary regimes where the executive enjoys a legislative majority and thus can count on quick, tidy, almost automatic approval of whatever is negotiated. But messy or not, it is the well-established American system. And Woodrow Wilson, formerly an acclaimed professor of political science, should have understood that.

He clearly did not. Rather than try to work with the Senate's treaty opponents, the president, always extremely self-confident (some describe him as "implacable") and contemptuous of others' opinions, grew ever more stubborn. He allowed only that he would accept non-binding, modest statements expressing the Senate's own interpretations of the treaty. He would hear of nothing requiring reopening renegotiations. He had made his concessions in Paris, he strongly felt; he need not make any in Washington. The mere thought, according to historians who have studied Wilson closely, of his returning to what for him had been the Paris Conference's ugly and grueling bargaining process was just too painful. It was totally unthinkable.

His rejection of treaty change was thus unequivocal; his adamancy admitted no parsing. "We cannot rewrite this treaty. We must take it or leave it," he asserted.[3] Any acceptance of the senators' "reservations," he added, would amount to "nullification." His inflexibility was prominently on display in a talk with the French ambassador. "I shall consent to nothing," Wilson told the envoy. "The Senate must take its medicine."[4]

What the Senate did was take its time, just as Lodge had planned. As the clock ticked on seemingly forever, Wilson's frustration (and anger) ran high and his patience ran thin. Soon it ran out. Feeling he dare wait no longer, he concluded that he could save his League of Nations only by going over the Senate's head and taking his case directly to the American people. In that pre-radio and pre-television age, going to the people meant literally just that—appearing in person before as many audiences across the country as a speaker could handle. And that is what Wilson did.

On September 2, 1919, in what history calls his "Western Tour," he set off in the presidential railway coach from Washington's Union Station for what was to be a three-week, nearly 10,000-mile whistle-stop circle through two dozen Midwest and far West states, the heartland of isolationist America. As the train rolled out of Washington, Wilson was wrapped in cheer and high hopes; his return was to be draped in crushing solemnity. He could not know it, but it was to be a trip whose tragic unintended consequences were to cripple him physically, limit him mentally and throw the presidency into a confusing, non-functioning limbo for seventeen months.

In those days, obviously, such a tour was vastly more punishing than it is now, when an *Air Force One* jumbo jet and a *Marine One* helicopter comfortably whisk a president from one speech platform to another. For Wilson it was an extraordinarily demanding marathon, requiring him to address scores and scores of welcoming, enthusiastic and curious crowds, stand interminably in open cars, review parades, speak (actually shout) without amplification hours each day to audiences as large as 40,000 and shake an endless army of hands.

First stop was Columbus, Ohio, then on to Indiana and Missouri, where he told war veterans in St. Louis that Senate rejection of the League would betray them because "you fought for something you did not get." After that the presidential train veered northward, with speeches and rallies all along a route from Iowa to the Dakotas and Washington State and then south and east through California and into Arizona. He pulled few punches, caustically, even nastily, telling audiences at fair grounds, civic centers, armories, circus tents, legislatures and sports stadiums that it was time for the Senate to "put up or shut up," that League critics were engaging in "pro-German propaganda" and that a League rejection equaled a "death warrant" on America's children.

After a somewhat slow start with mixed receptions, according to reports by the several dozen journalists and movie cameramen accompanying him, crowds grew warmer and then boisterously enthusiastic. When those audiences loudly cheered his words, they cheered him up. He began to feel that he was succeeding, that he was churning a tidal wave of support for the treaty and his League.

Perhaps he was. But history will never know. In the evening

of September 25, following an unusually long speech in Pueblo, Arizona, the trip's strains and exhaustive pace caught up with the president. He fell so ill, with such "unbearable" pain, as his memoirs describe it, that his personal physician urged canceling the tour. After objecting a bit, Wilson agreed. The train, curtains on his car now drawn, barreled back to Washington, arriving September 28. Though he was able to walk haltingly through Union Station to his car, he was still very ill. Four days later catastrophe struck. He fell to the floor in a White House bathroom where his wife, Edith, found him bloody and unconscious.

For the public the official word was that the president was bedridden from nervous exhaustion. The truth, according to specialists who have scrutinized his medical records over the decades, is that he had suffered a massive stroke. He was paralyzed on the left side, was greatly incapacitated and never again could rise from a chair without help. Though his health occasionally rallied, it always again quickly deteriorated. For the remaining seventeen months of the Wilson presidency, he could do but little work and barely spoke. As August Heckscher explains in his 1991 Wilson biography, the White House stopped functioning; bills became laws without a president's signature, personnel vacancies remained unfilled and decisions were indefinitely postponed.

Through all of this, America was told nothing of their president's true condition. The twice-daily official medical bulletins spoke only of Wilson's fatigue from overwork. It was, admits Heckscher, a Wilson admirer, "a cover-up as American history had not known." No one—not any cabinet member, not the vice president—had regular access to Wilson but his wife, his secretary and his physician. They, in a real sense, for that entire period became America's unelected and unaccountable chief executive, something inconceivable and unacceptable today.

As Wilson lay half-paralyzed in the White House, almost a hermit in what *New Yorker* editor David Remnick calls an "isolation ward," in many respects a prisoner of his wife who sought to shield him from all stress (and shield the nation from all truth about his condition), the Senate twice voted on the Treaty of Versailles. Twice it was defeated. In all the great powers that had signed it, ratification failed only in America. Absent America, on January 10, 1920, the treaty took effect; the rest of the world now was at peace with Germany. Six days later, the League of Nations convened its first council meeting.

America officially was to remain at war with Germany until Warren Harding became president in early 1921. He moved swiftly to negotiate a formal peace, known as the Treaty of Berlin. It was signed on August 25 and quickly was ratified by the Senate, restoring full American-German diplomatic relations on November 16 and granting the U.S. all benefits of the Treaty of Versailles, except, pointedly, League membership. America never joined the League.

America's rejection of the League of Nations often has been denounced as a catastrophic geopolitical mistake. Over the years, historians, diplomats, politicians and officials have pointed fingers (and worse) at the GOP-led Senate, accusing it of denying the League the American muscle which, they say, would have made it strong enough to stop the 1930s and 1940s aggressions by Imperial Japan, Fascist Italy and Nazi Germany. With a powerful League, goes this argument, World War Two may have been prevented; Hitler may have been stopped. Republicans in the 1940s and 1950s—even into the 1960s—found themselves derided as the party that had killed U.S. League membership, thus making them, went the charge, partly responsible for World War Two. In the 1960 presidential election, for instance, GOP campaigners had to rebuff accusations that their vice presidential candidate, Henry Cabot Lodge, Jr., in part bore responsibility for the war and even for Hitler because he was the grandson of the Senate leader and Wilson nemesis who had torpedoed the Versailles Treaty.

Today, such an argument collapses. Its definitive rebuttal is offered by the United Nations. That organization, of which, of course, America is a founder and robust member, repeatedly has demonstrated over its nearly seven decades the severe limitations on an international body's ability to stop aggression, settle disputes or even mitigate flare-ups. The U.N. was and remains helpless to do anything to resolve or even temper the world's most serious crises, such as the Cold War, the Viet Nam war, the genocidal massacres in Africa and the disputes keeping the Middle East a tinderbox. An American-backed League of Nations certainly would not then have succeeded where later the U.N. consistently has failed. The lesson of the U.N. record, despite what may be the organization's good intentions and sincere hand-wringing, is that no international organization can stand up to and adjudicate disagreements and clashes involving sovereign nations, to say nothing of major powers.

To argue or even fantasize that a League of Nations, with the U.S. as a member, could have blunted the brutal and determined aggressors of the 1930s and 1940s today therefore must be judged fantasy and self-delusion. To be sure, Lodge and the League's other opponents vastly exaggerated the dangers to America posed by League membership. Their opposition clearly was motivated much more by a politically driven determination to hand Wilson an embarrassing defeat than by a fear of the ostensible landmines embedded in some of the League Covenant clauses. American membership in the League was not likely to have imposed any serious restraints on the nation's sovereignty. But it is just as true that American membership would not have affected, even modestly, the course of 20th Century history. The League, for which Wilson at the Paris Peace Conference had traded away almost all his trump cards and so doing punished Germany in the myriad ways that he long had deplored, turned out to be irrelevant. And it would have been just as irrelevant had America joined.

It is an irony of history that, even today, much of Wilson's legacy is measured by his national security record: his basing foreign policy on lofty idealism and his losing the battle for the Versailles Treaty and the League. This has put Wilson fans, of which there have been and remain legions, on the defensive. It often has overshadowed his considerable, though controversial, very liberal domestic policy achievements, such as broadening government's reach and building a foundation for what later would be called the welfare state. Strangely, Wilson is not at all celebrated for being the prophet that he was. He warned against imposing a peace on Germany that would incite Germans to seek revenge. He was, as history grimly testifies, right. And he deserves credit for that. The tragedy of the 20th Century is that he ignored his own warning.

"November Criminals" and "Weimar Traitors"

Whether or not the Versailles Treaty was ratified by America made little difference to Germany. It still had to live with the treaty's terms. And they were to handicap the new Germany severely, with enormous consequences for that nation, its neighbors and much of the world, including, of course, America. Yet it would be inaccurate (and unfair) solely to blame the Versailles peace for the tragically convulsive fate of German democracy. The young Weimar Republic, so named because its constitution was drafted in the idyllic, culturally rich central German city of Weimar (home to the likes of Goethe, Schiller and the Bauhaus Movement), would have had rough going even without struggling under the weight of the treaty.

To start, Germany had no democratic tradition. Though momentum towards constitutional monarchy had been accelerating in the decades just before the war, it lacked deep roots. Importantly, the army officer corps and the civil service, two central pillars of the state inherited by the republic, were strongly antagonistic to democracy. A second serious weakness was the assertive, even militant, regionalism of Germany's component parts; unsettling postwar separatist movements undermining central government legitimacy broke out in Bavaria, Brunswick, Thuringia and elsewhere.

Then there was the challenge to the republic's control of internal security from war veterans, many still armed and many unemployed, who were forming private armies, some with names as innocent as "military clubs." Most prominent (and notorious) was the Free Corps (*Freikorps* in German), a loose alliance of groups whose aggregate membership at times topped 100,000, making them as large as the army permitted Germany by the Versailles Treaty. The army, in fact, backed these freelance military bands, giving them weapons, money, supplies and even barracks. It opportunistically saw the units as a way around the treaty's military manpower limits. So widely known was this support that the private armies commonly were called the "Black Army."

The Free Corps and other groups, whose individual members' profiles often seemed plucked straight from Hollywood's portrayal of French Foreign Legion thugs, pushed an array of special causes. But one issue united them: searing hatred of the Weimar Republic. They were its sworn enemies. For them, the answer to Germany's problems and balm for its humiliation were the republic's obliteration and the Hohenzollern monarchy's return. At times they dominated the streets, marching in menacing formations under swastika insignias (a polygon later adopted by the Nazis), brandishing weapons and unleashing the random violence which discredited city and national authorities, revealing their inability to maintain law and order.

The most sinister Free Corps action was surely its assassination campaign, targeting and killing hundreds of republic leaders and supporters. Its victims in the early 1920s included Matthias Erzberger (whose crime was having signed the Armistice) and Walther Rathenau (who not only was a very influential and wealthy Jew, thus an automatic target of anti-Semitic ultranationalists, but also, as foreign minister, was insisting that Germany fulfill Versailles

Treaty terms). Ultimately, most of the Free Corps would swell the ranks of the Nazis' brown-shirted SA storm troopers.[5]

The gravest immediate internal threat to the republic was communism. The large and growing German Communist Party in the first years after the war offered not even lip-service loyalty to the new democracy nor hid its determination to overthrow it by a Bolshevik-style revolution. The prospects of this were real, particularly since the communists were receiving money, agents and other support from Moscow's new rulers. Middle class Germans and other supporters of the Republic watched anxiously in Weimar's early years as huge demonstrations by red flag-waving communists increasingly were unsettling German cities and towns and as communist insurgencies were erupting in the central part of the country. Violence intensified as communist demonstrators clashed both with police and with rightist and nationalist private armies. There had been good reason for the nervous German delegate at the Armistice talks, cited in the previous chapter, to have exclaimed, after hearing how few weapons the German government would be allowed to keep: "But then we are lost! How are we going to defend ourselves against Bolshevism?"

Under-girding internal discontent and challenges to the Weimar Republic's authority was a crippled economy. The four years of feeding an insatiable war machine had distorted and weakened the once envied (and feared) German productive colossus. Unemployment shot up as millions of returning and demobilized soldiers were finding no jobs and as factories, having stopped turning out weapons, ammunition, uniforms and other battlefield goods, began firing workers. Prices, meanwhile, continued their wartime climb as a shortage of consumer goods was coupled with an expanding money supply. That was one of the war's most destructive legacies, since Imperial Germany had financed its military operations primarily through borrowing and printing money instead of taxation. This inflation, though just a whisper of the hyperinflation pain Germans were to feel in 1923, worrisomely compounded the Republic's burdens.

Unemployment, inflation, disquieted demobilized soldiers and other problems, of course, were not uniquely German. In various forms and to differing degrees most or all of them plagued the war's other former combatants, including America. Nor, of course, did these problems begin with the Versailles peace settlement; for that the war's victors cannot be blamed. What the Versailles Treaty crucially did was intensify greatly Germany's already festering postwar economic and social woes.

But there was to be more. Much more consequential, the deep conviction that the treaty had dealt with Germany extraordinarily unfairly and that Germany had been betrayed—in Paris at the peace conference by the Americans and in Berlin by the republic's politicians—pulled together the many strands of German postwar fury and despair, gave them sharp focus and then aimed them at one target. Whatever else they believed, however else they viewed the day's urgent issues, every German of every stripe seemed to hate the treaty: liberals, conservatives, reformers, moderate and radical socialists, centrists, democrats, monarchists, editorialists of all political shades, workers and owners, Catholic and Protestant clergy. Everyone. For the German people, historian Richard Watt says, the Versailles Treaty had become "the most vicious and wrathful document in the history of mankind." And in his classic intellectual history *The Mind of Germany*, Hans Kohn explains that "the lament of so many decent, conservative, liberal or socialist Germans about the burdens and cruelties inflicted by the Allies...undermined democracy."[6]

The internationally respected sociologist Max Weber, for example, openly expressed his outrage at the treaty. Jewish banker and liberal Max Warburg blasted it as "the worst act of world piracy." The majority socialists' parliamentary spokesman warned that socialists would never "rest in our zealous task to create...the power…to renounce the treaty." The *Frankfurter Zeitung,* a very influential democratic daily, approved the "bitter resentment" with which Germans were reacting to the peace, adding that "this triumph is too cheap, the superiority of the victors too ostentatious," the treatment of Germany "too unscrupulous." This situation, declared the paper, "must not and cannot remain so."

At the political spectrum's other end, the extreme nationalist *Deutsche Zeitung* screamed: "Vengeance! German nation! … Do not forget it! …Today German honor is being carried to the grave. Do not forget it! The German people will…press forward to reconquer the place…to which it is entitled. Then will come the vengeance for the shame of 1919." And an obscure Adolf Hitler began discovering that he could ignite intense passion and reap thundering shouts and applause simply by hammering the treaty and vilifying, in what became his trademark sarcastic and caustic delivery, the "November Criminals" (signers of the November 1918 armistice) and the "Weimar Traitors." Such lines, no matter how often yelled over the years, always were rewarded by truly hysterical audience responses, including increasingly from the kind of good, stolid German burghers who had never, over the generations, even flirted with public display of political emotion.

In this cauldron of discontent and despair, of hatred of the peace treaty, it became all too reflexively easy to make the Weimar Republic the culprit. "Wither" was to be the fate of any German hand daring to sign the treaty, had warned Chancellor Philipp Scheidemann, a socialist who did in fact resign rather than sign. His warning proved distressingly true. What ultimately "withered" was the Weimar Republic's legitimacy, because its leaders signed the treaty. Historian Marshall Dill explains in his textbook *Germany*: "The history of Germany from 1919 to 1939 is very largely the history of the Treaty of Versailles."[7] Had Woodrow Wilson not been secluded half-paralyzed in his White House bedroom, had he been aware of what was happening, he surely could have said: "I told you so."

Pinpricks and Worse

In the Weimar Republic's early months, as it was struggling for credibility, confronting threatened and even real putsches (the March 1920 Kapp Putsch actually grabbed power for five days and put the government to flight) and attempting, largely unsuccessfully, to disarm the private armies, Allied enforcement of the peace terms further fueled German popular anger. Inflaming feelings, for instance, were London's and Paris's efforts to try as war criminals Kaiser Wilhelm and some 900 other wartime leaders (including Generals von Hindenburg and Ludendorff, chancellors, cabinet members and four Hohenzollern princes). This was a right the Weimar Republic, in signing the treaty, had been forced to grant the Allies. Yet in exercising this right, London and Paris were reaching too far. Germany exploded in public fury at what its people saw as an Allied attempt to disgrace honorable and highly regarded German leaders. (Hindenburg remained fanatically revered until his 1934 death at age eighty-six.) This uproar plus criticism from Washington forced London and Paris to back down. The Kaiser never stood trial, first because the Netherlands, where he had sought refuge and was in exile, refused to hand him over and then because London and Paris were reluctant to push the Dutch on the matter. The number of accused war criminals, meanwhile, was reduced to a half-dozen minor functionaries.

Still, for Germans that was too much. It was another reminder of their nation's treatment by the victors. Such Allied actions, Wilson expert Arthur Link says, may have been merely "pinpricks," but they "served no purpose except to humiliate the German people."[8]

Pinpricks too were the 150,000 American, Belgian, British and French soldiers occupying parts of Germany and overseeing, as set by the treaty, destruction of German war material. Since Washington only reluctantly agreed to keep some troops in Germany, the remaining doughboys comprised but ten percent of the total occupying force. The Americans were headquartered in Koblenz, the British in Cologne and the French in Mainz. From there they fanned across Germany searching for weapons everywhere, even poking into factories to ensure that none were being made. The American touch was gentle, perhaps because the doughboys grew to like the Germans. According to Pershing biographer Donald Smythe, "the more the doughboys saw of the disciplined, clean, friendly Germans, the more they preferred them to the French."

In contrast to the Americans, the French were assertive and tough. While they may have been treating the Germans no worse than German occupiers of France had treated the French in 1871, such comparisons were lost on the German public. What mattered was that the stationing of foreign troops on German soil had been mandated by the Versailles Treaty. This offered up yet another rhetorical cudgel for hammering Weimar's democratic leaders. In some areas of Germany, occupation troops remained until 1930.

No mere pinpricks were the reparations payments imposed by the treaty. They were a huge issue and major burden for the republic throughout its thirteen-year existence. It was bad enough that endless squabbling over reparations bruised Germany's relations with America, Britain and France just when an embrace by those nations could have boosted the Weimar Republic's image and credibility inside Germany. Much worse was that the real and presumed pain of paying the reparations bill more than anything else continually reminded Germans how vindictively they were being treated.

Because the victors at the Paris Peace Conference, as described in the previous chapter, could not agree on a specific reparations total, they forced Germany to sign what Germans and others immediately denounced as "a blank check." Berlin had to agree to pay whatever bill it ultimately was handed. Woodrow Wilson had wanted to set a fixed total, but Britain's David Lloyd George and France's Georges Clemenceau balked. They feared that any sensible amount would seem grossly inadequate to and infuriate their countrymen. Indeed, back home the British and French peoples were demanding loudly and forcefully that Germany pay the cost of just about everything related to the war: for property damage from the fighting, for caring for the wounded, for war widows' and others' pensions and even for the interest on bonds and other debt incurred (such as loans from America) to finance the war. So much political heat were Allied leaders feeling on reparations that Lloyd George in Britain's December 1918 parliamentary election campaign had to reassure voters that they could trust him to squeeze the German lemon until "the pips squeak."

Whether those pips ever squeaked or not has been one of history's great controversies. For decades historians and economists have tried to decipher reparations' murky, opaque ledgers. They have tried to audit both how much a now smaller Germany could afford to pay (having lost, under the Versailles treaty, ten percent of its land and ten percent of its tax base) and how much in the end it really paid. Most experts now agree, though they hedge their calculations, that the ultimate cost to Germany was relatively modest. At conference after conference of the victors and Germany in the first half of the 1920s, the reparations bill kept being shaved. And of that reduced amount, Germany shelled out only a tiny portion. It was far, extraordinarily far, below the early reparations numbers tossed about at the peace conference where the French and British initially blithely talked of making Germany pay 500 billion or even 800 billion gold marks.

Those were truly astronomical sums, completely beyond Germany's existing and projected means. They would have been the equivalent in that year of $59 billion and $94 billion U.S. dollars respectively; in our day that would be a staggering $770 billion and $1.2 trillion U.S. dollars. By 1921, the Reparations Commission cut the bill to 132 billion marks, still a huge sum: about $16 billion U.S. dollars then or $203 billion U.S. dollars now. From there, the total continued to retreat. In the end, estimates historian Sally Marks in her study of the issue, Germany was told to pay 50 billion gold marks, equaling some $77 billion U.S. dollars today. Germany kept paying something until 1932 when the worldwide economic crisis prompted the Allies to cancel all outstanding reparations.[9]

The amount paid is of far less consequence to history than the problems created by the mere existence of the lingering and irritating issue. Reparations cast a worrisome cloud of uncertainty over the German economy, hampering internal and foreign investment. It also impeded policies for stimulating economic growth, since some German economists and politicians warned that the wealthier Germany appeared, the higher the payments the Allies would demand. British historian Niall Ferguson argues that German "tax reform was deliberately botched out of the desire to avoid reparations." He adds that some experts feel that reparations created a "disincentive" for Germany to stabilize economically and that the insistence that Germany pay "made impossible demands and promoted intolerable choices."[10]

Just as damaging, the periodic requirement that reparations be appropriated by the Reichstag, the republic's parliament (the same name as was used for that body in Imperial Germany), was a constant and bitter reminder of Versailles. It handed the anti-democratic forces a powerful recurring club to hammer the republic. After all, in appropriating the reparations installments, the government was forced to make the widely-hated case that Germany must fulfill the treaty's terms. Upon this the republic's enemies heaped scorn, adopting in one form or another the proud motto: "We will not pay." Instead of "fulfilling" the treaty, they demanded that it be ignored.

By far the worst pain was suffered in the aftershocks of an authentic economic earthquake triggered by a reparations issue. It began January 11, 1923 when French and Belgian troops marched into the Ruhr, Germany's industrial core. Their ostensible aim was to retaliate for Berlin having missed some minor reparations payments; it had fallen behind in shipping to the Allies coal and timber for telegraph poles. In reality, Paris and Brussels were grabbing an excuse to demonstrate to their peoples that they still could be tough on their enemy. But they had to act alone; America and Britain refused to participate. The French/Belgian plan was to collect the value of the delinquent reparations by confiscating the output of the Ruhr's industry and mines. To do this, they started taking control of Ruhr factories and railroads. Berlin protested ferociously, arguing correctly that the occupation was not allowed by the treaty. Outrage erupted across all sectors of Germany. "With a scream of indignation" is how Erich Eyck, in his classic history of the Weimar Republic, describes Germans' reaction to the occupation. "Never since August 1914 had the spirit of the German people been so united."[11]

Lacking any force to oppose the French and Belgians, Berlin called for passive resistance—asking the Ruhr's managers and workers to stop working. And they did. Soon, Dill writes, "a sullen quiet fell over the most productive industrial district on the continent." At times, the quiet was broken by violent clashes. The worst erupted in the city of Essen on March 31 when French forces machine-gunned a crowd at the Krupp factory complex, killing thirteen Germans. Two weeks later, in what became the most famous act of repression, the French arrested Free Corps soldier Albert Leo Schlageter, accusing him of derailing trains and other acts of sabotage (charges that most historians conclude were probably true). He was hauled before a French military court in Düsseldorf, found guilty and executed two weeks later.[12] Furor exploded throughout Germany, with enduring consequences. The French had created an instant reparations martyr to be exploited by the anti-republic nationalists and ultra-rightists. Memorials to Schlageter popped up all over the country, while Hitler extolled him in *Mein Kampf* and a play was written lionizing him. Later, in the Nazi years, a *Luftwaffe* (Air Force) fighter wing, a navy vessel and two Nazi storm trooper units all took his name.

318 | AMERICA'S GREATEST BLUNDER

With nothing being produced in the Ruhr and thus no factory output being sold, there was no money for striking workers' salaries. Were workers to remain unpaid, they would have had to return to their jobs, ending the resistance. To prevent this, the national government started paying the strikers. Lacking the actual resources to do so, the republic let loose its printing presses, turning out ton after ton of paper marks, flooding the country with a tsunami of inflated money. Though prices in Germany had been rising ever since the war's start in late summer 1914 and had been accelerating since 1919, painfully pinching consumers, that had been almost nothing, truly nothing, compared to what they now were beginning to face, not just in the Ruhr, but throughout their country.

As an increasing quantity of money began chasing a decreasing quantity of goods (since the Ruhr's factories had stopped production), prices kept climbing. And then, as the Ruhr's citizens needed ever more money for the ever higher-priced food and other goods, Berlin printed ever more marks. In fall 1923, dozens of mills (some sources say hundreds) were required to manufacture the paper needed by the hundreds of plants printing the bank notes. This fueled what became, according to the calculations of economists Steve Hanke and Alex K. F. Kwok, history's fourth worst hyperinflation (exceeded only, in descending order of severity, by Hungary in 1946, Zimbabwe in 2008 and Yugoslavia in 1994).[13]

History continually has been astonished by and has shuddered at how disastrous the German situation grew. In 1919, about nine Reichsmarks had bought one U.S. dollar; by the end of 1923, a dollar fetched 11.7 trillion Reichsmarks, a surely incomprehensible, unfathomable figure. In that period, the German cost of living index skyrocketed 1.25 trillion times, with a loaf of bread costing 428 billion Reichsmarks. Stores began closing briefly at midday so that staff could scribble higher prices on merchandise; workers, as soon as they got their pay envelopes, rushed to stores to convert their paper currency into almost anything tangible before prices jumped still further. They were wise to rush. Reichsmarks were losing value not just day by day, but hour by hour. Hanke and Kwok reckon that German prices doubled every 3.7 days, with prices in October 1923, the worst month of the crisis, soaring 29,500 percent. Even now, after almost a century, gasps and disbelief greet photos of Germans in 1923 pushing wheelbarrows or carrying bushel baskets brimming with paper currency and still not having enough cash to buy food for a simple meal.

London, New York and other financial centers watched all this with horror, understanding that their economies would be pounded were Germany to collapse economically. They were terrified by the growing prospects of what economists in our day call "contagion." Forced to take action, Britain and France followed Washington's lead and backed an American blueprint to halt Germany's inflation. This worked extremely well. So successfully was the German currency stabilized and so solidly was confidence in it restored that the economy by 1927 began to thrive, giving the Weimar Republic a brief taste of relative prosperity—until it ended abruptly with the worldwide financial collapse of 1929 and the ensuing Great Depression.

Hyperinflation's end and the onset of good times came too late for Germany's tender democracy. Enormous and fatal damage already had been done. Germany's inflation victims were the same as inflation's victims throughout the ages and in all places: those with fixed income assets, such as cash and bonds denominated in paper currency; those on pensions, such as war veterans, war widows and the retired; and those, such as civil servants, teachers, police and army officers, whose government wages did not keep pace with soaring prices. These were Germany's celebrated (and admired) burghers, its middle class, its artisans, shopkeepers, professionals and what later would be called white-collar workers who over generations had lived solid, responsible, productive lives, respecting the law, paying taxes, trusting officials. They prudently had bought government and corporate bonds and diligently had stashed money into bank savings accounts. And then, in 1923, they watched the value of all of that vaporize. Their living standards collapsed and the cherished symbols of their status vanished; many sank into absolute poverty, becoming to their horror and terrifying humiliation that for which they always had nothing but contempt, members of the despised proletariat. Crushed were their self-confidence and self-respect.

Not surprisingly, they grew bitter, angry and vengeful. Instead of standing firmly, as the middle class must in every democratic society, as democracy's backbone, the German middle class wavered, losing faith in the Weimar Republic and falling susceptible to a seductive radical message from the right, ultimately from Hitler's National Socialists, promising to restore to them their dignified place in society and their nation's respected place in the world. "The inflationary experience," economic historian Derek Aldcroft writes in his analysis of the Versailles legacy, "probably contributed more to the disintegration of democracy in Germany than any other factor." William Shirer, in his bestselling history of Hitler's rise to power, puts it even more directly. He says: "In their misery and hopelessness, [the middle class] made the Republic the scapegoat for all that had happened [to them]. Such times were heaven-sent for Adolf Hitler."[14]

Who or what bears the blame? In part, certainly, the Weimar Republic. The hyperinflation resulted directly from its policies, first its call for passive resistance to the Belgian and French Ruhr occupation and then its nonstop running of the printing presses to pay the passively resisting Ruhr workers and officials. No policymaker should have had any doubt, particularly not the skilled economists working for the republic, about what happens when money is debased or currency inflated. Devastating inflation, if not always hyperinflation, is assured.

But there is a more fundamental blame for the catastrophe

of 1923. It is rooted in the circumstances by which the Great War ended and the peace was crafted. The lopsided Armistice, codified in the Versailles Treaty, is what allowed France to pursue with little restraint its vindictiveness against a much-weakened Germany. Especially under France's new premier, the proudly anti-German Raymond Poincaré, continued punishment of Germany was a proclaimed French policy. To be sure, Germany in any event would have had to fight a bruising postwar battle against inflation. But it was the festering reparations issue and France's ability to exploit it that transformed that battle into a rout, greatly weakening the republic and strengthening its enemies.

Seriously weakening the republic too was a broadening undercurrent of tolerated criminality fostered by the Versailles Treaty. So corrosive of national sovereignty were many of the treaty's clauses, so painful were they, that compliance seemed, to Germany's leaders, irresponsible. Wherever possible, in one area after another and in one way or another, otherwise upright, honest and honorable German officials and citizens deliberately violated the treaty. Breaking the law was either encouraged by the government or winked at. British historian David Stevenson, in his study of the international relations aspect of the war, writes that Berlin grew "committed, as far as possible, to [treaty] evasion."[15] More vivid is the judgment of Thomas Mann, perhaps the 20th Century's most acclaimed German author. He said: "Having been robbed" by the Treaty of Versailles, "the Germans became a nation of robbers."[16] What emerged was a culture of lawlessness that gnawed away at the republic's claim to legitimacy.

Economic and tax policies, as noted above, deliberately were skewed to prevent Germany from appearing so prosperous that it would have to increase reparations payments to the Allies. The same motive prompted Germans to fudge the output statistics of their factories, the value of their foreign currency holdings and the size of their gold hoard. Denied by the Treaty sufficient military manpower to repress communist demonstrations and a feared likely communist uprising, the police and other officials tolerated and even encouraged ostensibly outlawed Free Corps bands, brandishing ostensibly outlawed weapons, to patrol the streets.

The most extensive treaty evasion involved the German Army. The Allied/American victors so drastically had limited its size and weaponry that those at the peace conference joked that it seemed more like a constabulary than a military. It was, among many other things, not to exceed 100,000 men; conscription and a general staff were banned; and it was denied tanks, airplanes, heavy artillery, battleships, submarines and poison gas. Such restrictions were intolerable for a major nation, even to the republic's socialist and liberal leaders. In short time, the German Army methodically sought ways around the treaty. Though a General Staff had been banned, an "Office of the Troops" was established to perform the same functions. To seemingly abide by the 100,000-manpower limit while actually rebuilding a strong reserve army, basic training of recruits was cut to four months. After that, the newly trained soldiers were dismissed and training began for a new class of 100,000. The result: each year minted 300,000 soldiers. None of that was secret; everyone in Germany knew what was being done to evade the treaty.

Just a bit more secret and just as illegal were the efforts to get around the Versailles weaponry limits. For this, Berlin signed secret agreements with Moscow, allowing German troops to train in Russia with tanks and war planes. As important, in Russia the German Army built clandestine military camps and ran arms factories turning out and testing, among other things, airplanes, BMW-powered tanks, artillery shells and poison gas—all banned by the Versailles Treaty. By 1933, the German air base at Lipetsk, in Russia's Don basin, had trained some 1,200 pilots. And among the German tank school instructors at the secret base near the Tartar city of Kama was Heinz Guderian who, with Erwin Rommel, a decade later was acclaimed as the architect of Germany's enormously devastating World War Two blitzkrieg *panzer* (tank) tactics.

For the Soviet Union, the German factories became the source of sorely-needed arms, access to developing technology and the chance to exercise under expert German generalship.[17] For Germany, the secret Russian connection reinforced to German leaders and the informed public that illegality was an acceptable response to the despised treaty. Britain's David Lloyd George, of all the victors' leaders perhaps the most shrewd and prescient observer of the Versailles peace, was right when he warned that "there is a possibility that a hungry Russia might be armed by an angry Germany."

Revising How America Viewed the War

Very quickly, within a few years, in fact, the pain that the Versailles peace was inflicting on the German Republic was attracting attention in America, Britain and elsewhere. Some sympathy for Germany was emerging. In addition, reparations were being seen not only as unreasonable and unfair but also as a mounting burden on the victors themselves. London, in particular, began realizing that the impediments imposed on the German economy by the peace were preventing Germany from again being the major customer for British exports and a reliable source of important imports which it had been before the war.

The first to voice criticism of the treaty's economic clauses was the thirty-six-year-old British economist John Maynard Keynes. (His subsequent economic output coalesced into what is known as "Keynesian" theory, still embraced by a large cadre of economists.) As the Treasury's financial representative in the British delegation at the Paris Peace Conference, Keynes grew appalled by the treaty's proposed economic penalties. He forcefully said so, warning that by strangling Germany economically, high reparations would damage the world economy. When his opinions were ignored, he quit the delegation, took his arguments public and within months, in late 1919, published the bestselling (and still in print) *The Economic Consequences of the Peace*. This book shook conventional thinking in Britain and America by portraying Germany not as an incorrigible villain but as a victim of the peace.

Four years later, the image of Germany-as-victim gained great credibility following the French/Belgian occupation of the Ruhr. Receiving extensive press coverage in the U.S. and Britain, it was seen as absolutely unwarranted and even cruel treatment of the Germans. Articles describing "French atrocities in the Ruhr," for example, appeared in *The Nation*, then as now one of America's leading and most acrid leftist journals. According to diplomatic historian Warren Cohen, the Ruhr occupation "aroused American sympathy for Germany" more than any other postwar event.[18]

By the mid-1920s, therefore, as the harshness and vengefulness of the Versailles peace grew better understood and as the public's once intensely-hot war fever started cooling, momentum built in America and Britain for taking a fresh look at the Great War. Academics and journalists began analyzing its causes, prosecution and peace-making. They dug through mountains of documents, interviewed key participants and began drawing conclusions that turned out to be at odds with what their governments throughout the war had been saying and, importantly, what they personally had believed. Because they first challenged and then demanded revisions of the prevailing views, they were called "revisionists."

A boon to their work was the avalanche of official papers, much of them secret, released by the new regimes in Berlin and Moscow; their leaders felt no need to protect the actions of their deposed predecessors. Open to public view now were highly confidential army mobilization plans and timetables, cables between key officials, minutes of top-level talks in the weeks preceding the war's August 1914 outbreak, agreements between combatants for callously dividing expected spoils of victory and reams of other war-related papers that governments typically guard for decades, if not longer. The material flooding out of Berlin and Moscow forced London and Paris to release some of their own documents.

Initially, revisionist writers focused mainly on the question of who started the war. The official Allied and American line, of course, had been that Germany and its ally Austria-Hungary alone were at fault. This was asserted in the Versailles Treaty's Article 231, the notorious "war guilt clause," forcing Germany to accept sole responsibility for the conflict. The revisionists soon began poking huge holes in this. Citing documents and events, they pointed fingers at the other combatants, accusing them of sharing the blame; some revisionists now placed Germany far down the guilt list, below Austria-Hungary, Russia and France. Reflecting the changing views is the title of a 1925 *Christian Century* article: "France and Russia Start the War."

To those who had argued, as was common, that aggressive Prussian nationalism and militarism, magnified by Kaiser Wilhelm's bombastic rhetoric, stoked the international tensions that were the roots of the war, revisionists offered refuting arguments. The new evidence, they insisted, proved that Germany in the decade and more before the war was less imperialistic than Britain, less nationalistic than France and less militaristic than Russia and France. In sum, said the revisionists—in a pithy verdict that became widely quoted, according to historian Selig Adler—though Germany and its allies had made the war possible, Britain and France, along with their ally Russia, had made it inevitable.[19]

The American revisionists looked beyond war guilt. They intensively investigated the steps that had taken their country onto the battlefield. Documents and other evidence prompted them to question and then refute the premise that America had a legitimate grievance against Germany. They derided Woodrow

Wilson's ostensible neutrality policy, condemning it as having been pursued inconsistently, even hypocritically. Typifying their tone and arguments were the titles of the October 1925 *Christian Century* article by Columbia University historian Harry Elmer Barnes, "Was America Deluded by the War?" and of the 1929 book by prolific author C. Hartley Grattan, *Why We Fought*.[20] Such writings had become so influential by the early 1930s, Wilson scholar Thomas Knock says, that they changed millions of American minds.[21]

Huge swaths of the American public no longer reflexively saw Germany as the villain starting the war and committing horrible atrocities; the Versailles Treaty now was broadly condemned; and America's entering the war increasingly was regarded as foolish. Such revisionist attitudes seemed to convert even President Franklin Roosevelt, according to experts who cite some of his 1935 statements and letters. In the Senate, meanwhile, Republican Arthur Vandenberg of Michigan was declaring that "we were suckered into that war."[22] Such skepticism on war-related policy was reinforced greatly in the public mind by the disillusion with the battlefield experience conveyed in the popular writings of e.e. cummings, John Dos Passos, F. Scott Fitzgerald and Ernest Hemingway. By 1937, a Gallup Poll of American attitudes was finding that sixty percent of respondents felt that it was a mistake for America to have entered the Great War and only twenty-eight percent believed that it was not.[23] The revisionists seemed destined to win their argument.

They did not. By the late 1930s, a sinister new German specter was looming. And one of its earliest victims was revisionism's influence. It shriveled under the impact of Nazi Germany's brutality and evil. "Hitler's march through Europe began to undermine what had appeared to be the victory of the revisionist interpretation of American intervention in 1917," concludes Cohen in his study of American revisionists. It became increasingly unacceptable for any respectable author to say anything sympathetic about what Germany had done at just about any time in its past. To suggest that Germany may not have been solely guilty for starting the Great War or may have been mistreated by the Versailles Treaty (or, for that matter, that Bismarck was actually a reformer) was now dismissed as appeasement and, worse, as making excuses for Adolf Hitler, his totalitarian repression inside Germany and his mounting military threat outside. To suggest that the lessons of 1917 should teach America that it must not intervene in what was becoming World War Two was denounced as Nazi sympathizing. In fact, those drawing that lesson, such as revisionists Harry Elmer Barnes and C. Hartley Grattan, once praised for their critique of how America got into the first war, now found themselves being investigated by Congressional committees.

In those years and for several decades after, German history was read backwards, with German behavior and actions over the ages viewed retrospectively through the lens of Nazi horrors, invasions and concentration and extermination camps. All of German history, it seemed, ran along a simple, direct line leading straight to Hitler and World War Two. Ostensibly serious scholars, for instance, scoured Martin Luther's life and writings for the roots of Nazism. This, of course, is now recognized as extremely flawed historiography. Historian Hew Strachan cautions in a 2003 *Foreign Affairs* article that "the knowledge of World War II must not be allowed to shape the search for guilty parties in World War I." Adding historical perspective, Henry Kissinger writes in *Diplomacy*: "For 200 years, Germany had been the victim, not the instigator, of the wars in Europe. In the Thirty Years' War, the Germans had suffered casualties estimated as high as thirty percent of their entire population, and all of the decisive battles of the dynastic wars of the 18th Century and of the Napoleonic Wars were fought on German soil."[24]

But such calls for perspective were not heard nor could even be issued as the deadly storm unleashed by Nazi Germany gathered force. In this storm's fury, the revisionist case died; the questions it raised in the 1920s and 1930s about what had propelled America into the Great War and the answers it offered disappeared. Today, however, three-quarters of a century later, history not only can return to those questions and chronicle how America found itself at war but can push much further. History now can also chronicle, as the revisionists obviously could not, the consequences flowing from America's declaring war. And these were consequences more horridly destructive than the revisionist critics in the early decades after the war ever could have imagined.

Beyond their imagination too, since they, of course, had no way to witness (as subsequent generations did) those consequences of the Great War's settlement, is a new question for history to pose: Could it have been different?

CONCLUSION

———————

AND HAD AMERICA NOT BLUNDERED INTO WAR?

THE QUESTION IS UNAVOIDABLE. Answers, of course, are speculative. And though history is an unforgiving master allowing no replays, it does encourage reinterpretation of events and reconsideration of how they could have unfolded differently. Every generation, it is said, revisits (and rewrites) history by posing its own questions, imposing its own framework and seeking its own relevance. Each exercise in historical reinterpretation selects and manipulates its own variables.

This exercise, this inquiry into America's fateful April 6, 1917 decision, manipulates just one variable: America's declaration of war on Germany and its entering that war on the Allied side. From that it raises for reconsideration just one question: If the U.S. had not sent eighty American Expeditionary Force supersize divisions to France, what might have been the consequences? One theoretical outcome is that Germany would have won the war. Another is the opposite, a British and French victory. A third is that the Western Front's guns would have gone quiet without a decisive winner, with a clichéd whimper instead of a bang, as all combatants, too physically exhausted and financially broke to fight any further, reluctantly and unhappily would drag themselves to a negotiating table to purchase peace with compromise. Of the three hypothetical outcomes, only one was realistic and likely.

Germany Wins the War

Had America not entered the war, might Germany have won? A German victory, after all, genuinely was feared at two points during the conflict: in the early weeks when the slashing momentum of its invading armies tore through Belgium, poured into France and seemed about to capture Paris and drive the hastily deployed British Army into the sea; and then again nearly four years later, when General Erich Ludendorff's devastating spring 1918 offensives, armed with brazen new tactics, drove his troops once more to within strike of Paris' gates. At both those moments, Allied generals, sniffing defeat, truly panicked. The French government fled Paris while the British believed they were doomed to encirclement and agonized aloud that their backs were to the wall. Had they been right, Germany's victory would have been decisive.

And such a victory would have been ugly for the defeated. The Allies almost certainly would have been treated as harshly by a conquering Germany as the Russians had been by the March 1918 peace Germany had inflicted on them. At that time, Russia wanted to end the war, no matter what the cost. Its new Bolshevik rulers, determined to pour all their resources into crushing rivals at home, had no desire to keep bleeding in fighting Germany and its Central Powers allies. Soviet dictator Vladimir Lenin put it plainly on February 23, threateningly warning that anyone opposing "an immediate, even though extremely onerous peace, is endangering Soviet power." Onerous indeed was what the Soviets had to accept in the crushing Treaty of Brest-Litovsk, named after the city in which it was negotiated in what today is Belarus. Germany took 300,000 square miles of Russian territory, a quarter of its industry and almost all of its coal and iron resources. Several months later it demanded 6 billion marks in reparations (about $10 billion U.S. dollars today).

The Allies in defeat would have fared little better. What Berlin had in mind for its enemies could have made a Versailles Treaty seem tame, at least according to sensational documents outlining German war aims published in 1961 by Hamburg University historian Fritz Fischer. A victorious Germany's appetite at armistice and peace tables might have been even more rapacious than were those of France's Ferdinand Foch and Georges Clemenceau. Berlin was planning to squeeze extensive territorial annexations and rich booty from a beaten Belgium, Britain and France. Its aim was to dominate its eastern neighbors militarily and its western neighbors economically. The diktat that would have ended the war would have been a German diktat, establishing Germany's geopolitical and economic supremacy on the continent.

That, in fact, was the recurring message of Teddy Roosevelt, Senator Henry Cabot Lodge and those others who, almost from the war's first moments, were urging the U.S. to back the Allies. "If Germany conquers France, England, or Russia," warned Lodge in September 1914, "she will dominate Europe and will subsequently seek to extend that domination if she can to the rest of the world."[1] And that, without question, would have endangered America and thus would have justified American military actions to prevent it.

But Germany, of course, whatever its expansionist dreams and plans, whatever its theoretical dangers, in reality never had the power to impose a diktat. Victory remained always beyond its reach. And that was not because America had entered the war; it was because Britain and France, without help from American forces, demonstrated repeatedly that they were capable of thwarting a German victory. The only moment when American arms arguably might have been needed to save the Allies from what appeared, momentarily, as looming defeat was in the war's initial weeks, in late summer and early fall 1914. If rushing to the imperiled Allies to save them was to justify America's going to war, then September 1914 was the time for that—not April 1917, when the Western Front had been frozen for nearly three years and was near certain to remain frozen. But, as history tells us, even in the scary moments of the war's first September, the Allies got along without America. Despite Germany's initial punishing onslaught, as Chapter 1 explains, the French Army survived and the British Army rallied. They then launched their celebrated Marne counterattack, pushing Germany far back and forcing it to live the nightmare that had haunted two generations of its generals: a two-front war, one in the west against France, the other in the east against Russia.

By the end of September 1914, a new reality had the Western Front in an unforgiving grip: Germany's forces were strong enough and soon were to be entrenched enough to hold on to the Belgian and French lands that they had conquered at the war's start, but they were not strong enough to destroy the British and French armies. This was confirmed time and again over four years of Western Front offensives and counteroffensives. Most convincingly, it was confirmed by Ludendorff's massive, roll-of-the-dice five offensives in spring 1918. In their first days, almost replaying the war's opening weeks, the attacking Germans pulverized the British and the French armies and sent them fleeing, horrifying their civilian leaders back home. But then, as described in Chapter 6, each of the five German thrusts faltered. Each time, intense British and French pressure drove back gravely weakened Germans. And once again, as in the war's first phase, the Allies did not need Americans to prevent a German victory.

Only in July, during the final spring offensive, were enough doughboys on the line to contribute anything significant to the Allies. But that contribution, though unquestionably heroic, was marginal. What most thwarted the German advance, as in the previous four spring offensives, were logistics failures and dwindling reserves. Ludendorff and Germany simply overreached in trying to destroy the Allied armies. Even with their extra troops hastily repositioned from the now-peaceful Russian Front and even with the new innovative storm trooper tactics, Germany could not overcome the British and French. By 1918, moreover, Niall Ferguson points out, Germany was lagging far behind the Allies in three critically new weapon systems: airplanes, motorized transport and tanks.[2]

The question thus can be answered: Even had America not gone to war, Germany would not have won on the Western Front. America's doughboys were not needed to save the Allies from defeat; they were needed only to hand them victory.

Britain and France Win the War

What about the second hypothetical outcome: Had America not entered the war, might Britain and France have won anyway? To this too history answers "no." The British and French situations closely mirrored the German. Their armies were strong enough and had become adept enough to absorb and then repel massive German assaults, but not strong enough to break the German Army. The horrifying record of one failed gargantuan Allied offensive after another—the Somme, the Nivelle Offensive, Passchendaele and others—testifies to that. In many respects, moreover, Britain and France in 1918 were weaker (as was Germany) than ever. Conscription ages in all three countries were being set both lower and higher, while standards were falling. Into their armies' ranks were inducted mere boys, old men and those previously rejected as unfit. In all three countries, some of the most able-bodied were being kept at home to turn out airplanes, munitions and other essential war products.

By 1918, therefore, both the Allies and Germans were exhausted, running out of men and stymied. Submarine warfare had failed the Germans, victim to the convoy system of British and American warships escorting merchantmen safely through perilous waters. That dashed Berlin's hopes of starving Britain. London's own hopes were dashed by the failure of its offensives to break through

German lines. And no revolutionary weapon development by either side was on the horizon; nothing offered any hope of transforming the conflict suddenly and dramatically as first tanks and then atomic bombs were to transform World War Two.

Meantime, inflation, food and coal shortages, rationing, scores of other daily deprivations and, above all, ever-lengthening casualty lists were fueling pressures from all home fronts to just somehow end the war. To make matters worse, mutinies and fear of mutiny were paralyzing much of the French Army, while Britain's civilian leaders were staging a kind of mutiny of their own. They were balking at sending to Douglas Haig, their Western Front commander, the replacements he sought for the staggering losses from his failed offensives. British Prime Minister David Lloyd George in effect was declaring: "Enough!" And "enough" was what Britain and France lacked to break through the rows of German trenches, set the German armies in flight and defeat them.

Ultimately, of course, they did just that. But that was thanks entirely to America's intervention. In summer 1918, the British Expeditionary Force, in particular, demonstrated (at last) a mastery of the Western Front's peculiar and, hitherto, daunting challenges. Its troops drove breathlessly forward, forced the Germans out of their trenches and into the open and then put them on the run, earning plaudits from generations of military experts and burnishing somewhat Haig's very tarnished reputation. It was Britain's finest battlefield hour since Waterloo, and probably still has not been surpassed. In its sector, France too fought extraordinarily well and successfully. Both British and French forces clearly deserve the honors won.

But they could not have won them without America. In that exhilarating Allied push during what became the "last 100 days," Supreme Commander Ferdinand Foch could risk escalating his conventional counterattack (against the last of Ludendorff's spring threats) into a daring all-out offensive only because he could count on the nearly two million American doughboys at the front. They were his margin of decisive superiority over the Germans. Almost one million of those doughboys just had arrived in France, in effect replacing the one million Allied soldiers killed or wounded in the German offensives. There was, of course, no one to replace Germany's one million casualties.

Soon, first at St. Mihiel and then in the Argonne Valley, the American troops were pounding the Germans and engaging and tying down whole German armies. Without that, Foch's offensive and the subsequent spectacular Allied gains would have been beyond reach. When German generals in October called for an armistice, they were prompted not by calculations that they were about to be beaten by Britain and France, but by the unforgiving math flashing that ultimately they were to be overwhelmed by a flood of Americans, 10,000 of whom were still landing in France every day.

Indeed, it had been the specter of that cresting doughboy flood that had prompted Ludendorff in the first place to launch his risky and costly spring offensives. He grimly had concluded that he had no choice but to strike before enough Americans arrived to tilt the Western Front's arithmetic irrevocably against him. The losses he suffered in those offensives, agree historians, were what made his armies vulnerable to the summer's Allied counterattacks. Absent Ludendorff's fears of how America would shift the battlefield's balance, there is no evidence that he would have gambled, rolling the dice on risky offensives.

Instead, with his still formidable forces (not depleted by the offensives' losses), he could have sat powerfully, even smugly, in France and Belgium, behind his Siegfried Line of trenches, artillery and machine guns. From those fortified positions, B.H. Liddell Hart writes in *The Real War*, "there seems little doubt" that Germany would have been able to resist Allied assault.[3] The Western Front thus would have remained stalemated. Without America's entry into the conflict, neither side in 1917 or after would have been capable of breaking out and ending the war militarily. The only resolution would have had to be political.

Neither Side Wins

And political is how, without American intervention, the deadlocked war would have had to end. To be sure, the very notion of negotiations, with the accompanying assumption of compromises, was extremely distasteful to the combatants' leaders. They had given too many speeches promising victory; they had launched too many offensives promising to crush the hateful enemy and end the war; and they too often had promised that their countrymen's great sacrifices would be rewarded. Painful it would be for them to admit that all of that was now impossible. Their peoples, though fervently wanting peace, also wanted something to justify the deaths of and injuries to so many of their sons and husbands. They wanted payback; in essence, they wanted vengeance. That a negotiated peace would not deliver.

But at some moment, distasteful or not, both sides' leaders would have had to admit that the reality of the Western Front offered no exit but compromise. They grudgingly, unhappily, reluctantly would have had to pull themselves to a conference table to stop the fighting. There they would bargain, change some lines on a map, accept some burdens for paying restitution and pocket some payments for damages. Because these talks would have been spawned by frustrating but undeniable stalemate rather than by battlefield triumph, neither the British, French nor German publics could have seen themselves as outright victors, expecting retribution and spoils. No one at the conference table would have had victory's muscle to demand revenge. No belligerent would have been branded with the sole guilt of having started the war. No one would have been humiliated—except, perhaps, the generals who had failed, after all the sacrifice, to bring home glory.

For such a peace of compromise there were honorable and

extremely encouraging precedents. The various Treaties of Westphalia signed in 1648, for example, negotiated an end to both the Thirty Years' War in the Holy Roman Empire and the Eighty Years' War between Spain and the Dutch Republic. These were, until World War One, Europe's most destructive conflicts. While they involved important territorial rivalries and dynastic challenges, at their core was a battle over something ostensibly permitting no compromise: matters of faith, with Roman Catholics and Protestants fighting ferociously and determinedly over competing views of how man gains eternal salvation. Yet compromise the belligerents did when they became too worn down to fight any more and convinced that neither side ever would conquer the other.

Negotiated compromise too ended France's Napoleonic wars when all sides met in Vienna in 1814. Though Napoleon I's armies had been defeated soundly and the French unquestionably had been the aggressor, the victorious states—mainly Austria, Britain, Prussia and Russia—treated France leniently. It was stripped of its recent conquests but allowed to keep the extensive land holdings taken over a century by war or through intimidation by its Bourbon kings. The victors were not out for vengeance; France was not humiliated. Being "generous to France," Henry Kissinger explains, "was no easy matter. [It] had been trying to dominate Europe for a century and a half." Still, the victors concluded, according to Kissinger, "that Europe would be safer if France were relatively satisfied rather than resentful and disaffected."

They were right. Their work in Vienna, as that in Westphalia, was a prescription for enduring peace. Says Kissinger, "the order that grew out of the Peace of Westphalia lasted 150 years; the international system created by the Congress of Vienna maintained itself for a hundred years."[4]

The delegations at Versailles in 1919 left no such legacy. Twenty years after they signed their treaty, war again erupted in Europe; it was a war in many respects more devastating than the conflict they had ended. Its casualties were higher; Germany terrorized much of Europe in ways unimaginable in modern times; and, after the war, Soviet power, rushing into the vacuum left by Germany's collapse, pushed far westward and for two generations brutalized Eastern Europe and terrified Western Europe with threats of invasion. That was the legacy of Versailles; it was the price paid for having ignored the lessons of the peacemakers at Westphalia and Vienna.

Had those lessons been honored, German history—and Europe's—could have followed a less torturous path. A peace that did not brand the Germans guilty of starting the war, strip them of key industrial regions, impose what were regarded as crippling reparations and reduce their military to the size of a police force could have allowed the democratic Weimar Republic a chance to take root. Its ability to maintain a full-sized military, for instance, may have given it the force to check those armed bands of the far left and far right that took control of German streets and unleashed the epidemic of random violence. Its middle class may not have been impoverished and demoralized (and thus attracted politically to the far right) by the hyperinflation resulting from the punitive Belgian and French occupation of the Ruhr. Its government could not have been denounced and discredited as "November criminals" (for signing the Armistice) and "Weimar traitors" (for trying to fulfill Versailles Treaty terms).

Without the humiliations imposed by the treaty, there would have been little to avenge. Weimar's opponents would have had difficulty finding other flashpoint slogans and issues with which to rally mass support. Without all of that, the German political center may not have disintegrated, leaving few committed supporters for the republic.

To be sure, the republic still would have had to deal with the enormous, potentially disruptive problems that had been rising towards a boil in the decades before the war: the enormous tensions spawned by industrialization, urbanization and modernity. It also would have had to confront the legacy of the war's destruction and the vast social changes spurred by the military and economic mobilizations required to put millions in uniform and send them into battle. And any postwar German government would have had to subdue inflation. But with a strong center in Germany, odds increase enormously that these problems would not have led to the republic's destruction.

Conjuring a vision of an enduring Weimar Republic is, of course, raw speculation. But it is speculation encouraged by recent history. For a time after World War Two, it was fashionable, perhaps plausible, to argue that Germans culturally or by temperament or by history were unsuited to democracy. Today that argument rings false. For more than a half-century, Germany (initially its western part) has been democratic, remaining stable through economic setbacks, collapses of parliamentary majorities, sustained and often intense external military and political pressures, mass demonstrations in 1968 and threats from a far right and a far left. Through it all, Germany has not wavered from its democratic course. But today's thriving German democracy, obviously, was not handicapped at its birth by World War Two's victors as the Weimar Republic had been by the Versailles peace.

In even the best of circumstances, admittedly, the survival of Germany's Weimar democracy would have been no sure bet. The republic might have failed even had it been spared the burdens of war guilt, reparations and humiliation. Germany's many other grave postwar problems could have sunk democracy and brought to power a dictatorship of the far left, on the Soviet model, or the far right, on an ultra-nationalist or fascist model. Yet even then, the 20th Century most likely would have avoided much of the horrors that ultimately engulfed it. Those leftist or rightist dictatorships undoubtedly would have imposed ugly, repressive rule inside Germany. But it is very far from certain that they also would have led their country into a new great war, carrying their brutality to other nations as Hitler's Germany did. Germans had no more appetite to begin fighting again than did those publics of the Great War's other combatants.

In our day, generations later, it may be difficult to understand how strong were Europe's desires for peace in the 1920s and 1930s. There had been so much bleeding, suffering and death in the Great War that no one wanted to go through it again. There was no stomach for fighting and no tolerance for glorifying and romanticizing combat. That is what made the 1928 German novel and 1930 film *All Quiet on the Western Front* so extraordinarily popular in dozens of countries. Saying that the Great War wiped out an entire European generation has become a cliché; but that makes it no less true. The Western Front's killing fields, its million-man offensives and their staggering tolls—all, it seemed, without purpose—were still vividly fresh in memory. They were but yesterday.

Abhorrent, absurd, mad were how huge numbers regarded any suggestion of once more heading into combat. Peace movements attracted great followings; nations negotiated pacts renouncing war, vowing nonaggression and limiting the sizes of their navies. The most extreme, and still controversial, outbreak of peace fever was the so-called "Oxford Oath." On February 9, 1933, members of the very influential Oxford Union debating society at England's Oxford University vowed never again to "bear arms for king and country." That was an extraordinary, even rebellious, declaration by Britain's elite youth. Similar pledges were made elsewhere in Britain and across Europe and even in America.

Reflecting deeply-felt peace sentiments too were the 1930s' appeasement efforts. Now rightly criticized for having rewarded Hitler's aggression, at the time they were a sincere and even plausible attempt to avoid another general war at almost any cost. The appeasers did not want to repeat the mistakes that they perceived had been made in summer 1914 when Europe's great powers, as Lloyd George later put it, "slithered" into war. At that time, it was argued, nations had rushed to battle, were too quick to order military mobilization and not willing enough to negotiate and consider compromise. Europe's leaders of the 1920s and 1930s vowed not to repeat that.

Such passions for peace and against a second war would have been just as strong in Germany, even a Germany ruled by a dictator of the right or the left. It would have been extremely risky, perhaps impossible, to try to override those feelings. What enabled a Hitler to do so was the punishing treatment that Germany had suffered under the Armistice and the Versailles Treaty. What turned Germans into warriors in 1939, what made them willing so soon to order their young men back into harm's way was a furor and anger stoked by revenge. It was the call for revenge, for overturning the treaty, for rectifying its shame and humiliations that allowed Hitler to mobilize Germany for war. Germans rallied to those who promised to get even for the Allied occupation of the Rhineland, for the French and Belgian invasion of the Ruhr, for being forced to bear sole guilt for starting the war, for reparations and for dozens of other slights and degradations, petty and gross.

Woodrow Wilson, David Lloyd George and others at times had warned that Germany should not be treated in ways that would spark an irrational and powerful revenge. But even they had no idea, would be unable to guess, just how powerful a lever revenge would be in the hands of a Hitler. Thus though postwar Germany might have been unstable, perhaps even ruled by a communist or fascist dictator, without the draconian peace imposed by the Allies and Americans, it stretches imagination beyond imagination that such a dictator could have taken Germany into war, a war which drowned Europe in Nazi brutality, destructiveness, racist violence and genocide. Such was the lasting offspring of the Versailles peace.

America's Fateful Decision and Greatest Blunder

How responsible was America for that? Specifically for those tragedies, not responsible at all. Responsible were those in Vienna, Paris, Moscow, Berlin, and London who actually triggered the Great War, those who demanded the punitive ceasefire and peace, those who in 1923 marched troops into the Ruhr to punish Germany for faltering in reparations payments, those inside Germany and outside who denied the Weimar Republic its chance and, of course, those who devised and executed Nazi policies. For those, America cannot be held directly to account; America was not a player and not a culprit.

Still. Still—at a crucial moment in history America made a decision on which history pivoted. America chose to take sides in Europe's Great War. America declared war against Germany even though it was not at all endangered by Germany. America dispatched enough fresh and eager divisions to the Western Front to shift its balance decisively in Britain's and France's favor. And America abandoned its vision of a peace without victory, instead allowing the armistice and peace talks to exclude Germany and become instruments of punishment and humiliation which spawned German demands for revenge. From all those flowed much of the century's subsequent tragedy. It is for creating the conditions in which those bred that America must accept responsibility.

The war ended as it did only because America had entered the war as it did. And the way the war ended came to determine the way the peace played out. Entering the Great War would prove to be, over the following decades, America's greatest blunder of the 20th Century.

Who and what were responsible for that blunder? This remains one of the 20th Century's most perplexing questions; historians have found answers perpetually elusive. Even nearly 100 years later, they do not seem certain why America actually went to war. Wilson scholar Thomas Knock admits that "there is no direct evidence that reveals why Wilson decided to lead the country into war."[5] Unlike in 1941, the nation's navy had not been sunk in a Pearl Harbor; unlike in 1898, its battleship *Maine* had not (ostensibly) been attacked in a Cuban port; unlike in 1950, its Cold War resolve had not been tested when a North Korea invaded a South Korea. By stark contrast, in 1917 American security was not at stake. In his April 2, 1917 stirring appeal to the Congress to declare war, Woodrow Wilson did not even claim that it was.

Yet America, gradually, over thirty-one months, convinced itself that it must fight. A number of forces ultimately joined together, as Chapters 2 and 3 relate, herding the nation to this conclusion. These forces included Congress; political leaders of all parties; Progressives and liberals as well as Teddy Roosevelt's interventionists; the Preparedness Movement's boosters and the growing number of National Security League members who warned that Germany was planning to invade the U.S.; hawkish newspaper owners and publishing houses turning out the dozens of alarmist bestsellers like John Bernard Walker's *America Fallen! The Sequel to the European War* and Hudson Maxim's *Defenseless America*; tocsin-beating clergymen; bankers, industrialists and farmers whose fortunes increasingly were tied to, even held hostage by, the fate of Britain and France on the battlefield.

Included too as forces driving America to war were German leaders unleashing their submarines to attack American and other neutral ships venturing into the war zone; and, of course, Britain's skillful propaganda campaign and its near-total censorship of war news which etched into the American awareness an image of Germans as inhuman and threatening beasts who impale Belgian children on bayonets. Culpable as well was the Progressive Movement's uplifting moralizing rhetoric which for decades had inspired (and mobilized) a generation of Americans, making them by 1917 receptive to seeing an America at war as a virtuous and moral crusade.

Over the months, as America watched the Great War, these diverse strands created an almost inertial force, knitting together a mood in which, for great numbers of Americans, a call to arms began seeming sensible, even inevitable. But only one American could issue such a call: the president.

And he did.

And by doing that, the Woodrow Wilson remembered by history must accept more responsibility than any other person, institution or factor for America having gone to war. Whatever his personal agonies and private doubts, however much he genuinely may have been to his core a man of peace, whatever his good intentions and whatever his fears that sending his nation into war could impede his ambitious domestic reforms, in the end he turned his back on all of that. In the end, he demanded of Congress that it give him war.

Wilson's champions and defenders—and there have been honored and distinguished legions of them over the century—will argue that by April 6, 1917, Wilson had no options. By that late date, they could say, war may have been unavoidable. But that is neither an adequate answer nor a convincing excuse. In the many months leading up to April 6, the president had countless opportunities to temper America's growing anti-German mood and to explain and demonstrate convincingly that both sides in the war were denying America its international rights. Through words and policies Wilson could have derailed his nation's momentum towards war. He did not. At too many turns his actions and, as critical, inactions contradicted or eroded his lofty words and his sensible inclinations about neutrality and peace. At too many crossroads he chose the path that ultimately led doughboys to the Western Front's trenches. Were history a prosecutor seeking a culprit for failure to keep America at peace, it could charge Wilson on many counts. Among them:

- Wilson failed, despite the soaring rhetoric of his promises, to pursue true neutrality. In ways large and small, he consistently favored the British and French over the Germans. In the key area of finance, this pro-Allied tilt had enormous consequences; it quickly aligned major U.S. economic interests with London and Paris. All belligerents desperately, truly desperately, needed American loans to keep on fighting. And American banks had the right to lend to all comers. But Wilson's policies gave only the Allies access to Wall Street's money spigot; it was shut tightly to the Germans. Without the funds to buy American food, munitions and other products, Germany ceased being a source of business and thus profit for U.S. factories, banks and farms and thus ceased being a driver of American prosperity and job growth. It is no wonder that major U.S. economic interests ultimately became an influential force favoring Allied victory.

- Wilson failed to defend America's freedom of the seas, arguably the bedrock of American security policy since the republic's founding. He took no action against Britain when it endangered U.S. shipping by mining the North Sea or when its tight blockade around Germany kept U.S. ships from getting to German ports or when its Royal Navy warships intercepted and then forced U.S. merchantmen to British docks to be inspected for contraband. All of that seriously violated America's right to international commerce. But Wilson did nothing. Hugely different was the story when it came to Germany. To Berlin, Wilson issued angry and tough ultimatums, directly threatening harsh reprisals when its submarines tried to keep American vessels from British ports. At an intellectual level, he actually understood the inconsistency, if not hypocrisy, of his policy. As a onetime political science professor, he recognized the equivalence of the

British and German actions: to prevent goods from reaching the other's ports, each was willing to violate America's rights. He surely agreed when essayist Walter Lippmann, a fellow liberal and supporter of the Allies, in February 1917 wrote that there is no reason "for regarding the submarine as more deadly than the blockade of Europe."[6] Tacitly acknowledging this, Wilson at one point proposed a tradeoff: London would allow some American and other neutral ships to reach Germany, while Berlin, in exchange, would curtail sharply its submarine attacks. Berlin accepted the deal; London did not. But instead of castigating Britain for intransigence, Wilson dropped the matter. For him, American freedom of the seas was a sovereign right to be enforced only against Germany, not against Britain. And by denouncing solely German violation of American rights, he focused American public anger against Germany.

• Wilson failed to wield America's considerable and growing economic leverage to press Britain and France first to respect American rights and neutrality and then, after the U.S. entered the war, to accept his outline for peace. He never even tried, even though Britain had become so dependent on America for food, manufactured goods, munitions and, of course, loans that by mid-1916, according to historian Ross Gregory, it "could not continue the war without the United States." On February 22, 1917, in fact, a British official was telling his government that "four weeks from today" they would be bankrupt. And just five months after that, the head of Britain's supply mission in the U.S. wrote to London: "We are down on our knees to the Americans." Yet Wilson never threatened to embargo American products or withhold financing to gain concessions from London. When, for example, London placed on a "blacklist" the names of eighty-seven U.S. firms it accused of helping Germany and then ordered the Royal Navy to stop neutral ships, search for and confiscate those firms' goods (even though they were not heading for Germany), all Wilson did was fume and complain. He took no action to defend the American firms.

- Wilson similarly failed to wield American geopolitical leverage. When he brought America into the war on the British and French side, he did so gratuitously. In contrast to the promises and rewards won by Italy, Japan and every other country as a payback for their support of the Allies, America made no demands and set no conditions for its help. Wilson did not even ask that, in exchange for troops and supplies, the Allies agree to the kind of non-punitive peace he long had advocated. Failure to obtain concessions when America easily could have done so was to hamstring Wilson grievously at the 1919 Paris peace talks. There he was unable to hold London and Paris to earlier promises since he had not demanded or obtained any promises.

- Wilson failed to use his renowned eloquence and his presidential bully pulpit (a term coined by his predecessor Teddy Roosevelt) to educate his nation about how the war's complexities were affecting America. This could have corrected, at least somewhat, Americans' distorted view that only Germans were trampling on America's rights. For example, Wilson could have explained how Britain's naval blockade was violating America's freedom of the seas by denying American ships their right to head for any port. He could have informed the public and indignantly complained that Britain was endangering all American vessels by deploying its so-called "Q ships"—armed British freighters disguised to masquerade as American merchantmen, even flying the

American flag, to lure German submarines to the surface and then attack them. This made every U.S. ship suspect to German submarine commanders who understandably saw them as a possible hostile and dangerous British warship in disguise. Wilson could have mobilized his famed rhetorical slashing ire to denounce London for "blacklisting" those eighty-seven American firms. He could have shared with the public the dismay he confided to his cabinet as late as March 20, 1917 when he complained about "German militarism on land and England's militarism on sea." And he could have alerted his countrymen that Britain was controlling and heavily censoring all of the war news they were receiving because it had cut the undersea cable between Germany and the U.S., that Britain was waging an intensive propaganda campaign inside America, that Britain and France had planted spies in the U.S. and that British and French soldiers on occasion, like the Germans, had committed atrocities. On all this, Wilson remained silent. So doing, he allowed to simmer and then build to an angry boil a public view that Germany uniquely was evil, dangerous and violating American rights.

- Wilson failed to insist that America be at the armistice table to ensure that a ceasefire follow the lines set by his extensive exchanges with Berlin. As a result, the French and British alone confronted the Germans, imposing on them, as Chapter 7 describes, an armistice vastly more punishing than anything Wilson had negotiated and than the Germans rightly had expected.

- Wilson failed in Paris to block the war's victors from imposing on Germany the kind of punishing peace about which he long had warned. As a negotiator, he was surprisingly ineffective, neither open to guidance from his staff nor alert to the nuances and details of the crucial issues on the table. Above all, far above all, he was too ready to trade away America's high-value cards simply to get British and French (and others') backing for his League of Nations. In exchange for the League, he abandoned all he ever had said or written about the dangers of a peace that planted seeds of revenge.

• And, most consequential, Wilson failed to ask, when debating whether to take America to war, what national interests were at stake. He did not pose the essential question: What are the factors affecting Americans' personal and national well-being and security for which the nation's sons will be risking their lives? The inescapable answer would have been that there were none. America was not threatened nor would it be. America would neither be advancing its interests nor even defending them. But simply to raise such a question would have been abhorrent to Wilson. He saw himself in international affairs, explain the many historians who have studied him intensively, as he did in domestic matters, as a missionary called to bring the New World's superior moral commandments to the old, replacing selfish balance of power calculations with the imperatives of his notions of justice and fairness. He boasted that America in entering the war was seeking nothing for itself, that it had signed no squalid "secret treaties" with their tantalizing (and aggrandizing) promises of spoils of victory. Instead, his was an altruistic America, ready to fight for ideals and for lofty principles. Its war was to be a war to end all wars, a war to make the world safe for democracy. When he personally brought the Versailles Treaty to the Senate for ratification in July 1919, he declared with pride that America had gone to war not for "our material interests...[but] as the disinterested champions of right." In embracing such views, of course, Woodrow Wilson became the first "Wilsonian," whose descendants on the left and even on the right insist that idealism be the lodestar of American foreign policy. To our day they have wielded what Henry Kissinger points out has been an outsize, even dominant, influence on America's foreign relations. Perhaps Wilson's fervent Wilsonianism, as much as anything else, is what in the end convinced him that he must take America to war. Only that, he could argue, would earn him a seat at the conference table where he would have his chance to proselytize and convert nations to his soaring moral vision of a new ordering of the world. Alas, at that conference table in Paris, as history well knows, he failed. It is a failure whose consequences America and the world could have been spared had Wilson weighed America's security and economic interests before asking Congress for war. In weighing those interests he would have found no justification for sending anyone into battle.

These are the counts by which history can charge Woodrow Wilson culpable, more so than any other person, faction or institution, for taking America to war. He was far from solely responsible; but he was most responsible. He could have stopped it. No summation of charges against him is probably more damning than that of George Kennan, one of the 20th Century's most prescient, creative and influential American diplomats. In his 1951 study *American Diplomacy*, he pitches his voice directly at Wilson, telling him, as if the president were in a defendant's dock: "You could have refrained from moralistic slogans, refrained from picturing your effort as a crusade, kept open your lines of negotiation to the enemy, declined to break up his empires and overthrow his political system, avoided commitments to the extremist war aims of your allies, retained your freedom of action, exploited your bargaining power flexibly."[7]

But, as we know, Wilson did not. What he did not know, could not know, was that his actions in the aggregate would coalesce into a national mistake that would launch his young century on a course in the West more tortuous, more self-destructive than any other since the wars of religion had ravaged Europe 300 years earlier. The decision to go to war would inflict great and prolonged suffering on America. It suffered first from the horrors its doughboys encountered on the Western Front and from the rationing, hardships and restrictions on liberties all its citizens encountered at home. Then within just a generation, America suffered again, from a second and even greater war, whose battlefield losses and home front deprivations dwarfed the first war's.

And more suffering was to come. As a direct result of the second war, the Soviet Union marched its Red Army as far west as the Elbe River, dividing Europe by what Winston Churchill despairingly called an Iron Curtain. This sparked a Cold War, a tense conflict—at times, of course, not very cold at all, as in Korea and Viet Nam—which pulled America into its vortex. For nearly a half-century, Americans patiently and at great cost shouldered the enormous burden of holding back the Soviet Union, of living in fear of nuclear attack, of knowing that suddenly they may be asked to fight again.

All that was the result of how the Great War had ended. And it had ended the way it did only because of America's fateful blunder on April 6, 1917. On that day, America had a choice and it chose. So doing, America shattered the Western Front's deadlock and won the war. America gave Britain and France their chance to punish and humiliate the newly democratic Germany. By its decision, America set the west, for what would be nearly a century, on its tortuous, agonizing and bloody course.

NOTES

Chapter 1 – Stalemate on the Western Front

1. Hew Strachan, *The First World War, Vol. I, To Arms* (New York: Oxford University Press, 2001) 42.

2. Niall Ferguson, *The Pity of War: Explaining World War I* (New York: Basic Books, 1999) 93, 248.

3. Ferguson, Ibid., 107.

4. John Keegan, *The First World War I* (New York: Knopf, 1999) 122.

5. Gary Sheffield, *Forgotten Victory: The First World War: Myths and Realities* (London: Headline Book Publishing, 2001) 119.

6. John Ellis, *The Social History of the Machine Gun* (New York: Arno Press, 1975) 177. Sheffield, Ibid., 5.

7. Douglas Porch, "Artois 1915," *The Great War: Perspectives on the First World War*, Robert Cowley, ed. (New York: Random House, 2003) 76.

8. Dennis E. Showalter, "The German Soldier of World War I: Myths and Realities," *A Weekend with the Great War: Proceedings of the Fourth Annual Great War Interconference Seminar*, Steven Weingartner, ed. (Wheaton, IL: Cantigny First Division Foundation, White Mane Publishing Co., with the Great War Society and the Western Front Association, 1997) 70.

9. Cowley, Robert, "The Somme: The Last 140 Days," *The Great War: Perspectives on the First World War*, Robert Cowley, ed. (New York: Random House, 2003) 344.

10. Russell F. Weigley, *The American Way of War: A History of United States Military Strategy and Policy* (New York: Macmillan, 1973) 346, citing Dwight D. Eisenhower, *Crusade in Europe*, 449.

11. Ellis, *The Social History of the Machine Gun*, 123.

12. Capt. B.H. Liddell Hart, *The Real War - 1914-1918* (New York: Little, Brown, 1964; originally published 1930) 215.

13. Strachan, *The First World War*, 188. Gerard J. Demaison, "From Verdun to the Maginot Line," *A Weekend with the Great War: Proceedings of the Fourth Annual Great War Interconference Seminar*, Steven Weingartner, ed. (Wheaton, IL: Cantigny First Division Foundation, White Mane Publishing Co., with the Great War Society and the Western Front Association, 1997) 20.

14. Laurence Moyer, *Victory Must Be Ours: Germany in the Great War, 1914-1918* (New York: Hippocrene Books, 1995) 147-148.

15. S.L.A. Marshall, *World War I* (New York: Mariner Books, 2001) 246.

16. Hew Strachan, "The War to End All Wars?" *Foreign Affairs* 82.1(Jan/Feb 2003).

Chapter 2 – America Watches a War

1. Herbert J. Bass, ed., *America's Entry into World War I: Submarines, Sentiment, or Security?* (New York: Holt, Rinehart and Winston, 1964) 1.

2. Kathleen Burk, "Great Britain in the United States, 1917-1918: The Turning Point," *The International History Review* 1.2 (Apr 1979) 228-245. Harry Elmer Barnes, "The World War of 1914-1918," *War in the Twentieth Century*, Willard Walter, ed. (New York: Random House, 1940) 71-82, excerpted in Herbert J. Bass, *America's Entry into World War I*, 21.

3. William C. Widenor, *Henry Cabot Lodge and the Search for an American Foreign Policy* (Berkeley: University of California Press, 1980)167.

4. Ross Gregory, *The Origins of American Intervention in the First World War* (New York: Norton, 1971) 194.

5. Reinhard R. Doerries, *Imperial Challenge: Ambassador Count Bernstorff and German American Relations, 1908-1917* (Chapel Hill, NC: University of North Carolina Press, 1989) 64-65. Thomas Fleming, *The Illusion of Victory: America in World War I* (New York: Basic Books, 2003) 63-65.

6. David M. Kennedy, *Over Here: The First World War and American Society* (New York: Oxford University Press, 1980) 11. Ernest R. May, *The World War and American Isolation, 1914-1917* (Chicago: Quadrangle, 1966, originally published 1959) 173-174. H. W. Brands, *Woodrow Wilson* (New York: Times Books, 2003) 71.

7. Thomas Knock, *To End All Wars: Woodrow Wilson and the Quest for a New World Order* (Princeton, NJ: Princeton University Press, paper edition, 1995) 50.

8. Susan Zeiger, "She Didn't Raise Her Boy to Be a Slacker: Motherhood, Conscription, and the Culture of the First World War," *Feminist Studies* 22.1 (1996) 10-12.

9. Stewart Halsey Ross, *Propaganda for War: How the United States Was Conditioned to Fight The Great War of 1914-1918* (Jefferson, NC: McFarland, 1996) 28.

10. Ross, Ibid., 33-34.

11. Ross, Ibid., 20.

12. Jonathan A. Epstein, "German and English Propaganda in World War I, a paper given to The New York Military Affairs Symposium on December 1, 2000" (New York: City University of New York Graduate Center) 6-7.

13. Epstein, Ibid.

14. Niall Ferguson, *The Pity of War: Explaining World War I* (New York: Basic Books, 1999) 232.

15. Ross, *Propaganda for War*, 45-40. C. Hartley Grattan, *Why We Fought* (New York: Bobbs-Merrill, 1969, originally published 1929) 72.

16. Ross, Ibid., 51-60. Knock, *To End All Wars*, 60.

17. Dennis E. Showalter, "The German Soldier of World War

I: Myths and Realities," *A Weekend with the Great War: Proceedings of the Fourth Annual Great War Interconference Seminar.* Steven Weingartner, ed. (Wheaton, IL: Cantigny First Division Foundation, White Mane Publishing Co. with the Great War Society and the Western Front Association, 1997) 63.

18. Knock, *To End All Wars*, 60.

19. Epstein, "German and English Propaganda in World War I," 16.

20. Epstein, Ibid., 14.

21. Ross, *Propaganda for War*, 116-117.

22. Keith Windschuttle, "Was World War I Necessary?' *New Criterion* 18.4 (Dec 1999) 9ff, citing Niall Ferguson.

23. Laurence Moyer, *Victory Must Be Ours: Germany in the Great War, 1914-1918* (New York: Hippocrene Books, 1995) 196.

24. Clara Eve Schieber, *The Transformation of American Sentiment Toward Germany, 1870-1914* (Boston: Cornhill, 1923) 14-37.

25. Manfred Jonas, *The United States and Germany: A Diplomatic History* (Ithaca, NY: Cornell University Press, 1984) 23-26.

26. Jonas, Ibid., 60. Schieber, *The Transformation of American Sentiment Toward Germany*, 111-133.

27. Gregory, *The Origins of American Intervention in the First World War*, 8.

28. Jonas, *The United States and Germany*, 51.

29. Schieber, *The Transformation of American Sentiment Toward Germany*, 187, 275-276.

30. Brands, *Woodrow Wilson*, 59.

31. Gregory, *The Origins of American Intervention in the First World War*, 60.

32. May, *The World War and American Isolation*, 167.

33. Hew Strachan, *The First World War. Vol. I, To Arms* (New York: Oxford University Press, 2001) 222. John Keegan, *The First World War* (New York: Knopf, 1999) 265.

34. Capt. B.H. Liddell Hart, *The Real War – 1914-1918* (New York: Little, Brown, 1964, originally published 1930) 212.

35. Gregory, *The Origins of American Intervention in the First World War*, 93.

36. Keegan, *The First World War*, 274. L.L. Farrar, "The Strategy of the Central Powers, 1914-1917," *The Oxford Illustrated History of the First World War*, Hew Strachan, ed. (New York and Oxford: Oxford University Press, 1998) 36.

37. Knock, *To End All Wars*, 61, 74. May, *The World War and American Isolation*, 217-218, 232-233, 250-252. Jonas, *The United States and Germany*, 109, 114-115. August Heckscher, *Woodrow Wilson* (New York: Scribner's, 1991) 384-387. Daniel Malloy Smith, *The Great Departure: The United States and World War I, 1914-1920* (New York: Knopf, 1965), 61-66. Gregory, *The Origins of American Intervention in the First World War*, 95.

38. May, *The World War and American Isolation*, 197.

39. May, Ibid., 25-26. Gregory, *The Origins of American Intervention in the First World War*, 40-41. Smith, *The Great Departure*, 40-41.

40. Moyer, *Victory Must Be Ours*, 122.

41. Moyer, Ibid., 133. Edwin M. Borchard and William P. Lage, *Neutrality for the United States* (New Haven, CT: Yale University Press, 1937) 33-34, excerpted in Herbert J. Bass, ed., *America's Entry into World War I*, 28-29.

42. May, *The World War and American Isolation*, 61-62. Louis Guichard, Member of France's Chamber of Deputies, "Germany under the Great Blockade," *The Living Age* (Apr 1929). 111-118.

43. Liddell Hart, *The Real War*, 472.

44. Moyer, *Victory Must Be Ours*, 262. Roger Chickering, *Imperial Germany and the Great War, 1914-1918* (Cambridge, UK: Cambridge University Press, 1998) 122-123.

45. Chickering, Ibid., 126. Kennedy, *Over Here*, 7.

46. Ernest R. May, *The World War and American Isolation*, 137,

328-329.

47. Smith, *The Great Departure*, 40-43.

48. Moyer, *Victory Must Be Ours*, 122.

49. Knock, *To End All Wars*, 34-35.

Chapter 3 – Choosing War

1. Arthur S. Link, *Wilson the Diplomatist: A Look at His Major Foreign Policies* (Chicago: Quadrangle Books, 1963, originally published in 1957) 68. Thomas Knock, *To End All Wars: Woodrow Wilson and the Quest for a New World Order*, (Princeton, NJ: Princeton University Press, 1992, paper edition, 1995) 106.

2. Charles Seymour, *American Neutrality, 1914-1917: Essays on the Causes of American Intervention in the World War* (New Haven, CT: Yale University Press, 1935) 26-36, see also Herbert J. Bass, ed., *America's Entry into World War I: Submarines, Sentiment, or Security?* (New York: Holt, Rinehart and Winston, 1964) 14.

3. Meirion and Susie Harries, *The Last Days of Innocence: America at War 1917-1918* (New York: Random House, 1998, Vintage Books edition) 70.

4. Rod Paschall, *The Defeat of Imperial Germany, 1917-1918* (Chapel Hill, NC: Algonquin Books, 1994, originally published 1989) 15.

5. Mayer, George H. Mayer, *The Republican Party, 1854-1964* (New York: Oxford University Press, 1967) 304.

6. Thomas Fleming, *The Illusion of Victory: America in World War I* (New York: Basic Books, 2003) 82, citing W.B. Fowler, *British-American Relations 1917-1918: The Role of Sir William Wiseman*, 22-23.

7. Arthur S. Link, "Wilson and the Struggle for Neutrality," *The Impact of World War I*, Link, ed. (New York: Harper and Row, 1969) 12.

8. Link, *Wilson the Diplomatist*, 16-17.

9. Harries, *The Last Days of Innocence*, 69. Niall Ferguson, *The Pity of War: Explaining World War I* (New York: Basic Books, 1999) 251.

10. Paul Birdsall, "Neutrality and Economic Pressures, 1914-1917," *Science and Society*, 3 (Spring, 1939) 217-228, excerpted in Bass, ed., *America's Entry into World War I*, 56.

11. Edward B. Parsons, "Why the British Reduced the Flow of American Troops to Europe in August-October 1918," *Canadian Journal of History* 12 (Dec 1977) 175-179.

12. Ross Gregory, *The Origins of American Intervention in the First World War* (New York: Norton, 1971) 29. Hew Strachan, "Economic Mobilization: Money, Munitions and Machines," *The Oxford Illustrated History of the First World War*, Hew Strachan, ed. (New York and Oxford: Oxford University Press, 1998) 147. J. W. Thacker, *History: Review of New Books* (Winter 2002) 61, review of Hew Strachan, *The First World War: Vol. I: To Arms*. Niall Ferguson, *The Pity of War*, 329. Link, *Wilson* the *Diplomatist*, 44.

13. Kathleen Burk, "Great Britain in the United States, 1917-1918: The Turning Point," *The International History Review* 1.2 (Apr. 1979) 228-245.

14. Gregory, *The Origins of American Intervention in the First World War*, 109. Burk, Ibid., 228-245.

15. Daniel Malloy Smith, *The Great Departure: The United States and World War I, 1914-1920* (New York: Knopf, 1965) 37. Birdsall, "Neutrality and Economic Pressures, 1914-1917," 56. Newton D. Baker, *Why We Went to War* (New York: Harper, 1936) 127.

16. Fleming, *The Illusion of Victory*, 71. David M Kennedy, *Over Here: The First World War and American Society* (New York: Oxford University Press, 1980, paperback edition) 305-307. Gary Sheffield, *Forgotten Victory: The First World War, Myths and Realities* (London: Headline Book Publishing, 2001) 55. Niall Ferguson, *The Pity of War*, 328.

17. Benjamin O. Fordham, "Revisionism" Reconsidered: Exports and American Intervention in the First World War," presented

at the American Political Science Association 1 Sep 2005," 1.

18. Fordham, Ibid., 6. Gregory, *The Origins of American Intervention in the First World War*, 130-131.

19. John Patrick Finnegan, *Against the Specter of the Dragon: The Campaign for American Military Preparedness* (Westport, CT: Greenwood Press, 1974) 65-68. John Whiteclay Chambers II, *To Raise an Army: The Draft Comes to Modern America* (New York: The Free Press, 1987) 83. Michael Pearlman, *To Make Democracy Safe for America: Patricians and Preparedness in the Progressive Era* (Urbana, IL: University of Illinois Press, 1984) 58.

20. *New York Times*, 14 May 1916: 1. Finnegan, Ibid., 104-105, 177-178.

21. Finnegan, Ibid., 104-105.

22. Finnegan, Ibid., 93-95. Eric Van Schaack, "The Coming of the Hun! American Fears of a German Invasion, 1918," *The Journal of American Culture* 28.3 (2005).

23. *Variety* 13 Aug 1915. *New York Times* 7 Aug 1915. *Moving Picture World* 21 Aug 1915 and 25 Sep 1915. Schaack, Ibid.

24. Gregory, *The Origins of American Intervention in the First World War*, 67. Harry Elmer Barnes, "The World War of 1914-1918," *War in the Twentieth Century*, Willard Walter, ed. (New York: Random House, 1940), excerpted in Bass, ed., *America's Entry into World War I*, 18.

25. Ernest R. May, *The World War and American Isolation, 1914-1917* (Chicago: Quadrangle, 1966, originally published 1959) 414. Birdsall, "Neutrality and Economic Pressures, 1914-1917," 57-58. L.L. Farrar, "The Strategy of the Central Powers, 1914-1917," *The Oxford Illustrated History of the First World War,* Hew Strachan, ed. (New York and Oxford: Oxford University Press, 1998) 37.

26. Strachan, "Economic Mobilization: Money, Munitions and Machines," 147.

27. May, *The World War and American Isolation*, 217. Laurence Moyer, *Victory Must Be Ours: Germany in the Great War, 1914-1918*

(New York: Hippocrene Books, 1995) 185. Roger Chickering, *Imperial Germany and the Great War, 1914-1918* (Cambridge, UK: Cambridge University Press, 1998) 92. Reinhard R. Doerries, *Imperial Challenge: Ambassador Count Bernstorff and German American Relations, 1908-1917* (Chapel Hill, NC: University of North Carolina Press, 1989) 222, footnote 143.

28. Arthur S. Link, "Wilson Moves to the Center of the Stage of World Affairs," Arthur S. Link, ed., *The Impact of World War I* (New York: Harper and Row, 1969) 39-40. Gregory, *The Origins of American Intervention in the First World War,* 116. Knock, *To End All Wars,* 107-111. Link, *Wilson the Diplomatist, xiii,* 44. August Heckscher, *Woodrow Wilson* (New York: Scribner's, 1991) 415-416, 422. Smith, *The Great Departure,* 75-76.

29. Heckscher, Ibid., 435.

30. Manfred Jonas, *The United States and Germany: A Diplomatic History* (Ithaca, NY: Cornell University Press, 1984) 111. May, *The World War and American Isolation,* 416.

31. George F. Kennan, *American Diplomacy, 1900-1950* (Chicago: University of Chicago Press, 1951), excerpted in Bass, ed., *America's Entry into World War I,* 103.

32. Fordham, "'Revisionism' Reconsidered," 1.

33. C. Hartley Grattan, *Why We Fought* (New York: Bobbs-Merrill, 1969, originally published 1929) 401. Barnes, "The World War of 1914-1918," 18.

34. Warren I. Cohen, *The American Revisionists: The Lessons of Intervention in World War I* (Chicago: University of Chicago Press, 1967) 183.

35. Chambers, *To Raise an Army,* 144-145. Edward M. Coffman, *The War to End All Wars: The American Military Experience in World War I* (New York: Oxford University Press, 1968) 8.

Chapter 4 – Mobilizing the Nation

1. John Patrick Finnegan, *Against the Specter of the Dragon: The Campaign for American Military Preparedness* (Westport, CT: Greenwood Press, 1974) 5-6, 184-185. General William Robertson to General A.J. Murray, 13 February 1917, *The Military Correspondence of Field Marshal Sir William Robertson, Chief, Imperial General Staff, December 1915-February 1918*, David R. Woodward, ed., *Publications of the Army Records Society* 5 (London: 1989) 149.

2. Rod Paschall, *The Defeat of Imperial Germany, 1917-1918* (Chapel Hill, NC: Algonquin Books, 1994, originally published 1989) 52. Edward M. Coffman, *The War to End All Wars: The American Military Experience in World War I* (New York: Oxford University Press, 1968) 31, 37.

3. Newton D. Baker, *Why We Went to War* (New York: Harper, 1936) 119-120.

4. Gary Mead, *The Doughboys: America and the First World War* (New York: Overlook Press, 2000) 13. Coffman, *The War to End All Wars*, 48.

5. S.L.A Marshall, *World War I* (New York: Mariner Books, 2001, originally published 1964) 281.

6. McCarthy, Michael J.. "Planning the AEF: The Need for an Expeditionary Force," *'Lafayette, We Are Here,' The War College Division and American Military Planning for the AEF in World War I* (The Great War Society, Doughboy Center, www.worldwar1.com.) "You're Not Going to Send Soldiers Over There Are You! The American Search for an Alternative to the Western Front," *Military Affairs* 36.1 (Feb 1972). Stephen Pope and Elizabeth-Anne Wheal, *The Macmillan Dictionary of the First World War* (London: Macmillan Reference Books, 1997) 441.

7. McCarthy, Ibid.. John Mosier, *The Myth of the Great War: A New Military History of World War I* (New York: Harper Collins, 2001) 305.

8. John J. Pershing, *My Experiences in the World War, Vol. I* (New York: Frederick A. Stokes, 1931, Tab Edition) 38.

9. Coffman, *The War to End All Wars*, 122-124. Raquel Hendrickson, "Lafayette, We Are Here! The Yanks Arrive in Europe" (The Great War Society, Doughboy Center, www.worldwar1.com.). Meirion and Susie Harries, *The Last Days of Innocence: America at War 1917-1918* (New York: Random House, 1998, Vintage Books edition) 116. Donald Smythe, *Pershing: General of the Armies* (Bloomington, IN: Indiana University Press, 1986) 14-16, 20. Pershing, Ibid., 58-59.

10. Laurence Stallings and M.S. Wyeth, *The Story of the Doughboys: The AEF in World War I* (New York: Harper and Row, 1963) 3. Mead, *The Doughboys*, 66. Alfred E. Cornebise, *The Stars and Stripes: Doughboy Journalism in World War I* (Westport, CT: Greenwood Press, 1984) 101-103.

11. John Whiteclay Chambers II, *To Raise an Army: The Draft Comes to Modern America* (New York: Free Press, 1987) 144.

12. Chambers, Ibid., 41, 53-54.

13. Chambers, Ibid., 236.

14. Allen Davis, "The Flowering of Progressivism," *The Impact of World War I*, Arthur S. Link, ed. (New York: Harper and Row, 1969) 52-53.

15. Chambers, *To Raise an Army*, 150.

16. Davis, "The Flowering of Progressivism," 45-46.

17. Thomas Knock, *To End All Wars: Woodrow Wilson and the Quest for a New World Order* (Princeton, NJ: Princeton University Press, paper edition, 1995) 129.

18. Arthur S. Link, ed., *The Impact of World War I* (New York: Harper and Row, 1969) 34. William E. Leuchtenburg, "The Impact of the War on the American Political Economy," *The Impact of World War I*, Arthur S. Link, ed. (New York: Harper and Row, 1969) 60. Knock, Ibid., 129-130. Davis, "The Flowering of Progressivism," 46-47, 50. David M Kennedy, *Over Here: The First World War and American Society* (New York: Oxford University Press, 1982, paperback edition) 258.

19. http://www.treasurydirect.gov/govt/reports/pd/histdebt_histo3.htm. http://www.usgovernmentspending.com/federal_debt_chart.html.

20. Susan Zeiger, "She Didn't Raise Her Boy to Be a Slacker: Motherhood, Conscription, and the Culture of the First World War," *Feminist Studies* 22.1 (1996) 13. Kennedy, *Over Here*, 27-28.

21. Harriett Williams, "American Universities and World War I," *American Decades CD-ROM* (Farmington Hills, MI: History Research Center for Gale Research, 1998).

22. Harries, *The Last Days of Innocence*, 90. Stewart Halsey Ross, *Propaganda for War: How the United States Was Conditioned to Fight The Great War of 1914-1918* (Jefferson, NC: McFarland, 1996) 251.

23. David McLean and Monica Siems, "World War I: A Call to Arms," *American Decades CD-ROM* (Farmington Hills, MI: History Research Center for Gale Research, 1998), cites "Billy Sunday Fires Hot Shot at Kaiser," *New York Times*, 19 Feb1918; "Sunday, Coatless, Flays Kaiserism," *New York Times*, 28 May 1917.

24. Ross, *Propaganda for War*, 262, cites Michael T. Isenberg, *War on Film: The American Cinema and World War I, 1914-1941* (Rutherford, NJ: Farleigh Dickinson University Press, 1981) 149, 151.

25. Creighton Peet, "Hollywood at War, 1915-1918: A Little Reminder of What the Movies Could Do in the Days of the Beast of Berlin," *Esquire* (Sep 1936) 60, 109.

26. The Internet Movie Database. *www.silentera.com. http://movies.nytimes.com/movie/97524/The-Kaiser-the-Beast-of-Berlin/overview*. Harries, *The Last Days of Innocence*, 294.

27. Ross, *Propaganda for War*, 244-248. Harries, ibid., 172.

28. Harriett Williams, "American Universities and World War I," *American Decades CD-ROM* (Farmington Hills, MI: History Research Center for Gale Research, 1998). *"Antiwar Press during World War I, 1914-1918,"* (Farmington Hills, MI: History Research Center for Gale Research, 1997). *"Antiwar Sentiment in the 1910s, 1910-1919."* (Farmington Hills, MI: History Research Center for Gale Research, 1997). Mark Sonntag, "Fighting Everything German in Texas, 1917-1919," *The Historian* 56.4 (1994) 655ff. Chambers, *To Raise an Army*, 209. Ross, Ibid., 270. Harries, *The Last Days of Innocence*, 296. Thomas

Fleming, *The Illusion of Victory: America in World War I* (New York: Basic Books, 2003) 106. Kennedy, *Over Here*, 81-82.

Chapter 5 – Doughboys Head for the Western Front

1.Gary Sheffield, *Forgotten Victory: The First World War: Myths and Realities* (London: Headline Book Publishing, 2001) 105. Rod Paschall, *The Defeat of Imperial Germany, 1917-1918* (Chapel Hill, NC: Algonquin Books, 1989, originally published 1989) 11.

2. Hew Strachan, *The First World War. Vol. I, To Arms* (New York: Oxford University Press, 2001) 253.

3. S.L.A Marshall, *World War I* (New York: Mariner Books, 2001; originally published 1964) 288, 290.

4. Rod Paschall, *The Defeat of Imperial Germany, 1917-1918* (Chapel Hill, NC: Algonquin Books, 1989) 327 329.

5. Capt. B.H. Liddell Hart, *The Real War – 1914-1918* (New York: Little, Brown, 1964, originally published 1930) 337. S.L.A Marshall, *World War I*, 304-305. Paschall, *The Defeat of Imperial Germany*, 59. John Keegan, *The First World War I* (New York: Knopf, 1999) 355.

6. Keegan, Ibid., 361-364, 367. Liddell Hart, Ibid., 340-343. Sheffield, *Forgotten Victory*, 214. Paschall, Ibid., 60, 76-77. Strachan, *The First World War*, 253.

7. Liddell Hart, Ibid., 343.

8. John Terraine, *To Win a War, 1918: The Year of Victory* (New York: Doubleday, 1981) 27.

9. John Ellis, *The Social History of the Machine Gun* (New York: Arno Press, 1975) 141-142. Keegan, *The First World War*, 395. Sheffield, *Forgotten Victory*, 99.

10. Gail Braybon, "Women, War, and Work," *The Oxford Illustrated History of the First World War,* Hew Strachan, ed. (New York and Oxford: Oxford University Press, 1998) 152.

11. David F. Trask, *The AEF and Coalition Warmaking, 1917-1918* (Lawrence, KS: University of Kansas Press, 1993) 33. Donald Smythe, *Pershing: General of the Armies* (Bloomington, IN: Indiana University Press, 1986) 59. Anne Cipriano Venzon, ed., *The United States in the First World War: An Encyclopedia* (New York: Garland Publishing, 1995) 617. Laurence Stallings and M.S. Wyeth, *The Story of the Doughboys: The AEF in World War I* (New York: Harper and Row, 1963) 26. S.L.A Marshall, *World War I*, 308. Gary Mead, *The Doughboys: America and the First World War* (New York: Overlook Press, 2000), 162-163. Edward M. Coffman, *The War to End All Wars: The American Military Experience in World War I* (New York: Oxford University Press, 1968) 139-140.

12. Smythe, Ibid., 9, 101, 111.

13. Smythe, Ibid., 69. Mead, *The Doughboys*, 167. Sheffield, *Forgotten Victory*, xviii, 85-86, 105, 262.

14. Smythe, Ibid., 18, 64.

15. Trask, *The AEF and Coalition Warmaking*, 245.

16. Smythe, *Pershing*, 30. Coffman, *The War to End All Wars*, 131, 138-139. John J. Pershing, *My Experiences in the World War, Vol. I* (New York: Frederick A. Stokes, 1931, Tab Edition), 127, 138, 315.

17. Mead, *The Doughboys*, 153-154.

18. Coffman, *The War to End All Wars*, 135-137, 144. Stallings, *The Story of the Doughboys*, 22.

19. John J. Pershing, *My Experiences in the World War, Vol. II* (New York: Frederick A. Stokes, 1931, Tab Edition)114, 230.

20. Pershing, Ibid., 188-189.

21. Mark Grotelueschen, *Doctrine Under Trial: American Artillery Employment in World War I* (Westport, CT: Greenwood Press, 2001) 13. Paschall, *The Defeat of Imperial Germany*, 167-168.

22. Alfred E. Cornebise, *The Stars and Stripes: Doughboy Journalism in World War I* (Westport, CT: Greenwood Press, 1984) xi, 6, 99.

23. Pershing, *My Experiences in the World War: Vol. I,* 153. *Vol. II,* 237-238.

24. Pershing, Ibid., Vol. II, 238. Paschall, *The Defeat of Imperial Germany,* 167-168. Smythe, *Pershing,* 72-73.

25. Hans Binneveld, *From Shellshock to Combat Stress* (Amsterdam: 1997) 145.

26. Mead, *The Doughboys,* 124, 217. Pershing, *My Experiences in the World War: Vol. II,* 215. Smythe, *Pershing,* 70.

27. Pershing, Ibid., 28-29.

28. Thomas Fleming, "Iron General." *The Great War: Perspectives on the First World War,* Robert Cowley, ed. (New York: Random House, 2003) 426. Pershing, Ibid., 246-247.

29. Pershing, Ibid. 32.

30. Pershing, Ibid., Vol. I., 33.

31. David Trask, "The Entry of the USA into the War and its Effects," *The Oxford Illustrated History of the First World War,* Hew Strachan, ed. (New York and Oxford: Oxford University Press, 1998) 244.

32. Pershing, *My Experiences in the World War: Vol. II,* 20-24, 32. Coffman, *The War to End All Wars,* 231-232.

33. Smythe, *Pershing,* 90. Pershing, Ibid., 80-81.

34. Pershing, Ibid., 130-131, 309. Mead, *The Doughboys,* 152.

35. Terraine, *To Win a War,* 60.

36. Pershing, *My Experiences in the World War: Vol. I,* 254-255.

37. Trask, *The AEF and Coalition Warmaking,* 54-55. Pershing, *My Experiences in the World War: Vol. I,* 295, *Vol. II,* 35.

38. David M Kennedy, *Over Here: The First World War and American Society* (New York: Oxford University Press, 1982) 176. Pershing, *My Experiences in the World War: Vol. I,* 95.

Chapter 6 – America Breaks the Stalemate
1. David F. Trask, *The AEF and Coalition Warmaking, 1917-1918* (Lawrence, Kansas: University of Kansas Press, 1993) 74.

2. Holger Herwig, "The German Victories, 1917-1918," *The Oxford Illustrated History of the First World War,* Hew Strachan, ed. (New York and Oxford: Oxford University Press, 1998) 259.

3. Capt. B.H. Liddell Hart, *The Real War – 1914-1918* (New York: Little, Brown, 1964 edition, originally published 1930) 368.

4. Benjamin O. Fordham, "Revisionism Reconsidered: Exports and American Intervention in the First World War" (Presented at the American Political Science Association Sep 1, 2005) 7. McKercher, "Economic Warfare," 128-129.

5. Paul G. Halpern, "The War at Sea," *The Oxford Illustrated History of the First World War,* Hew Strachan, ed. (New York and Oxford: Oxford University Press, 1998) 116. Roger Chickering, *Imperial Germany and the Great War, 1914-1918* (Cambridge, UK: Cambridge University Press, 1998) 92. Rod Paschall, *The Defeat of Imperial Germany, 1917-1918* (Chapel Hill, NC: Algonquin Books, 1994, originally published 1989) 196-197. Laurence Moyer, *Victory Must Be Ours: Germany in the Great War, 1914-1918* (New York: Hippocrene Books, 1995) 189-190. Liddell Hart, *The Real War*, 310-311.

6. Paschall, *The Defeat of Imperial Germany*, 131.

7. Donald Smythe, *Pershing: General of the Armies* (Bloomington, IN: Indiana University Press, 1986) 57.

8. John J. Pershing, *My Experiences in the World War, Vol. I* (New York: Frederick A. Stokes, 1931, Tab Edition) 356, 378, 396-397. Meirion and Susie Harries, *The Last Days of Innocence: America at War 1917-1918* (New York: Random House, 1998, Vintage Books edition) 231. S.L.A Marshall, *World War I* (New York: Mariner Books, 2001, originally published 1964) 366, 378. John Keegan, *The First World War* (New York: Knopf, 1999) 405. Trask, *The AEF and Coalition Warmaking*, 58.

9. John Terraine, *To Win a War, 1918: The Year of Victory* (New York: Doubleday, 1981) 44-45. Winston Churchill, *The World Crisis, Vol. II*, 1281, cited by Laurence Moyer, *Victory Must Be Ours*, 242. Herwig, "The German Victories, 1917-1918," 260-261. Paschall, *The Defeat of Imperial Germany*, 135ff.

10. Pershing, *My Experiences in the World War: Vol. I*, 354-355.

11. Keegan, *The First World War*, 400. Paschall, *The Defeat of Imperial Germany*, 140-142.

12. Herwig, "The German Victories, 1917-1918," 262. Keegan, Ibid., 404. Terraine, *To Win a War*, 48-49. S.L.A. Marshall, *World War I*, 364. Tim Travers, *How the War Was Won: Command and Technology in the British Army on the Western Front, 1917-1918* (South Yorkshire, U.K.: Pen & Sword Military Classics, 1992) 50-53, 90-91, 98-99. Trask, *The AEF and Coalition Warmaking*, 51-53. Paschall, Ibid., 146. Chickering, *Imperial Germany and the Great War*, 180. Liddell Hart, *The Real War*, 373, 391.

13. Paschall, *The Defeat of Imperial Germany*, 152.

14. Pershing, *My Experiences in the World War: Vol. II*, 65.

15. Trask, *The AEF and Coalition Warmaking*, 70.

16. Hew Strachan, *The First World War, Vol. I, To Arms* (New York: Oxford University Press, 2001) 298.

17. O'Brien Browne, "March 21, 1918," *The Great War: Perspectives on the First World War*, Robert Cowley, ed. (New York: Random House, 2003) 402-403. Dan Todman, review of Alexander Watson, *Enduring the Great War: Combat, Morale and Collapse in the German and British Armies, 1914-1918*, *War in History*, 16.2 (Apr 2009) 252. Travers, *How the War Was Won*, 107-108.

18. Paul von Hindenburg, *Out of My Life, Vol. II* (1921) 351-352, cited by Trask, *The AEF and Coalition Warmaking*, 56.

19. S.L.A Marshall, *World War I*, 352.

20. Keegan, *The First World War*, 407.

21. Tim Travers, "The Allied Victories, 1918," *The Oxford Illustrated History of the First World War*, Hew Strachan, ed. (New York

and Oxford: Oxford University Press, 1998) 280. Trask, *The AEF and Coalition Warmaking*, 91.

22. Chickering, *Imperial Germany and the Great War*, 186-187.

23. Charles F. Horne, ed., *Source Records of the Great War*, Vol. VI, http://www.firstworldwar.com/source/amiens_gibbs.htm

24. Terraine, *To Win a War*, 84.

25. Liddell Hart, *The Real War*, 430.

26. Russell F. Weigley, *The American Way of War: A History of United States Military Strategy and Policy* (New York: Macmillan, 1973) 135, 141, 143, 145. Smythe, *Pershing*, 202-203, 219.

27. Edward M. Coffman, *The War to End All Wars: The American Military Experience in World War I* (New York: Oxford University Press, 1968) 340. Strachan, *The First World War*, 311. Gary Mead, *The Doughboys: America and the First World War* (New York: Overlook Press, 2000) 189.

28. Pershing, *My Experiences in the World War: Vol. II*, 16.

29. Pershing, Ibid., *Vol. I*, 227.

30. Harries, *The Last Days of Innocence*, 240.

31. David Zabecki, review of *America's Deadliest Battle: Meuse-Argonne, 1918*, by Robert H. Ferrell, *War in History 17.3* (Jul 2010) 372. S.L.A Marshall, *World War I*, 372. Tim Travers, foreword to Mark Grotelueschen, *Doctrine Under Trial: American Artillery Employment in World War I* (Westport, CT: Greenwood Press, 2001) xi. Todman, review of Alexander Watson, *Enduring the Great War*, 252.

32. Richard Fogarty, review of *A Fraternity of Arms: America and France in the Great War*, by Robert B. Bruce, *War in History* 12.3 (Jul 2005) 351-354. Trask, *The AEF and Coalition Warmaking*, 101.

33. Trask, Ibid., 66.

34. Robert Lee Bullard, *Personalities and Reminiscences of the War I* (Garden City, NY: Doubleday, Page, 1925) 197-198.

35. James H. Hallas *Doughboy War: The American Expeditionary Force in World War I* (Boulder, CO: Lynne Rienner, 2000) 98. Terraine,

To Win a War, 77.

36. Trask, *The AEF and Coalition Warmaking*, 132.

37. Trask, Ibid., 71.

38. John Mosier, *The Myth of the Great War: A New Military History of World War I* (New York: Harper Collins, 2001) 321-323. S. L.A Marshall, *World War I*, 385-386, 395. Smythe, *Pershing*, 139. Terraine, *To Win a War*, 56.

39. Coffman, *The War to End All Wars*, 363.

40. Pershing, *My Experiences in the World War: Vol. II*, 267.

41. Laurence Stallings and M.S. Wyeth, *The Story of the Doughboys: The AEF in World War I* (New York: Harper and Row, 1963) 97. Liddell Hart, *The Real War*, 463.

42. Moyer, *Victory Must Be Ours*, 276.

43. Liddell Hart, *The Real War*, 463.

44. Smythe, *Pershing*, 233.

45. Coffman, *The War to End All Wars*, 311-312, 335.

46. John Bowers, "The Mythical Morning of Sergeant York," *The Great War: Perspectives on the First World War*, Robert Cowley, ed. (New York: Random House, 2003) 450. Mead, *The Doughboys*, 319-322. Coffman, Ibid., 324.

47. S.L.A Marshall, *World War I*, 445-446.

48. Smythe, *Pershing*, 205-206, 209, 225.

49. Thomas Fleming, "Iron General," *The Great War: Perspectives on the First World War*, Robert Cowley, ed. (New York: Random House, 2003) 427-428.

50. Mead, *The Doughboys*, 299, 307.

51. Smythe, *Pershing*, 204, 206.

52. Coffman, *The War to End All Wars*, 340. Paschall, *The Defeat of Imperial Germany*, 191. Smythe, Ibid., 216-217. S.L.A Marshall, *World War I*, 447.

53. Smythe, I bid., 246-247.

54. S.L.A Marshall, *World War I*, 433.

55. Terraine, *To Win a War*, 204.

56. Smythe, *Pershing*, 226-227. S.L.A Marshall, *World War I*, 446.

57. Paschall, *The Defeat of Imperial Germany*, 214. Smythe, Ibid., 226.

58. Terraine, *To Win a War*, xv.

59. Travers, "The Allied Victories, 1918," 289-290. Stallings, *The Story of the Doughboys*, 182-183. Mead, *The Doughboys*, 325, 333. Niall Ferguson, *The Pity of War: Explaining World War I* (New York: Basic Books, 1999) 311. Keegan, *The First World War*, 416. Harries, *The Last Days of Innocence*, 416-418.

60. Harry R. Rudin, *Armistice: 1918* (New Haven, CT: Yale University Press, 1944) 168, 177. Smythe, *Pershing*, 219-220, 231. Mead, Ibid., 323. Strachan, *The First World War*, 316. Liddell Hart, *The Real War*, 385. Paschall, *The Defeat of Imperial Germany*, 166-167. Travers, *How the War Was Won*, 153-154, 157.

61. Ferguson, *The Pity of War*, 295, 299. Mead, Ibid., 353.

62. Mead, Ibid., 397.

Chapter 7 – Culmination: Armistice and Versailles

1. Richard M. Watt, *The Kings Depart. The Tragedy of Germany: Versailles and the German Revolution* (New York: Barnes and Noble Books, 2000, originally published 1968) 11.

2. George F. Kennan, *American Diplomacy, 1900-1959* (Chicago: The University of Chicago Press, 1951), excerpted in Herbert J. Bass, ed., *America's Entry into World War I: Submarines, Sentiment, or Security?*(New York: Holt, Rinehart and Winston, 1964) 104. Arthur S. Link, "Wilson Moves to the Center of the Stage of World Affairs," *The Impact of World War I* (New York: Harper and Row, 1969), Arthur Link, ed., 40-41. Thomas Knock, *To End All Wars: Woodrow Wilson and the Quest for a New World Order* (Princeton, NJ: Princeton University Press, 1992, Princeton Paper edition, 1995) 112.

3. Arthur S. Link, *Wilson the Diplomatist: A Look at His Major Foreign Policies* (Chicago: Quadrangle Books, 1963, originally published 1957) 469, 480.

4. Harry R. Rudin, *Armistice: 1918* (New Haven, CT: Yale University Press, 1944) 1, 267. Gary Sheffield, *Forgotten Victory: The First World War: Myths and Realities* (London: Headline Book Publishing, 2001) 69-70. David Stevenson, *The First World War and International Politics* (Oxford: Clarendon Press, 2001 edition, originally published 1988) 193-197.

5. *Congressional Record*, 65th Congress, 2nd Session, 56 (Washington), 680-681.

6. Rudin, *Armistice: 1918*, 12-13, 35, 127-130.

7. Koppel S Pinson, *Modern Germany: Its History and Civilization.* (New York: Macmillan, 1954) 321. Watt, *The Kings Depart*, 144-146.

8. Bullitt Lowry, *Armistice 1918* (Kent, OH: Kent State University Press, 1996) 36.

9. John J. Pershing, *My Experiences in the World War: Vol. II* (New York: Harper and Row, 1931, Tab Edition) 365. Link, "Wilson Moves to the Center of the Stage of World Affairs," 43.

10. Niall Ferguson, *The Pity of War: Explaining World War I* (New York; Basic Books, 1999) 313-314, 317. Rudin, *Armistice: 1918*, 393. William Mulligan, *War in History,* 18.1 (Jul 2011) 133, review of Scott Stephenson, *The Final Battle: Soldiers of the Western Front and the German Revolution of 1918.*

11. Meirion and Susie Harries, *The Last Days of Innocence: America at War 1917-1918* (New York: Random House, 1998, Vintage Books edition) 412-414.

12. August Heckscher, *Woodrow Wilson* (New York: Scribner's, 1991) 487. Lowry, *Armistice 1918*, 77, 80, 83-84. David F. Trask, *The AEF and Coalition Warmaking, 1917-1918* (Lawrence, KS: University of Kansas Press, 1993) 158. Harries, Ibid., 409. Knock , *To End All Wars*, 182-183. John Terraine, *To Win a War, 1918: The Year of Victory*

(New York: Doubleday, 1981) 217. Watt, *The Kings Depart*, 34-35. Stevenson, *The First World War and International Politics*, 230.

13. S.L.A Marshall, *World War I* (New York: Mariner Books, 2001) 444. Rudin, *Armistice: 1918*, 285-289. Lowry, Ibid., 47-48, 67-68. Terraine, Ibid., 206-207. Ferguson, *The Pity of War*, 314. Rod Paschall, *The Defeat of Imperial Germany, 1917-1918* (New York: Da Capo Press, 1994, originally published 1989) 210, 231. Donald Smythe, *Pershing: General of the Armies* (Bloomington, IN: Indiana University Press, 1986) 220. David Zabecki, *War in History* 17.3 (Jul 2010) 372, review of Robert H. Ferrell, *America's Deadliest Battle: Meuse-Argonne, 1918* (Lawrence, Kansas: University Press of Kansas, 2007).

14. Terraine, *To Win a War,1918*, 196-197.

15. Pershing, *My Experiences in the World War: Vol. II*, 233, 367.

16. Seward W. Livermore, *Woodrow Wilson and the War Congress, 1916-1918* (Seattle: University of Washington Press, 1966) 210-211, 215, citing *Congressional Record*, 65th Congress, 2nd Session (Washington) 9392-94,11156-63. Thomas Fleming, *The Illusion of Victory: America in World War I* (New York: Basic Books, 2003) 278. Knock , *To End All Wars*, 169.

17. Capt. B.H. Liddell Hart, *The Real War – 1914-1918*, (New York: Little, Brown; 1964 edition, originally published 1930) 384.

18. Ferguson, *The Pity of War*, 317.

19. Terraine, *To Win a War, 1918*, 195-196.

20. Gary Mead, *The Doughboys: America and the First World War* (New York: The Overlook Press, 2000) 336. Smythe, *Pershing*, 231-232. Edward M. Coffman, *The War to End All Wars: The American Military Experience in World War I* (New York: Oxford University Press, 1968) 355. Joseph E. Persico, *Eleventh Month, Eleventh Day, Eleventh Hour: Armistice Day 1918, World War I and Its Violent Climax* (New York: Random House, 2004) 3, 12, 54, 131, 318. Paschall, *The Defeat of Imperial Germany*, 223.

21. Persico, Ibid., 375-376, 378.

22. Bullitt Lowry, *Armistice 1918*, 72.

23. Watt, *The Kings Depart*, 204-207. Laurence Moyer, *Victory Must Be Ours: Germany in the Great War, 1914-1918* (New York: Hippocrene Books, 1995) 331-332.

24. Mead, *The Doughboys*, 396-397.

25. Watt, *The Kings Depart*, 44, citing Herbert Hoover, *The Ordeal of Woodrow Wilson* (1958) 64.

26. Knock , *To End All Wars*, 195.

27. Henry Kissinger, *Diplomacy* (New York: Simon and Schuster, 1994) 232.

28. John A. Thompson, *Reformers and War: American Progressive Publicists and the First World War* (Cambridge, UK: Cambridge University Press, 1987) 243, citing "Á Tale That Is Told," *The Saturday Evening Post*, 4 Oct 1919, 162.

29. Link, *Wilson the Diplomatist*, 22.

30. Fleming, *The Illusion of Victory*, 364.

31. Zara Steiner, "The Peace Settlement," *The Oxford Illustrated History of the First World War*, Hew Strachan, ed. (New York and Oxford: Oxford University Press, 1998) 294. Knock, *To End All Wars*, 246-250. Harries, *The Last Days of Innocence*, 429. Link, *Wilson the Diplomatist*, 119. Fleming, Ibid., 365. Stevenson, *The First World War and International Politics*, 249-250. Margaret MacMillan, *Paris 1919: Six Months That Changed the World* (New York: Random House Trade Paperbacks, 2002) 312, 322, 325-334.

32. Livermore., *Woodrow Wilson and the War Congress*, 210, citing *Indianapolis News*, 29 May 1918.

33. Peter A. Poole, *America in World Politics: Foreign Policy and Policy-Makers Since 1898* (New York: Praeger, 1975) 60. H. W. Brands, *Woodrow Wilson* (New York: New York Times Books, 2003) 102-103. George H. Mayer, *The Republican Party, 1854-1964* (New York: Oxford University Press, 1967) 351-353. Harries, *The Last Days of Innocence*, 408. Watt, *The Kings Depart*, 37, 47. Livermore., Ibid., 1,

148-152, 224. Fleming, *The Illusion of Victory*, 291, 298, 314. David M Kennedy, *Over Here: The First World War and American Society* (New York: Oxford University Press, 1980, paperback edition) 240, 242-244. Knock , *To End All Wars*, 184. Stevenson, *The First World War and International Politics*, 246.

    34. MacMillan, *Paris 1919*, 168, 176.

    35. Link, *Wilson the Diplomatist*, 112.

    36. Kissinger, *Diplomacy*, 240.

    37. Watt, *The Kings Depart*, 95

    38. Warren I. Cohen, *The American Revisionists: The Lessons of Intervention in World War I* (Chicago: University of Chicago Press, 1967) 70, 72-75, 85. Len Shurtleff, review of Holger Herwig, *The Marne 1914: The Opening of World War I and the Battle That Changed the World*, *Relevance*, Winter 2011, 47-48. Keith Windschuttle, "Was World War I Necessary?" *New Criterion*, 18.4 (Dec 1999) 9ff. Terence Zuber, "The Schlieffen Plan Reconsidered," *War in History* 6.3 (Jul 1999) 97, 101. Stewart Halsey Ross, *Propaganda for War: How the United States Was Conditioned to Fight The Great War of 1914-1918* (Jefferson, NC: McFarland, 1996) 18. Knock , *To End All Wars*, 250. Ferguson, *The Pity of War*, xxxvii, 53, 64, 68, 73, 81, 98-99, 151, 156-158, 161, 163-164, 167, 172, 443-444. Watt, Ibid., 441-443. Strachan, *The First World War*, 15-21, 35-39, 47-48. Stevenson, *The First World War and International Politics*, 259. Sheffield, *Forgotten Victory*, 39. Samuel R. Williamson, Jr. "The Origins of the War," *The Oxford Illustrated History of the First World War*, Hew Strachan, ed. (New York and Oxford: Oxford University Press, 1998) 9-25. Keegan, *The First World War*, 19, 60-61, 63, 67. Moyer, *Victory Must Be Ours*, 51, 58, 71, 74, 86. Roger Chickering, *Imperial Germany and the Great War, 1914-1918* (Cambridge, UK: Cambridge University Press; 1998) 8, 14. *The Economist*, 12 May 2001, 89, review of Hew Strachan, *The First World War*. Annika Mombauer, *War in History*, 12.1 (Jan 2005) 108-110, review of Richard F. Hamilton and Holger Herwig, eds. *The Origins of World War I.*

39. Ferguson, Ibid., xxxv. Keegan, Ibid., 27, 48, 59.

40. Sheffield, *Forgotten Victory*, 333.

41. Hew Strachan, "The War to End All Wars?" *Foreign Affairs*, 82.1 (Jan/Feb 2003).

42. Sheffield, *Forgotten Victory*, 39.

43. Kennan, *American Diplomacy*, 102.

44. MacMillan, *Paris 1919*, 461. Watt, *The Kings Depart*, 397.

45. Watt, Ibid., 407. MacMillan, Ibid., 467. Stevenson, *The First World War and International Politics*, 276.

46. Watt, Ibid., 412. MacMillan, Ibid., 461.

47. Pinson, *Modern Germany*, 396. Moyer, *Victory Must Be Ours*, 356-357. Watt, Ibid., 414.

48. MacMillan, *Paris 1919*, 477. Sheffield, *Forgotten Victory*, 25. Watt, Ibid., 9-10.

Chapter 8 -- Legacy of a Victor's Peace

1. William C. Widenor, *Henry Cabot Lodge and the Search for an American Foreign Policy* (Berkeley: University of California Press, 1980) 208, citing Lodge letters to Theodore Roosevelt, 19 Feb and 1 Mar 1915.

2. John A. Thompson, *Reformers and War: American Progressive Publicists and the First World War* (Cambridge, UK: Cambridge University Press, 1987) 235-239, 242, 244. Thomas Knock, *To End All Wars: Woodrow Wilson and the Quest for a New World Order* (Princeton, NJ: Princeton University Press, 1992, Princeton Paper edition, 1995) 252-253, 256-257. August Heckscher, *Woodrow Wilson* (New York: Scribner's, 1991) 589, 604. Arthur S. Link, *Wilson the Diplomatist: A Look at His Major Foreign Policies* (Chicago: Quadrangle Books,1963, originally published 1957) 133-134. Warren I. Cohen, *The American Revisionists: The Lessons of Intervention in World War I* (Chicago: University of Chicago Press, 1967) 33. Thomas Fleming, *The Illusion of Victory: America in World War I* (New York: Basic Books, 2003) 379.

3. Woodrow Wilson, *The Public Papers of Woodrow Wilson*, Ray S. Baker and William E. Dodd, eds., Authorized Edition, Vol. 1 (New York: 1924) 30-44.

4. Heckscher, *Woodrow Wilson*, 618-619, 629-631. Link, *Wilson the Diplomatist*, 131.

5. Erich Eyck, *A History of the Weimar Republic, Vol.* I, translated by Harlan P. Hanson and Robert G.L. Waite (Cambridge: Harvard University Press, 1962, original German edition, 1954) 140, 148, 155, 181, 240. Richard M. Watt, *The Kings Depart. The Tragedy of Germany: Versailles and the German Revolution.* (New York: Barnes and Noble Books, 2000, originally published 1968) 505-510.

6. Hans Kohn, *The Mind of Germany: The Education of a Nation* (New York: Scribner's, 1960) 317-318. Watt, Ibid., 504. Selig Adler, "The War-Guilt Question and American Disillusionment, 1918-1928," *The Journal of Modern History,* 23.1 (Mar 1951).

7. Marshall Dill, *Germany: A Modern History* (Ann Arbor, MI: University of Michigan Press, 1961) 278. Derek Aldcroft, "The Versailles legacy," *History Review*, 29 (1997) 8.

8. Link, *Wilson the Diplomatist*, 121-122. Watt, *The Kings Depart*, 502.

9. Sally Marks, "Reparations Reconsidered: A Reminder," *Central European History*, 2.4 (Dec 1969) 356, 363. Niall Ferguson, *The Pity of War: Explaining World War I* (New York; Basic Books, 1999) 403-404, 407-408, 412, 414. "Dawes Plan Formulated, September, 1922-September, 1924," (Gale Research, 1997). Currency conversion assumptions: In 1919, about 8.5 German Goldmarks equaled 1 U.S. dollar. Reparations were denominated in Goldmarks not in inflated German paper marks. Calculations thus divide the Goldmarks reparations total by 8.5 to get the equivalent U.S. dollars at the time of the Versailles Conference. To convert U.S. dollars of 1919 to U.S. dollars in 2010, use U.S. $1 in 1919 = U.S. $13.09 in 2010. Source: www.dollartimes.com/calculators/inflation.htm.

10. Ferguson, Ibid., 255-272, 408, 411.

11. Eyck, *A History of the Weimar Republic, Vol. I*, 233.

12. Eyck, Ibid. *Vol. I*, 235, 237. Fritz Stern, *The Politics of Cultural Despair: A Study in the Rise of the Germanic Ideology* (Berkeley: University of California Press, 1961) 251.

13. Steve Hanke and Alex K. F. Kwok, "On the Measurement of Zimbabwe's Hyperinflation," *Cato Journal*, 29.2 (Spring/Summer 2009) 356.

14. Aldcroft, "The Versailles legacy," 8. William L. Shirer, *The Rise and Fall of the Third Reich: A History of Nazi Germany* (New York; Simon and Schuster, 1959) 62.

15. David Stevenson, *The First World War and International Politics* (Oxford: Clarendon Press, 2001 edition, originally published 1988) 317.

16. "The Treaty of Versailles and Nazism," *History in Dispute, Vol. 4: World War II, 1939-1943*, Dennis Showalter, ed. (London: St. James Press, 2000) reproduced in History Resource Center, Gale Group.

17. Arvo Vercamer and Jason Pipes, "German Military in the Soviet Union, 1918-1933," (www.feldgrau.com). Watt, *The Kings Depart*, 517. Kohn, *The Mind of Germany*, 314. Shirer, *The Rise and Fall of the Third Reich*, 62.

18. Marks, "Reparations Reconsidered: A Reminder," 56.

19. Adler, "The War-Guilt Question and American Disillusionment, 1918-1928," 11, 16-17, 22. 28. Cohen, *The American Revisionists*, 75.

20. Cohen, Ibid., 74-75, 107, citing *Christian Century*, XLII (8 Oct 1925) 1231 and XLII (5 Nov 1925) 1375.

21. Knock, *To End All Wars*, 271-272.

22. Cohen, *The American Revisionists*, 161-162.

23. D. F. Fleming, "Our Entry in the World War in 1917: The Revised Version," *Journal of Politics*, 2.1 (Feb 1940) 84. Cohen, Ibid., 87, 189, citing *Public Opinion Quarterly* (Fall, 1941) 476-477.

24. Hew Strachan, "The War to End All Wars?" *Foreign Affairs*, 82.1 (Jan/Feb 2003). Henry Kissinger, *Diplomacy* (New York: Simon and Schuster, 1994) 169.

Conclusion – And Had America Not Blundered Into War?

1. William C. Widenor, *Henry Cabot Lodge and the Search for an American Foreign Policy* (Berkeley: University of California Press, 1980) 188, citing *New York Times*, 24 Sep 1914, 5.

2. Niall Ferguson, *The Pity of War: Explaining World War I* (New York; Basic Books, 1999) 282, 286, 290, 303.

3. Capt. B.H. Liddell Hart, *The Real War – 1914-1918*, (New York: Little, Brown; 1964 edition, originally published 1930) 385, 472.

4. Henry Kissinger, *Diplomacy* (New York: Simon and Schuster, 1994) 81, 806.

5. Thomas Knock, *To End All Wars: Woodrow Wilson and the Quest for a New World Order* (Princeton, NJ: Princeton University Press, 1992, Princeton Paper edition, 1995) 118.

6. Warren I. Cohen, ed., *Intervention, 1917: Why America Fought. Problems in American Civilization* (Boston: Heath, 1967) 6, citing Walter Lippmann, "In Defense of the Atlantic Community," *New Republic*, 17 Feb 1917, 59-61.

7. George F. Kennan, *American Diplomacy, 1900-1959* (Chicago: The University of Chicago Press, 1951), excerpted in Herbert J. Bass, ed., *America's Entry into World War I*, 107.

BIBLIOGRAPHY

Abrams, Ray H. *Preachers Present Arms: A Study of Wartime Attitudes and Activities of the Churches and Clergy in the United States, 1914-1918.* New York: Roundtable Press, 1933. Print..

Adams, R.J.Q *The Great War, 1914-1918: Essays on the Military, Political and Social History of the First World War.* London: Macmillan, 1990. Print.

Adler, Selig. "The Congressional Elections of 1918." *South Atlantic Quarterly* (Oct 1937). Print.

Adler, Selig. "The War Guilt Question and American Disillusionment, 1918-1928." *The Journal of Modern History* 23.1 (Mar 1951). Print.

Afflerbach, Holger. "Wilhelm II as Supreme Warlord in the First World War." *War in History* (Nov 1998). Print.

Albertini, Luigi. *The Origins of the War of 1914.* New York: Enigma Books, 2005. Print.

Aldcroft, Derek. "The Versailles Legacy." *History Review* 29 (Dec 1997). Print.

Allen, Henry T. *The Rhineland Occupation.* Indianapolis: Bobbs-Merrill, 1927. Print.

Allen, Howard W. "Republican Reformers and Foreign Policy, 1913-1917." *Mid-America* 44 (Oct 1962). Print.

Allen, Keith. "Sharing Scarcity: Bread Rationing and the First World War in Berlin, 1914-1923." *Journal of Social History* 32.2 (1998). Print.

Almond, Gabriel A.. *The American People and Foreign Policy.* New York: Praeger, 1960. Print.

Ambrosius, Lloyd. *Wilsonian Statecraft: Theory and Practice of Liberal Internationalism during World War I.* Wilmington, DE: SR Books, 1991. Print.

American Battle Monuments Commission. *American Armies and Battlefields in Europe: A History, Guide and Reference Book.* Washington: Government Printing Office, 1928. Print.

Arnett, Alex M. *Claude Kitchin and the Wilson War Policies.* Boston: Little Brown, 1937. Print.

Ashworth, Tony. *Trench Warfare 1914-1918: The Live and Let Live System.* London: Macmillan, 2000. Print.

Ashworth, William. *A Short History of the International Economy 1850-1950.* London: Longman, 1961. Print.

Asprey, Robert B. *At Belleau Wood.* New York: Putnam, 1965. Print.

Audoin-Rouzeau, Stephane and Annette Becker. *14-18: Understanding the Great War.* New York: Hill and Wang, 2002. Print.

Axelrod, Alan. *Selling the Great War: The Making of American Propaganda.* New York: Palgrave Macmillan, 2009. Print.

Ayres, Col. Leonard P. *The War with Germany: a Statistical Summary.* Washington: Government Printing Office, 1919. Print.

Baker, Newton D. *Why We Went to War.* New York: Harper, 1936. Print.

Baehr, Harry. "A Cycle of Revisionism Between Two Wars." *Essays in American Historiography,* Donald Henry Sheehan, ed. New York: Columbia University Press, 1960. Print.

Bailey, Stephen. "The Berlin Strike of January 1918." *Central European History* 13 (1980). Print.

Bailey, Thomas A. *The Man in the Street: The Impact of American Public Opinion on Foreign Policy.* New York: Macmillan, 1948. Print.

Bailey, Thomas A. "The United States and the Blacklist during the Great War." *Journal of Modern History* 6 (1934). Print.

Banks, Arthur. *A Military Atlas of the First World War.* South Yorkshire, UK: Pen & Sword Books, 2001. Print.

Barnes, Harry Elmer. "Professor Barnes on War Origins." *Christian Century* 42 (Oct. 8, 1925). Print.

Barnes, Harry Elmer. "Russia and France Start the War." *Christian Century*, 42 (Nov. 5, 1925). Print.

Barnes, Harry Elmer. "The World War of 1914-1918." *War in the Twentieth Century*. Willard Walter, ed. New York: Random House, 1940. Print.

Barnett, Corelli. *The Swordbearers: Supreme Command in the World War*. Bloomington, IN: Indiana University Press, 1975. Print.

Bartlett, Merrill L. *Lejeune: A Marine's Life, 1867-1942*. Columbia, SC: University of South Carolina Press, 1991. Print.

Bass, Herbert J., ed. *America's Entry into World War I: Submarines, Sentiment, or Security?* New York: Holt, Rinehart and Winston, 1964. Print.

Bauer, Raymond, Ithiel de Sola Pool and Lewis Dexter. *American Business and Public Policy: The Politics of Foreign Trade*. Chicago: Aldine-Atherton, 1972. Print.

Beard, Charles. *National Governments and the World War*. New York: Macmillan, 1919. Print.

Beard, Charles. "New Light on Bryan and War Policies." *New Republic* (Jun 17, 1936). Print.

Beaver, Daniel R. *Newton D. Baker and the American War Effort 1917-1919*. Lincoln: University of Nebraska Press, 1966. Print.

Beckett, Ian F.W. *The Great War, 1914-1918*. New York: Longman, 2001). Print.

Bernstorff, Johann Heinrich von. *Memoirs of Count Bernstorff*. New York: Random House, 1936. Print.

Bernstorff, Johann Heinrich von. *My Three Years in America*. New York: Scribner's, 1920. Print.

Bessel, Richard. *Germany after the First World War*. Oxford: Clarendon Press, 1993. Print.

Birdsall, Paul. "Neutrality and Economic Pressures, 1914-1917." *Science and Society* 3 (Spring, 1939). Print.

Birdsall, Paul. *Versailles Twenty Years After*. New York: Reynal and Hitchcock, 1941. Print.

Birnbaum, Karl E. *Peace Moves and U-Boat Warfare: A Study of Imperial Germany's Policy Towards the United States, April 18, 1916-January 9, 1917*. Stockholm: Almqvist and Wiksell, 1958. Print.

Blakey, George. *Historians on the Homefront: American Propagandists for the Great War*. Lexington: University Press of Kentucky, 1970. Print.

Blewett, Daniel. *American Military History: A Guide to Reference and Information Sources*. Englewood, CO: Libraries Unlimited, 1995. Print.

Bliss, Tasker H. "The Armistices." *American Journal of International Law* 16 (Oct 1922). Print.

Boemeke, Manfred F., Roger Chickering and Stig Förster. eds. *Anticipating Total War: The United States and Germany, 1871-1914*. Cambridge, UK: Cambridge University Press, 1999. Print.

Boemeke, Manfred F., Gerald D. Feldman and Elizabeth Glaser, eds. *The Treaty of Versailles: A Reassessment after 75 Years*. Washington: Cambridge University Press, 1998. Print.

Bonadio, Felice A. "A Failure of German Propaganda in the United States, 1914-1917." *Mid-America* (Jan 1959). Print.

Borchard, Edwin M. and William P. Lage. *Neutrality for the United States*. New Haven, CT: Yale University Press, 1937. Print.

Bowers, John. "The Mythical Morning of Sergeant York." *The Great War: Perspectives on the First World War*. Robert Cowley, ed. New York: Random House, 2003. Print.

Braim, Paul F. *Test of Battle: The AEF in the Meuse-Argonne Campaign*. Newark, DE: University of Delaware Press, 1987. Print.

Brands, H.W. *Woodrow Wilson*. New York: Times Books, 2003. Print.

Braybon, Gail. "Women, War, and Work." *The Oxford Illustrated History of the First World War*. Hew Strachan, ed. New York and Oxford: Oxford University Press, 1998. Print.

Brendon, Vyvyen. "Imperial Germany and the Great War, 1914-1918." *History Review* 48 (1999). Print.

Brendon, Vyvyen. "The Great War 1914-1918." *History Review* (1999). Print.

Broadberry, Stephen and Mark Harrison, eds. *The Economics of World War I*. Cambridge, UK and New York: Cambridge University Press, 2005. Print.

Brock, Peter. *Pacifism in the United States, from the Colonial Era to the First World War*. Princeton, NJ: Princeton University Press, 1968. Print.

Broun, Heywood. *The A.E.F.: With General Pershing and the American Forces*. New York: D. Appleton, 1918. Print.

Brown, O'Brien. "March 21, 1918." *The Great War: Perspectives on the First World War*. Robert Cowley, ed. New York: Random House, 2003. Print.

Bruce, Robert B. *A Fraternity of Arms: America and France in the Great War*. Lawrence, KS: University Press of Kansas, 2003. Print.

Brumberg, Stephan F. "New York City Schools March Off to War." *Urban Education* (Jan 1990). Print.

Bruntz, George S. *Allied Propaganda and the Collapse of the German Empire in 1918*. New York: Arno Press, 1972. Reprint of 1938 edition. Print.

Buchanan, Albert Russell. "American Editors Examine America's War Aims and Plans in April 1917." *Pacific Historical Review* 9 (Sep 1940). Print.

Buchanan, Albert Russell. *European Propaganda and American Public Opinion, 1914-1917*. Stanford: Stanford University Press, 1935. Print.

Buchanan, Albert Russell. "Theodore Roosevelt and American Neutrality." *The American Historical Review* 43 (Jul 1938). Print.

Buckley, John Patrick. *The New York Irish: Their View of American Foreign Policy, 1914-1921.* New York: Arno Press, 1976. Print.

Buehrig, Edward H. "Woodrow Wilson and Collective Security: The Origins." *The Impact of World War I.* Arthur Link, ed. New York: Harper & Row, 1969. Print.

Buehrig, Edward H. *Woodrow Wilson and the Balance of Power.* Bloomington, IN: Indiana University Press, 1955. Print.

Bullard, Robert L. and Earl Reeves. *American Soldiers Also Fought.* New York: Longman, 1936. Print.

Burk, Kathleen. *Britain, America and the Sinews of War, 1914-1918.* Boston: G. Allen and Unwin, 1985. Print.

Burk, Kathleen. "Great Britain in the United States, 1917-1918: The Turning Point." *The International History Review* 1.2 (Apr 1979). Print.

Burk, Kathleen. "The Mobilization of Anglo-American Finance during World War I." *Mobilization for Total War: The Canadian, American and British Experience, 1914-1918, 1939-1945.* N. F. Dreisziger, ed. Waterloo, Ontario: Wilfrid Laurier University Press, 1991. Print.

Cantril, Hadley, ed. *Public Opinion, 1935-1946.* Princeton, NJ: Princeton University Press, 1951. Print.

Capozzola, Christopher. "The Only Badge Needed is Your Patriotic Fervor: Vigilance, Coercion and the Law in World War I America." *Journal of American History* 88.4 (Mar 2002). Print.

Capozzola, Christopher. *Uncle Sam Wants You: World War I and the Making of the Modern American Citizen.* New York: Oxford University Press, 2010. Print.

Carlisle, Rodney. *Sovereignty at Sea: U. S. Merchant Ships and American Entry into World War I.* Gainesville, FL: University Press of Florida, 2009. Print.

Chambers, F. P. *The War Behind the War, 1914-1918: A History of the Political and Civilian Fronts.* New York: Harcourt, Brace, 1939. Print.

Chambers, John Whiteclay II. *To Raise an Army: The Draft Comes to Modern America.* New York: The Free Press, 1987. Print.

Chambers, John Whiteclay II. "World War I and the Liberal Pacifist in the United States." *The American Historical Review* (Dec 1970). Print.

Chatfield, Charles. *The American Peace Movement: Ideals and Activism.* New York: Twayne Publishers, 1992. Print.

Chickering, Roger. *Imperial Germany and the Great War, 1914-1918.* Cambridge, UK: Cambridge University Press, 1998. Print.

Child, Clifton James. *The German-Americans in Politics 1914-1917.* Madison, WI: University of Wisconsin Press, 1939. Print.

Cipriano, Anne, ed. *The United States in the First World War: An Encyclopedia.* New York: Garland Publishing, 1995. Print.

Clark, John Maurice. *The Costs of the World War to the American People:* New Haven, CT: Yale University Press, 1931. Print.

Clarkson, Grosvenor B. *Industrial America in the World War: The Strategy behind the Lines 1917-1918.* New York: Houghton Mifflin, 1923. Print.

Clements, Kendrick. *William Jennings Bryan, Missionary Isolationist.* Knoxville, TN: University of Tennessee Press, 1982. Print.

Clifford, John Garry. *The Citizen Soldiers: The Plattsburg Training Camp Movement, 1913-1920.* Lexington, KY: University Press of Kentucky, 1962. Print.

Clough, Shepard Bancroft and Charles Woolsey Cole. *Economic History of Europe.* Boston: Heath, 1946. Print.

Coetzee, Frans, and Marilyn Shevin-Coetzee, eds. *Authority, Identity and the Social History of the Great War.* Providence, RI: Berghahn Books, 1995. Print.

Coffman, Edward M. "American Command and Commanders in World War I." *New Dimensions in Military History: An Anthology.* Russell F. Weigley, ed. San Rafael, CA: Presidio Press, 1975: 177-195. Print.

Coffman, Edward M. "The American Military and Strategic Policy in World War I." *War Aims and Strategic Policy in the Great War, 1914-1918.* Barry Hunt and Adrian Preston, eds. London: Croom Helm, 1977. Print.

Coffman, Edward M. *The War to End All Wars: The American Military Experience in World War I.* New York: Oxford University Press, 1968. Print.

Cohen, Bernard Cecil. *The Public's Impact on Foreign Policy.* Boston: Little, Brown, 1973. Print.

Cohen, Warren I., ed. *Intervention, 1917: Why America Fought.* Englewood, NJ: Heath, 1967. Print.

Cohen, Warren I. *The American Revisionists: The Lessons of Intervention in World War I.* Chicago: University of Chicago Press, 1967. Print.

Connors, Michael F. *Dealing in Hate: The Development of Anti-German Propaganda.* London: Britons Publishing, 1966. Print.

Coogan, John W. *The End of Neutrality: The United States, Britain and Maritime Rights, 1899-1915.* Ithaca, NY: Cornell University Press, 1981. Print.

Coombs, Rose. *Before Endeavors Fade: A Guide to the Battlefields of the First World War.* London: Battle of Britain Prints International, 1983. Print.

Cooper, John Milton. ed. *Causes and Consequences of World War I.* New York: Quadrangle Books, 1972. Print.

Cooper, John Milton. "Progressivism and American Foreign Policy: A Reconsideration." *Mid-American* (Oct 1969). Print.

Cooper, John Milton. *The Vanity of Power: American Isolationism and the First World War, 1914-1917.* Westport, CT: Greenwood Press, 1969. Print.

Cooper, John Milton. *The Warrior and the Priest: Woodrow Wilson and Theodore Roosevelt.* Cambridge, MA: Belknap Press, 1983. Print.

Cornebise, Alfred E. *The Stars and Stripes: Doughboy Journalism in World War I.* Westport, CT: Greenwood Press, 1984. Print.

Cornebise, Alfred E. *War as Advertised: The Four-Minute Men and America's Crusade 1917-1918.* Philadelphia: American Philosophical Society, 1984. Print.

Costrell, Edwin. *How Maine Viewed the War, 1914-1917.* Orono, ME: Maine University Press, 1940. Print.

Cowley, Robert, ed. *The Great War: Perspectives on the First World War.* New York: Random House, 2003. Print.

Cowley, Robert. "The Somme: The Last 140 Days." *The Great War: Perspectives on the First World War.* Robert Cowley, ed. New York: Random House, 2003. Print.

Cowley, Robert. "The Stakes of 1915." *The Great War: Perspectives on the First World War.* Robert Cowley, ed. New York: Random House, 2003. Print.

Cowley, Robert. "The Unreal City: The Western Front as the World's Largest Metropolis." *A Weekend with the Great War: Proceedings of the Fourth Annual Great War Interconference Seminar.* Steven Weingartner, ed. Wheaton, IL: Cantigny First Division Foundation (Shippensburg, PA), White Mane Publishing Co., with the Great War Society and the Western Front Association, 1997. Print.

Craig, Gordon Alexander. *Germany, 1866-1945.* New York: Oxford University Press, 1978. Print.

Craig, Gordon Alexander. *The Politics of the Prussian Army, 1640-1945.* New York: Oxford University Press, 1964. Print.

Cramer, C. H. *Newton D. Baker: A Biography.* Cleveland: World Publishing, 1961. Print.

Creel, George. *How We Advertised America: The First Telling of the Amazing Story of the Committee on Public Information that Carried the Gospel of Americanism to Every Corner of the Globe.* New York: Harper, 1920. Print.

Crighton, John C. *Missouri and the World War, 1914-1917: A Study in Public Opinion.* Columbia, MO: University of Missouri Press, 1947. Print.

Crowder, Enoch. *The Spirit of Selective Service.* New York: The Century Co., 1920. Print.

Crowell, Benedict and Robert Forrest Wilson. *How America Went to War: An Account from Official Sources of the Nation's War Activities, 1917-1920.* New Haven, CT: Yale University Press, 1921. Print.

Crozier, Emmet. *American Reporters on the Western Front, 1914-1918.* New York: Oxford University Press, 1959. Print.

Cruttwell, C. R. M. F. *A History of the Great War, 1914-1918.* Oxford: Clarendon Press, 1936. Print.

Cuff, Robert D. *The War Industries Board: Business-Government Relations During World War I.* Baltimore: Johns Hopkins University Press, 1973. Print.

Cummins, Cedric C. *Indiana Public Opinion and the World War, 1914-1917.* Indianapolis: Indiana Historical Bureau, 1945. Print.

Czernin, Ferdinand. *Versailles, 1919.* New York: Putnam, 1964. Print.

Daniels, H. G. *The Rise of the German Republic.* London: Nisbet, 1927. Print.

Daniels, Josephus. *The Wilson Era: Years of War and After, 1917-1923.* Chapel Hill, NC: University of North Carolina Press, 1946. Print.

Davis, Allen. "The Flowering of Progressivism." *The Impact of World War I,* Arthur Link, ed. New York: Harper and Row, 1969. Print.

Davis, Belinda J. *Home Fires Burning: Food, Politics, and Everyday Life in World War I Berlin.* Chapel Hill, NC: University of North Carolina Press, 2000. Print.

DeBenedetti, Charles. *Origins of the Modern American Peace Movement, 1915-1929.* Millwood, NY: KTO Press, 1978. Print.

DeBauche, Leslie Midkiff. *Reel Patriotism: The Movies and World War I.* Madison, WI: University of Wisconsin Press, 1997. Print.

DeBauche, Leslie Midkiff. "The United States Film Industry and World War One." *The First World War and Popular Cinema: 1914 to the Present.* Michael Paris, ed. New Brunswick, NJ: Rutgers University Press, 2000. Print.

Demaison, Gerard J. "From Verdun to the Maginot Line. *A Weekend with the Great War: Proceedings of the Fourth Annual Great War Interconference Seminar.* Steven Weingartner, ed. Wheaton, IL: Cantigny First Division Foundation (Shippensburg, PA), White Mane Publishing Co., with the Great War Society and the Western Front Association, 1997. Print.

Devlin, Patrick. *Too Proud to Fight: Woodrow Wilson's Neutrality.* New York: Oxford University Press, 1975. Print.

DeWeerd, Harvey. *President Wilson Fights His War: World War I and the American Intervention.* New York: Macmillan, 1968. Print.

Dill, Marshall, Jr. *Germany: A Modern History.* Ann Arbor, MI: University of Michigan Press, 1961. Print.

Doerries, Reinhard R. *Imperial Challenge: Ambassador Count Bernstorff and German American Relations, 1908-1917.* Chapel Hill, NC: University of North Carolina Press, 1989. Print.

Dreisziger, N.F. *Mobilization for Total War: The Canadian, American, and British Experience, 1914-1918, 1939-1945.* Waterloo, Ont.: Wilfrid Laurier University Press, 1981. Print.

Dupuy, Ernest R. *Five Days to War: April 2-6, 1917.* Harrisburg, PA: Stackpole Books, 1967. Print.

Edwards, J. C. "America's Vigilantes and the Great War 1916-1918." *Army Quarterly* 106.3 (Jul 1976). Print.

Eisenhower, John S. D. with Joanne Thompson Eisenhower. *Yanks: The Epic Story of the American Army in World War I*. New York: The Free Press, 2001. Print.

Eksteins, Modris. "History or Histrionics? Recent Writing on the Great War." *Canadian Journal of History* (Dec 1985). Print.

Eksteins, Modris. "Memory and the Great War." *The Oxford Illustrated History of the First World War*, Hew Strachan, ed. New York: Oxford University Press, 1998. Print.

Eksteins, Modris. *Rites of Spring: The Great War and the Birth of the Modern Age*. Boston: Houghton Mifflin, 1989. Print.

Ellis, John. *The Social History of the Machine Gun*. New York: Arno Press, 1975. Print.

Englander, David. "Mutinies and Military Morale." *The Oxford Illustrated History of the First World War*. Hew Strachan, ed. New York: Oxford University Press, 1998. Print.

Epstein, Jonathan A. "German and English Propaganda in World War I, a paper given to The New York Military Affairs Symposium on December 1, 2000." New York: City University of New York (CUNY) Graduate Center. Print.

Esposito, David M. *The Legacy of Woodrow Wilson: American War Aims in World War I*. Westport, CT: Praeger, 1996. Print.

Evans, Martin, ed. *American Voices of World War I. Primary Source Documents*. London and Chicago: Fitzroy Dearborn, 2001. Print.

Evans, Martin. *Retreat Hell! We Just Got Here! The American Expeditionary Force in France, 1917-1918*. Botley, Oxford: Osprey Publishing, 1998. Print.

Eyck, Erich. *A History of the Weimar Republic*, translated by Harlan P. Hanson and Robert G.L. Waite. Cambridge, MA: Harvard University Press, 1962 and 1963. Print.

Farrar, L.L. *Divide and Conquer: German Efforts to Conclude a Separate Peace*. Boulder, CO: East European Quarterly, 1978. Print.

Farrar, L.L. "The Strategy of the Central Powers, 1914-1917." *The Oxford Illustrated History of the First World War*. Hew Strachan, ed. New York: Oxford University Press, 1998. Print.

Farwell, Byron. *Over There*. New York: Norton, 1999. Print.

Feldman, Gerald. *The Great Disorder: Politics, Economics, and Society in the German Inflation, 1914-1924*. New York: Oxford University Press, 1993. Print.

Ferguson, Niall. "Germany and the Origins of the First World War: New Perspectives." *Historical Journal* (Sep 1992). Print.

Ferguson, Niall. *The Pity of War: Explaining World War I*. New York: Basic Books, 1999. Print.

Ferrell, Robert H. *America's Deadliest Battle: Meuse-Argonne, 1918*. Lawrence, KS: University Press of Kansas, 2007. Print.

Ferrell, Robert H. *Woodrow Wilson and World War I, 1917-1921*. New York: Harper and Row, 1985. Print.

Ferro, Marc. *The Great War 1914-18*. London: Routledge and K. Paul, 1973. Print.

Finch, George A. "The Treaty of Peace with Germany in the United States Senate." *American Journal of International Law* 14 (Jan and Apr 1920). Print.

Finnegan, John Patrick. *Against the Specter of the Dragon: The Campaign for American Military Preparedness*. Westport, CT: Greenwood Press, 1974. Print.

Fischer, Fritz. *Germany's War Aims in the First World War*. New York: Norton, 1967. Print.

Fischer, Fritz. "Twenty-Five Years Later: Looking Back at the 'Fischer Controversy' and its Consequences." *Central European History* (Sep 1988). Print.

Fischer, Fritz. *World Power or Decline: The Controversy over Germany's Aims in the First World War*. New York: Norton, 1974. Print.

Fleming, Denna Frank. "Our Entry in the World War in 1917: The Revised Version." *Journal of Politics* 2 (Feb 1940). Print.

Fleming, Thomas. "Iron General." *The Great War: Perspectives on the First World War*. Robert Cowley, ed. New York: Random House, 2003. Print.

Fleming, Thomas. *The Illusion of Victory: America in World War I*. New York: Basic Books, 2003. Print.

Foch, Ferdinand and Thomas Bentley Mott. *The Memoirs of Marshal Foch*. Garden City, N.Y.: Doubleday, 1931. Print.

Fogarty, Richard. Review of *A Fraternity of Arms: America and France in the Great War,* by Robert B. Bruce. *War in History* 12.3 (Jul 2005). Print.

Fordham, Benjamin O. "Revisionism Reconsidered: Exports and American Intervention in the First World War." Presented at the American Political Science Association Sep 1, 2005. Print.

Freidel, Frank. *Franklin D. Roosevelt: The Apprenticeship*. Boston: Little Brown, 1952. Print.

Freidel, Frank. *Over There: The Story of America's First Great Overseas Crusade*. Boston: Little, Brown, 1964. Print.

French, David. "The Strategy of the Entente Powers, 1914-1917." *The Oxford Illustrated History of the First World War*. Hew Strachan, ed. New York and Oxford: Oxford University Press, 1998. Print.

Garraty, John A. *Henry Cabot Lodge: A Biography*. New York: Knopf, 1953. Print.

Gatzke, Hans W. *Germany and the United States: A "Special relationship?"* Cambridge, MA: Harvard University Press, 1980. Print.

Gelfand, Lawrence E. *The Inquiry: American Preparation for Peace, 1917-1919*. New Haven, CT: Yale University Press, 1963. Print.

Gienow-Hecht, Jessica. "Trumpeting Down the Walls of Jericho: The Politics of Art, Music and Emotion in German-American Relations, 1870-1920." *Journal of Social History* (Spring 2003). Print.

Gilbert, Bentley and Paul P. Bernard. "French Army Mutinies of 1917." *Historian* 22. Print.

Gilbert, Charles. *American Financing of World War I*. Westport, CT: Greenwood Press, 1970. Print.

Gilbert, Martin. *The First World War: A Complete History*. New York: Holt, 1994. Print.

Goldstein, Erik. *Winning the Peace: British Diplomatic Strategy, Peace Planning, and the Paris Peace Conference, 1916-1920*. Oxford: Clarendon Press, 1991. Print.

Goodspeed, D. J. *Ludendorff: Genius of World War I*. Boston: Houghton Mifflin, 1966. Print.

Gottlieb, Wolfram Wilhelm. *Studies in Secret Diplomacy during the First World War*. London: George Allen and Unwin, 1957. Print.

Graber, Doris A. *Public Opinion, the President, and Foreign Policy*. New York: Holt, Rinehart and Winston, 1968. Print.

Graham, Otis L. *The Great Campaigns: Reform and War in America, 1900-1928*. Englewood Cliffs, N.J.: Prentice-Hall, 1971. Print.

Grattan, C. Hartley. *Why We Fought*. New York: Bobbs-Merrill, 1929. Print.

Great War Society. Doughboy Center. www.worldwar1.com. Web.

Gregory, Ross. *The Origins of American Intervention in the First World War*. New York: Norton, 1971. Print.

Grotelueschen, Mark. *The AEF Way of War: The American Army and Combat in World War I*. New York: Cambridge University Press, 2007. Print.

Grotelueschen, Mark. *Doctrine Under Trial: American Artillery Employment in World War I*. Westport, CT: Greenwood Press, 2001. Print.

Groves, Charles. *Henry Cabot Lodge: The Statesman.* Boston: Small, Maynard, 1925. Print.

Gudmundsson, Bruce I. *Stormtrooper Tactics: Innovation in the German Army, 1914-1918.* Westport, CT: Praeger, 1989. Print.

Guichard, Louis. "Germany under the Great Blockade." *The Living Age* (Apr 1929). Print.

Guttmann, William and Patricia Meehan. *The Great Inflation: Germany 1919-1923.* Farnborough, UK: Saxon House, 1975. Print.

Hallas, James H. *Doughboy War: The American Expeditionary Force in World War I.* Boulder, CO: Lynne Rienner, 2000. Print.

Halpern, Paul G. "The War at Sea." *The Oxford Illustrated History of the First World War.* Hew Strachan, ed. New York and Oxford: Oxford University Press, 1998. Print.

Hamilton, Richard F. and Holger Herwig, eds. *The Origins of World War I.* New York: Cambridge University Press, 2003. Print.

Hanke, Steve and Alex K. F. Kwok. "On the Measurement of Zimbabwe's Hyperinflation." *Cato Journal* 29.2 (Spring/ Summer 2009). Print.

Hannigan, Robert E. *The New World Power: American Foreign Policy, 1898-1917.* Philadelphia: University of Pennsylvania Press, 2002. Print.

Harbord, James G. *The American Army in France 1917-1919.* Boston: Little, Brown, 1936. Print.

Harries, Meirion and Susie. *The Last Days of Innocence: America at War 1917-1918.* New York: Random House, 1998. Print.

Harrison, E.D.R. "Germany after the First World War." *History Today* (Jul 1995). Print.

Hart, Peter: *1918: A Very British Victory.* London: Weidenfeld and Nicolson, 2008. Print.

Hase, Ragnhild Fiebig von and Ursula Lehmkuhl. *Enemy Images in American History.* Providence, RI: Berghahn Books, 1997. Print.

Heckscher, August. *Woodrow Wilson*. New York: Scribner's, 1991. Print.

Herman, Gerald. *The Pivotal Conflict: A Comprehensive Chronology of the First World War, 1914-1919*. New York: Greenwood Press, 1992. Print.

Herman, Sondra R. *Eleven Against War: Studies in American Isolationist Thought, 1898-1921*. Stanford, CA: Hoover Institution Press, 1969. Print.

Herwig, Holger and Neil M. Heyman. *Biographical Dictionary of World War I*. Westport, CT: Greenwood Press, 1982. Print.

Herwig, Holger and David Trask. "The Failure of Imperial Germany's Undersea Offensive against World Shipping, February 1917-October 1918." *Historian* 33 (Aug 1971). Print.

Herwig, Holger. *The First World War: Germany and Austria-Hungary 1914-18*. London: Arnold, 1997. Print.

Herwig, Holger. "The German Victories, 1917-1918." *The Oxford Illustrated History of the First World War*. Hew Strachan, ed. New York and Oxford: Oxford University Press, 1998. Print.

Herwig, Holger. Review of *The German Offensives of 1918*, by Martin Kitchen. *War in History* 10.3 (Jul 2003). Print.

Higham, Robin D.S. and Dennis E. Showalter. *Researching World War I: A Handbook* . Westport, CT: Greenwood Press, 2003. Print.

Hilton, O.A. "Freedom of the Press in Wartime, 1917-1919." *The Southwestern Social Science Quarterly* (1948). Print.

Hilton, O.A. "Public Opinion and Civil Liberties in Wartime, 1917-19." *The Southwestern Social Science Quarterly* (1947). Print.

Hoehling, A.A. *The Fierce Lambs*. Boston: Little, Brown, 1960. Print.

Hogan, J. Michael. "Woodrow Wilson, 'The Pueblo Speech' (25 September 1919)." http://archive.vod.umd.edu/internat/wilson1919int.htm#_edn88. Web. 14 Jan 2010.

Holmes, Richard. Review of *Yanks: The Epic Story of the American Army in World War I*, by John S.D. Eisenhower. *The Historian* 65.3 (2003). Print.

Hoover, Herbert; *The Memoirs of Herbert Hoover: Years of Adventure, 1874-1920.* New York: Macmillan, 1951. Print.

Horn, Martin. "A Private Bank at War: J.P. Morgan & Co. and France, 1914-1918." *Business History Review* (Spring 2000). Print.

Horn, Martin. *Britain, France, and the Financing of the First World War.* Montreal: McGill-Queen's University Press, 2002. Print.

Horne, John, ed. *A Companion to World War I.* Chichester, UK: Wiley-Blackwell, 2010. Print

Horne, John and Alan Kramer. *German Atrocities, 1914: A History of Denial.* New Haven, CT: Yale University Press, 2001. Print.

Horne, John. "German atrocities, 1914: fact, fantasy, or fabrication?" *History Today* 52.4 (Apr 2002). Print.

Howard, Michael. "Europe 1914." *The Great War: Perspectives on the First World War.* Robert Cowley, ed. New York: Random House, 2003. Print.

Howard, Michael. *The First World War.* Oxford: Oxford University Press, 2002. Print.

Howard, Michael. "The Great War." *The National Interest* (Summer 2001). Print.

Howard, Michael. "World War One: The Crisis in European History and the Role of the Military Historian." *Journal of Military History* (Oct 1993). Print.

Hunt, Barry and Adrian Preston, eds. *War Aims and Strategic Policy in the Great War, 1914-1918.* London: Croom Helm, 1977. Print.

Hunt, Michael. *Ideology and U.S. Foreign Policy.* New Haven, CT: Yale University Press, 1987. Print.

Hunt, Richard N. *The Creation of the Weimar Republic: Stillborn Democracy?* Lexington, MA: Heath, 1969. Print.

Isenberg, Michael T. *War on Film: The American Cinema and World War I, 1914-1941*. Rutherford, NJ: Farleigh Dickinson University Press, 1981. Print.

Israel, Frederick L., ed. *Major Peace Treaties of Modern History, 1648-1967*. New York: Chelsea House Publishers, 1967. Print.

Jaher, Frederic Cople. "Reel Patriotism: The Movies and World War I." *The Historian* 61.3 (1999). Print.

Jarausch, Konrad. "Revising German History: Bethmann Hollweg Revisited." *Central European History* (Sep 1988). Print.

Jarausch, Konrad. *The Enigmatic Chancellor: Bethmann Hollweg and the Hubris of Imperial Germany*. New Haven, CT: Yale University Press, 1973. Print.

Jedell, Hugh. "Why German Propaganda Failed." *New York Times Book Review* (Sep 3, 1932). Print.

Jensen, Joan M. *The Price of Vigilance: The American Protective League*. Chicago: Rand McNally, 1968. Print.

Johnson, Donald. *The Challenge to American Freedom: World War I and the Rise of the American Civil Liberties Union*. Lexington, KY: University of Kentucky Press,

Johnson, James P.. "The Wilsonians as War Managers: Coal and the 1917-18 Winter Crisis." *Prologue* 8 (1977). Print.

Joll, James. *The Origins of the First World War*. London: Longman, 1984. Print.

Jonas, Manfred. *The United States and Germany: A Diplomatic History*. Ithaca, NY: Cornell University Press, 1984. Print.

Kazin, Michael. *The Populist Persuasion: An American History*. New York: Basic Books, 1995. Print.

Keegan, John. "European Tragedy, European Mystery." *Yale Review* (Apr 1999). Print.

Keegan, John. "Jutland." *The Great War: Perspectives on the First World War*. Robert Cowley, ed. New York: Random House, 2003. Print.

Keegan, John. "The Breaking of Armies." *The Great War: Perspectives on the First World War*. Robert Cowley, ed. New York: Random House, 2003. Print.

Keegan, John. *The Face of Battle*. New York: Viking Press, 1976. Print.

Keegan, John. *The First World War*. New York: Knopf, 1999. Print.

Keene, Jennifer D. *Doughboys, the Great War, and the Remaking of America*. Baltimore: Johns Hopkins University Press, 2001. Print.

Kennan, George F. *American Diplomacy, 1900-1950*. Chicago: University of Chicago Press, 1951. Print.

Kennan, George F. *Russia and the West under Lenin and Stalin*. Boston: Little, Brown, 1961. Print.

Kennan, George F. *The Fateful Alliance: France, Russia, and the Coming of the First World War*. New York: Pantheon Books, 1984. Print.

Kennedy, David M. *Over Here: The First World War and American Society*. New York: Oxford University Press, 1982. Print.

Kennedy, Ross A. *The Will to Believe: Woodrow Wilson, World War I and America's Strategy for Peace and Security*. Kent, OH: Kent State University Press, 2009. Print.

Kennett, Lee. "A.E.F. through French Eyes." *Military Review* 52 (Nov 1972). Print.

Kent, Bruce. *The Spoils of War: The Politics, Economics and Diplomacy of Reparations, 1918-1932*. Oxford: Clarenden Press, 1989. Print.

Kent, Frank R. *The Democratic Party, a History*. New York: Century, 1928. Print.

Kerr, Thomas J. "German-Americans and Neutrality in the 1916 Elections." *Mid-America* 43 (1961). Print.

Keynes, John Maynard. *The Economic Consequences of the Peace*. New York: Harcourt, Brace and Howe, 1920. Print.

Kissinger, Henry. *Diplomacy*. New York: Simon & Schuster, 1994. Print.

Kitchen, Martin. Review of *Helmuth von Moltke and the Origins of the First World War,* by Annika Mombauer. *War in History* (Apr 2003). Print.

Kitchen, Martin. *The German Offensives of 1918.* Stroud, Gloucestershire: Tempus, 2001. Print.

Knock, Thomas J. *To End All Wars: Woodrow Wilson and the Quest for a New World Order.* Princeton, NJ: Princeton University Press, 1992. Print.

Kohn, Hans. *The Mind of Germany: The Education of a Nation.* New York: Scribner's, 1960. Print.

Koistinen, Paul A.C. *Mobilizing for Modern War: The Political Economy of American Warfare, 1865-1919.* Lawrence, KS. University Press of Kansas, 1997. Print.

Kraft, Barbara S. and Donald Smythe. "How T.R. Tried in Vain to Fight in World War I." *Smithsonian* 4 (Oct 1973). Print.

Lansing, Robert. *War Memoirs of Robert Lansing, Secretary of State.* Indianapolis: Bobbs-Merrill, 1935. Print.

Lasswell, Harold D. *Propaganda Technique in the World War.* New York: Knopf, 1927. Print.

Lentin, A. *Lloyd George, Woodrow Wilson, and the Guilt of Germany: An Essay in the Pre-History of Appeasement.* Baton Rouge, LA: Louisiana State University Press, 1985. Print.

Leonard, Thomas. *Above the Battle: War Making in America from Appomattox to Versailles.* New York: Oxford University Press, 1978. Print.

Leopold, Richard. "The Problem of American Intervention, 1917: An Historical Retrospect." *World Politics* 2.3 (Apr 1950). Print.

Leuchtenburg, William E. "The Impact of the War on the American Political Economy." *The Impact of World War I.* Arthur Link, ed. New York: Harper and Row, 1969. Print.

Levering, Ralph B. *The Public and American Foreign Policy, 1918-1978.* New York: William Morrow, 1978. Print.

Liddell Hart, Captain B.H. "How Myths Grow – Passchendaele." *Military Affairs* 28 (1964-1965). Print.

Liddell Hart, Captain B.H. *Reputations: Ten Years After.* Boston: Little, Brown, 1928. Print.

Liddell Hart, Captain B.H. *The Real War – 1914-1918.* New York: Little, Brown, 1964, originally published 1930. Print.

Liddle, Peter, John Bourne and Ian Whitehead, eds. *The Great World War, 1914-1945.* London: HarperCollins, 2000. Print.

Lieven, D. C. B. *Russia and the Origins of the First World War.* New York: St. Martin's, 1983. Print.

Link, Arthur Stanley, ed. *The Impact of World War I.* New York: Harper and Row, 1969. Print.

Link, Arthur Stanley, and William M. Leary. *The Progressive Era and the Great War, 1896-1920.* New York: Appleton-Century-Crofts, 1969. Print.

Link, Arthur Stanley. *Wilson the Diplomatist: A Look at His Major Foreign Policies.* Chicago: Quadrangle Books, 1963. Print.

Link, Arthur Stanley. *Wilson: The Struggle for Neutrality, 1914-1915.* Princeton, N.J.: Princeton University Press, 1960. Print.

Link, Arthur Stanley. *Woodrow Wilson and the Progressive Era, 1910-1917.* New York: Harper, 1954. Print.

Link, Arthur Stanley and John W. Chambers. "Woodrow Wilson as Commander-in-Chief." *The United States Military Under the Constitution of the United States, 1789-1989.* Richard H. Kohn, ed.. New York: New York University Press, 1991. Print.

Link, Arthur Stanley. *Woodrow Wilson: Revolution, War and Peace.* Arlington Heights, IL: AHM Publishing, 1979. Print.

Livermore, Seward W. *Woodrow Wilson and the War Congress, 1916-1918.* Seattle: University of Washington Press, 1966. Print.

Lowry, Bullitt. *Armistice 1918.* Kent, OH: Kent State University Press, 1996. Print.

Luckau, Alma. *The German Delegation at the Paris Peace Conference.* New York: Columbia University Press, 1941. Print.

Ludendorff, Erich. *Ludendorff's Own Story, August 1914-November 1918; The Great War from the Siege of Liège to the Signing of the Armistice as Viewed from the Grand Headquarters of the German Army*. New York: Harper, 1919. Print.

Luebke, Frederick C. *Bonds of Loyalty: German Americans and World War I*. DeKalb, IL: Northern Illinois University Press, 1974. Print.

Lutz, Ralph Haswell. "Studies of World War Propaganda, 1914-1933." *Journal of Modern History* 5 (Dec. 1933). Print.

Lutz, Ralph Haswell, and W.L. Campbell. *The Causes of the German Collapse in 1918: Sections of the Officially Authorized Report of the Commission of the German Constituent Assembly and of the German Reichstag, 1919-1928*. Stanford: Stanford University Press, 1934. Print.

Lyons, Michael J. *World War I: A Short History*. Englewood Cliffs, NJ: Prentice Hall, 1994. Print.

Lyons, Timothy J. "Hollywood and World War I, 1914-18." *Journal of Popular Film* 1 (1972). Print.

MacMillan, Margaret. *Paris 1919: Six Months That Changed the World*. New York: Random House, 2002. Print.

March, Peyton C. *The Nation at War*. Garden City, NY: Doubleday, 1932. Print.

Marks, S. "Reparations Reconsidered: A Reminder." *Central European History* 2.4 (1969). Print.

Marshall, George C. *Memoirs of my Services in the World War, 1917-1918*. Boston: Houghton Mifflin, 1976. Print.

Marshall, S.L.A. *World War I*. New York: Mariner Books, 2001; originally published 1964. Print.

Martel, Gordon. *The Origins of the First World War*. London: Longman, 1996. Print.

Maurice, Frederick Barton. *The Last Four Months, How the War Was Won*. Boston: Little, Brown, 1919. Print.

Maxim, Hudson. *Defenseless America.* New York: Hearst's International Library, 1915. Print.

May, Ernest R. *The World War and American Isolation, 1914-1917.* Chicago: Quadrangle, 1966; originally published 1959. Print.

May, Henry F. *The End of American Innocence: A Study of the First Years of Our Own Time, 1912-1917.* Chicago: Quadrangle, 1964. Print.

Mayer, Arno J. *Political Origins of the New Diplomacy, 1917-1918.* New Haven, CT: Yale University Press, 1959. Print.

Mayer, George H. *The Republican Party, 1854-1964.* New York: Oxford University Press, 1967. Print.

Mayoralas, Antonio. *The Trench War on the Western Front, 1914-1918.* Alpedrete, Madrid: Andrea Press, 2009. Print.

McAdoo, W. G. *Crowded Years: The Reminiscences of William G. McAdoo.* Boston: Houghton Mifflin, 1931. Print.

McCarthy, Michael J. "Planning the AEF: The Need for an Expeditionary Force." *'Lafayette, We Are Here,' The War College Division and American Military Planning for the AEF in World War I.* The Great War Society, Doughboy Center, www.worldwar1.com. Web.

McKercher, B.J.C. "Economic Warfare." *The Oxford Illustrated History of the First World War.* Hew Strachan, ed. New York and Oxford: Oxford University Press, 1998. Print.

Mead, Gary. *The Doughboys: America and the First World War.* New York: Overlook Press, 2000. Print.

Millett, Allan R. "Belleau Wood: One Man's Initiation." *The Great War: Perspectives on the First World War.* Robert Cowley, ed. New York: Random House, 2003. Print.

Millett, Allan R. and Peter Maslowski. *For the Common Defense: A Military History of the United States of America.* New York: Free Press, 1984. Print.

Millett, Allan R. "Over Where? The AEF and the American Strategy for Victory, 1917-1918." *Against All Enemies: Interpretations of American Military History from Colonial Times to the Present*, Kenneth J. Hagan and William R. Roberts, eds. New York: Greenwood Press, 1986. Print.

Millett, Allan R. *Semper Fidelis: The History of the United States Marine Corps*. New York: Macmillan, 1980. Print.

Millis, Walter. *Road to War: America, 1914-1917*. Boston: Houghton Mifflin, 1935. Print.

Mombauer, Annika. *Helmuth von Moltke and the Origins of the First World War*. Cambridge, UK: Cambridge University Press, 2001. Print.

Mombauer, Annika. *The Origins of the First World War: Controversies and Consensus*. Harlow, UK: Longman, 2002. Print.

Mombauer, Annika. Review of *The Origins of World War I*. Richard F. Hamilton and Holger H. Herwig, eds. *War in History* (Jan 2005). Print.

Moos, Malcolm Charles. *The Republicans: A History of their Party*. New York: Random House, 1956. Print.

Moran, Daniel. "The Fortress Peace: Germany in the Great War." *A Weekend with the Great War: Proceedings of the Fourth Annual Great War Interconference Seminar*. Steven Weingartner, ed. Wheaton, IL: Cantigny First Division Foundation (Shippensburg, PA), White Mane Publishing Co. with the Great War Society and the Western Front Association, 1997. Print.

Morrissey, Alice M. *The American Defense of Neutral Rights 1914-1917*. Cambridge, MA: Harvard University Press, 1939. Print.

Mosier, John. *The Myth of the Great War: A New Military History of World War I*. New York: Harper Collins, 2001. Print.

Moyer, Laurence. *Victory Must Be Ours: Germany in the Great War, 1914-1918*. New York: Hippocrene Books, 1995. Print.

Mueller, John E. *War, Presidents and Public Opinion.* New York: Wiley, 1973. Print.

Nafziger, Ralph Otto. *The American Press and Public Opinion during the World War, 1914 to April 1917.* Madison, WI: University of Wisconsin, 1936. Thesis – PhD. Print.

Nenninger, Timothy K. "American Military Effectiveness in the First World War." *Military Effectiveness: The First World War.* Allan R. Millet and Williamson Murray, eds. Boston: Allen and Unwin, 1988. Print.

Nenninger, Timothy K. "Tactical Dysfunction in the AEF." *Military History* (Oct 1987). Print.

Noyes, Alexander Dana. *The War Period of American Finance, 1908-1925.* New York: Putnam, 1926. Print.

O'Brien, Patrick. "The Economic Effects of the Great War." *History Today* (Dec 1994). Print.

O'Connell, Robert L. "Die Pariskanone." *The Great War: Perspectives on the First World War.* Robert Cowley, ed. New York: Random House, 2003. Print.

O'Connor, Richard. *The German-Americans: An Informal History.* Boston: Little, Brown, 1968. Print.

Odom, William. "Under the Gun: Training the American Expeditionary Forces, 1917-1918." *Military Review* 80.4. Print.

Offer, Avner. *The First World War: An Agrarian Interpretation.* Oxford: Clarendon Press, 1989. Print.

Offner, Arnold A. *The Origins of the Second World War: American Foreign Policy and World Politics, 1917-1941.* New York: Praeger, 1975. Print.

O'Grady, Joseph P., ed. *The Immigrants' Influence on Wilson's Peace Policies.* Lexington, KY: University of Kentucky Press, 1967. Print.

O'Shea, Stephen. *Back to the Front: An Accidental Historian Walks the Trenches of World War I.* New York: Walker, 1997. Print.

Osiander, Andreas. *The States System of Europe, 1640-1900: Peacemaking and the Conditions of International Stability.* New York: Clarendon Press, 1994. Print.

Palmer, Frederick. *Newton D. Baker: America at War.* New York: Dodd, Mead, 1931. Print.

Papers Relating to the Foreign Relations of the United States: The World War. Supplements to 1914, 1915, 1916 and 1917. Washington: Government Printing Office, 1928-32. Print.

Paris, Michael, ed. *The First World War and Popular Cinema: 1914 to the Present.* New Brunswick, NJ: Rutgers University Press, 2000. Print.

Parsons, Edward B. "Why the British Reduced the Flow of American Troops to Europe in August-October 1918." *Canadian Journal of History* 12 (Dec 1977). Print.

Paschall, Rod. "D Day 1917." *The Great War: Perspectives on the First World War.* Robert Cowley, ed. New York: Random House, 2003. Print.

Paschall, Rod. *The Defeat of Imperial Germany, 1917-1918.* Chapel Hill, NC: Algonquin Books, 1989. Print.

Pearlman, Michael. *To Make Democracy Safe for America: Patricians and Preparedness in the Progressive Era.* Urbana, IL: University of Illinois Press, 1984. Print.

Peet, Creighton. "Hollywood at War, 1915-1918: A Little Reminder of What the Movies Could Do in the Days of the Beast of Berlin." *Esquire* (Sep 1936). Print.

Pershing, John J. *Final Report of Gen. John J. Pershing, Commander-in-Chief, American Expeditionary Forces.* Washington: Government Printing Office, 1919. Print.

Pershing, John J. *My Experiences in the World War, Volumes I & II.* New York: Frederick A. Stokes, 1931. Print.

Persico, Joseph E. *Eleventh Month, Eleventh Day, Eleventh Hour: Armistice Day 1918, World War I and Its Violent Climax.* New York: Random House, 2004. Print.

Petersen, Svend. *A Statistical History of the American Presidential Elections.* New York: Ungar, 1963. Print.

Peterson, Horace C. and Gilbert Fite. *Opponents of the War, 1917-1918.* Madison, WI: University of Wisconsin Press, 1957. Print.

Peterson, Horace C. *Propaganda for War: The Campaign Against American Neutrality, 1914-1917.* Norman, OK: University of Oklahoma Press, 1939. Print.

Pinson, Koppel S. *Modern Germany: Its History and Civilization.* New York: Macmillan, 1954. Print.

Piper, John F. *The American Churches in World War I.* Athens, OH: Ohio University Press, 1985. Print.

Ponsonby, Arthur. *Falsehood in War-Time, Containing an Assortment of Lies Circulated throughout the Nations during the Great War.* New York: Dutton, 1928. Print.

Pope, Stephen, and Elizabeth-Anne Wheal. *The Macmillan Dictionary of the First World War.* London: Macmillan Reference Books, 1997. Print.

Porter, Kirk H. and Donald Bruce Johnson, eds. *National Party Platforms: 1840-1964.* Urbana, IL: University of Illinois Press, 1966. Print.

Prior, Robin and Trevor Wilson. "Eastern Front and Western Front, 1916-1917." *The Oxford Illustrated History of the First World War.* Hew Strachan, ed. New York and Oxford: Oxford University Press, 1998. Print.

Purseigle, Pierre, ed. *Warfare and Belligerence: Perspectives in First World War Studies.* Leiden: Brill Academic Publishers, 2005. Print.

Rainey, James W. "The Questionable Training of the AEF in World War I." *Parameters* 22 (1992-1993). Print.

Read, James Morgan. *Atrocity Propaganda, 1914-1919.* New Haven, CT: Yale University Press, 1941. Print.

Reynolds, David. "American Isolationism." *History Today* (Mar 1984). Print.

Reynolds, David. "The Origins of the Two 'World Wars:' Historical Discourse and International Politics." *Journal of Contemporary History* (Jan 2003). Print.

Ritter, Gerhard. *The Sword and the Scepter: The Problem of Militarism in Germany.* Vol. 4. *The Reign of German Militarism and the Disaster of 1918.* Coral Gables, FL: University of Miami Press, 1969. Print.

Roberts, Priscilla. "Willard D. Straight and the diplomacy of international finance during the First World War." *Business History* (Jul 1998). Print.

Rosenau, James N., ed. *Domestic Sources of Foreign Policy.* New York: Free Press, 1967. Print.

Rosenau, James N. *Public Opinion and Foreign Policy.* New York: Random House, 1961. Print.

Ross, Stewart Halsey. *Propaganda for War: How the United States Was Conditioned to Fight The Great War of 1914-1918.* Jefferson, NC: McFarland, 1996. Print.

Rudin, Harry R. *Armistice: 1918.* New Haven, CT: Yale University Press, 1944. Print.

Ryder, A.J. *The German Revolution of 1918.* Cambridge, UK: Cambridge University Press, 1967. Print.

Savage, Carlton. *Policy of the United States Toward Maritime Commerce in War, 1776-1918.* Washington: Government Printing Office, 1934-1936. Print.

Schaffer, Ronald. *America in the Great War: The Rise of the War Welfare State.* New York: Oxford University Press, 1991. Print.

Schieber, Clara Eve. *The Transformation of American Sentiment Toward Germany, 1870-1914.* Boston: Cornhill, 1923. Print.

Schiff, Viktor and Geoffrey Dunlap. *The Germans at Versailles.* London: Williams and Norgate, 1930. Print.

Schröder, Hans. *Confrontation and Cooperation: Germany and the United States in the Era of World War I, 1900-1924.* Providence, RI: Berg, 1993. Print.

Scott, James Brown, ed. *Official Statements of War Aims and Peace Proposals, December 1916 to November 1918.* Washington: Carnegie Endowment for International Peace, 1921. Print.

Scott, Peter T. "The Secrets of Wellington House: British Covert Propaganda, 1914-1918." *Antiquarian Book Monthly* (Aug-Sept and Oct-Nov 1996). Print.

Seymour, Charles. *American Diplomacy during the World War.* Hamden, CT: Archon Books, 1934. Print.

Seymour, Charles. *American Neutrality, 1914-1917: Essays on the Causes of American Intervention in the World War.* New Haven, CT: Yale University Press, 1935. Print.

Seymour, Charles. "American Neutrality: The Experience of 1914-1917." *Foreign Affairs* (Oct 1935). Print.

Seymour, Charles. *The Intimate Papers of Colonel House.* Boston: Houghton Mifflin, 1926-1928. Print.

Shannon, David A. *The Socialist Party of America: A History.* New York: Macmillan, 1955. Print.

Sharp, Alan. *The Versailles Settlement: Peacemaking in Paris 1919.* New York: St. Martin's, 1991. Print.

Sheffield, Gary. *Forgotten Victory: The First World War: Myths and Realities.* London: Headline Book Publishing, 2001. Print.

Sheffield; Gary, ed. *War on the Western Front: In the Trenches of World War I.* Oxford: Osprey Publishing, 2007. Print.

Shirer, William L. *The Rise and Fall of the Third Reich: A History of Nazi Germany.* New York: Simon and Schuster, 1959. Print.

Shotwell, James T. *At the Paris Peace Conference.* New York: Macmillan, 1937. Print.

Showalter, Dennis E. "The German Soldier of World War I: Myths and Realities." *A Weekend with the Great War: Proceedings of the Fourth Annual Great War Interconference Seminar.* Steven Weingartner, ed. Wheaton, IL: Cantigny First Division Foundation (Shippensburg, PA), White Mane Publishing Co. with the Great War Society and the Western Front Association, 1997. Print.

Showalter, Dennis E. "Manoeuvre Warfare: The Eastern and Western Fronts, 1914-1915." *The Oxford Illustrated History of the First World War.* Hew Strachan, ed. New York and Oxford: Oxford University Press, 1998. Print.

Showalter, Dennis E. "The Treaty of Versailles and Nazism." *History in Dispute, Vol. 4: World War II, 1939-1943.* Benjamin Frankel, ed. Detroit: St. James Press, 2000. Print.

Shurtleff, Len. Review of *The Marne 1914: The Opening of World War I and the Battle That Changed the World,* by Holger Herwig. *Relevance* (Winter 2011). Print.

Sims, William Snowden. "The Truth About German Submarine Atrocities." *Current History* 18. Print.

Siney, Marion C. *The Allied Blockade of Germany, 1914-1916.* Ann Arbor, MI: University of Michigan Press, 1957. Print.

Small, Melvin. *The American Image of Germany, 1906-1914.* Ann Arbor, MI: University Microfilms, 1966. Print.

Smith, Daniel Malloy. "National Interest and American Intervention: 1917, an Historiographical Appraisal." *Journal of American History* 52 (Jun 1965). Print.

Smith, Daniel Malloy. *Robert Lansing and American Neutrality 1914-1917.* Berkeley: University of California Press, 1958. Print.

Smith, Daniel Malloy. *The Great Departure: The United States and World War I, 1914-1920.* New York: Knopf, 1965. Print.

Smith, Gene. *When the Cheering Stopped: The Last Years of Woodrow Wilson.* New York: William Morrow, 1964. Print.

Smythe, Donald. "AEF Strategy in France, 1917-1918." *Army Quarterly* 115.2 (Apr 1985). Print.

Smythe, Donald. *Pershing: General of the Armies*. Bloomington, IN: Indiana University Press, 1986. Print.

Smythe, Donald. "St. Mihiel: The Birth of an American Army." *Parameters* (Jun 1983. Print.

Snyder, Louis L. *The Weimar Republic: A History of Germany from Ebert to Hitler*. Princeton, NJ: Van Nostrand, 1966. Print.

Sonntag, Mark. "Fighting Everything German in Texas, 1917-1919." *The Historian* 56.4. Print.

Spector, Ronald. "You're Not Going to Send Soldiers Over There Are You! The American Search for an Alternative to the Western Front." *Military Affairs* 36.1 (Feb 1972). Print.

Spence, Richard B. "K.A. Jahnke and the German Sabotage Campaign in the United States and Mexico, 1914-1918." *Historian* (Fall 1996). Print.

Spencer, Samuel R. *Decision for War, 1917: The Laconia Sinking and the Zimmermann Telegram as Key Factors in the Public Reaction against Germany*. Rindge, NH: R.R. Smith, 1953. Print.

Squires, James Duane. *British Propaganda at Home and in the United States from 1914 to 1917*. Cambridge, MA: Harvard University Press, 1935. Print.

Stallings, Laurence and M.S. Wyeth. *The Story of the Doughboys: The AEF in World War I*. New York: Harper and Row, 1963. Print.

Steiner, Zara. "The Peace Settlement." *The Oxford Illustrated History of the First World War*. Hew Strachan, ed. New York and Oxford: Oxford University Press, 1998. Print.

Stephenson, Scott. *The Final Battle: Soldiers of the Western Front and the German Revolution of 1918*. Cambridge, UK: Cambridge University Press, 2009. Print.

Stern, Fritz. *The Politics of Cultural Despair: A Study in the Rise of the Germanic Ideology*. Berkeley: University of California Press, 1961. Print.

Stevenson, David. *The First World War and International Politics*. New York: Oxford University Press, 1988. Print.

Stevenson, David. *The Outbreak of the First World War: 1914 in Perspective*. New York: St. Martin's, 1997. Print.

Stevenson, David. "War Aims and Peace Negotiations." *The Oxford Illustrated History of the First World War*. Hew Strachan, ed. New York and Oxford: Oxford University Press, 1998. Print.

Stone, Ralph. *The Irreconcilables: The Fight Against the League of Nations*. Lexington, KY: University Press of Kentucky, 1970. Print.

Strachan, Hew. "Economic Mobilization: Money, Munitions and Machines." *The Oxford Illustrated History of the First World War*. Hew Strachan, ed. New York and Oxford: Oxford University Press, 1998. Print.

Strachan, Hew. *The First World War. Vol. I, To Arms*. New York: Oxford University Press, 2001. Print.

Strachan, Hew, ed. *The Oxford Illustrated History of the First World War*. New York and Oxford: Oxford University Press, 1998. Print.

Strachan, Hew. "The War to End All Wars?" *Foreign Affairs* 82.1 (Jan/ Feb 2003). Print.

Strachan, Hew, ed. *World War I: A History*. New York: Oxford University Press, 1998. Print.

Sutton, Walter A. "Progressive Republican Senators and the Submarine Crisis, 1915-1916." *Mid-America* 47 (Apr 1965). Print.

Syrett, Harold C. "The Business Press and American Neutrality, 1914-1917." *Mississippi Valley Historical Review* 32 (Sep 1945). Print.

Tansill, Charles C. *America Goes to War*. Gloucester, MA: Peter Smith, 1963, originally published 1938. Print.

Tarrant, V E. *The U-Boat Offensive, 1914-1945*. Annapolis, MD; Naval Institute Press, 1989. Print.

Taylor A.J.P. *The First World War: An Illustrated History*. London: H. Hamilton, 1963. Print.

Taylor, James. "The Drama of the Larder: Germany's Food Crisis 1914-1918." *Imperial War Museum Magazine* (1995). Print.

Terraine, John. *To Win a War, 1918: The Year of Victory*. New York: Doubleday, 1981. Print.

Thompson, John A. *Reformers and War: American Progressive Publicists and the First World War*. Cambridge, UK: Cambridge University Press, 1987. Print.

Thompson, John A. "Woodrow Wilson and World War I: A Reappraisal." *Journal of American Studies* 19 (Dec 1985). Print.

Tillman, Seth. *Anglo-American Relations at the Paris Peace Conference of 1919*. Princeton, NJ: Princeton University Press, 1961. Print.

Todd, Lewis Paul. *Wartime Relations of the Federal Government and the Public Schools, 1917-1918*. New York: Arno Press, 1971, originally published 1945. Print.

Trachtenberg, Marc. *Reparation in World Politics: France and European Economic Diplomacy, 1916-1923*. New York: Columbia University Press, 1980. Print.

Trachtenberg, Marc. "Versailles After Sixty Years." *Journal of Contemporary History* 17 (1982). Print.

Trask, David F. *The AEF and Coalition Warmaking, 1917-1918*. Lawrence, KS: University of Kansas Press, 1993. Print.

Trask, David F. "The Entry of the USA into the War and its Effects." *The Oxford Illustrated History of the First World War*. Hew Strachan, ed. New York and Oxford: Oxford University Press, 1998. Print.

Trask, David F. "Woodrow Wilson and International Statecraft: A Modern Reassessment." *Naval War College Review* 36 (Mar-Apr 1983). Print.

Trask, David F. "Woodrow Wilson and World War I." *American Diplomacy in the Twentieth Century.* Warren F. Kimball, ed. St. Louis: Forum Press, 1980. Print.

Travers, Tim. *How the War Was Won: Command and Technology in the British Army on the Western Front, 1917-1918.* South Yorkshire: Pen & Sword Military Classics, 1992. Print.

Travers, Tim. "July 1, 1916: The Reason Why." *The Great War: Perspectives on the First World War.* Robert Cowley, ed. New York: Random House, 2003. Print.

Travers, Tim. "The Allied Victories, 1918." *The Oxford Illustrated History of the First World War.* Hew Strachan, ed. New York and Oxford: Oxford University Press, 1998. Print.

Travers, Tim. *The Killing Ground: The British Army, the Western Front, and the Emergence of Modern Warfare, 1900-1918.* London: Unwin Hyman, 1990. Print.

Trommler, Frank and Joseph McVeigh, eds. *America and the Germans: An Assessment of a Three Hundred Year History.* Philadelphia: University of Pennsylvania Press, 1985. Print.

Tryon, Warren S. "The Draft in World War I." *Current History* 54 (1968). Print.

Tuchman, Barbara. *The Zimmermann Telegram.* New York: Macmillan, 1958. Print.

Tucker, Spencer, ed. *The European Powers in the First World War: An Encyclopedia.* New York: Garland Publishing, 1996. Print.

United States Department of the Army. *United States Army in the World War, 1917-1919.* Washington: Government Printing Office, 1948. Print.

United States Senate, Committee on Foreign Relations. *Treaty of Peace with Germany. Hearings.* Washington: Government Printing Office, 1919. Print.

Van Schaack, Eric. "The Coming of the Hun! American Fears of a German Invasion, 1918." *The Journal of American Culture* 28.3. Print.

Vaughn, Stephen. *Holding Fast the Inner Lines: Democracy, Nationalism, and the Committee on Public Information*. Chapel Hill, NC: University of North Carolina Press, 1980. Print.

Veale, F.J.P. "The Wicked Kaiser Myth: Demonstrating the Unreliability of Unanimous verdicts of Public Opinion." *Social Justice Review* (Apr 1960). Print.

Venzon, Anne Cipriano, ed. *The United States in the First World War: An Encyclopedia*. New York: Garland Publishing, 1995. Print.

Viereck, George S. ed. *As They Saw Us: Foch, Ludendorff and Other Leaders Write Our War History*. Garden City, NY: Doubleday, Doran, 1929. Print.

Vincent, C. Paul. *The Politics of Hunger: The Allied Blockade of Germany 1915-1919*. Athens, OH: Ohio University Press, 1985. Print.

Votaw, John F. *The American Expeditionary Forces in World War I*. Oxford: Osprey Publishing, 2005. Print.

Waite, Robert G.L. *Vanguard of Nazism: The Free Corps Movement in Postwar Germany, 1918-1923*. Cambridge, MA: Harvard University Press, 1952. Print.

Walworth, Arthur. *America's Moment, 1918: American Diplomacy at the End of World War I*. New York: Norton, 1977. Print.

Ward, Larry Wayne. *The Motion Picture Goes to War: The U.S. Government Film Effort during World War I*. Ann Arbor, MI: UMI Research Press, 1985. Print.

Watt, Richard M. *The Kings Depart. The Tragedy of Germany: Versailles and the German Revolution*. New York: Barnes and Noble, 2000, originally published 1968. Print.

Webster, Charles K. *The Congress of Vienna, 1814-1815*. New York: Barnes and Noble, 1963. Print.

Wecter, Dixon. *When Johnny Comes Marching Home*. Boston: Houghton Mifflin, 1944. Print.

Weigley, Russell F. *History of the United States Army*. New York: Macmillan, 1967. Print.

Weigley, Russell F. *The American Way of War: A History of United States Military Strategy and Policy*. New York: Macmillan, 1973. Print.

Weinberg, G.L. "The Defeat of Germany in 1918 and the European Balance of Power." *Central European History* 2.3 (1969). Print.

Weingartner, Steven, ed. *A Weekend with the Great War: Proceedings of the Fourth Annual Great War Interconference Seminar*. Wheaton, IL: Cantigny First Division Foundation (Shippensburg, PA), White Mane Publishing Co. with the Great War Society and the Western Front Association, 1997. Print.

Widenor, W.C. *Henry Cabot Lodge and the Search for an American Foreign Policy.* Berkeley: University of California Press, 1980. Print.

Williams, Harriet. "American Universities and World War I." *American Decades CD-ROM*. Farmington Hills, MI: History Research Center for Gale Research, 1998. CD.

Williams, John. *The Other Battleground: The Home Fronts-- Britain, France and Germany, 1914-1918*. Chicago: Regnery, 1972. Print.

Williamson, Samuel R. "The Origins of the War." *The Oxford Illustrated History of the First World War*. Hew Strachan, ed. New York and Oxford: Oxford University Press, 1998. Print.

Wilson, Keith. *Decisions for War, 1914*. New York: St. Martin's, 1995. Print.

Wilson, Woodrow. "An Address to a Joint Session of Congress," 2 April 1917. *The Papers of Woodrow Wilson*, Arthur S. Link, ed. Princeton, NJ: Princeton University Press, 1966.

Wilson, Woodrow. *The Public Papers of Woodrow Wilson, Authorized Edition*, Ray S. Baker and William E. Dodd, eds. New York: Harper, 1925-1927. Print.

Wimer, Kurt. "Woodrow Wilson Tries Conciliation: An Effort that Failed." *The Historian* (Aug 1963). Print.

Windschuttle, Keith. "Was World War I Necessary?' *New Criterion* 18.4 (Dec 1999). Print.

Winter, Jay M. "Catastrophe and Culture: Recent Trends in the Historiography of the First World War." *Journal of Modern History* 64.3 (Sep 1992). Print.

Winter, Jay M. "Propaganda and the Mobilization of Consent." *The Oxford Illustrated History of the First World War*. Hew Strachan, ed. New York and Oxford: Oxford University Press, 1998. Print.

Winter, Jay M., Geoffrey Parker, and Mary Habeck, eds. *The Great War and the Twentieth Century*. New Haven, CT: Yale University Press, 2000. Print.

Wittke, Carl Frederick. *German-Americans and the World War*. Columbus, OH: Ohio State Archeological and Historical Society, 1936. Print.

Wittke, Carl Frederick. *The German Language Press in America*. Lexington, KY: University of Kentucky Press, 1957. Print.

Wittke, Carl Frederick. *The Irish in America*. Baton Rouge, LA: Louisiana State University Press, 1956. Print.

Woodward, David R. *Trial by Friendship: Anglo-American Relations, 1917-1918*. Lexington, KY: University of Kentucky Press, 1993. Print.

Wrigley, Chris, ed. *The First World War and the International Economy*. Northampton, MA: E. Elgar, 2000. Print.

Wynn, Neil A. *From Progressivism to Prosperity: World War I and American Society*. New York: Holmes and Meier, 1986. Print.

Yockelson, Mitchell. *Borrowed Soldiers: Americans Under British Command, 1918*. Norman, OK: University of Oklahoma Press, 2008. Print.

Zabecki, David. Review of *America's Deadliest Battle: Meuse-Argonne, 1918*, by Robert H. Ferrell. *War in History* 17.3 (Jul 2010). Print.

Zeiger, Susan. "She Didn't Raise Her Boy to Be a Slacker: Motherhood, Conscription, and the Culture of the First World War." *Feminist Studies* 22.1 (1996). Print.

Zuber, Terence. "The Schlieffen Plan Reconsidered." *War in History* 6.3 (Jul 1999). Print.

INDEX

and moves towards democracy, 259-261, 272, 290, 293, 308-323, 338-339, 342
Gibbons, Cardinal James, 42, 101
Glynn, Governor Martin, 82
Goldman, Emma, 155
"Good God, did we really send men to fight in that?" 166
Grant, General Ulysses S., 17, 217
Grattan, C. Hartley, 326-327
Great Britain: able to thwart a German victory, 331, 333; blockade of Germany, 47, 57, 67-73, 84-85, 89, 91-92, 104-106, 117, 168-169, 197, 255, 270, 346; British Expeditionary Force (BEF), 12; Could Britain have won the war? 333-336; critical of Versailles Treaty terms, 296-297; Grand Fleet, 22, 64, 73; home front conditions, 168-169; military mission in the U.S., 127-129; Passchendaele offensive: see Offensives, Passchendaele; purchasing missions in the U.S., 86, 89; Royal Navy, 57, 63, 73, 81, 198, 282, 345, 347
Grey, Lord Edward, 10
Guderian, General Heinz, 323
Haig, General Douglas, 18, 24, 162, 164-168, 202, 212-215, 245, 260, 262-263, 265, 272, 275, 334; "Rather die than accept such [armistice] conditions." 263
Hanke, Steve, 318-319
Harbord, General James, 226
Harding, President Warren, 306
Harper's Weekly Magazine, 49, 51
"He kept us out of war!" 77, 82
Hillis, Newell Dwight, 150
Hindenburg, General Paul von, 106, 157, 169, 196, 198-203, 208-209, 256-257, 271, 313
Hindenburg Line, 215-216, 244
Hitler, Adolf, 2, 49, 264, 289, 306, 312, 317, 320, 326-327, 340-341
Hoboken piers, 110, 172, 175, 276
Holtzendorff, Admiral Henning von, 106-107
Hoover, President Herbert, 42, 277

CPSIA information can be obtained at www.ICGtesting.com
Printed in the USA
LVOW05*1442051213

364043LV00003B/70/P